Democracy Heading South

Democracy Heading South

National Politics in the Shadow of Dixie

Augustus B. Cochran III

UNIVERSITY PRESS OF KANSAS

Published by the University Press of Kansas (Lawrence, Kansas 66049),
which was organized by the Kansas Board of Regents and is operated and
funded by Emporia State University, Fort Hays State University, Kansas
State University, Pittsburg State University, the University of Kansas, and
Wichita State University

Library of Congress Cataloging-in-Publication Data

Cochran, Augustus B., 1946–

Democracy heading South : national politics in the shadow of Dixie /
Augustus B. Cochran III.

p. cm.

Includes bibliographical references and index.

ISBN 0-7006-1089-8 (alk. paper)

1. United States—Politics and government—1989–   2. Southern
States—Politics and government—1865–   3. Political culture—United
States.   4. Political culture—Southern States.   5. Democracy—United
States.   6. Political participation—United States.   I. Title.

E839.5 .C635 2000

320.973—dc21   00-011729

British Library Cataloguing in Publication Data is available.

Printed in the United States of America

10 9 8 7 6 5 4 3 2 1

The paper used in this publication meets the minimum requirements of the
American National Standard for Permanence of Paper for Printed Library
Materials Z39.48-1984.

With love and gratitude to my parents,
Mildred Lloyd Cochran and Augustus Bonner Cochran,
who passed down the finer features of a Southern heritage,
and to my children, Margaret MacLean Cochran and
Augustus Miller Cochran, in hopes that they will find
aspects of their Southern legacy useful in building
a more democratic South and nation.

Contents

Acknowledgments

All of us have copious intellectual debts, and mine stretch from my earliest teachers to my most recent students. My father, Bonner Cochran, was in a real sense my first teacher of politics. He awoke in me an interest in public affairs by "argufying" (as he said, in his own personal language) about current events, forcing me to defend my opinions on every great, and little, question. Had he lived to argue about the ideas presented here, this would have been a better book. To my sister, Becky Cochran Akin, and especially my mother, Mildred Lloyd Cochran, I owe multiple debts of gratitude for their support and help; it is a gratitude that mere words cannot express. Suffice it to say that computerized spell and grammar checks pale in comparison to having a fourth-grade teacher for a mother.

My thanks to my professors at Chapel Hill, in particular Thad Beyle and Merle Black, for my foundation in political science and for their generous responses to my intermittent queries about Southern politics over the years.

My thanks to Eric Uslaner for his advice on the publication process and to Michael Briggs of the University Press of Kansas for his early and consistent interest in this project. Thanks go as well to Stanford, Fagan, and Giolito for the time off to write this manuscript, as well as for the opportunity to experience some of the battles of the haves versus the have-nots from the trenches.

My debts are legion at Agnes Scott. I thank my students over the years for their questions and comments, which helped the ideas in this book become, I hope, progressively sharper and more insightful—at least more insightful than they were when I first tried them out in the classroom. Thanks to Sala Rhodes, Sheika Serritt, and Melanie Minzes for helping me find some of the information that appears in this book.

Susan Dougherty and Amy Whitworth deserve special gratitude for rescuing the manuscript from various technological swamps more times than any of us care to recall.

Will Reid gave generously of his time, reading the entire manuscript and sharing his usual good judgment and sound advice. Jessica Crawford well exceeded her student research assistant's duties by continuing to read drafts even after leaving for law school. Their editorial and substantive suggestions improved this book markedly.

A special debt is owed to Miller and Molly Cochran, whose workaholic father was even tougher to deal with during the course of writing this manuscript. My son Miller had to endure almost daily reports of progress (or, too frequently, the lack thereof) on "The Book." Molly not only rendered valuable editorial assistance but also encouraged me—or, more accurately, prodded me in her inimitably gentle way—to get this book written.

I also want to say a special word of thanks to my colleague Catherine Scott. Her constant teasing about my accent ("I 'cain't' show any 'biuz' when analyzing the 'gub'ment' ") served to remind me that I possess a real Deep South heritage. Her comments encouraged me to believe that I might have something worthwhile to say about that heritage, and her criticisms ensured that what I have said is better than it would have been without her suggestions. Thanks, Cathy.

Introduction

This book is both about the South and not about the South. It describes the way politics in Dixie once was, roughly in the first half of the twentieth century, and it traces the dramatic changes that brought Southern politics more into line with national politics in the second half of the century. But the real point of this book is to look neither to the past nor to the South but rather toward the future of American politics. The brief foray into Southern politics in chapters 2 and 3 is not merely to understand what has been going on below the Mason-Dixon line for its own sake. Instead, it is my contention that Southern politics contains the key to illuminating what has been happening in recent years in politics in the country as a whole. By viewing national politics through the prism of Southern politics, we can see in sharper relief some of the threatening clouds on America's horizon, trends that bode ill for our democracy.

In the 1990s, the South attained a position of prominence in national affairs unparalleled since before the Civil War. Southerners occupied the apex of political power. Executive leadership was firmly in the hands of Southerners and seemed destined to remain there, regardless of which party captured the White House in the year 2000. Almost simultaneously, a clique of conservative Southerners engineered and led the Republican takeover of Congress. Beyond the governmental sphere, the South acquired unprecedented influence in economic, social, and cultural affairs. The abolition of the Jim Crow system of segregation by law and the end of the Democrats' one-party monopoly in Southern politics brought tangible benefits to the region as a whole as the South exerted new leverage in the nation that it had only reluctantly rejoined.

The "Southernization of America" is in some ways as sinister as it

is singular. Over the years, several observers of Southern politics sounded alarms about the transformations at work. They noted that if Southern and national politics were becoming more aligned, this convergence was a two-way street.[1] If politics in the South increasingly mirrored politics in the rest of the country, it was at least partly because national politics more and more resembled the politics of Dixie.

This book examines the forces behind the "Dixification" of our national political life. My claim is that this trend is not the result of Southerners attaining new clout in the federal government—that is more a symptom than a cause of the changes afoot. Nor is the convergence primarily the result of a conservative tilt in the country's values or ideology caused by a turn to some supposedly traditional Southern political culture. If themes that appear to be familiarly Southern loom large in public life today, that is merely the surface reflection of deeper changes wrought in our political foundations. Although the South has wielded more weight in the country in recent years, its influence is merely part of a complex and multicausal explanation for the changes in our politics. My argument in this book is that our national political, and especially electoral, institutions, for all sorts of complicated and interrelated reasons, are coming increasingly to resemble the irrational and undemocratic politics of the old Solid South.

The Solid South system that dominated the political life of the region for the first half of the twentieth century was built on one-party domination, disenfranchisement of huge segments of the population, and white supremacy. In a country that aspired to be the world's greatest democracy, the region was ruled undemocratically by a tiny, autocratic elite. In a region mired in poverty and economic underdevelopment, politics conspired to reinforce backwardness and to thwart development. The Solid South "strangled the aspirations of generations of blacks and whites" who inhabited the region.[2]

From the angle of the Southern past, we are better able to detect worrisome trends in our national political life. Although they are strong as organizations, the vigor of American political parties as instruments of popular will is waning. The routine preeminence of a single party prevailing in the Solid South may seem remote from today's contentious partisan conflict, but party competition as currently practiced is failing to ensure coherence and accountability in

national politics anymore. Barriers to voting may have fallen, but participation in politics across the country has ebbed to an almost all-time low. Raw racism may not taint our politics as overtly as it once did in the Solid South of old, but it lies just below the surface of many of the social issues and "culture wars" that rage so furiously in American politics today.

If our electoral and political institutions are indeed assuming some of the traits of old Solid South structures, the experience of Southern history suggests that the future of democracy and sound governance in the nation may be in some jeopardy. The absence of healthy party competition, low participation in politics, and racialized campaigns produced appalling pathologies in the Solid South. In the first half of the twentieth century, the South spawned the nation's most notorious demagogues. Southern elections were at once empty, issueless affairs at one level and, at another level, maniacally focused on a single issue: white supremacy. Corruption ran rampant. Most Southerners sat on the sidelines, alternately entertained and appalled by the clownish antics of the "colorful characters" who dominated their politics. And politicians served up "bread and circuses" (actually, white bread and barbecue) for the masses while quietly serving the interests of the elite planters and wealthy industrialists.

This picture of the Solid South seems a far cry from national politics today, if taken as a literal description. But as a lens through which to analyze and understand the defects and trends of contemporary politics, these symptoms do not seem all that foreign from national political institutions that are troublesomely unresponsive to the will of the public. Our political leaders are increasingly irresponsible and remote from the electorate. Ever-larger numbers of citizens are questioning whether elections mean much in this era of incumbent-friendly, big-buck, high-tech, mass-media politics. Although the public arena is filled with sophisticated, well-crafted, and well-financed messages, public dialogue speaks less and less to the real concerns of ordinary people. Corruption and scandal increasingly tarnish the daily headlines. Participation in politics is plummeting. And as electoral politics seems to lose its deliberative and democratic content, the gap between the wealthy elites and the increasingly hard-pressed middle classes is becoming a gulf that threatens democracy itself. While politics represents a sideshow to most Americans, the big issues still go

unaddressed: structural transformation of the economy means severe hardships for many American workers; disintegrating communities pose dire threats to American families; a society that proclaims the ideals of justice and equality is divided along widening class, gender, and ethnic lines, diminishing us all; and governments that cannot solve these dilemmas undercut our faith in democracy. To the extent that institutional defects, and not merely the foibles of a few leaders or temporary trends in culture or ideology, are responsible for recent "Southern" symptoms, we must conclude that the problem runs deep, is serious indeed, and promises to persist.

The politics of the old Solid South merely provides a portent of one possible future scenario. An examination of Southern politics reveals structures underlying many surface changes in national politics that do not augur well for the future of our democracy, but this analysis also points to steps we could take to shape our future in a more humane and democratic vein. The Solid South of the past, in other words, is a signpost that points to a not-so-democratic future for the United States, *unless* we citizens learn from the past and take action. That, ultimately, is the point of looking at the Old South as a bell-wether—to use the Solid South as a beacon to steer us off the shoals of "Southern-style" politics before American democracy "heads south" for good.

A Note on Values and Bias, Methods and Metaphors

Readers will have no trouble detecting that my political values color the points I make here, and it would be astounding if everyone agreed with all my views. Political science, after all, is about politics. This book develops an argument about the drift of our politics, and it would be silly, even sinister, to try to disguise my point of view in the name of some false, value-free sense of objectivity. Instead, I have tried to be honest and straightforward in making my arguments and in presenting evidence to support them, including citing some contrary views and even my own doubts at times. Readers should also note, however, that my central focus here is political institutions and processes, not the substance of public policy. I argue that our political system is failing to address adequately many of the important problems facing our

nation, but this book does not propose solutions to our society's problems. Readers might agree or disagree with my own notions about desirable public policies, but people of various political stripes could probably agree that it is ultimately the public's ideas that should shape policy in a democracy. Rather than to persuade readers to my substantive political positions, my purpose here is to raise questions about the responsiveness and efficacy of our contemporary political institutions and processes as means for enacting the public will. I ask readers to reflect on how, in the current context, we citizens can decide what choices we want to make, make our decisions known, translate those options accurately into public policies, and hold leaders accountable for their actions. The primary political value undergirding these arguments is the belief that, in a robust democracy, ultimately the people must make the political decisions that affect their lives. Many who would advocate different choices on issues of substantive public policy can share my concern for the fate of self-government in America today.

My method in making these arguments is comparative: I ask the reader to compare the politics of the South in a bygone era to the evolving politics of the United States today. My analysis highlights core political structures that caused pathologies in the old Solid South and points to similarities with the electoral structures that are shaping current national politics. My purpose in making this comparison is to ask whether similar structures will not likely generate similar problematic symptoms. I am not arguing that the South or its politics caused the emergence of similar structures in national politics, nor do I maintain that the South is somehow responsible for the symptoms that may be flowing from these political processes. The South has played a role in the recent development of U.S. politics, and I trace the dual convergence of the region's and the nation's politics in chapters 3 and 4. There have, however, been other, more significant causative factors in the evolution of current American political structures, forces such as the escalating role of mass media, in particular, television and even newer electronic media; the overweening importance of money in modern elections; the heightening racial and ethnic conflicts in the contemporary era; the transformation from a manufacturing to a service and information economy; and the globalization of our national economy and society, to name just a few. The point of my argument

is not to identify the sources of our current flawed electoral structures but to analyze the probable consequences of such structures by reminding readers of the problems that flowed from similarly flawed structures in the old Solid South.

If this comparison is valid, then the Solid South can serve as a case study of the defects that result from electoral structures that cannot sustain healthy party competition, nor nurture widespread public participation, nor resist the temptation to exacerbate prejudices and ethnic and racial animosities for electoral advantage rather than solving problems plaguing the polity. Part of the appeal of this comparison is that the pathologies of the Old South's politics make such a powerful metaphor for the ills of undemocratic politics.[3] Despite its formally democratic institutions, the Solid South practiced a politics that contradicted every democratic norm. Along with some notably respectable leaders, its elections produced a menagerie of demagogues ranging from relatively harmless buffoons to virulent racists and proto-fascists. Its governments ruled in the interests of an elite few while the vast majority either were excluded from participation or lacked the wherewithal to ensure their voice in Southern governments. The South spent much of the last century mired in poverty, underdevelopment, illiteracy, and bigotry, and its undemocratic politics presented a barrier rather than a vehicle for resolving these problems. The politics of the Solid South represents a stark warning of how a society suffers when its supposedly democratic institutions fail to present genuine choices to an active and engaged citizenry.

There are dangers in using the Solid South as a metaphor for the undemocratic future we may face. Professor Larry Griffin, director of Vanderbilt's program in American and Southern Studies, has identified severe liabilities in using "southern referents" as a "moral compass to orient readers." Although recognizing that the region's genuine distinctiveness and pained past endow the very word "South" with a powerful metaphoric impetus, he warns that metaphors can blind as well as illuminate, muddle as well as clarify thought. In particular, the use of "the South as an American problem" can deflect questions about " 'which America?' " and " 'which South?' "[4] The tendency to identify particular social problems with the region focuses attention away from social ills in other regions and, even more importantly, away from national dimensions of social problems.[5] More egre-

giously, equating wrongs with region ignores the heterogeneity of the South, often conflating the South with the Confederacy and its heirs and legacy. Griffin points out that "the South" is actually rich in its diversity of races, regions, economics, and, as I note in chapter 8, political traditions.[6]

Although I use the South as a lens through which to view recent national developments, I pinpoint the problems on particular aspects of the South's political institutions—its partyless elections, its narrow franchise, and its racial politics. I am not pointing to aspects as amorphous as the culture or "character" of the region, or of its inhabitants. By comparing the region's historical political structures with the evolving electoral processes of the nation, I wish to challenge the conventional wisdom that all is well with democracy in the United States and the world. The comfortable view holds that the United States is the world's greatest democracy in a world where democracy is securely triumphant, and that the South, long the backwater bastion out of step with the rest of the country, has now, at long last, conquered its poverty and racism and rejoined the democratic Union. To draw analogies with the Solid South of old is to question the complacency of this picture of democracy's future. Ultimately I hope that the metaphor of a "Southern future" is sufficiently engaging politically as well as intellectually to motivate readers to take actions to head off democracy from "heading south."

Of course, making metaphors is also inherently contentious, a veritable political act in itself.[7] Readers are invited to question the questioner. Every comparison invites contrasts as well, and surely there are salient differences as well as striking similarities between the political structures of the old Solid South and those of the current United States. There are also countertrends afoot nationally that work against the analogy. The concluding chapter discusses some of these developments, but readers should be vigilant to differences and cognizant of the limits of the analogy at every step of the argument.

Despite these caveats, some may still be tempted to read me as identifying the "evils" I seek to highlight with "the South" or with "Southerners" per se. That is decidedly not my intent, nor is it the message of this book that increasing Southern influence is somehow a threat. I reiterate: nothing in this book is meant to imply that Southerners are personally or politically pathological. Rather, it is the

political institutions of the Solid South that pose dangers to the health of democracy.

Lest anyone doubt my own attitudes about and loyalties to the South and Southerners, I should apprise readers that I am Southern to my very core. I have lived all but two of my increasingly numerous years in the South. Moreover, I am descended from ancestors who inhabited the region since before the Revolutionary War. To the best of my knowledge, there is not a "yamdankee" in any branch of my family tree. My forebears fought and led Southern contingents in both the Revolutionary War and the Civil War—real flesh-and-blood colonels, not the mythical ones that some Southern white families allegedly concoct. I was raised in the (then, but no longer) sleepy, Deep South college town of Athens, Georgia, in a milieu that was so Southern, not to say parochial, that when I announced that I was going to college in Davidson, North Carolina, just north of Charlotte, a friend inquired incredulously, "Why do you want to go up North to college?"

What I condemn in this book, then, is not the South or Southerners but certain political institutions of the Solid South. Personally, I feel that the South has much to offer the nation as a whole, ranging from cooking to literature to lifestyle. The region even has lessons to teach from its difficult experiences in righting its race relations, learned in the courageous struggle for equality and dignity waged by Southern African Americans. If we still aren't what we ought to be, at least "we ain't what we was."[8]

But perhaps the South's best legacy would be if its discredited politics could stand as a warning against the trends that increasingly taint our national politics and that threaten what has always been and remains today America's grandest experiment and noblest aspiration: democracy.

1 / *Dixie Déjà Vu*
Southern Politics All Over Again

The Bottom Rail on Top

"For over four decades now, since John F. Kennedy was elected in 1960, everyone elected President of the United States has been a Southerner." True or false?

If this statement appeared on an SAT-type objective test, the obviously correct answer would be "false." But in the complex real world of politics, where truth is rarely short-answer simple, the statement captures an often overlooked shift of power in American politics in recent decades.

From 1960 to 2000, only Jimmy Carter (1977–1981) from Georgia and Bill Clinton (1993–2001) from Arkansas were unambiguously Southern.[1] Both Lyndon Johnson (1963–1969) and George Bush (1989–1993) were from Texas.[2] The most clearly non-Southern president of the era, Gerald Ford (1974–1977) of Michigan, was not in fact *elected* but succeeded to the presidency in the wake of Watergate (okay, trick question).

That leaves Richard Nixon (1969–1974) and Ronald Reagan (1981-1989), both Californians (from southern California, no less). A prototypically Sun Belt state, California could be defined as "Southern," but that rigs the definition. Besides, there is a more important sense in which these two Republican presidents were Southern. Nixon began, and Reagan accomplished, a fundamental reorientation that reversed many of the old verities of American politics. Nixon pursued a conscious "Southern strategy" in winning the presidency twice and in loosening the Democrats' grip on the federal government. Reagan, although he did not openly talk of an explicitly Southern strategy, launched his 1980 campaign for the White House from Philadelphia, Mississippi, best known as the site of the murders of three civil rights

workers during the Freedom Summer of 1964. There, candidate Reagan affirmed, "I believe in states' rights," a slogan long identified with Southern resistance to federal civil rights initiatives.[3] Once in office, the Reagan administration redirected policy in ways Nixon could only dream of, erecting a framework of budget deficits and conservative attitudes that still constrains policy options today. These two conservative California Republicans turned the nation's politics sharply to the right—and to the South.

For over a hundred years after the Civil War, it was taken for granted that Southerners were precluded from holding the office of president, although they held positions of entrenched if less visible power in Congress. Events since the 1960s have repealed this axiom of American politics, but by the mid-1990s, this truism was only one of many that had been turned topsy-turvy. In a political system that observers had long judged to be one of the world's most stable, today's political climate is in turmoil: the tried-and-true rules of American politics no longer apply, and the conventional wisdom serves as an unreliable guide to current realities.

One political commonplace that may now be relegated to a bygone era is the Republican "lock" on the electoral college and thus the White House.[4] For several decades, Democrats seemed to have lost the near monopoly on the presidency they enjoyed during the New Deal era. In the post-1960s political order, the norm was Republican presidents, although Democrats retained majority control of Congress. Democrat Jimmy Carter's rejection by the voters after an agonizing single term only confirmed this pattern.

Yet by the late 1990s, a Democrat presided over the executive branch for only the second time in three decades. More amazingly, Bill Clinton managed to win reelection despite disastrously low initial approval ratings based on his early performance, when he enjoyed Democratic majorities in Congress. After the 1994 Republican sweep of Congress, Clinton faced almost unanimous predictions that he too, like Carter, was destined for an early exile after an undistinguished one-term presidency. Yet he coasted to an easy victory in 1996, but without carrying congressional Democrats with him. Despite suffering the ignominy of being the only elected president to be impeached, the "Comeback Kid" rebounded to avoid conviction on the charges and to exact electoral revenge on his tormentors in the 1998 midterm elections.

An even more unforeseen shock, however, occurred on Capitol Hill, where the "earthquake" election of 1994 cracked Democratic control of the House of Representatives for the first time since 1952.[5] Although some pundits read the Republican Revolution of 1994 as a fluke reaction against the temporarily unpopular Clinton, neither the standoff 1996 congressional elections nor the relative retrenchment of the 1998 midterm elections dislodged the Republican majorities in the House and Senate. After a generation of expecting Republican presidents to face Democratic Congresses, the pattern had been stood on its head in the mid-1990s; a Democratic president confronted Republican congressional majorities for the first time since the anomalous Republican Congress that Democratic president Harry Truman "gave hell" in 1947–1949.

Southern Coup?

Less noted is the fact that by the 1990s, Southerners, long excluded from national leadership, dominated both the executive and legislative branches of government as well as both parties.[6] Not only was President Clinton a former Arkansas governor, but his vice-president and heir apparent, Al Gore, was a former senator from Tennessee. While the "Bubba Brothers" dominated the Democratic party, the Republican party in Congress was also under the sway of Southerners. Former Speaker of the House Newt Gingrich, the polarizing leader of the 1994 Republican Revolution, represented the north Atlanta suburbs. Several of his chief lieutenants hailed from similar terrain in Texas. Dick Armey, the Republican majority leader, represented suburban Houston, while Republican whip Tom Delay's district was suburban Dallas. When Gingrich's reign as Speaker ended abruptly in the aftermath of his party's disappointing showing in the 1998 midterm elections, House Republicans elected Robert Livingston of Louisiana as their leader. Speaker-elect Livingston had to step aside because of revelations of marital infidelity, and Dennis Hastert, who followed him, is from Illinois. However, many party and committee leadership slots remain staffed with Southerners. In fact, purveyors of Washington political gossip often designate Delay as the real power behind the throne in the House.[7]

On the Senate side, the leader of the majority Republicans was Trent Lott of Mississippi, who defeated Mississippi's other senator, Thad Cochran, for the post. Southerners have historically played leading roles in the Senate, but in the 1990s, they were Republicans rather than Democrats. Connie Mack of Florida chaired the Senate Republican Conference, and Paul Coverdell of Georgia was its secretary.[8] GOP committee chairs included Jesse Helms of North Carolina, chair of Foreign Relations, and Strom Thurmond, chair of the Judiciary Committee as well as president pro tempore of the Senate. From the other side of the aisle, in a remarkable instance of reverse carpetbagging, First Lady Hillary Rodham Clinton launched a foray into the North after New York's seat in the U.S. Senate.

A continuation of Southern political leadership was ensured by the nomination stage of the 2000 election, regardless of whether the electorate voted for partisan continuity or for change. Vice-President Al Gore inherited the status of the anointed nominee-designate by virtue of his service in the Clinton administration. For a time, tentative candidacies by previous presidential aspirant Lamar Alexander, former governor of Tennessee, and first-term Tennessee senator Fred Thompson raised the possibility that the 2000 presidential contest could have been an all-Tennessee affair. The most innovative candidacy featured the first serious campaign for the presidency by a woman, Elizabeth Dole. She is a North Carolinian, perhaps somewhat of a surprise, since the South is reputedly the most traditional region of the country. Although he proved not to be the expected consensus candidate, the almost foreordained Republican nominee was George W. Bush, Jr., son of the former president and governor of Texas. The resulting presidential matchup featuring "Li'l Bubba" Gore and George "Dubya Junior" Bush virtually guarantees a Southerner residing in the White House well into the twenty-first century.[9]

Déjà Vu All Over Again

Not only was the nation's leadership the most heavily Southern in its origins since the Civil War, but policies since the 1960s also began to assume a distinctly "Southern" cast, with some unanticipated twists to confound settled expectations. This development may not be sur-

prising, given the number of Southerners in policy-making positions by the mid-1990s. Yet many of the policy currents had begun to flow earlier, and there were deeper forces, with sources dating from a previous period of Southern history, seething beneath the surface of these changing policy tides.

Most remarkable was the end of the Second Reconstruction in civil rights and the backlash against women's progress made in the 1960s and 1970s. While reversals in affirmative action received most of the media attention, gains for African Americans were rolled back on a number of fronts, including voting rights, income equality, job training, and housing. The Harvard Project on School Desegregation reported with some alarm that the nation's schools were returning to the extremely segregated status that had characterized Southern and border state schools before *Brown v. Board of Education* (1954) outlawed school segregation. Not only had most Northern and Western states escaped the more stringent court-imposed remedies for segregation, but Southern schools, which had achieved a significant measure of desegregation under the vigorous enforcement of the 1964 Civil Rights Act and the sweeping Supreme Court decisions of the 1960s, were now reverting to segregation as well. After the reluctance of five Republican administrations to back energetic enforcement of civil rights laws, courts dominated by Republican appointees were now willing to countenance this regression under the guise of declaring districts to be "unitary," having removed the vestiges of past discrimination. Gary Orfield, the nation's leading expert on school desegregation, wrote that the arguments and assumptions about resegregation made by courts and political leaders in the 1990s bore a strange resemblance to the 1890s in the wake of the 1896 *Plessy v. Ferguson* decision validating "separate but equal" policies. Orfield suggested that the whole nation was living in an era not unlike the South in the period between *Plessy* (1896) and *Brown* (1954).[10] These two landmark court decisions, incidentally, make convenient bookends for dating the period of the traditional Solid South.[11]

Other policies sponsored by the Clinton administration seemed more "Southern" than traditionally Democratic. Welfare reform, which the president promised would end "welfare as we know it," was passed through Republican initiative and with presidential approval over the loud objections of liberal Democrats in both Congress and the administration. Trade policies, too, pitted a Democratic president in

alliance with Southern Democrats and Republicans in Congress against the core of the traditional New Deal Democrats, Northeast liberals and labor. The administration's premier urban program, "empowerment zones," differed little from the standard Republican elixir for urban ills, "enterprise zones." And the president's anticrime initiatives had distinctly Republican overtones (100,000 more police on the streets) mixed with more liberal elements (gun control and "midnight basketball" community programs).[12]

Prisons, in fact, attained the status of a major growth industry during the 1990s. The cost of building jails averaged $7 billion annually in the decade, and the yearly bill for keeping prisoners incarcerated amounted to $35 billion. The prison industry employed more than 523,000 people, including 350,000 guards, in addition to the 600,000 police and estimated 1.5 million private security guards in the nation. By the year 2000, human rights groups were claiming that the country's prison population had topped the 2 million mark, meaning that more Americans were imprisoned on a per capita basis than in any other nation. With only 5 percent of the world's population, the United States housed 25 percent of the world's prisoners. Although the phenomenal expansion of prisons surely had its roots in earlier law-and-order administrations, the rate of growth under a Democratic administration was remarkable: the incarceration rate rose from 1 in every 217 residents in 1990 to 1 in every 149 in 1998. Not surprisingly, the yoke of imprisonment fell heaviest on minorities, with 1 of 9 African American men and 1 in 25 Latino males in their twenties and early thirties behind bars, compared with 1 of 65 Anglo males.[13]

Although Clinton could claim an impressive number of accomplishments during his years in office, "the whole seemed to be less than the sum of the parts."[14] Health care, of course, was the biggest fiasco. The administration's plan, which was remarkably market oriented and cost conscious in an attempt to avoid the anticipated charge of being a traditional tax-and-spend Democratic program, was shot down amid withering attacks as being too liberal, too expensive, and too big-government oriented. This crushing defeat ushered in the turn against government that culminated in the Republican Revolution of 1994.[15] Although it soon became apparent that rumors of revolution were greatly exaggerated, the remainder of the Clinton term mostly followed the policy agenda shaped decisively by the Republican con-

servatives in the House. Major health care initiatives were replaced by limited Band-Aid measures, despite the fact that the number of uninsured Americans continued to grow. New departures in environmental protection or urban livability failed to surface in a political climate in which moderate and cautious "New Democrats" faced an ideologically doctrinaire, conservative Congress. Even small initiatives achieved through reluctant bipartisanship, amid substantial bickering of a personal as well as a partisan nature, were accomplished in spite of an overarching agreement on deficit reduction as the top national priority. Such a Republican-leaning agenda prompted even President Clinton to exclaim that "we're Eisenhower Republicans here and we are fighting Reagan Republicans!"[16]

The Democrats, standing in the shadow of Reaganomics, offered little by way of alternative programs to ameliorate the pain entailed by rapid restructuring of the economy in response to globalization. Although the Clinton administration presided over the longest stretch of prosperity in memory, the displacement of old liberalism by neoliberalism in the Democratic party meant that economic policies were more solicitous of the interests of American corporations than of the needs of ordinary Americans, at least those receiving short shrift in the information economy. The Democrats' default ensured that a surprising number of issues with arguably popular appeal remained off the policy table. Pat Buchanan, running on the far right in the 1996 Republican presidential primaries, had demonstrated the great appeal of job security to the voters, a theme not picked up by the Clinton campaign. The departure of Secretary of Labor Robert Reich from the second-term cabinet left the Clinton team without a steadfast advocate for the plight of American workers. Reich's retirement also reduced the chances that the Democrats would address another major, if somewhat subterranean, national crisis—the dramatic decline of the middle class. Altogether, the economic policies pursued in an era of retrenchment by government and American corporations followed a "low road" to international competitiveness—cost-conscious cutting of wages, jobs, taxes, infrastructure, and research and development. Stephen Cummings suggested that this low road followed past conservative economic policies originating in part in the dependent and underdeveloped Old South, a source that inevitably raises questions about this low road's destination.[17]

In other words, policy in the 1990s resembled the traditional policies of Southern states: fiscally conservative; market oriented, with a decided tilt toward big business; punitive toward the poor; insensitive to if not downright discriminatory toward the interests of racial and ethnic minorities and women; and neglectful of the everyday needs of average folks.[18]

Mud 'Rastling

As a bewildered nation looked on, President Clinton's second term was tainted by the impeachment fiasco. Resembling nothing more than a barnyard brawl at times, the entire affair over "The Affair" seemed more like trash TV than drama worthy of the highest offices in the land. The whole spectacle—personal, unseemly, lacking in decorum—surely made Miss Manners's flesh crawl. And once again, the prime-time actors were almost entirely Southern.

The chief protagonist, Clinton, had preached a "rhetoric of responsibility"[19] in a pitch for "value voters,"[20] but he could not live it. In risking everything in an affair with a White House intern, Clinton evidenced traces of that strange blend of hedonism and Puritanism that W. J. Cash claimed characterized the "mind of the South." In publicly proclaiming while privately flaunting old-fashioned morality, Clinton, a Southern Baptist, resembled those Southern low-churchers whom Southern novelist Leroy Percy described as faithfully attending revival services but then fighting and fornicating in the bushes afterward.[21]

Clinton's tormentors spoke, or railed, in a Southern accent, too. The president's chief nemesis, independent counsel Kenneth Starr, hailed from the small Southern town of Vernon, Texas, a mere 350 miles from the president's birthplace of Hope, Arkansas.[22] The impeachment forces in the House were led first by Georgian Gingrich, then by Livingston of Louisiana. Many of the House prosecutors represented Southern constituencies, and the most extreme proponents of impeachment, for example, Tom Delay of Texas and Bob Barr of Georgia, had a distinctly Southern cast.

While evincing a "pox on both your houses" attitude, the American public, according to polls, found the whole episode not terribly edifying, indeed, not even very significant or substantive. Although

most Americans were genuinely shocked that our politics could have come to such a pass, the sad truth is that the whole impeachment imbroglio was reminiscent of the worst of the down-and-dirty politics of Dixie of old. Although not necessarily resembling a "comic opera,"[23] to most citizens, the entire episode was a diversion, a sideshow, though not so much entertaining as riveting. It distracted much public energy and attention away from society's real ills. In doing so, it functioned in much the same way that politics had in Dixie.

Dixie Rising

The emergence of Southern prominence has not been limited to politics. In the 1980s, much discussion of the economy deplored the decline of the Northern manufacturing Rust Belt and heralded the rise of the Sun Belt. In retrospect, we can see that much of the mobility of investment and jobs to the South was only the first wave of a larger flow of capital from the United States to less developed countries. Yet the South, with its economy more centered in the booming service sector, remains poised to continue to reap a major regional share of the benefits of the transition to a "postindustrial" economy.[24]

The South's economic upsurge has been accompanied by rapid population growth. Migration from the rest of the country resulted in growing urbanization and suburbanization. It also produced a direct shift in political power, as Southern states gained seats in Congress through reapportionment. Although strongly concentrated in Florida and Texas, reapportionment netted the region as a whole a gain of nineteen seats in the House of Representatives from the 1960 to the 1990 censuses.[25] Southern cities also grew because of population shifts within the region, and international migration grew especially rapidly, beginning in the 1980s. These migrations transformed the region from a mostly rural population in black and white to an increasingly cosmopolitan, multicultural mix more closely resembling the rest of the country.

Perhaps population growth and changes facilitated what other observers have claimed to detect: a rising tide of Southern cultural hegemony. Writing in the *New York Times*, David Galef asserted that Southern culture was "spreading faster than kudzu":

The blues have come to Carnegie Hall, there's an Off Broadway revival of Patsy Cline, and Garth Brooks has taken over Central Park. John Grisham, the best-selling novelist from Mississippi, keeps turning out movie-friendly thrillers on a yearly basis. In the art scene, folk objects like McArthur Chism's bottle-cap art from the rural South are selling faster than hotcakes—or rather biscuits, which the Acme Bar and Grill in Manhattan features for weekend brunches, along with red-eye gravy. Upscale floral decorators now include cotton bolls in their arrangements, and the plantation look is big in furniture.[26]

Other signs of the new legitimacy of mythical Southern nostalgia include the 1999 rerelease of *Gone With the Wind* and the advent of a Southern party, which advocates, apparently with a straight face, Southern secession, only this time by legal means. In a more pragmatic vein, the success and spread of CNN, headquartered in Atlanta; the popularity and victories of the Atlanta Braves, televised on Ted Turner's Superstation network, and indeed, the emergence of Turner's broadcasting holdings as one of the leading international communications empires; the hosting of the 1996 Olympic games in Atlanta; and the near-universal adoption of the useful "y'all" in pop-speak all betoken a Southern cultural revival that might support the recent tilt in our politics.

Nor was the South's influence limited to pop culture. In 1997, President Clinton appointed fellow Southerners to head both the National Endowment for the Arts (William Ivey, a Michigan native but former Vanderbilt University professor who had directed the Country Music Foundation in Nashville since 1971) and the National Endowment for the Humanities (William Ferris, a Mississippi native who founded the University of Mississippi's Center for the Study of Southern Culture). Of course, the prime impetus for these appointments may have stemmed from an effort to blunt the attacks on these national endowments by Senator Jesse Helms (R-N.C.) and his fellow conservatives, who felt that "liberal" cultural elites had lost touch with the populace and were sponsoring morally degenerate projects. Whatever its impetus, Southern leadership of national cultural institutions has not gone unnoticed, producing "a certain undercurrent of disdain among scholars who view Southern culture as an oxymoron."[27]

The conservative turn in national culture was best exemplified by

the "virtue crusade" led by the likes of William Bennett. These "Virtuecrats" bemoaned the loss of authority in contemporary society and the failure of traditional institutions such as families, schools, and churches to inculcate character. Former senator Sam Nunn (D-Ga.) even cosponsored a Character Counts Caucus in Congress, an institution whose reputation was badly tarred even before the impeachment mess dragged down the good names of some of its members.[28] A division of labor among Virtuecrats led some (the "Scouts") to emphasize volunteerism as the salvation of the nation, some (the "McGuffeys") to stress moral education, and others (the "Preachers") to advocate establishing a Christian nation. All shared a faith in the efficacy of punishment in building character, favoring prison construction, mandatory "three strikes and you're out" sentencing, "boot camps" for young offenders, "deadbeat dad" statutes, denial of welfare benefits for unwed teen mothers, police sweeps through housing projects, and even caning and curfew ordinances. Not surprisingly, this harsh pro-punishment message resonated especially well in the South, where the "spare the rod and spoil the child" ethos persists. Calls for "traditional values" found a wider national audience as well, because "chaos, or the fear of it, has made Americans nostalgic for a more orderly age."[29]

The stress on older values matches the temperament of Southern culture, which is "universally regarded as traditional and conservative."[30] Daniel Elazar characterized the South's political culture as "traditional," in contrast to the more "moralistic" (in today's political climate, a better term might be "communitarian" or even "public spirited") bent of the Puritan-influenced extreme northern parts of the country and the more "individualistic" tendencies of the middle regions.[31] Given the hierarchical nature of most traditional institutions, it is not difficult to see that the renewed interest in "traditional values" can easily carry very conservative baggage. Michael Lind argues that the Republican Right represents the resurgence of traditional Southern and Southwestern political culture. He concludes that "since the new Republican movement has much more in common with the old Dixiecrats than with neoconservatives, the most fruitful way to analyze and predict its course is not to read *The Public Interest* [a neoconservative policy magazine] but to examine the history of state and local politics in the South." Lind warns that

"the South exports some of the country's best literature, music and food—but it also exports its worst politics." Lind asserts that traditional Southern culture has provided a rich soil for racism, patriarchy, heterosexism, and xenophobic patriotism but a barren sustenance for civil liberties, dissent, and diversity.[32]

Peter Applebome, a prophet of Southern ascendance, maintains that the South is setting the tone for the nation. On race in particular, he notes that

> there's probably no better place to start trying to understand race in America than to make sense of the utterly unexpected way the civil rights revolution turned out to be the best thing that ever happened to the white South, paving the way for the region's newfound prosperity, but a mixed blessing for Southern blacks, who won a measure of integration into a white world at the expense of some of the enduring and nurturing institutions of their old black one.

But Applebome makes an even stronger claim, arguing that

> at a time when a Democratic president like Bill Clinton is coming out for school prayer, going along with sweeping Republican legislation shredding welfare and taking his cues from a consultant, Dick Morris, who formerly worked for Southern arch-conservatives like Jesse Helms and Trent Lott; when race is a fractious national obsession; when the nation's population is moving steadily South; when the Supreme Court is acting as if Jefferson Davis were chief justice; when country music has become white America's music of choice and even stock car racing has become a $2 billion juggernaut; when evangelical Christians have transformed American politics; when unions are on the run across the nation much as they always have been in the South; when whites nationwide are giving up on public education just as so many Southerners did after integration—in times such as these, *to understand America, you have to understand the South.*[33]

Why Is This Scene So Familiar?

As the United States faces a new century, its politics seems woefully inadequate to meet the needs of the nation. Particularly in an era

when the United States can no longer count on dominating the world economy, the political system seems incapable of producing policies to address adequately the pressing needs in fields such as education; economic training, job security, and retirement security; health care; sexism, racism, poverty, and the growing class gap; declining communities and multicultural conflicts; and environmental degradation.[34] To anyone with historical memory of the South in the first part of this century, this fin de siècle litany of problems and the bankruptcy of the political system that should be addressing them should sound hauntingly familiar. As one astute observer of the Southern and national political scene exclaimed in 1998,

> What stamped Georgia politics in the late forties has been enlarged and exported. The negative campaigning, the unregulated solicitation and misuse of campaign funds, the crushing weight of corporate power, the civic passivity and low voter turnout—all have come to typify our national political behavior. It's as if the gallus-snapping, shirt-sleeved demagogues of Georgia's yesterday have merely moved north, acquired Armani suits and new accents, and gone on network television.[35]

In *Southern Politics in State and Nation,* written in 1949 at the threshold of the second half of the twentieth century, V. O. Key, Jr., the foremost analyst of Southern (and perhaps American) politics of his day, suggested that politics was the number one problem of the South. This claim must have appeared counterintuitive if not outrageous. Although politics in the South of that day was the bailiwick of buffoons and scoundrels, many other problems must have appeared far more urgent than the sad state of Southern politics. For example, virulent racism, pervasive violence, grinding poverty, rampant illiteracy, abysmal health, a bankrupt agriculture, depleted natural resources and a degraded environment, and a painful, chaotic transition from a rural to an urban, industrial society could all lay claim to the dubious distinction of being most critical. Key's point, however, was that politics is the way societies attempt to organize responses to their problems. In the process, "we determine who governs and in whose interests the government is run." Although many would have judged politics irrelevant, or at best peripheral, to the greatest needs of the South at midcentury, Key saw that workable solutions to these problems required

an organized and responsive politics, which he found sorely lacking in the region at that time.[36]

Especially in an era when national leadership has passed into almost exclusively Southern hands, Key's complaint seems uniquely pertinent. Politics is now the number one problem of the United States. Many citizens are so deeply touched by cynicism toward the American political system that they have essentially tuned politics out of their lives.[37] Observing that the current climate could be called a "culture of nonparticipation," noted political commentator Wilson Carey McWilliams writes that "millions of Americans believe or suspect that democratic politics, even at its best, has become largely irrelevant; in America's developing postindustrialism, economics and technology seem to call the tune even where government plays the fiddle."[38] Government may not be the problem, as Ronald Reagan proclaimed, but increasing numbers of Americans think that it is not part of the solution.[39] Unfortunately, no satisfactory solutions to the nation's woes are likely to be forthcoming unless a more vibrant democratic politics can be recovered.

Many Americans, both citizens and pundits, blame our ills on our leaders. Given Americans' intellectual habit of perceiving only individuals and not social structures to be real and significant, it is hardly surprising that Newt Gingrich should be widely demonized for the sharp rightward tilt of American politics. Conversely, many on the liberal side of the spectrum hold Bill Clinton responsible for rushing rightward rather than resisting the conservative tide after 1994.[40] That the most prominent leaders are now Southern correlates easily with the rightward drift of our politics.

The success of Southern politicians and the widespread acceptance of dominant Southern political values, however, are mere symptoms of the striking resemblances between American politics at the end of the century and Southern politics at the century's midpoint. Underneath these surface similarities lie structural features that shaped politics in the early-twentieth-century South and that increasingly drive national politics as we enter a new century. Although American politics does not share the one-party dominance that made the old solidly Democratic South distinctive, the contemporary political system exhibits the critical core characteristics that shaped the Solid South before 1950: lack of meaningful party competition, low levels of pop-

ular participation, and an emphasis on racial conflict to the detriment of economic issues. Today, our political parties are fiercely competitive and offer the voters distinct choices, but voter loyalty to parties is on the wane, and partisan identification gives less guidance to citizens' political choices than in the past. More and more barriers to voting have been removed, but fewer and fewer citizens find compelling reasons to vote; less than one-half of the eligible voters turned out in the 1996 presidential election, normally the high-water mark of participation in American politics. Racism is subtler in this country than in past eras, but the emotion-charged politics of crime, affirmative action, and welfare reform is tinted with thinly disguised racial overtones. These developments in our contemporary national politics suggest that it is these structural aspects of our political system, rather than the geographic origins of our leadership, that is "Southernizing" national politics. If our political system is evolving traits like that of the older Southern system, the emerging trends are liable to prove deeper and more enduring, regardless of who our elected leaders are or what part of the country they call home.

These new developments in our politics also augur poorly for the future of American democracy. These traits—enfeebled party competition, a narrow electorate, and racialized politics—today as well as then, result in policies that favor powerful political and economic elites to the disadvantage of the vast majority of average citizens. Ironically, the Democratic Solid South was decidedly undemocratic,[41] and the structures that undermined democracy then threaten the vitality of our national democratic institutions now. An analysis of the structural traits of Southern politics in the first half of the twentieth century, along with a tracing of the paths by which Southern politics and national politics have come to be so similar, serves to illuminate the odd political configurations that have come to overshadow the American political landscape. After all, as Ira Katznelson reminds us, "the most significant shifts in the central tendencies of American politics in the past six decades—the New Deal, the civil rights revolution, and the sharp turn toward conservatism and Republicanism—all have had the South at their core." Such an analysis also highlights how our current political difficulties hinder attempts to solve our social ills as we enter a new century.[42]

History does not repeat itself in any straightforward or simple way,

and obviously, a literal return to the Jim Crow policies and race-baiting politics of the Solid South is not merely unlikely but unthinkable. There have been too many dramatic social, economic, and political, not to mention technological, changes in the last half century to conceive of Southern, much less national, politics being hijacked by a planter aristocracy and redneck good ole boys. Nonetheless, political developments from the 1960s to the 1990s have created sufficient parallels between contemporary politics nationally and politics in the old Solid South that an understanding of Southern politics can shed light on recent movements in American politics. In addition, an examination of Southern politics of the past might provide a timely warning about future directions in American politics. Given national trends in recent decades, the idea of the Solid South as a portent of developments on the horizon in American politics is, sadly, not as outlandish as it might first appear. As long as three decades ago, the noted student of party politics Walter Dean Burnham somberly predicted that if the party system continued to disintegrate, "American politics would come to resemble the formless gubernatorial primaries that V. O. Key described in his classic *Southern Politics.*"[43] One can only hope that such gloomy prophecies will spur citizens to act to ensure that our future does not mirror the uglier facets of Southern politics past.

The Past as Prologue

If the example of traditional Southern politics is to illuminate contemporary developments in national politics, we need to examine the most significant structural features that shaped Southern politics. Chapter 2 outlines the origins and main traits of the solidly Democratic Southern political system that was erected at the turn of the twentieth century and lasted into the 1960s. Key's classic analysis of the characteristics of this system and its consequences for Southern politics internally, in Southern states, and externally, in national politics, explains why politics was the South's number one problem and why the South was the nation's number one political problem.

Chapter 3 traces the convergence of Southern and national politics that occurred largely from the 1960s to the 1990s from the angle of changes in the South, using Georgia and North Carolina as proto-

typical cases through which to grasp these developments. Dramatic changes created a South no longer out of step with the rest of the nation. Socially, legal changes and the civil rights movement dismantled de jure segregation and put race relations on the same footing as in the rest of the country. Politically, the conspicuous growth of two-party politics is the most manifest sign of change. This convergence was a dual one. At the same time that the South was rejoining the nation socially and politically, national trends have "Southernized" American politics. In particular, the demise of the New Deal, the decline of parties generally, and the displacement of economic and class politics with racial and cultural politics have rendered the nation's politics increasingly problematic, in ways reminiscent of Key's description of old-style Southern politics. Chapter 4 examines these developments at the national level.

If there is consensus that the old political order of the New Deal has been upended, there is no agreement on the current state of our political party system. Political scientists hotly debate whether our parties have realigned, perhaps producing a new majority party, or whether they are simply in the process of dealigning, entering an extended period of decline. The cases for partisan realignment and dealignment are reviewed in chapter 5. There is substantial evidence that the South has shifted partisan allegiance, contributing to a Republican majority in the country as a whole. This movement represents a dramatic change from the Democratic dominance of the New Deal era from 1932 to the 1960s, but some analysts dispute whether the new partisan balance constitutes a stable party system. The new party lineup is closely competitive and highly fluid. The parties' weaknesses create a partisan realignment with many of the characteristics of a dealigned party system, one in which parties and partisanship have only diminishing influence in channeling the politics and policies of the era.

Chapter 6 examines national politics in the post–New Deal era, comparing the contemporary political scene with the structure of Southern politics described by Key: weak partisan competition, a shrinking electorate, and racialized politics. Chapter 7 then describes some of the symptoms produced by politics lacking coherence, continuity, and accountability as a result of these structural flaws. The political deficiencies we suffer as we enter the new century hinder

efforts to solve the problems we face as a nation, especially those brought on by the globalization of the economy. This current economic restructuring parallels the older South's traumatic transition from an agricultural to an industrial and urban society, a transformation rendered more painful than necessary because of the region's warped politics. The lesson to be learned for the contemporary transformation is that irrational and undemocratic politics will place the burdens of transition squarely on the shoulders of average citizens, while benefits will be reaped by the privileged. Chapter 8 concludes by exploring political reforms that might avoid such consequences by enhancing participation in politics and government accountability to popular majorities.

Look Away, Dixieland

To recapitulate briefly, conventional wisdom holds that in the second half of the twentieth century, the South finally and fully rejoined the rest of the nation, ending its backward social segregation by extending opportunity to African Americans, overcoming its legacy of grinding poverty by integrating itself into the modern economy, and renouncing its yellow-dog Democrat, one-party politics by welcoming Republican competition. This view, while not wrong, is only half the story, because the nation has in a sense seceded from its previous, more salutary politics and seems headed toward joining the South in its older brand of unhealthy politics. No one expects the country to be reduced to a politics of race baiting, stump demagoguery, and behind-the-scenes Bourbon elite skullduggery. Yet a gnawing sense is pervasive that politics in this country is changing in disturbing ways. Although remaining formally democratic, politics just does not "work" for most people anymore. The malaise that antedated Jimmy Carter's administration and lingered through Clinton's exhibits symptoms of the sick politics of the Solid South.

The antics of Old Southern politics, although often eerily entertaining, were no laughing matter. They produced, or at least reinforced, a society that was the "sick man" of the country—uneducated, illiterate, unproductive, backward, poor, unhealthy, racist, and sexist—in a word, undemocratic. These conditions were not products of some

distinctive, distorted Southern personality or culture; they were shaped and maintained by political institutions and leadership. Southern elites alone benefited from the politics of the Solid South. African Americans by and large were disenfranchised, as were many poor whites and women, and their needs were regularly ignored by Southern state governments. Although Southern whites constituted the constituencies of Southern politicians, their interests, too, except perhaps their need for symbolic gratification, were regularly sacrificed for the tangible interests of the planter-industrialist elites. The problems of ordinary Southerners that called desperately for new departures were neglected; the elites' stakes in the status quo were protected. The notion, then, that national politics may be approaching this model of politics is not a reassuring thought.

If our current national politics is coming to resemble Old Southern politics, we should take heed and act now. By understanding Southern politics of the past, perhaps we can better comprehend and escape our present political conundrums and redirect our future toward a more responsible and democratic politics. In the next chapter, we turn first to a look at "ole-timey" politics in Dixie, for if politics nationwide has become "Dixified," then the whole country should heed this bit of Southern wisdom: "The past is never dead. It's not even past."[44]

2 / Politics in the Land of Cotton
Old Times There Should Not Be Forgotten

Not a Comic Opera

To claim that contemporary American politics bears any resemblance to "ole-timey" Southern politics seems a bit outlandish. In fact, seeing any similarity between contemporary Southern politics and traditional Southern politics requires a bit of a stretch (and thank goodness, most would add). After all, the bigots and buffoons who stalked the Southern political landscape as recently as fifty years ago, rhetorically refighting the Civil War and vowing to protect the "Southern way of life" against intervention by the federal "gub'-ment," have been replaced by moderate political leaders equally at home in the halls of government in Washington seeking to win federal grants as in corporate boardrooms pursuing capital investments in their states. The traditional fire-and-brimstone stump speeches delivered by men in white linen suits with red suspenders at barbecues in the sweltering summer heat have been replaced by televised campaign ads as slick and cool as any thirty-second spot in the nation. In the most dramatic difference, Southern elections now involve partisan competition, not traditional one-party Democratic dominance, with the advantage inclining, in fact, to the Republicans. For example, although no Southern state elected a Republican governor between 1900 and 1950, in 1997, eight of the eleven Southern governors were Republicans. If there are comparisons to be drawn between traditional Southern politics and contemporary politics, whether Southern or national, they must be sought not on the surface, where so much appears different, but in deeper, structural similarities, where subtler continuities reside.

To lay a proper foundation for comparing contemporary politics,

whether in the South or in the United States, with traditional Southern politics, we must start at the beginning. In Southern politics, the point of departure is always V. O. Key's classic analysis written in 1949. Key, a political scientist from Texas, began *Southern Politics in State and Nation* by noting that in his day, many commentators viewed politics in Dixie as "a comic opera staged on a grand scale for the amusement of the nation."[1] Indeed, the antics of regional politicians seemed to justify the view that Southern politics was mainly a form of entertainment, if a bit on the low-brow side. Although Southern politics produced serious, dignified leaders such as Walter F. George and Richard B. Russell, including both respected liberals (e.g., Senator Lister Hill of Alabama) and conservatives (e.g., Senator Harry F. Byrd of Virginia), "colorful" characters were also plentiful: Huey Long, who served simultaneously as Louisiana governor and senator, whose real passions included coaching the Louisiana State University Tigers and who once received the German ambassador while attired in his pajamas after a night of hearty partying;[2] Gene Talmadge, four-time governor of Georgia, who, when caught spending state funds without authorization, assured his die-hard supporters (poor dirt farmers known as the wool hat boys), "Yeah, it's true. I stole, but I stole for you, the dirt farmer";[3] and "Big Jim" Folsom, beloved (and liberal) governor of Alabama whose political career came to a sad end when he appeared on an election-eve broadcast so drunk that he could not introduce his children by name.[4]

But if Southern politics had its comic and colorful side, there was an ugly underside as well. The violent race baiting that often polluted campaign rhetoric not only reflected the white majority's prejudice but also inflamed racial hatred and incited racial violence.[5] The electoral antics that vaulted buffoons to public attention unfortunately sometimes elevated them to public office. Many governments in Southern states were corrupt,[6] incompetent, or ineffective. As a result, Southern social problems festered with little or no relief provided by government policies. Long impoverished relative to other regions of the nation, the South was singled out by President Roosevelt during the Great Depression as "the nation's No. 1 economic problem."[7] Even into the 1950s and beyond, the region lagged far behind on measures of literacy, poverty, health, wealth, income, industry, and other indicators of socioeconomic development.[8] Dixie's inability to solve these problems

was rooted in its politics, according to Key, thus making politics "the South's number one problem."[9]

Bourbon Democracy

Key's genius was that he pierced beneath the "droll facade" of comedy and chaos to identify structures that he claimed were responsible for the South's political underdevelopment. Rather than blaming the region's distinctiveness on its history of defeat in the Civil War or its unique "redneck" culture or its poverty or backward economy, Key located the main source of the problem within its political practices and institutions. Specifically, Key characterized the problematic nature of Southern politics as rooted in a political system that was (1) based solidly on one-party Democratic dominance; (2) predicated on the disenfranchisement of virtually all African Americans, but also of large numbers of whites, especially poor ones; and (3) dedicated to the preservation of white supremacy.[10]

Although founded on a generalized racism pervasive in Southern society, this system was the creation of a Southern minority, a planter elite, according to Key. The core of Southern politics was located in the black belt, counties so called less because of their black earth than because African Americans made up a majority of their populations. African Americans came to be concentrated in these areas because the fertile soil supported large plantations and hence numerous slaves before the Civil War. These areas, however, were not governed by their black majorities, but rather by the plantation-owning whites, whose position, Key astutely observed, was analogous to white colonizers in the third world. Just as colonists could not allow democracy without yielding power to the indigenous majority, so black-belt whites could not countenance genuine democracy and still cling to their power and privilege.

Most of the South, particularly the Piedmont hill regions and mountains, did not share the interests of the planter elite. In these areas, where whites were the clear majorities, obsession with maintaining white supremacy was a less pressing item on the political agenda. These up-country areas tended to be less wealthy, populated by poorer farmers operating smaller farms with less productive soil. In states

that were still primarily agricultural, these non–black-belt residents tended to need more government services and were willing to tax the wealthy to finance them. Thus, the majority of Southern whites were less committed to maintaining the racial and economic status quo, and the concomitant passive, "small" state governments, than were the wealthy whites of the black-belt counties. That the planter minority was able to maintain dominance in the midst of a nominally democratic society is a twisted tribute to their political skills and to the perverse logic of the political system they devised and foisted on the rest of Southern society.

Key did not contend that black-belt elites always triumphed. In fact, the poorer white majority was often successful in electing "populist" candidates who promised redistributive policies and active government programs to help the "little man." A few officials actually pursued popular reforms once elected. Huey Long, for all his antics and violations of democratic procedures, pursued tax-and-spend policies that benefited the masses of Louisiana. He also did not partake of the traditional obsession with racial politics. Despite not frontally attacking racial injustices, Long, like his contemporary Franklin Roosevelt, designed programs to help all in need, rather than whites only, thus including African Americans among the beneficiaries of his policies.[11] Most politicians elected with poor white votes, however, confined their populism to political rhetoric; once off the stump and in the halls of government, they were too corrupt or incompetent to carry through and enact programs favored by their constituency.

In any event, Key did not think that these isolated populist victories conclusively defined the contours of Southern politics. Instead, the black-belt core won at the decisive turning points of Southern history, in effect by trumping the economic interests of the vast majority with their concerns for racial dominance. First, on the eve of the Civil War, the slave-owning plantation elite managed to convince a majority of whites who owned no slaves to secede from the Union and to fight a bloody struggle to defend slavery. Second, at the end of the nineteenth century, Southern elites successfully staved off an economic rebellion by poor whites and blacks who, in many localities, had fused in alliances of Populist (predominantly poor white) and Republican (predominantly poor black) parties to challenge Democratic party rule. Elite victory was attained by raising the specter of racial equality

(touted as African American rule, of course) and was embodied in the system that shaped the region's "uniquely deviant political history" until well past the midpoint of the twentieth century.[12]

The central institutions of Southern politics became, first, the Solid Democratic South. The Democratic party was sold as "the white man's party"; for whites to go outside the Democratic primary to challenge the political status quo became racial treason. Second, as the national government turned its gaze elsewhere, Southern states gutted the Fifteenth Amendment's grant of the vote to African American males by enacting various devices to disenfranchise black voters. Many of these means, for example, poll taxes and literacy tests, ironically also disenfranchised many whites, especially the poor populist farmers.[13] The third pillar, racist politics aimed at maintaining white supremacy, rested on the foundations of a one-party Democratic politics with a narrow base of wealthier voters, making planter control and a diversion from economic populism more attainable. During this period, Southern states enacted Jim Crow statutes that codified white supremacy and strict segregation—laws that remained in force until the civil rights movement and court decisions began to dismantle them in the 1950s.[14]

Although Key stressed the role that so-called top-drawer Southerners played in instituting the disenfranchisement and segregation of African Americans, latent and manifest racism among the white masses ensured a receptive audience for racist politics. If elite politicians issued the battle cry of racial solidarity, it was a call to which the mass of poor Southern whites responded. Likewise, the national government responded with "benign neglect" as Southern states rolled back the constitutional rights of many of their citizens. Key noted that "as in the case of the colonials, that white minority can maintain its position only with the support, and by the tolerance, of those outside—in the home country or in the rest of the United States." At the same time, political elites in many Northern localities were enacting "reforms" designed to break the power of ethnic partisan machines that had been used by immigrant majorities to attain power in many cities.[15] Viewed nationally, the effect of these diverse innovations in both South and North was to reduce drastically the size of the electorate, creating a "hole" of nonvoters at the lower ends of the socioeconomic class and racial and ethnic spectrums.[16]

Even though the larger society was implicated in the creation of the Solid South system, it was nonetheless an impressive achievement by an elite minority that managed to protect its interests and impose its priorities in a nominally majoritarian democracy where the majority might have asserted different concerns. Internally, within Southern state politics, the Solid Democratic South meant that all significant political conflict was confined within the Democratic party, an all-white constituency skewed to a narrow electorate. Within this tightly constricted arena, racial politics displaced economic issues. Despite occasional flashes of lower-class insurgency, white supremacy trumped populist tax-and-spend and redistributive policies opposed by the wealthy planters. Externally, "unity on the national scene was essential in order that the largest possible bloc could be mobilized to resist any national move toward interference with southern authority to deal with the race question as was desired locally."[17] Thus, within the federal system, the strength of a united Solid South was harnessed to prevent "intervention" by the national government against racial injustices that so blatantly violated basic American principles and legal norms.

The achievement of the black-belt elite, then, was to institutionalize a Solid South system that was designed to, and effectively did for decades, protect the undemocratic dominance of the planter elites and their interests in the racial and economic status quo both from the potentially democratic governments of Southern states and from the federal government. This achievement, not surprisingly, carried a high price tag in terms of democracy in Southern states and even in national politics.

Kaleidoscopic Politics

Having excluded African Americans by various legal and extralegal means from voting and participating in public affairs, and having defeated the Populist party challenge by intimidation and appeals to white loyalty, the Democratic party dominated the field as the only realistic route to winning political power. The "white primary" of the Democratic party attracted more voters than the general election, because winning the Democratic nomination was tantamount to victory. One-party politics Southern style, of course, meant something

very different from one-party domination in authoritarian states, where an official party controls all the government, including the state bureaucratic machinery and state police, and monopolizes public affairs. In contrast, the political life of Southern states was only nominally under the sway of the Democratic party. Although almost all political participants were Democrats in name, the party as an organization was a hollow shell. Paradoxically, in the politics of Dixie, the Democratic party was everything, yet nothing. Instead of the tight stranglehold of an authoritarian one-partyism, politics in the Solid South, although occurring within the confines of the Democratic party, was wide open and highly disorganized.

The problem for politics within the Southern states, as Key correctly diagnosed, was not only that this one-party politics rested on a narrow base. Certainly, treating the Democratic party as a private club that excluded almost all African Americans, most women, and many poor white men distorted political contests and skewed policy in favor of the planter elite. "The blunt truth is that politicians and officials are under no compulsion to pay much heed to classes and groups of citizens that do not vote." A further distortion, Key stressed, resulted from the lack of party competition. Although nominations were generally determined by wide-open primary contests for popular votes rather than controlled by party cadres in caucuses or conventions, the very nature of one-party politics introduced additional deformities into the democratic process. Key's main insight was to suggest that one-party politics is functionally equivalent to a "non-party system." When all political players are Democrats, being a Democrat is meaningless. Unlike in competitive party systems, where party labels denote contrasting political tendencies, if everyone in politics is a "Democrat," candidates convey no more information about themselves or their platforms by labeling themselves "Democrats" than if they simply chose to call themselves "humans" or any other label that describes all participants. One-party Democratic politics was, in effect, a species of partyless politics that produced a disorganization that undermined democratic politics in the sense of popular rule.[18]

Without party organization and, even more critically, party competition, the politics of the South lacked several qualities necessary for popular self-government.[19] First, partyless politics lacked coherence. Instead of a fathomable number of party tickets, Southern elec-

torates faced a bewildering gaggle of candidates running for each office. Moreover, rather than running as members of party "teams," candidates for each office tended to maintain their distance and independence from candidates for all other offices. In effect, all candidates chose "to go into business for themselves," ensuring that although a group of Democrats was certain to be elected to office, being a "Democrat" was meaningless in terms of cooperation, platform, or allegiance.[20] Southern states did have factions within the Democratic party, ranging from highly fluid and disorganized multifactional states such as Florida and Arkansas to the tightly factional Long versus anti-Long politics of Louisiana. Most states fell somewhere on the continuum in between, with various bases for state party factionalism. Georgia, for example, loosely divided into factions around the personality of Gene Talmadge. North Carolina had its "Simmons machine," followed by a "Shelby Dynasty" formed around geographical conflicts as well as leadership rivalries. Even the best-organized factions, however, only remotely approximated parties in their coherence.[21] In Georgia, for instance, such was the electoral benefit of associating with the Talmadges that sometimes multiple candidates claimed to wear the mantle of "Ole Gene" or his son, Herman, but it was often tough to tell which candidate actually ran with their blessings. The result was not a *total* lack of coherence to Southern state politics, but without the organization of political players into a manageable number of coherent party teams, political patterns resembled a kaleidoscope, complex and confusing.[22]

One-party factional politics was lacking not only coherence but also continuity; like a kaleidoscope when turned, each new election or political battle was likely to introduce a new, equally incomprehensible lineup of factional forces. Obviously, such a fluid pattern lacked continuity across time. Allies in one fray could be opposed in the next, while former adversaries could easily find themselves bedfellows of convenience in a later contest. Time was not the only dimension of incoherence, however. In governments where power has been divided into separate legislative, executive, and judicial branches, some level of cooperation is necessary for policy making and administration. Yet the jealousies of institutional, ideological, and personal rivalries make conflict inevitable. Parties offer at least some hope of spanning constitutionally separated branches of government. In the South, however,

where being a Democrat was a nearly universal albeit meaningless label, having Democrats in control of the various branches of state government produced little if any consensus on program. In Georgia in 1970, to cite just one example, the voters elected progressive Jimmy Carter governor and segregationist Lester Maddox, his sworn political enemy, lieutenant governor. Using his prerogatives as presiding officer of the senate, Maddox used his term in office to sandbag the governor's initiatives, including Carter's vaunted reorganization of state government. Both were Democrats, but they could not have been further apart in terms of ideology and policy, resulting in a state government divided against itself. Even within the executive branch of state governments, state constitutions created plural executives, with many functions administered by independently elected commissioners (e.g., labor commissioner, insurance commissioner, commissioner of agriculture, secretary of state) or boards (Public Service Commission, State School Board, Transportation Board). Even a minimum of administrative continuity was difficult to achieve when executive leadership was lodged in the hands of nominally Democratic but actually independent politicians.

Continuity was lacking across levels of the federal system, as well as across branches of government. During the 1930s, for example, Georgia voters endorsed Franklin Delano Roosevelt's New Deal with overwhelming majorities for FDR in the 80 to 90 percent range in the presidential elections. During this same period, however, Gene Talmadge, a die-hard opponent of FDR and his New Deal, won the governorship four times. Federal and state elections were almost completely unsynchronized, and different levels of the federal system were unable to act with coordination and continuity.[23]

Furthermore, the isolation of Solid South politics from national political tides had a reciprocal effect, reinforcing the one-party system. The distancing of state politics from national political contests deprived Southern states of the visible controversy that could have sustained democratic debates: "if in no other way the one-party system, by its insulation of the South from national campaigns, deprives the southern electorate of the stimulation of most grand questions of public policy." Cut off from external allies in other parts of the country and unstirred by participation in national debates, fewer citizens were drawn into politics, harming the chances of political competi-

tion by "slic[ing] from the electorate the persons who would form the basis for a large faction or, in a two party state, the basis for a party."[24]

The bottom line for Key was that one-party politics lacked responsibility. Given the one-party monopoly enjoyed by the Democrats, the voters lacked the means for imposing accountability on their leaders. Although voters could kick the bums out of office one at a time, it was difficult to identify which bum was responsible for problems, given the lack of coherence and continuity that characterized partyless politics. Even presuming that individual politicians could be replaced, it was impossible for the voters to endorse new programs or directions because there were no rival organizations offering reasonably clear alternatives. Each election, indeed, each office, constituted a new and separate competition for power. Under these chaotic conditions, the public had no way to pass judgment on previous officeholders or to endorse new departures proposed by opposing teams of political players. Without parties, in other words, ties of responsibility linking government and the ultimately sovereign people were nearly severed.

The Price of Partyless Politics

The effects of incoherence, discontinuity, and irresponsibility on Southern politics were numerous, detrimental, and severe. One result was elections that were almost devoid of issues. The plethora of candidates running for office meant that substantive discussions of policy were necessarily precluded. Serious dialogue was almost impossible because candidates had difficulty attracting the public's attention to their proposals, and any proposals that seemed to win popular support were immediately "copycatted," adopted by other candidates as their own. In the absence of sustained discussion of tough issues, valence issues dominated, that is, issues on which all agreed. The only "debate" involved trying to appear most fervently dedicated to the proposition preferred by almost everyone. As Key noted, "When two distinct groups with some identity and continuity exist, they must raise issues and appeal to the masses if for no other reason than the desire for office. . . . [I]n those states with loose and short-lived factions campaigns often are the emptiest sorts of debates over personalities, over means for the achievement of what everybody agrees on."[25]

Extremism thrived in a politics devoid of issues other than those beyond question or criticism, where the competition revolved around who was the most zealous of true believers. In states where the enfranchised white voters were virtually universal in their support for segregation, maintaining the caste system and keeping African Americans "in their place" were nonetheless perennial campaign issues, not between segregationists and integrationists, but rather among candidates vying to prove the ardor of their support for Jim Crow. A legendary example of this extremism is the election-eve statement by George Wallace after losing the Alabama governor's race in 1958 to John Patterson, perceived as more hard line on race than the somewhat populist Wallace. Even Patterson attributed his victory to Wallace's being "considered soft on the race question," but Wallace swore that "no other son-of-a-bitch will ever out-nigger me again." He went on, of course, to be elected governor four times (not including his wife Lurleen's term) and to become the very embodiment of segregationist resistance, pledging in his 1963 gubernatorial address to fight for "segregation today, segregation tomorrow, segregation forever."[26]

Instead of issues, personalities dominated electoral contests, but "the lack of continuing groups of 'ins' and 'outs' profoundly influence[d] the nature of political leadership." By downplaying the importance of party leadership or issue content, elections by default centered on outstanding personalities, producing some strong leaders, but also opening the door for candidates who attracted attention for other, idiosyncratic, even gratuitous reasons or, worse, who were notorious demagogues. Demagogic politics did not reflect some sick Southern cultural trait but rather the structure, or lack of it, in the one-party political system.[27] Demagogues reaped an electoral premium in disorganized politics because their antics helped them stand out from the rabble of their competitors. At least voters could remember the names of colorful characters, and buffoons do get attention. Lester Maddox's ability to ride a bicycle backward was no indicator of competence to govern, but it was a "talent" that generated reams of photo footage. In an age before television, the penchant of Southern politicians for rousing rhetoric, especially of the mudslinging variety, was less a cultural talent than a survival technique in elections that were anarchistic wars of all against all. The apogee of artful, and deceptive, rhetorical excess was achieved by George Smathers in his

successful challenge of Senator Claude Pepper of Florida in 1950. Smathers's campaign speech tarnished Pepper with inspired, insinuating malapropisms: "Are you aware that Claude Pepper is known all over Washington as a shameless extrovert? Not only that, but this man is reliably reported to practice nepotism with his sister-in-law, and he has a sister who was once a thespian in wicked New York. Worst of all, it is an established fact that Mr. Pepper, before his marriage, practiced celibacy."[28]

In party competition, party organizations discipline as well as support leaders. They do so because the party interest is both broader and more enduring than the immediate self-interest of individual candidates; the party hopes to win not just one office but majority control of government, not only in this election but in future elections as well. Thus, "organization both elevates and restrains leaders; disorganization provides no institutional brake on capriciousness when the will in that direction is present."[29]

Candidates may attain recognition by means other than demagoguery, of course. Incumbents tend to have more name recognition and stand out in the crowd of challengers. Southern states often imposed severe limits on gubernatorial term lengths and succession to ensure competition for the office, but Southern representatives in Congress were only rarely defeated at the polls, accumulating massive seniority and thus power within the national government to protect sectional interests. Family name can also distinguish a candidate in an otherwise indistinguishable field of rivals. In Georgia, for over half a century, Gene Talmadge and his son Herman held statewide elected office almost continuously. The Harry Byrd dynasty of Virginia exemplifies the patrician Southern oligarchy. In North Carolina, the succession of father and son politicians was sufficiently striking to call into question the extent to which governing is a public rather than a private affair in that state.[30]

One consequence of issueless politics filled instead with histrionics, demagoguery, and vacuous name recognition was a tilt toward the status quo; no matter how badly change might be needed, even desired, proposals for change were not likely to be seriously entertained. "The chances are that the one-party or nonparty system facilitates the combination of those satisfied with current arrangements and encourages as well the inclination of the politician to let sleeping

dogs lie," wrote Key. As a result of letting sleeping dogs lie, issues tended to be decided by "nondecisions," by never explicitly making a decision because the matter never came to public attention for serious consideration.[31]

This pattern advantaged the status quo because nondecision facilitates drift, whereas change generally requires conscious choice. Many issues were never put on the agenda for discussion; instead, showboating and reaffirmations of safe nonissues that already enjoyed a broad consensus displaced these concerns. Even if issues were raised and promises made, without mechanisms of electoral accountability, there was no assurance of governmental follow-through by the victorious candidates. Lacking continuity, Southern political systems could not ensure enough cooperation and planning to get programs passed and implemented. The same tired issues could be raised in election after election, the same tried-and-true promises made, but campaign promises were unlikely to be translated into government action without parties. It is small wonder that Southern partyless politics resembled a "merry-go-round."[32]

Partyless politics also was peculiarly prone to corruption. Normally, the restraint of individual candidates by party organizations that take a bigger-picture view of the partisan interest serves as a hedge against corruption. Parties also provide a legitimate source of support for candidates, who otherwise have to turn elsewhere for the resources, especially money, to run for office. In the South, the absence of the continuity provided by parties corrupted the policy-making process in a broader sense, too. Without an organization of political leaders with at least broad agreement on political principles and some incentive to cooperate across terms and branches and levels of government, making policy tended to be an ad hoc affair, with the passage of each policy requiring a series of accommodations of specific interests. Deals substituted for general, coherent policy. Key observed that "factional fluidity and discontinuity probably make a government especially susceptible to individual pressures and especially disposed toward favoritism. . . . In a loose, catch-as-catch-can politics highly unstable coalitions must be held together by whatever means is available."[33] For example, roads got built where powerful legislators wanted them, not as mapped out by a state transportation plan. Branches of the state university were advanced according to local political pressures rather

than directed by an orderly development scheme for the state's higher education system.

Conversely, "an organized politics is also better able to establish general standards, to resist individual claims for preference, and to consider individual actions in the light of general policy."[34] Policy formulated through deals among elites in the absence of public discussion of issues and electoral accountability, however, was likely to be corrupt in this broader sense, in that it did not conform to an overall notion of the public good, as well as in the more literal sense that a politics of backroom deals tempted the players to line their pockets.

For the electorate, the consequences of disorganized, factional politics were severe. Most obviously, voters tended to be confused by vaguely defined and fluid factions. Their informational task in choosing candidates to represent them was "not simplified by the existence of continuing competing parties with fairly well-recognized, general-policy orientations." Instead of identifiable and stable political organizations, voters were faced with factions that "form[ed] and reform[ed]" and were "confronted with new faces, new choices, and [had to] function in a sort of state of nature."[35] Not surprisingly, the corollary of this confusion was low participation rates, especially among voters with lower socioeconomic status and less education, for whom the burden of obtaining information in such a chaotic system was especially heavy. Other factors, of course, also conspired to depress turnout in Southern elections, not the least of which was the disenfranchisement by legal devices of almost all African Americans and many poorer whites. In addition, a traditional political culture downgraded the role of women in politics and doubtless contributed to a lower voter turnout rate among Southern women. Even for those not pushed out of politics by legal or extralegal means, however, the confused, issueless politics of Southern states lacked the pull to attract significant numbers of voters to the polls.

Key's ultimate interest was in determining who benefited from this type of politics. He thought that state politics generally revolved around the conflict between the haves and the have-nots because of the crucial state governmental functions of taxing and spending. The elite haves rather than the have-nots won in Southern politics, despite being vastly outnumbered at the polls. Part of the explanation centered on the narrowed electorate that excluded many have-nots: "The

have–have not match is settled in part by the fact that substantial numbers of have-nots never get into the ring. For that reason professional politicians often have no incentive to appeal to the have-nots." His argument emphasized, however, the essentially partyless nature of one-party politics:

> Organization is not always necessary to obstruct; it is essential, however, for the promotion of a sustained program in behalf of the have-nots, although not all party or factional organization is dedicated to that purpose. It follows, if these propositions are correct, that over the long run the have-nots lose in a disorganized politics. They have no mechanism through which to act and their wishes find expression in fitful rebellions led by transient demagogues who gain their confidence but often have neither the technical competence nor the necessary stable base of political power to effectuate a program.[36]

The flip side of Key's argument is that the elite won. The one-party Solid South Democratic system constructed primarily to serve the interests of the black-belt planter elite in maintaining its racial hegemony also performed admirably to protect the economic interests of the wealthy from challenge from below. Despite occasional campaigns by populist-style candidates who shook their fists at the rich and ranted about representing the "little man," little of substance came of such "fitful rebellions," even when successful, because they lacked any organized clout to sustain a program of change and redistribution. Instead, most political conflicts were merely contests over "who is the 'best man' or the 'most competent' man to carry out what everyone is agreed upon," masking control, no matter who happened to be governor, by conservative groups "who squabble among themselves for the perquisites of office."[37]

In essence, Key was charging that politics without parties was irrational and undemocratic. Politics in the Old South was irrational because it avoided addressing critical issues, it failed to elevate qualified leaders, and it resulted in corrupt policy making and policies lacking general coherence. Solidly Democratic politics was undemocratic, except in name, because large numbers of potential voters were excluded from the system, or they failed to vote because of the confusion and lack of clear alternatives. The vast majority of the South-

ern population, who were have-nots in Key's day, lost to dominant elites who tended to be more organized and who in any event benefited from the status quo, which tended to persist in the absence of an organized and sustained challenge from below. Thus, popular sovereignty, the keystone of democratic values, remained an unrealized ideal because of the lack of institutional mechanisms to effect the will of the majority of the citizens. Liberty, too, suffered in a political framework erected on the systematic repression of a substantial portion of the population. And of course equality remained a hollow phrase in Southern societies divided by race, class, and gender and in which the elite haves regularly won office and policies favoring their interests. Far from democracy, Southern electoral politics was government of, by, and for the elites.[38]

Exceptionalism as the Rule

Protection of the black-belt planters' interest at the state level was only one aspect of the Solid South system. An elite local minority concerned with maintaining its domination over the majority population had to be wary as well of interference from the national government in a nation at least nominally dedicated to democratic principles of liberty, equality, and popular sovereignty through majority rule. The Solid South's most visible face was external, turned toward Washington. The basic premise of the Solid South was that the one-party system would contain all regional conflict within the Democratic party so that the region could present a united front to the rest of the nation, especially on racial issues.

Maximizing regional clout was achieved primarily through two mechanisms. First, the two-thirds rule, in existence until 1936, required that any Democratic presidential contender receive at least two-thirds of the national convention's votes to win the party's nomination. This rule ensured that a unified South could cast a sufficiently large bloc of votes to exercise a veto over candidates disfavored by Southern delegates. Second, Southerners, lacking weighty representation within the Republican party, relied on their power bases in Congress to guard against encroachments by national governments led by Republican presidents. Their power was greatly enhanced by the

seniority system for allocating crucial committee assignments and chairs and for ranking minority leaders, which was instituted at roughly the same time as the Solid South system was put in place. Because incumbents enjoyed significant name-recognition advantages and tended to be reelected more securely in one-party primaries than in competitive party elections, Southern representatives tended to serve longer in Congress than members from other regions. The seniority system that based leadership on longevity expanded the South's power within the national legislature well beyond what the region's proportionate numbers would have warranted.

Just as the Solid South system had lamentable consequences internally for Southern state politics, so it created problems externally for the American political system. One ironic result noted by Key was its contribution to the centralization of power in our federal system. Because Southern states failed to address issues of importance to the region, their "default" generated inevitable pressures for federal action. Even though generations of Southern politicians built careers posturing against "interference" from Washington, historically, the South has disproportionately benefited from national investments in military bases and depended on federal funding to ameliorate the ills that Southern states lacked the capacity or the will to solve.

The major external distortions resulting from the Solid South flowered with the advent of the political realignment that came to fruition during the Great Depression of the 1930s. With Franklin Roosevelt's elections, conservative Southern Democrats constituted a crucial pillar of the otherwise liberal electoral coalition composed of urban ethnics, minorities, labor, and intellectuals. Although Roosevelt attempted to restructure the Democratic party by purging such conservatives as Georgia senator Walter George, he ultimately failed and had to settle for de-emphasizing rather than revitalizing the party. How ironic that the undemocratic Democratic South, whose leadership rested on a system that excluded or grossly underrepresented the poor and working class, women, African Americans, and indeed the majority of average citizens, provided necessary support for the national Democratic party that sought to bring a New Deal to the down-and-out as well as the average citizens of America. Many peculiarities flowed from this "odd couple" arrangement, and they shaped American politics in distinctive ways.

Many observers in Key's time viewed Southern politics as strange—perhaps quaint, perhaps diabolical, but definitely distinctive. Likewise, there has been a parallel but separate tradition of citing American "exceptionalism"—noting that U.S. politics seems not to fit the expected patterns observed in most comparable Western industrialized democracies. Stressing Americans' adherence to liberal (philosophically) ideals such as antistatism, individualism, populism, and egalitarianism, Seymour Martin Lipset explains American distinctiveness as a reflection of American opinions, ideology, and cultural values. Lipset also notes that Americans' religiosity, for example, helps make the United States an "outlier" compared with similar nations. While 94 percent of Americans express faith in God, only 70 percent of Britons and 67 percent of Germans do. Religious fundamentalism is even more notable, with 69 percent of Americans believing that the Devil exists, compared with only about 33 percent of Britons and 18 percent of Germans.[39] Others have stressed other factors, especially in trying to explain the lack of a strong socialist strain in American politics. These factors range from historical peculiarities, such as the absence of a feudal past, to economic explanations, such as economic opportunity and the open frontier, to social factors, such as the racial and ethnic diversity of the country, to political explanations, such as early universal suffrage and repression of leftist groups. Jill Quadagno criticizes theories that rely on the early democratization of the United States, its liberal ideology, or its weak working class as explanations of American exceptionalism. She argues that racism limited American democracy and commitment to liberal values and weakened its working class. Michael Goldfield, too, recently traced the history of the United States, arguing that race was crucial in determining the political development of the country at every critical juncture. What most observers have failed to note, however, is that often Southern distinctiveness is the secret to American uniqueness.[40] The South, with its unique brand of politics, can help explain America's weak parties, stunted labor movement, and truncated welfare state.

The weakness of American political parties is one important way that American politics has differed from that of similar democracies. American parties have been much less ideologically unified, less programmatic, and less disciplined. Historically, they have achieved less

agreement on programs, and consequently, they have contested elections more on factors such as traditional loyalties, candidates, and pure public relations hoopla than on platforms. Although party platforms are far from meaningless as guides to the parties' policy orientation,[41] policy initiative in the American system lies more with the president than with party organizations, and straight party voting in American legislatures has been the exception rather than the rule, as in European political systems. These characteristics stem naturally from the fact that American parties are "umbrella" organizations, having no ideological or loyalty tests for membership. Unlike parties in most democracies, American parties do not even control their nominations and thus cannot enforce any modicum of agreement on policy or ideological questions. This weakness, along with the existence of only two major parties, means that the range of political opinions within each party is quite broad. Scholars have identified many sources for American party weakness, including the fragmentation embodied in a Constitution of separated powers and federalism and the size and diversity of the nation.[42] The diversity within the Democratic party, however, has historically been much greater than that within the Republican party. This disunity—at times, disarray—within the majority party has meant that party governance in America has been weak, and that the U.S. party system fell far shorter of the responsible party model than did the parties of other democratic nations. The peculiar role of the South as the misfit in the Democratic coalition has frustrated attempts to build strong, programmatic, responsible parties in the twentieth century.

A related American exceptionalism has been the weakness of the labor movement in this country. Union organizing flourished with the passage of the National Labor Relations Act (NLRA) in 1935, with union membership rising steeply from 13 percent of the labor force in 1935 to 35 percent in 1955. Still, density of union membership never reached the proportions achieved in many industrial democracies and has fallen to among the lowest in the world in recent years. The South has acted as a drag that has long held back organizing. Many explanations for the lower rate of unionization in the South focus on slower industrialization, the rural setting, an antiunion and traditionally deferential culture, and racial divisions. Less frequently emphasized is the hostility of state and local governments and political leaders,

who often have met union organizing drives with unrelieved hostility to assertions of worker rights. Have-not workers could expect little sympathy from their political leaders, whose support was rooted in a politics that systematically slighted have-not interests. Southern governments responded to organizing campaigns with injunctions, arrests, protection for scabs, illegal harassment, and, of course, the notorious "right to work" laws passed under the Taft-Hartley amendments to the NLRA.[43]

The vast reservoir of unorganized, cheap labor in the South has hobbled unions nationally because, when challenged by Northern unions, businesses could threaten to head south with some credibility. Although the union movement launched a major campaign to organize the South in the late 1940s, "Operation Dixie" ultimately failed, leaving American labor disadvantaged in its position vis-à-vis business. Although the national business offensive against labor reached epic proportions in the 1980s after President Reagan busted PATCO, the flight controllers' union, the decline began much earlier and was rooted in the failure of the labor movement to take root in the South. Once again, the South being out of line with the nation set the stage for the United States being out of step with comparable democracies.[44]

A final exceptionalism arguably flows rather directly from the previously noted weaknesses of American labor and political parties. Given that social democracy and the welfare state have been the constructions of labor movements and labor parties throughout Western Europe, not surprisingly, the United States is rather notable in its lack of a social democratic movement and in the underdevelopment of its welfare state.[45] The United States was not only slower to adopt welfare-state policies. When, in the depths of the Great Depression, a welfare state was at last adopted, the political coalition that enacted those policies, the Democratic New Deal of Franklin Roosevelt, rested not only on Northern progressive political forces but also necessarily on the reactionary forces of the Solid South. The South was, in effect, a "nation within a nation": "By 1935 the North was industrialized and democratic. . . . The South was neither industrialized nor democratic."[46] The inclusion of the South as a contradictory pillar within the shaky New Deal coalition no doubt helps explain many of the limits of New Deal policies, which some view as a pale shadow of

social democracy in this country. Liberal Democratic administrations that depended on Southern committee chairs and votes in Congress and Southern votes at the polls could not afford to alienate Southern politicians who were responsive to interests antagonistic to the welfare measures favored by the other elements of the New Deal coalition.

The necessary resulting compromises put in place fewer and more attenuated welfare measures than were enacted in most industrial democracies, and many of the disparities remain to this day. The United States never enacted or funded the full panoply of measures to ensure the security of its citizens that comparable industrial democracies did in response to demands by labor and social democratic parties. The Southern "hole" in the labor movement and in the New Deal Democratic coalition resulted in gross omissions in the American welfare state, such as no national health insurance or national health system, no general children's allowances, no paid parental leaves, and no mandated vacations.[47]

Another unique characteristic of the American welfare state is its decentralization. This was an accommodation to local power centers generally, perhaps, but specifically, it was a concession to Southern elites who were determined not to allow their hegemony to be challenged from below by have-nots, especially African Americans, provided with an independent, national source of resources. For example, social assistance programs ("welfare"), unemployment insurance, and housing programs are implemented by local authorities and often reflect local prejudices. Moreover, not only did the South block civil rights measures directly aimed at improving the lot of African Americans, but even the general welfare and labor legislation of the New Deal contained "racialized exclusions" to protect Southern employers' interests in a low-wage, segregated workforce. For example, the Social Security Act did not cover agricultural or domestic workers, relegating most Southern poor and black workers to the mercies of local welfare agencies, which were careful not to tread on the toes of local employers by providing too much assistance. The NLRA and other labor legislation also failed to extend federal protections to many dependent Southern workers. As Katznelson succinctly states, "the South made an American version of European social democracy impossible."[48]

Southern Politics in State and Nation

The regional result of the Solid South system was to facilitate elite domination in a political system that was irrational in its failure to cogently address the region's pressing social ills and undemocratic in its failure to respond to the interests of the majority of its citizens. The national consequences, while not as dramatically deforming, roughly paralleled the effects at the state and local levels. Public policy in the United States responded less fully to the social problems of the depression and to citizens' continuing need for measures to protect their security and welfare in the modern industrial setting. Although elite rule was certainly more firmly established in the Solid South, democratic responsibility was also undermined in the nation by the weakness of institutions such as unions and parties that generally give voice to the less powerful and hold leaders more accountable to the interests of the mass of citizens.

The undemocratic Democratic Solid South represented not only a pox on its own house but also a plague on national political life. The malformations of the strange breed of Southern politics disturbed political alignments and distorted public policies. More lastingly, the Solid South undermined the strength of the American party system and helped define the contours of the "welfare-warfare" hybrid national security state.[49] If politics has been the number one problem of the South, the South has been the number one political problem of the nation.

3 / *Dual Convergence*
The Reconstruction of the Unreconstructed South

Old Times There

The description of "ole-timey" Southern politics presented in chapter 2 is likely to elicit one of two contradictory reactions: everything is different now, or nothing has changed. One response to V. O. Key's analysis of traditional Southern politics is to conclude that it is irrelevant today, except perhaps as a yardstick by which to measure the progress that the region has made. The temptation is to look at the specifics of Key's description written in 1949 and to assert that the strange world of traditional Southern politics bears little resemblance to the contemporary realities of Southern life. Nothing has been immune from the sweeping changes that have transformed the region in recent decades. Have-not dirt farmers have been displaced by prosperous suburbanites. The colorful demagogues of yesterday have been replaced by gray-suited, carefully coifed, soft-spoken, moderate, and, for the most part, very dull politicians. Most importantly, Jim Crow segregation, the very raison d'être of the Solid South system, has been swept away by a potent combination of the outside intervention of national antidiscrimination law and an indigenous civil rights movement. Not surprisingly, the Democratic party monopoly has likewise vanished, with Southern states now enjoying closely competitive or even Republican-leaning party systems. Key's South seems almost as remote and strange to today's Southerners as it always did to the rest of the country.

Another reaction seems equally valid, if directly opposed: that nothing has really changed about Southern politics. Elections seem to turn on meaningless public relations ploys and campaign hoopla. Public choices are submerged as candidates focus exclusively on "mom and

apple pie" valence issues. All pledge improved education, more jobs, and reduced crime, but are these really issues? Who is on the opposing side of this "debate"? Is anyone against education or for unemployment and crime? Yet state governments still fail to address effectively these same issues, as Southern states lag behind the nation in indices of social welfare even as the Southern economy booms. Participation in state politics is still abysmally low, reflecting low popular attention to and comprehension of state and local governments. Although the traditional planter aristocracy has been displaced by a business class, the elite is still in the driver's seat in Southern politics and is still taking the populace for a ride.[1]

Both reactions are correct, at different levels. The modern-day South is different in all the particulars that made its politics a unique spectacle in Key's day. The South has indeed changed; today the region is practically indistinct from the rest of the nation in most observable aspects. But even as it has changed, certain deeper continuities remain. Several of the underlying structural characteristics that shaped Southern politics have been little modified, rendering Key's description hauntingly familiar. Even more telling, perhaps, the rest of the country has been changing, too. In some startling ways, national politics has come to resemble Southern politics. Although the more visible traits of traditional Southern politics have long since been shed, the underlying foundations that remain intact do not seem as distinctive as they once did. These subtle but profound similarities mean that Key's critique of disorganized mass politics still resonates in the region, and increasingly on a national level as well.

Since Key completed his book in 1949, a dual convergence has been at work in the South and in the nation. One prong of the forces at work has "Northernized" the South, mainstreaming the once distinct region into a section that closely resembles the rest of the country on most indicators. The other prong of the dual transformation has produced a "Southernization" of the North, paving the way for Southern politicians to assume national leadership roles and for traditionally Southern concerns and patterns increasingly to dominate American politics. The Southern metamorphosis is most striking, but it is the triumph of "Southernized" politics at the national level that bodes most significant for the future of democracy in America.

The Americanization of Dixie[2]

Many facets of Southern society have changed dramatically since mid-century, and not surprisingly, these changes have been working to produce equally noticeable political changes. Although the South still stands apart from the rest of the country on many indicators, the gaps are closing, and the trends toward convergence are unmistakable.

If V. O. Key was correct in identifying race as the driving force behind the Solid South system and the black-belt whites as the core of the political South, the decline in the percentage of African Americans in the Southern population holds special significance. Whereas blacks made up 32 percent of the region's population in 1920, in 1950, they constituted only 25 percent; by 1980, that proportion dropped to 20 percent. Interestingly, this decrease was paralleled by an increase in the percentage of blacks in the rest of the United States, from 10 percent in 1950 to 12 percent in 1980. These figures reflect the immense internal migration of Southern blacks out of the region to areas of greater economic opportunity and less racial discrimination. This migration occurred in massive numbers after the turn of the twentieth century, picked up steam during World War II, and was further accelerated by the advent of the tractor and the mechanization of Southern agriculture. In the three decades after World War II, 5 million African Americans left the South. Since the mid-1970s, however, the direction of the flow has reversed, and around 100,000 African Americans have moved south every year.[3]

Reverse migration into the region has further diminished the distinctiveness of the South's racial composition. An in-migration has occurred primarily since the 1960s, as Northern whites were drawn to the region by urbanization and industrialization, the heavy concentration of military bases, and the boom in retirement communities in certain areas of the South.[4] From 1990 to 1997 alone, more than 5 million adults relocated to the South from other parts of the country. In a dramatic shift, the percentage of Southern whites born outside the South rose from 8 percent in 1950 to 20 percent in 1980. Since the 1980s, international immigration into both nation and region has further blurred the lines between the two by contributing to a less distinct racial and ethnic mix in the Southern population. Whites have declined from 76 percent to 68 percent of the Southern population

since the mid-1970s, while the percentage of African Americans has remained relatively steady at just under 20 percent. Hispanics have increased from 5 to 11 percent, with other minorities, although much smaller in absolute numbers, growing rapidly as well.[5]

Restructuring of the U.S. economy brought even more in-migration, as the Northern manufacturing base stagnated and declined while the South's newer, more service-based economy boomed. Over 43 million jobs have been lost since 1979, and the pain was unevenly distributed across the country. The Sun Belt's population exploded, while Rust Belt growth lagged far behind. Over half the growth in jobs in the 1990s occurred in the South, and two of the states growing fastest in manufacturing employment are located there. Far from being the economic laggard that it had been in the first half of the 1900s, by the end of the century, the *Economist* was calling the South "a locomotive powering the American economy."[6]

V. O. Key's South was primarily a rural region. By midcentury, only Florida, Texas, and Louisiana were as much as half urban. In 1920, fewer than 25 percent of the region's residents lived in urban areas (defined as localities with populations greater than 2,500), compared with roughly 60 percent of non-Southerners. Southern states ranged from a mere 13 percent urban population in Mississippi to 37 percent in Florida. By the 1980s, however, population shifts had tilted the region toward urbanism, with all Southern states except North Carolina and Mississippi being majority urban, and with Florida (84 percent) and Texas (80 percent) exceeding the national average (76 percent) for urban populations. By the 1990s, seven of ten Southerners lived in metropolitan areas of 250,000 to 2 million inhabitants; in only Mississippi and Arkansas did rural residents outnumber the people residing in these new metropolitan places. The region also claimed five "mega-metro" cities of over 2 million: Houston, Atlanta, Dallas, Tampa–St. Petersburg–Clearwater, and Miami.[7]

Generational replacement has contributed to a population with fewer ties to the traditional South. Utilizing a cohort analysis, Merle Black and Earl Black divided the Southern electorate into three groups based on when they attained voting age: the Solid South generation, which reached maturity before 1946; the post–World War II generation, which began voting between 1946 and 1964; and the post–voting rights generation, which became eligible to vote after 1964. The Blacks found

significant differences among these groups, with the two younger cohorts displaying significantly less loyalty to the Democratic party. The natural rhythm of population cohort replacement is contributing to the convergence of the South toward national political patterns.

Economic development has caused further changes. Industrialization and the growth of commerce, stimulated by the New Deal and World War II and accelerated by the rise of the Sun Belt economy, have diversified the once agricultural Southern economy. This broadening of the economic base has led to a rise of new economic and political leadership, as the old planter elite has had to yield power to new elites based on different interests.[8]

New occupational structures have resulted from the economic transformation. Agricultural employment dropped from about 7 percent to just over 2 percent, now paralleling the national pattern. Industrial in-migration has strengthened the region's manufacturing base; factory jobs rose from 6 million to 7 million between 1970 and 1996, even as the Rust Belt was losing a significant proportion of its manufacturing jobs. Despite the South's economic development, the Blacks note that historically, the region has followed a path of "conservative modernization," and some distinct patterns remain. Southern industry tends to be dispersed rather than concentrated in urban areas, perpetuating a pattern of company towns typical of the region. Southern industry is often nonunionized, yielding lower union density rates than in the North. Until recently, many industries, epitomized by textiles and poultry processing, were low-skill, low-productivity, and low-wage operations, although the region also registered gains in automobile assembly, steelmaking, and pharmaceuticals. Last, Southern industries historically have been unusually dependent on federal contracts and orders. The result is a less developed working-class culture, with middle-class hegemony being even more firmly established than elsewhere in the country.[9]

The changing occupational structure supports a new class structure. The have-nots of Key's day are declining, as agricultural and low-skilled jobs are being replaced with factory and office work. As farm owners and laborers were displaced, the proportion of the Southern working and middle classes came to resemble the rest of the country: in 1980, the Southern working class constituted 45 percent of the labor force, versus 42 percent for the non-South; the Southern middle class,

at 52 percent, approached the share of the nation's occupations that were middle class, 56 percent. Since the 1970s, the South has followed national occupational trends, with increases in managerial, professional, and other service jobs and declines in operative, unskilled, and agricultural jobs. There is a growing middle class, broadly defined; particularly significant are much larger numbers of industrial working-class and African American middle-class members.[10] The in-migration has also had some impact on the occupational and class structure, because disproportionate numbers of newcomers held white-collar managerial or professional jobs.

Rising educational levels both reflect and affect the scaling up of the occupation and class distributions. In 1938, when Roosevelt termed the region "the nation's No. 1 economic problem," only 19 percent of Southerners had a high school education, and a scant 4 percent had college degrees. By the late 1990s, the South compared favorably with the rest of the nation, with 79 percent of its adults having high school diplomas (versus 82 percent nationwide) and 21 percent having college degrees (compared with 24 percent for the nation).[11]

The region's income showed similar gains relative to the nation's. In 1938, the average income of Southerners was a mere 52 percent of the income of non-Southerners. The richest Southern state ranked lower in per capita income than the poorest state outside the region. By century's end, Southerners' per capita personal income was 92 percent of the U.S. average. Other quality-of-life measures reflected the region's poverty. The region's health problems were legion. Malaria alone infected more than 2 million Southerners annually and reduced the industrial output of the South by one-third. The number of physicians per population was merely one-third the nation's average in 1938, but the ratio should reach the national average by early in the twenty-first century. In the depression, half of the Southern population needed to be rehoused, but "the typical Southerner today is more likely to live in a newer house and is more likely to own that house than is typical of citizens nationwide."[12]

The civil rights movement and the civil rights laws have, of course, produced the most visible and sweeping changes in the region. Gone are the Jim Crow segregation laws, and if there is still racial separation and inequality, they follow the pattern of de facto segregation familiar in much of the country. A corresponding secular change in

racial attitudes has accompanied the transformation of social mores. Whereas white Southern attitudes on race relations were uniquely out of line with those of all other groups when Key wrote, today, polls document only slightly more racist attitudes among Southern respondents. There has also been recorded a decline in the "siege mentality" of regional defensiveness that formed one of the attitudinal buttresses of the traditional status quo.[13]

Many of the political changes observed in recent decades in the South flow rather predictably from these socioeconomic changes. More social and economic diversity has led to more divergent and conflicting group interests, which in turn has elicited more diverse opinions, ideologies, and organizations. The development of this new social, economic, ideological, and political diversity has furnished a basis for partisan competition, because political pluralism has resisted being confined within the narrow bounds of one-partyism. Not surprisingly, wider-ranging participation, especially as previously excluded African Americans enter political life, and emerging party competition are moving to center stage as the drama of Southern political development unfolds.

The Long March to Republicanism: Georgia and North Carolina

Political change in the South can be gauged by tracing the evolution of politics over the course of the twentieth century in Georgia and North Carolina. Although no two states can represent all the divergent patterns of the region, Georgia and North Carolina illustrate a number of illuminating differences. In terms of their reputations and ideological configurations, the two states began the modern era as nearly polar opposites. Commentators regularly associated Georgia with the core of the rural Solid South and with its most egregious and benighted features. By contrast, Democrats, although predominant, had less of a stranglehold on North Carolina, with its smaller black belt and larger industrial and urban bases, and the state enjoyed a reputation for progressivism and moderation. Ironically, the two states have nearly flip-flopped since Key wrote. North Carolina, a Peripheral South state, arrived at party competitiveness, with a Republican edge,

earlier and more pervasively than has Georgia, a Deep South state.[14] Now they represent almost different ends of the region's partisan spectrum, with Georgia's erratic Republican party failing to attain the steady success of North Carolina's firmly established GOP. Meanwhile, Georgia—or, more properly perhaps, Atlanta—has seized the high ground of business dynamism and urban progressivism in the region. Moreover, while moderate Democrats competing with more conservative Republicans constitute the broad middle ground of both states' political landscape, Georgia has nurtured some of the nation's most liberal politicians, such as congressional members John Lewis and Cynthia McKinney. North Carolina, in contrast, has been the home base of some of America's most extreme conservatives in the personae of Senator Jesse Helms and his disciples.

Despite these differences, the two states have followed similar paths in some respects, being inundated with simultaneous waves of Republican advances. Geographically and temporally, Republican voting spread first from its traditional foothold in the Appalachian Mountains to the Piedmont cities with the appearance of Eisenhower Republicanism in the 1950s. In the mid-1960s, the Goldwater and Wallace defections loosened racial reactionaries' ties to the Democratic party and brought major gains to the Republicans in the most racially conservative portions of these two states, eastern Carolina and south Georgia. Finally, in the 1980s, Ronald Reagan cemented an alliance between the Republicans and the religious right. Occurring in tandem was a tide of Republicanism spilling over from the top of the ballot in presidential elections to support Republicans running for state and eventually local offices further down the ballot.

BEFORE 1950: THE SOLID SOUTH

In the decades preceding the publication of Key's *Southern Politics* in 1949, both Georgia and North Carolina were Solid South states, firmly aligned in the Democratic column in both state and national politics. Georgia was more of a core Southern state, classified not only in geographic terms but also, more importantly, in terms of Key's emphasis on black-belt whites as the backbone of the political South. In 1940, 11.3 percent of Georgia's white population resided in majority-black counties, while only 4.5 percent of North Carolina's white population

hailed from the black belt. The two states' commitment to the Democratic party is borne out by their overwhelmingly Democratic voting in presidential elections between 1900 and 1948, with the exception of 1928. That year, North Carolina bolted when the Democrats nominated "wet" Al Smith, a Catholic who opposed Prohibition, while Georgia remained firmly in the Democratic camp. Although Georgia was presumably as "dry" and Protestant as its neighbor slightly to the north, its loyalty to the Democrats even in 1928 is testimony to Key's contention that the planter elite would maintain its central concern for race while subordinating all other issues. Georgia, a state more dominated by black-belt whites, was prepared to stick with the Democrats as long as the party nominee posed no threat to the Southern style of race relations, even though this loyalty compromised other nonracial values.[15]

The two states differed in another politically significant respect. The larger Appalachian Mountain region in North Carolina provided stronger support for a local Republican party. Mountainous terrain had afforded no base for plantation agriculture, hence western Carolina had little stake in slavery. These mountain counties had opposed secession, had contested the economic and racial conservatism of the dominant planter elites, and had voted Republican in opposition to the Solid South since the 1860s. Georgia, too, had a few Republican counties in the north Georgia mountains, but Republican voters in Georgia were not numerous enough to pose a significant threat to Democratic dominance. The dearth of Republicans is hard to exaggerate, as illustrated by the surely apocryphal story of the Georgia county that registered two Republican votes in one election. Election officials immediately threw out both votes on the certain knowledge that "somebody must of voted twiced."

In North Carolina, in contrast, the presence of a sizable concentration of Republicans, even if amounting only to a minority, was sufficiently threatening to instill in that state's Democratic party some cohesion and organization that were absent in Georgia's majority party. And just as organized competition from the Republicans tended to beget counterorganization from the Democrats, so an organized Democratic leadership tended to call forth an organized factional challenge within the Democratic party. Thus, politics within North Carolina's Democratic party revolved around bifactional rivalries in the first half of the twentieth century.

Georgia also experienced competition between two Democratic factions during much of this period, but the basis of factional conflict was different. Politics in Georgia centered on the polarizing figure of Eugene Talmadge, who was a leading candidate for statewide office in most elections from 1926 until his death in 1946. Although Georgia's factional patterns were more personal, ill-defined, and fluid than North Carolina's more enduring factional coalitions, both states ranked high on bifactionalism as opposed to the even more chaotic multifactional politics of most Southern states.

Gene Talmadge was a magnetic personality and perennial candidate who managed to split the Georgia electorate into pro- and anti-Talmadge factions. He created a die-hard following among the state's rural populace, especially the poor dirt farmers known as the "wool hat boys." Southern agriculture, always vulnerable to market forces and natural ravages because of its monoculture base in cotton, had fallen on permanent hard times as early as the 1910s with the arrival of the boll weevil that devastated large areas of cotton land. Talmadge spoke to the fears and frustrations of farmers suffering through hard times, and it is tempting to speculate that Talmadge's appeal to the desperately poor and isolated rural electorate was grounded at least in part on his sheer entertainment value for people who were too poor to purchase amusement before an era of cheap mass entertainment. Talmadge was an electrifying campaigner whose rallies were the pre–pop culture era's equivalent of a rock concert.

Ole Gene knew all the tricks of exciting a crowd. If the meeting was indoors, his advance people staged them in buildings too small to accommodate the anticipated crowd, knowing that having supporters hanging out the windows would create a sense of momentum and appeal that an underfilled hall would lack. If the meeting was a multi-candidate affair, Gene invariably showed up late, creating a sense of tension as the crowd speculated on whether he would show. He generally timed his arrival to coincide with his rival's speech, detracting from his opponent's message and demonstrating visible support as his loyalists disrupted his competitor's speech with cheers for the tardy Gene. He had plants in the audience to yell questions and affirming exclamations, giving his speeches the interactive style of a religious revival. His stump style was made for an era of "hot," live-audience campaigning, including a phrase-making ability designed to appeal to

an audience acclimated to oral rather than written communication. Talmadge spoke in the rural idiom of his followers. His biographer, William Anderson, notes that although he was a highly educated man (with a Phi Beta Kappa key and a law degree), he knew just how to fire up his largely uneducated, unsophisticated constituents: "He was fiery, indignant, angry, corny, and iconoclastic. His language could be earthy, profane, grammatically atrocious, and very provincial. In isolated rural areas it was tailored to be understood by the most ignorant farmhand. It was a simple, uncluttered, blunt discourse, punctuated with Bible passages and rural humor."[16] Even his trademark red suspenders, which he snapped as if to punctuate his more memorable lines, contributed to his entertainment value.

"The Wild Man from Sugar Creek," as Talmadge was nicknamed, also managed by these antics to identify with his downtrodden constituency by flaunting the social conventions of "polite society." When caught spending unauthorized government funds as state commissioner of agriculture, he retained his loyal following by confessing, "Yeah, it's true. I stole, but I stole for you, the dirt farmer!" He rhetorically aligned himself with the plight of farmers beleaguered by the extended agricultural depression. "The dirt farmer ain't got but three friends in the whole world," he used to shout to rural followers who felt increasingly left out of a modernizing, urbanizing, industrializing society, "God Almighty, the Sears Roebuck catalogue, and Ole Gene." Part of his appeal was his race baiting. Although integration was never a political issue during this era, Talmadge's intemperate tirades against African Americans provided symbolic reassurance to poor white farmers whose fortunes were fast fading. Even if the poor dirt farmers were losing their whole world, Ole Gene seemed to assure his desperate followers that they still had their white skin, which in the rigid caste system of the Jim Crow South, entitled them to membership in the upper caste. If he offered nothing else, he reaffirmed their sense of racial superiority and solidarity by pandering to and inflaming their prejudices.

Georgia's two factions did not turn only on the salience of Gene Talmadge's personality, however. Fundamentally, the conflict in state politics reflected an urban-rural split. Key entitled his chapter on Georgia "Rule of the Rustics." Talmadge often bragged that he never campaigned in a county with a streetcar. This split was institutionalized

in the county unit system, an electoral scheme operating in statewide primary elections from 1917 until it was ruled unconstitutional by the U.S. Supreme Court in 1962. Counties determined electoral outcomes in statewide Democratic primaries, casting their votes as units won by pluralities in each county. Although more populous urban counties were allocated more votes, the three-to-one ratio of unit votes nowhere matched the larger population disparities. The unit votes of small, rural counties greatly outweighed the votes of urban areas, contributing to the domination of state politics by increasingly depopulated rural areas. The urban-rural rift approximated a geographical division, with north Georgia inclined to support Talmadge opponents while Ole Gene carried his south Georgia base.

There was also a class and policy basis for the factionalism. Talmadge appealed more to the poorer whites, whom we would probably characterize today as "rednecks," while anti-Talmadge candidates won most of their votes from the more respectable middle classes. Paradoxically, Gene also enjoyed significant support from the upper classes of the state, including the Atlanta business elite. Despite his populist rhetoric, Talmadge was profoundly conservative when it came to policy. He believed in a sound pro-business approach to state government, preferring to keep taxes low and services sparse. Even during the depression, he believed in a balanced budget, pay-as-you-go funding for capital improvements, and minimum regulations. He was an ardent, if somewhat covert, opponent of Franklin Roosevelt's New Deal. The same wool hat boys who elected Gene Talmadge governor four times during this period simultaneously gave unprecedented backing to the New Deal, with FDR's margins of support reaching an incredible 92 percent in 1932 and never dipping below 82 percent.[17] Although Talmadge cobbled together a top-and-bottom class coalition, his supporters did not benefit equally. While his upper-crust backers got pro-business policies, his dirt farmer constituency received little by way of help from Talmadge administrations. Programmatic help came from Washington; state government offered little in the way of progressive policies, such as education, health, or roads, to spur socioeconomic development and ease the poverty of the state's rural areas. Besides reducing the cost of automobile tags to $3, Talmadge supplied only rhetoric, especially racist reaffirmation, and entertainment to ease the pain as the wool hat boys' way of life disappeared. As one

country newspaper editor replied when asked what Talmadge had done for Georgians, "He gave us a three-dollar tag. And a dern good show."[18]

By dent of his personality and style, Talmadge cemented a following that was personally loyal to him. He constituted the core of a factional division that overrode the "friends and neighbors" voting pattern so typical of Southern elections, that is, the phenomenon of voting purely on the basis of local loyalties since so little else was at stake in elections. Up to a point, he could also deliver his faction's votes to other Talmadge candidates; his endorsements seemed effective in statehouse races, but he proved unable to swing votes in congressional, local, or state legislative races. The anti-Talmadge forces, which included progressive constituencies such as city voters, labor, enfranchised African Americans, the urban press, and the middle classes, could sometimes carry elections when they united behind a single strong candidate. For instance, the progressives of E. D. Rivers (1937–1941) and Ellis Arnall (1943–1947) were elected with the votes of these groups, and Talmadge lost both of his Senate bids against entrenched incumbents. Talmadge's opponents, however, were even less coherent than his supporters, and they often lost when they failed to rally around a common challenger to Gene or his designated candidate, enabling Talmadge to dominate state politics from the 1920s until the 1940s. He was elected state commissioner of agriculture three times and ran for governor five times, winning four contests. His power was so great that during his last campaign for governor the joke circulated that if told that Ole Gene planned to move Stone Mountain, the average Georgian would ask without batting an eye, "Where's he gonna put it?"[19]

North Carolina politics and government in the first half of the twentieth century present a stark contrast, nicely captured in Key's chapter title: "North Carolina: Progressive Plutocracy." Its factional politics was more coherent, and the state's respectable element played a more prominent role in its governance. Most remarkable was the business establishment's commitment to more progressive policies.

North Carolina politics was dominated by two "machines" during this era. From 1900 to 1930, the faction that coalesced around Senator Furnifold M. Simmons predominated. From about 1930 on, the "Shelby Dynasty," a clique of state officeholders, controlled the state through clientelistic, patronage-based politics. Both of these machines

were based in the western Piedmont portions of the state, although they often balanced their slates with easterners to appeal to voters there. Key noted North Carolina's deviation from his dominant thesis that the black belts constitute the core of the political South. He pointed out that the black belts were historically weaker in North Carolina because (1) there were more white tenant farmers as opposed to planter elites in these areas of the state, (2) North Carolina black-belt farms were smaller than the plantations found in these regions in other Southern states, and (3) the state had more cities to offset the influence of black-belt counties. To explain why the machines developed in the west, Key applied his "competition breeds organization which breeds counter-organization" hypothesis. Republicanism attained significant levels in the mountains of North Carolina's westernmost counties, sometimes totaling one-third of the vote cast in statewide elections. This threat was sufficient to develop a sense of the Democratic party as something more than a hollow facade, especially among Democrats in the west. "By compelling the Democratic party to fight, the Republicans gave it a backbone composed of those counties in which it has to fight." The development of a dominant party faction, however, invited factional opponents to organize and compete, resulting in a factional politics that produced a modicum of organization, discipline, and responsibility. The happy result, Key argued, was that "partly from the nature of its political organization North Carolina does not suffer the erraticism, the instability, and the incapacity to act that characterize most Southern states with an unorganized politics."[20]

Key almost euphorically, if a bit naively, described the prevailing mood of the state as "energetic and ambitious. The citizens are determined and confident; they are on the move. . . . In any competition for national judgment they deem the state far more 'presentable' than its southern neighbors." According to Key, this mood realistically reflected state policies. Industrialization had created a business elite that exercised prevailing influence through the leading political machines. The urban-based manufacturing and financial elite had perceived its stake in state politics and wielded its influence to win policies that responded to the needs of this "economic oligarchy." Key maintained, however, that this elite had "not been blind to broad community needs." Rather, it identified the interests of "corporate capital" as aligned with policies

that effectively advanced the economic development of the state. For example, as early as the 1920s, when most Southern state governments remained mired in the fiscally conservative practices of pay-as-you-go capital improvement programs that limited development projects, North Carolina embarked on a massive highway building program financed by borrowed money. The state raised salaries for teachers and civil servants, funded health programs, and invested heavily in its university system. One governor characterized the oligarchy's vision as a "capitalistic system liberally and fairly interpreted." Key pointed out that while many North Carolina politicians might be described as "stodgy and conservative," they were never "scoundrels or nincompoops."[21]

Although Key mentioned that race relations were a "two-sided picture," he doubtless overstated the "harmonious" relations between the races in North Carolina and failed to assess accurately North Carolina's "reputation for fair dealings with its Negro citizens."[22] Nonetheless, the extreme race baiting characteristic of so much Southern politics of this period, including in Georgia, was largely absent in North Carolina. More organized factions and an economic elite that was conservative but also civic-minded produced a politics that was relatively progressive for the Solid South of the day.

1950–1970: REACTIONS TO CIVIL RIGHTS

With different factional systems and divergent prevailing political climates, not surprisingly, Georgia and North Carolina lurched even further apart in the era when Southern politicians had to respond to the challenges of racial desegregation. While Georgia embraced Massive Resistance and elected mostly politicians of the old school, North Carolina took tentative steps in the direction of at least token integration, led by moderates. North Carolina Republicans also emerged as a force to be reckoned with in this era, while Georgia Republicans remained for the most part marginalized.

Although Joseph Bernd calls 1954 to 1962 the "era of good feeling" in Georgia politics, all was not quiet, to say the least. The 1954 Supreme Court decision in *Brown v. Board of Education* brought race to the center stage of Southern politics. After an initially moderate reaction to the decision, hard-line opponents of any change used the

threat of integration to defeat moderates around the South. In Georgia, the Talmadge faction used resistance to desegregation as an issue to revive its ebbing electoral appeal. Other factors combined with the segregationist tenor of the times to defeat resoundingly the anti-Talmadge forces. Charges of corruption tainted some anti-Talmadge administrations, and several opposition leaders deserted to the Talmadge faction. Once expectations of Talmadge victories were established, other tendencies reinforced them, such as self-fulfilling prophecies that the Talmadge forces were invincible and a bandwagon effect that encouraged support for the likely winners. Most of all, however, opposition to integration was the dominant white voter obsession, moving other issues to the back burner, and Talmadge candidates personified Massive Resistance, regardless of costs.[23]

Herman Talmadge, Gene's son, was unstoppable. When the elder Talmadge died before beginning his fourth term as governor, the state was pitched into near governmental anarchy as three claimants asserted their credentials to be governor. In the absence of a clear constitutional succession, the state legislature elected Herman to succeed his father. When the state supreme court bestowed the office instead on lieutenant governor–elect M. E. Thompson, Herman defeated Thompson in the special election held in 1948 to fill the remainder of the term, repeating the feat in 1950 for a full term. Young Herman next turned his sights to Washington and a Senate seat. Georgia was represented in the Senate by two veritable institutions: Richard B. Russell, who was first elected in 1930 and who had defeated Gene Talmadge for reelection in 1936, and Walter F. George, first elected in 1932, who in 1938 had survived both a challenge by Gene and the opposition of the fabulously popular Franklin Roosevelt. In 1956, however, when Herman made it known that he wanted a Senate seat, Robert Woodruff, head of the Atlanta-based Coca Cola Company, reportedly spoke to President Eisenhower (a Republican—suggesting how little party meant in the one-party South) while playing golf on the Masters course in Augusta. Ike in turn suggested to the venerable George that it might be time to retire. Rather than risk a nasty reelection fight and likely defeat, Senator George chose to leave the field to young "Hummon," who waltzed into the Senate. Herman Talmadge held that seat without serious challenge until upset 51 to 49 percent by Mack Mattingly, an upstart Republican, in 1980.[24]

During this era, contests for state offices were mostly intra-Talmadge affairs, with Marvin Griffin winning the governorship in 1954 and Ernest Vandiver winning in 1958 with 80 percent of the vote. By the early 1960s, however, it appeared that the tide might be turning. In 1962, the U.S. Supreme Court ruled that the county unit system was unconstitutional, and Carl Sanders, a young, urbane state senator from Augusta, won the governor's race that year. At long last it seemed that the forces of "dynamic Georgia," the northern metropolitan and urban areas, might vanquish the Talmadge forces rooted in "static Georgia," comprising the black belt and the poorest, most rural, agricultural counties of the southern and eastern portions of the state.[25] Indeed, former governor Marvin Griffin's quip upon losing to Sanders, "somebody's been eatin' my barbecue that ain't been votin' for me," might have provided a suitable epitaph for the demise of the old rural-dominated politics.

Obsession with racist resistance, however, made premature any such speculation about the death of reactionary forces in Georgia. In 1966, Lester Maddox ran for governor as the candidate of die-hard segregation. In normal circumstances, the public would have perceived Maddox, who had never held elective office and had been soundly defeated in a run for mayor of Atlanta in 1962, as a fringe candidate. The passage of the 1964 Civil Rights Act, however, which required, among other things, integrated public accommodations and brought the first substantial school desegregation, also elicited a vehement backlash. Maddox symbolized firebrand opposition to civil rights, having brandished pistols and pickax handles to deter would-be African American customers at his Pickwick restaurant in Atlanta. With the enforcement of integrated public accommodations, Maddox closed the Pickwick rather than desegregate service. In 1966, he defeated widely admired, progressive, anti-Talmadge former governor Ellis Arnall in the Democratic primary for governor, and the Republicans, led by conservative but respectable Howard "Bo" Callaway, smelled likely victory. When Arnall received 50,000 write-in votes in the general election, however, the election was thrown into the Georgia House of Representatives because no candidate had a majority. The Democratic House remained loyal to its party and elected Maddox governor, despite Callaway's plurality and Maddox's reputation as a novice and extremist. True to the tradition of elite rule even when populist can-

didates won office, Mills B. Lane, president of the C & S Bank, supposedly told Maddox the obvious—that he was unqualified to govern the state—and offered his help, which Maddox accepted. Whether for this or other reasons, the Maddox administration was not the disaster that many expected, with the unpredictable governor sometimes even championing progressive causes such as prison reform.[26]

Even as late as 1970, Georgia appeared mired in the politics of the past as Jimmy Carter, a young former state senator with a progressive record, defeated Carl Sanders by appealing to the rural, racist, "static" Georgia constituency who had won the state's electoral college votes for George Wallace in 1968. In addition to praising Wallace and inviting him to Georgia to speak, Carter managed to tar Sanders with a class brush by pinning the nickname "Cuff Links Carl" on the former governor, who had prospered working in a large Atlanta law firm after his term in office. From the perspective of 1970, then, the last two decades appeared to be an epoch dominated by the conservative, "static" political forces in the state, based in the rural areas and resistant to any moderation on racial issues. Rather than the dawn of a new day, the lone progressive administration of Carl Sanders appeared to be a deviation, a mere bump on a country road.

The fortunes of Republicans also appeared bleak as a long-term proposition, despite significant achievements in discrete elections. The state cast its electoral college votes for Barry Goldwater in 1964, the first time Georgia had voted for a Republican presidential candidate in the century. In 1968, five constitutional officers (the secretary of agriculture, comptroller general, state treasurer, and two Public Service commissioners) read what they perceived to be the handwriting on the wall and switched parties to the GOP. None of this "Statehouse Clique" was ever elected to office again, however, and despite Bo Callaway's strong challenge in 1966, the Republicans failed to score a statewide victory during this period.[27] On the surface, then, Georgia entered the 1970s frozen in the same political mode that it had entered the 1950s—solidly Democratic, with the rural and reactionary forces firmly in charge.

North Carolina followed a different path. The Shelby Dynasty had disintegrated into multiple factions after 1940, and competition among the east, the west, and the Piedmont middle, with the last holding the edge, had replaced the bifactional east-west rivalry.[28] Nonetheless, the

state's tradition of business leadership and moderately progressive policy remained intact.

In 1948, although W. Kerr Scott was elected governor from the east and represented an insurgency of the rural and black-belt areas against the economic oligarchy, his administration was aggressively liberal, building roads and schools in rural areas, for example. Succeeding William Umstead upon that governor's death in 1954, Luther Hodges was elected governor for a full term in 1956. Labeled "the business governor," Hodges epitomized the progressive plutocracy. His administration passed tax breaks for corporations and individuals but also built roads and vocational schools, promoted the Research Triangle Park as a joint private-public venture in research and development, and passed a state minimum wage. He also led the state in a more moderate reaction to desegregation, symbolized by the token integration in 1957 of eleven black students into formerly white schools in three North Carolina cities. In 1960, President Kennedy tapped the highly acclaimed Hodges to be his secretary of commerce.[29]

Hodges was followed in the governor's mansion by Terry Sanford, who, if anything, seemed to embody the New South even more perfectly. Having supported Kerr Scott and served in the Hodges administration, the young, progressive Sanford managed to support national Democrat John Kennedy in 1960 and still defeat I. Beverly Lake, the segregationist Wake Forest law professor who had argued the Southern states' position in the *Brown II* (1955) desegregation implementation case before the Supreme Court. Sanford led a progressive administration that built roads and the North Carolina School of the Arts, attracted industry, and even raised the minimum wage, although these programs were partly funded by removing the sales tax exemption from food, earning him the nickname "Food Tax Terry."[30]

In 1964, Dan Moore, a moderate, defeated liberal L. Richardson Pryor and segregationist I. Beverly Lake for the governorship. In the 1968 Democratic primary, Robert Scott, son of former governor Kerr Scott, continued the tradition of moderate progressivism by defeating J. Melville Broughton, Jr., son of the World War II governor, and Reginald Hawkins, the state's first black gubernatorial candidate in the twentieth century. In the general election that fall, however, in a portent of things to come, Scott defeated Republican James Garner, a thirty-two-year-old political novice, by the relatively thin margin of

52.7 to 47.3 percent. Meanwhile, the state cast its electoral votes for Republican Richard Nixon for president.[31]

From 1950 to 1970, then, Georgia met the challenge of desegregation with a defiant stance of Massive Resistance. Moderates managed only one significant victory; other than the brief interlude of Carl Sanders's administration, the Talmadge faction and hard-line segregationists ruled supreme. Despite revolts against the Democrats at the presidential level and some stirrings in state politics, Republicans made little permanent headway in Georgia during this era. North Carolina, in contrast, continued its tradition of progressive and moderate leadership. The state certainly did not embrace integration, but its resistance to desegregation was flexible enough to encompass some token and incremental integration. Most significantly for the future of the state's politics, the Republican party gained a significant foothold in contests for both national and state offices. By the decade of the 1970s, North Carolina Republicans were poised to seize leadership from state Democrats. As Preston Edsall and J. Oliver Williams concluded in 1972, "the most important fact about North Carolina politics is that the era of one-party dominance is nearing an end."[32]

THE END OF "WHITES ONLY" POLITICS: THE VOTING RIGHTS ACT

In 1940, so thorough was the Solid South's disenfranchisement of African Americans that black voter registration stood at a paltry 3 percent of the black voting-age population in the region. That percentage rose after World War II, a war that pitched democratic principles against the racist ideology of fascism and provided many African American soldiers escape from strict segregation in experiences beyond the Jim Crow South. It took almost two decades of struggle to increase African American registration to slightly less than a third of the black population in the early 1960s. Three national civil rights laws and, even more important, heroic efforts by the civil rights movement, especially the Southern Nonviolent Coordinating Committee (SNCC), dramatically raised that figure by 1964, when 43.3 percent of eligible African Americans were registered regionwide. Still, black registration lagged behind comparable figures for Southern whites (approximately 73.4 percent) and for blacks outside the South, and great disparities existed, with the fewest blacks registered in those areas where most

blacks lived. Mississippi had only 6.7 percent of its African American citizens registered, and the average for the five Deep South states was only 28.9 percent.[33]

In 1965, Congress passed the Voting Rights Act (VRA), arguably "the most effective civil rights law ever passed."[34] Section 4 of the act abolished literacy tests in areas where registration or turnout was under 50 percent in 1964. Alabama, Georgia, Louisiana, Mississippi, South Carolina, Virginia, and 40 of North Carolina's 100 counties were covered. In these areas, the VRA froze election laws, with any changes requiring preclearance from the Justice Department or the court of appeals of the District of Columbia circuit. Southern legislatures had previously thwarted voting rights laws by enacting new barriers to black voting as old obstacles were declared illegal. The preclearance provision preempted this "legislate and litigate" strategy by requiring approval from Washington for any new electoral enactments in the covered areas. Finally, the VRA authorized the attorney general to send federal registrars to covered jurisdictions to ensure that qualified persons were free to register.

The surge in black registration was immediate and striking. South-wide, black registration leapt from 43.1 percent just before passage of the act to 62 percent three years after enactment. In four years, black registration in Mississippi swelled almost tenfold, while in Alabama the rate more than doubled. The changes were less dramatic in Georgia and North Carolina, where notable gains in registration by African Americans preceded the act. In Georgia, black registration increased from 44 percent to 56 percent in four years, although the percentage has not continued to grow reliably since. Nonetheless, the number of African Americans registered grew from 270,000 in 1964 to 607,782 in 1990. In North Carolina, registration in the forty covered counties increased from 32.4 percent in 1964 to 54 percent in 1976. Although whites continued to lead African Americans in registration for decades after passage of the VRA, by 1990, the percentage of registered eligible blacks (63 percent) approached that for whites (69 percent). Although the few registered Southern blacks historically turned out to vote at rates well below those for the region's white voters, by 1980, that gap, too, had virtually disappeared.[35]

It would be naive to equate voting with political power, and the upsurge in black registration and turnout has not automatically

resulted in an end to racial injustices. In the short run, whites in some states—for example, Alabama, where they were spurred on by arch-segregationist governor George Wallace—responded to the removal of legal impediments to black voting with a surge in white registration. This white mobilization was counteracted by a black countermobilization and was probably temporary. The long-term trend has been a declining white numerical registration advantage.[36] More generally, William Keech demonstrated that the extent to which black voting translated into black power depended on the reactions of whites. Where whites constituted the majority, racially polarized voting could leave enfranchised blacks a permanently politically impotent minority. Some Southern jurisdictions responded to black voting by creating electoral rules designed to dilute the impact of those votes, setting up a multidecade legal battle to ensure that minorities are afforded "an equal opportunity to participate in the political process and to elect representatives of their choice." Finally, many questions of public importance respond only feebly to electoral politics; for example, economic development and social inequities are only marginally responsive to electoral outcomes if contenders for political power do not directly challenge economic structures.[37]

Despite the limitations of voting, especially for minorities, the VRA produced remarkable changes in the formerly all-white politics of the South. Recent decades have seen significant numbers of African Americans elected to public office, reaching almost 3,000 officeholders by 1985. After the VRA was passed, the number of blacks elected to office in Georgia grew from 3 to 495 in 1990, including a supreme court justice, 27 of 180 representatives, and 8 of 56 senators in the state's General Assembly. African American representatives held three of the state's U.S. House seats after the 1992 redistricting. North Carolina has one black supreme court justice, two black appeals court judges, and eleven other black superior court judges elected statewide. In its legislature, by 1990, 5 of 50 senators and 13 of 120 representatives were black, and in that year, an African American was elected speaker of the house. Forty-four county commissioners, 83 school board members, 260 city council members, and 18 mayors were black. The state has also seen blacks elected to two of eleven congressional seats and a close challenge by an African American, Harvey Gantt, to an incumbent senator, Jessie Helms.[38]

While these numbers do not constitute proportionate representation for the South's African American population, they do represent real if hard-won progress in political participation. There can be no doubt that the entry of African American citizens into the region's politics has had profound effects on the tenor and substance of public affairs. Not least has been the impact of black participation on the realignment of the region's partisanship. Black voters have played a major role in moderating the Democratic party and diversifying its base and leadership. The advent of black participation in the Democratic party has also been a significant factor in the appeal of the Republican party for many white voters.

AFTER 1970: POST–CIVIL RIGHTS POLITICS

When he signed the 1964 Civil Rights Act, President Lyndon Johnson supposedly quipped, "I think I just lost the South."[39] The alienation and countermobilization of white segregationist voters, however, were at least partially offset by the advent of African Americans enfranchised by the VRA as well as other developments in the region. The result of this change was a complex mixture of political change and continuity affecting both Georgia and North Carolina.

Although campaigning for the Wallace vote, Jimmy Carter positioned himself in Georgia's 1970 gubernatorial election as an economic populist. Once in office, Governor Carter made it clear that he would not continue to mine the vein of Wallace's racial resistance. Instead, he used his inaugural address to announce that "the time for racial discrimination is over," signaling that a new breed of Deep South moderate governors had arrived on the scene.[40] He made good on his inaugural words by forming a biracial commission on discrimination, appointing African Americans to office, hiring black highway patrol officers for his security detail, and hanging a portrait of Dr. Martin Luther King, Jr., in the state capitol. The major thrust of his administration was a reorganization of state government agencies, undertaken in the name of economy and efficiency, reducing 300 state agencies to 22 departments. The reforms, however, also threatened to disrupt the established cozy relationships between Georgia's special interests and state government. Lester Maddox, who as lieutenant governor presided over the state senate, led the resistance to Carter's plan. The conflict in some ways pre-

saged Carter's presidential administration: having run as a populist out-sider, Carter championed mainly technocratic policies against the entrenched interests. As voters grew tired of both the Democratic lead-ers in Congress and President Carter in 1980, so Georgians pronounced a pox on both Carter's and Maddox's houses in the mid-1970s. Carter left office with little popularity in his home state, while Maddox was unable to translate his high visibility and early lead in the gubernato-rial race of 1974 into a second term as governor.

In the 1974 Democratic gubernatorial primary, more than seven viable candidates jockeyed for the inevitable runoff. Maddox came in first, with 36.1 percent of the vote. But Maddox was a polarizing fig-ure, with a fixed bloc of support that was relatively inelastic. He was able to expand his vote total to only 40.1 percent in the runoff. The rest of the candidates in essence split the anti-Maddox total. George Busbee, an eighteen-year veteran of the Georgia house of representa-tives, won a berth in the runoff with only 20.8 percent of the total vote. Once in the runoff, however, he inherited the anti-Maddox man-tle and handily defeated Maddox, 59.9 to 40.1 percent.[41] Busbee proved popular, if a far cry from Georgia's traditionally colorful governors. In a state embarrassed by years of national attention to Lester Maddox's antics, perhaps he proved popular precisely because he was so down-right dull. Unlike the squabbling outsiders Carter and Maddox, Bus-bee epitomized the practical insider in state politics. When the state constitution was amended to allow gubernatorial succession—itself an implicit recognition that more competitive party politics was on the horizon, if not imminent—Busbee was reelected to a second term without significant opposition in the Democratic primary or from the Republicans. He was followed as governor by Joe Frank Harris, another veteran of the state house of representatives who also proved popular, although he was even more lackluster than Busbee. Although he too was easily reelected to a second term, other than his quintessentially Southern double first name, Joe Frank seemed to have little in com-mon with the raucous governors of years past, except his conser-vatism, of course.

Zell Miller attained the governor's mansion in 1990. Miller had been elected lieutenant governor in the post-Watergate election of 1974 with promises to reform the senate previously controlled by Maddox and his cronies.[42] Over his long incumbency as lieutenant

governor (1975–1991), Miller backed away from some of his own reforms, although Herman Talmadge tarred him with the "liberal" label when the two faced off in the primary for Talmadge's Senate seat in 1980. Miller defeated Republican Johnny Isaacson for governor in 1990. In office, his populist instincts based on his poor mountain background shone through; he supported using lottery proceeds to pay for Hope Scholarships to fund free college tuition for good students, and he removed the sales tax from food. Despite keeping his progressive promises, his administrations became more conservative in response to the growing Republican challenge, for example, establishing boot camps for young offenders and privatizing many state functions, including state parks such as Stone Mountain. His flexibility and willingness to compromise earned him the nickname "Zig Zag Zell" from critics, but in 1994, he narrowly won reelection 51 to 49 percent over Republican Guy Millner, a multimillionaire who had never held elective office but who willingly spent freely to fund his own campaign. By 1998, the Republicans could look forward to a realistic chance of capturing the governorship and possibly even majority control of the entire state government.

Republicans' first statewide victories came for national offices. Georgia began to desert the Democrats with Wallace's independent candidacy in 1968; the Republicans won overwhelmingly with Richard Nixon over George McGovern in 1972. Native son Jimmy Carter brought the state back into the Democratic column in 1976 and 1980, as did Arkansas native Bill Clinton in 1992. In other elections since 1960, however, Democratic presidential nominees failed to win the state's electoral votes, even when Clinton ran for a second term in 1996.

As early as 1972, the Republicans were able to mount a serious challenge to succeed Senator Richard B. Russell, who died in office. Republican Fletcher Thompson garnered 46 percent of the vote for the open seat, losing to Sam Nunn. Once in office, however, Nunn became practically a political institution, handily winning reelection by comfortable margins ranging up to 83 percent of the vote in 1978, and in 1990, Nunn even received the implicit endorsement of the Republican as well as Democratic party. Likewise, incumbent senator Herman Talmadge remained a fixture in Georgia politics throughout the 1950s, 1960s, and 1970s. After a series of personal tribulations and

political scandals, however, Talmadge was challenged by Lieutenant Governor Zell Miller in the 1980 Democratic primary. Although successfully fending off this strong challenge, Talmadge met defeat at the hands of Republican Mack Mattingly, an Indiana native who had never held elective office before.[43]

The Republicans' foothold in Georgia's congressional delegation proved slippery throughout the 1980s, however. Democratic Representative Wyche Fowler defeated Senator Mattingly in the Democratic comeback year of 1986. The House delegation remained overwhelmingly Democratic until 1992. Redistricting after the 1992 census led to the creation of majority minority districts, but also to a consequent "bleaching" of surrounding districts. By the Republican Revolution of 1994, a political landslide transformed the state's House delegation from nine Democrats and one Republican in 1990, to seven and four in 1992, then to eight Republicans and three Democrats in 1994. This partisan divide was replicated in 1996, as all eleven incumbents were reelected. Secretary of State Max Cleland's narrow victory over Republican Guy Millner in 1996 allowed the Democrats to retain retiring senator Sam Nunn's seat, proving that moderate Democrats could still win statewide races.

Despite increasingly vigorous competition from Republicans for lower offices, the "bifurcated electoral system" of the 1970s and 1980s, with Republican strength concentrated at the top of the ticket, cast a surprisingly long shadow into the 1990s in Georgia.[44] The General Assembly remained solidly Democratic until the 1990s, and Republican gains were slow until big gains occurred after the 1994 election, a year that also saw the first Republican victories in statewide elections for constitutional offices. These mid-1990s gains, plus the fact that the state's population was growing most rapidly in the areas and among groups that were most likely to vote Republican, especially in the suburban "donut" surrounding Atlanta, caused many observers of state politics to predict that by 1998, Republicans would at last dislodge Georgia from its Democratic moorings. Backlash against what some saw as the Republican obsession with impeaching William Jefferson Clinton, combined with a clever Democratic "containment strategy," allowed the state's Democrats to retain their grip on the governor's mansion and a majority in the General Assembly, although the effort to roll back superior Republican numbers in the state's congressional

delegation was feeble. Republican gubernatorial candidate Guy Millner (making his third self-financed run for statewide office in the 1990s)
bought television ads opposing affirmative action, and the ads of the
party's candidate for lieutenant governor were laced none too subtly
with themes of drugs and race. The voters, however, were not buying
these attempts to inject wedge issues into the election. Taking a page
from Clinton's 1996 playbook, Roy Barnes, from suburban Cobb
County, defeated Guy Millner by focusing on "kitchen table" economic
issues and other everyday, practical concerns of middle-class, suburban
voters. Barnes proved to be an unusually liberal and activist governor
for Georgia, but he also proved adept at the New Democrat–style tactics of stealing the Republicans' thunder by co-opting their positions.[45]
Still, despite moderating its political tone as early as 1970, Georgia had
retained its solidly Democratic heritage longer than almost any Southern state, with Republican victories being confined to national offices
until the mid-1990s.

North Carolina, in contrast, was poised on the edge of Republican
government by the beginning of the 1970s. At the presidential level,
solidly Democratic voting had been shaken earlier than in Georgia,
with Eisenhower victories in 1952 and 1956 and a narrow margin for
Richard Nixon in 1960. By the 1970s, North Carolina was practically
a safe state for Republican presidential candidates; in 1976, Southerner
Jimmy Carter was the only Democrat to carry the state's electoral
votes during this entire era, a feat that not even Arkansan Bill Clinton could match.[46]

In 1972, moderate mountain Republican Jim Holshouser was
elected governor in a year when Richard Nixon swamped George
McGovern for president. At the same time, Jesse Helms, who drew
his strength from the eastern part of the state and from the extreme
right side of the political spectrum, won an open Senate seat against
moderate Democratic Representative Nick Galifinikas. Moderate
Democrats proved that they were still viable, with victories by Robert
Morgan for the Senate in 1974 and Jim Hunt for governor in 1976.
Helms and his "Jessecrat" followers proved that Republicanism was
no fluke in North Carolina; "Senator No" won reelection in 1978
over populist insurance commissioner John Ingram, and Helms's
crony John East, a political science professor with no electoral experience, rode Helms's coattails to the Senate in 1980 by defeating

incumbent Morgan. Helms retained his Senate seat by defeating challenger Jim Hunt in "the battle of the titans" in 1984, a race in which the candidates spent $28 million. He held onto his seat despite two energetic challenges from Harvey Gantt, the African American ex-mayor of Charlotte, in 1990 and 1996. Although the Republicans lost the junior Senate seat to former governor Terry Sanford in the Democratic comeback year of 1986, in 1992 they retook it with a victory by Jessecrat Lauch Faircloth. In the meantime, the governorship was traded back and forth between the parties, with Republican Jim Martin winning in 1984 and 1988, and Democrat Hunt winning reelection in 1992 and 1996.[47]

Republicans also established a firm foothold in the North Carolina House congressional delegation earlier. Although Democrats outnumbered Republicans seven to four in 1972, the Democratic tilt in the delegation varied from nine to two to a mere six to five during the 1970s and 1980s. In the 1990s, there were rapid swings. After the 1992 elections, Democrats still held an eight-to-four edge. In 1994, however, the Republicans reversed this margin, taking eight congressional seats to the Democrats' four. In 1996, the Democrats came back to split the delegation evenly at six each. A pattern of growing Republican strength was also clear in the state legislature. The Republicans won control of the house in their 1994 election sweep but narrowly failed to wrest control of the state senate from the Democrats. In 1996, the Republicans retained a majority in the house but lost seats in both the house and the senate.[48]

In summary, Georgia and North Carolina represent variations on a theme in their partisan evolution, with both states following the same route in their "long march into the Republican column," but at a different pace.[49] North Carolina started from a stronger base of competitive and moderate politics and evolved sooner toward two-party, even Republican-leaning, political competition. Both states experienced earlier and steadier Republican voting at the presidential level first, with the national legislative offices of Senate and House lagging somewhat behind in their competitiveness. State offices were tougher nuts for the Republicans to crack, with Republican challenges coming first at the gubernatorial level, and other statewide constitutional offices and state legislative offices being the last to fall to the Republican insurgents. In short, Republicans had earlier successes with the more

visible offices at the top of the ticket, with success trickling down over the course of time.

The result by the mid-1990s was that two formerly solid Democratic states had become competitive, with at least a Republican edge in North Carolina and a similar tilt possibly developing in Georgia. At the same time, the ideological ground had shifted from the pre-1950 pattern, wherein the Democratic party provided the home for the states' most conservative elites and the Republican party housed the minority mountain moderates. By 1990, the lineup had almost completely reversed itself: the Republicans represented the most conservative groups in both states, while the state Democratic parties, although containing liberal wings, were dominated by middle-of-the-roaders.

Split-level Realignment

It is easy to be impressed with Republican victories in the formerly solidly Democratic South. In the course of a lifetime, voters who came of age without ever meeting an acknowledged Republican now see their state elections dominated by the GOP. But if the change is impressive in magnitude and in speed, perhaps the truly remarkable aspect is that the shift to Republicanism did not occur more monolithically, earlier, and faster. To understand why, one has only to remember that the basis of the solidly Democratic South was the preservation of white supremacy. After 1948, with the national Democratic party taking the lead, if slowly at first, in pressing for an end to Southern Jim Crow segregation and for civil rights for African Americans, why did the South not shift massively and immediately to the Republican party? The surprise is not the rise of Republicanism but rather that the Democrats were able to remain at all competitive after their party seized the initiative in civil rights policy. How were Southern Democrats able to stem, or at least retard, the onslaught of Republicanism and resist the replacement of the Solid Democratic South with a Solid Republican South?

In the first place, it is all too easy with the benefit of hindsight to overstate the differences between the parties on civil rights issues during this period, especially before 1964.[50] Even after the post-Goldwater shift toward conservatism within the Republican party, there were

attempts to downplay, or perhaps disguise, direct opposition to civil rights. Often the goals of civil rights were accepted, or at least given lip service, while the means for enforcement were rejected. Similarly, it is easy to overstate how committed national Democrats were to civil rights, too. Second, Jim Crow was by and large dismantled by forces beyond the easy reach of electoral politics. The legal changes were often initiated by unelected federal judges and justices; although popular sentiments and elected branches of government do influence the courts, the insulation of the federal courts from the electoral arena somewhat diffuses legal changes as a partisan issue. Also, the civil rights movement operated outside the field of electoral politics. Elections clearly played a role in determining how governments would respond to the movement, but the direct impetus for dismantling segregation was contested more in the streets than at the polls. Third, with voter registration drives and especially after passage of the 1965 Voting Rights Act, African American voters provided a reliable constituency for Southern Democratic politicians. As segregationists deserted traditional party loyalties for a more conservative alternative, Democratic ranks could be at least partially replenished with newly enfranchised African American voters. But finally and most important, Southern Democratic politicians proved particularly adept at fashioning "night and day" coalitions of diverse groups, enabling them to hang onto power at the state level even when majorities of Southern white voters were deserting in droves the national Democratic party at the presidential level.[51]

The "night and day" Democratic coalitions contained some rather strange bedfellows: rural white farmers and urban liberals, courthouse gangs and blacks, labor unions and business leaders. What could cement these bizarre alliances together? One advantage enjoyed by these Democratic coalitions was experienced, homegrown leadership. Republicans, being the "new kids on the block," often had to resort to running candidates with little experience in electoral politics. Moreover, these novices were often newcomers to the area. Former House Speaker Tip O'Neill once said, "all politics is local," and perhaps more than most, Southerners feel an allegiance to place and a suspicion of "outsiders." These considerations of roots and experience represent boons over and above the already imposing advantages of incumbency in American politics. The Republicans required time to build a leadership pool that could match the reservoir maintained by the Democrats.[52]

Republican strategy may have extended the period of "playing catch-up ball" by not developing "farm teams" of candidates early enough. Joseph Aistrup maintains that Republicans too often attempted to win by running for high-visibility offices without first laying the groundwork by running candidates for local and lower-level state offices. Of course, the Republicans, faced with the reality of scarce resources in terms of candidates, money, and volunteers, confronted a genuine dilemma: if top-of-the-ticket candidates were hurt by a lack of supporting candidates further down the ticket, low-level candidacies would be disadvantaged by not having visible campaigns for higher offices to turn out potential Republican voters whose support would trickle down to less publicized races.[53]

Southern Democrats also developed innovative campaign tactics to appeal to their own diverse constituencies. In some ways, these candidates ran almost segregated campaigns, appealing to African American voters in settings invisible to their white constituents. For example, candidates could be fairly certain that promises made and positions taken while campaigning at black churches would be unlikely to get back to white voters. Even mass-media advertising could be surgically targeted at particular elements of the coalition, a tactic facilitated by the cultural gulf between the races. Messages could be "narrowcast": ads running on country music radio stations could take one tone, while the messages on rap music stations could safely sound rather different.[54]

Another way to appeal to disparate interests was to downplay ideological issues in favor of distributive issues, in other words, pork-barrel politics. Incumbents made special efforts to win spending projects for their constituents—for example, roads, grants, and building projects—and were zealous in offering services to their constituents, such as facilitating appointments to military academies, interceding with Social Security, and obtaining favorable regulatory consideration for small business owners. By "bringing home the bacon," or satisfying the needs of diverse groups and areas for specific programs, Democratic politicians could "deliver" to a broad constituency that might not agree on policy principles but would vote on self-interest.[55]

Traditional loyalties provided a further appeal. Politics is not all interest calculation, and political scientists have long maintained that

party identification is emotionally freighted and stable, not based on momentary considerations of interest. Party officials are aware of the pull of traditional loyalties; in 1996, Georgia Democratic party officials distributed "I'm a yellow-dog Democrat" pins referring to the legendary Southern party loyalist who would supposedly vote Democratic even if a yellow dog headed the ticket. Party identification has shifted over time, but perhaps not as fast as expected, given the salience of racial issues in the South. In Georgia in the 1970s, about 55 percent of the electorate considered themselves Democrats, while only 12 percent called themselves Republicans. In 1987, after the "Reagan Revolution," Democratic identification had fallen to 51 percent and Republican identification had risen to 23 percent. By 1996, 38 percent of the state's voters considered themselves Democrats, 34 percent Republicans, and 28 percent independents. In North Carolina, Democrats outnumbered Republicans 60 percent to 21 percent in 1960, but the advantage had declined to 51 percent to 30 percent in 1986. In 1996, 42 percent of the voters identified with the Democrats, 39 percent with the Republicans, and 18 percent were independents. Even among white voters, 34 percent identified with the Democrats, but 47 percent considered themselves Republicans, and 20 percent were independents.[56]

Also, Southern Democrats have taken steps to insulate state politics from national political tides. For example, in Georgia in the 1970s, the state Democratic party promoted a bumper sticker saying "I'm a Georgia Democrat," with the loud and clear, if unstated, implication that "I'm not a national Democrat." Not content to sloganeer, the state legislature first passed a 1972 law making it impossible to vote a straight ticket for both president and vice-president and state and local offices, but voters could vote a straight party ticket for all state and local offices. As statewide competition heated up, the legislature abolished straight ticket voting altogether in 1995, requiring that voters vote on each race separately. Georgia, in contrast to North Carolina, also held its gubernatorial elections in off years, when no presidential contest could threaten to inject national issues into state politics.

Most important for Southern Democratic electoral prospects, successful state Democratic candidates sought to avoid "wedge" issues that would divide their "night and day" coalitions. One way to do so, of course, was to co-opt issues that might appear to be "Republican"

issues in national politics. For instance, Democratic candidates assumed "tough" stances on crime. An even safer strategy was to de-emphasize social and cultural issues in favor of economic issues, especially the promotion of jobs and economic growth.

One way to understand how Southern Democrats avoided wedge issues that would splinter the diverse constituencies composing their coalition is to recognize that they resisted casting themselves in conservative or liberal ideological terms. After the initial reaction against integration, many politicians adopted the label "moderate." A more analytically useful label, however, is "modernizer." In a scheme that fits other Southern states as well, Paul Luebke described North Carolina politics in terms of a struggle between "traditionalists" and "modernizers." Both camps favor economic growth, but their approach to development varies markedly. The traditionalists want business growth, but not at the cost of disturbing the status quo in social and economic relations. They prefer to let growth occur under business leadership, with the state government playing a minimal role, primarily offering the inducement of low taxes. Traditionalists tend to be wary of high-tech, high-wage work for fear of subverting stable labor markets and labor relations, and they do not favor programs to help minorities or women economically. In terms of the Carolina economy, traditionalists find their base in textiles, apparel, and furniture. Politically, their home has been in the state legislature in North Carolina and, in recent decades, in the Republican party, especially among the Jessecrat wing.

Modernizers favor more active state government to promote development of the region's economy. They are willing to spend money to fuel the "growth machine" and are willing to tax in order to raise the revenues to fund the needed expenditures. They are committed to pursuing higher-tech, higher-wage jobs and reducing the dependency on the traditional low-wage industries of the South. If economic development undermines some of the traditional social relations and structures, the modernizers say, "So be it." Modernizers are not liberals, however. Their economic policy is trickle-down in approach; they believe that the way to stimulate growth is through government support for business, with the benefits trickling down to employees and the community. They are not redistributive or even egalitarian, as are the neopopulists. In the social field, although modernizers are not will-

ing to block industrial development to preserve traditional social hierarchies of race, gender, and class, neither do they initiate policies to further the advancement of women, minorities, or the economically disadvantaged. Rooted in higher-tech, more "modern" economic sectors, modernizers have predominated in the governor's office, in the Democratic party, and in the moderate wing of the Republican party.[57]

The success of Southern Democrats in fending off Republican gains had resulted by the early 1990s in a split-level realignment.[58] Southern electoral patterns tended to be bifurcated between the top of the ticket, where Republican victories were increasingly reliable, and lower state and local offices, where Democrats held on tenaciously with some, though decreasing, success. The gap was closing, however, and by decade's end, analysts rated both Georgia and North Carolina, along with their sister Southern states, if not a toss-up, at least realistically competitive. All in all, Southern politics as we commence a new century does not look very different from politics in other areas of the country. The regional political system that had appeared so backward and out of step with national politics in the first half of the century had, in the course of the second half of the century, lost much of its distinctiveness.

4 / *Dual Convergence II*
The North Marches South

The Sequel

Because of changes in Southern society and politics that moved the region closer to national norms,[1] by the 1990s, the peculiarities of Southern politics that V. O. Key described at midcentury were more differences of degree than of kind. But if major changes were restructuring politics in Dixie, not all the transformations were occurring south of the Mason-Dixon line. Politics in the rest of the nation had been changing, too, constituting the second prong of a dual convergence. In the country as a whole, the Democrats began to lose their edge in national politics at about the same time as the solidly Democratic South lost its grip on that region's politics, and the trends were obviously related. After 1968, it became increasingly apparent that the New Deal Democratic political hegemony established by Franklin Roosevelt in the Great Depression of the 1930s had run its course. Although the Democrats usually continued to hold fairly sizable majorities in Congress until the mid-1990s and to control more state governments than the Republicans, after the election of Lyndon Johnson in 1964, only two presidents were Democrats. Ironically, both were Southern Democrats: Carter of Georgia and Clinton of Arkansas. In a sense, the Republican campaign against New Deal Democracy nationally has resembled the Republican assault on the Solid Democratic South, with presidential victories at the top of the ticket spilling down to congressional, state, and local offices. At the beginning of the twenty-first century, the national political configuration paralleled the Southern political pattern that had evolved in recent decades.

The national political alignment paralleled the emerging political configuration of the South in ways beyond its pattern of competition

between the parties. Within each party, the leading factions that coalesced had their forerunners in the South. The burgeoning conservative movement, strongly fortified by the religious right, had its testing ground on Southern soil. The leading neoliberals among the national Democrats had their counterparts in Southern "modernizers"—in fact, the most successful national neoliberals, Bill Clinton and Al Gore, hailed from the South. Moreover, the contestation of issues in national politics came to correspond closely to the issues and tactics forged in Southern politics.

The South did not cause the evolution in Northern politics that completed the other half of the dual convergence of national and Southern politics, at least not in any simple or straightforward way. Addressing the problem of Jim Crow segregation in the South unleashed forces that have had a major impact in realigning both the region's and the nation's politics. The South, however, has not been exclusively, or even primarily, influential in shaping the structural similarities that have the potential to move American politics toward the irresponsible and undemocratic politics of the Solid South. The causes of that political restructuring are complex and too numerous to analyze here, but they surely include the rise of mass-media politics, in particular, television's impact on elections and governance; the correlative melding of public relations and politics; the proliferation of interest groups and their growing power; the hemorrhaging of money into our electoral system; social transformations that undermined many traditional forms of community; the resulting decline in social capital and increase in individual isolation; economic transformations that radically revised how we work, shop, and live; and the globalization not only of our economy but also of our culture. Rather than analyzing the causes of political change in the United States, chapter 6 analyzes the nature of the structural similarities that have emerged between national electoral institutions and the old Southern system, and chapter 7 examines possible consequences of this restructuring. In this chapter, we simply retrace the course followed as our politics aligned regionally and nationally.

In a nutshell, when the national government, led by Democrats, finally moved in the 1960s to dismantle the system of Jim Crow legal segregation in the South, it dealt the death blow to the rickety New Deal coalition that had led the nation since the 1930s. The Democrats'

championing of civil rights led to partisan white flight by many Southerners. But race did more than yank the pillar of the solidly Democratic South out from under the New Deal coalition. Focusing attention on racism in the South surfaced pervasive and deep-seated problems of discrimination in other parts of the country. As Jill Quadagno writes, "No longer a regional embarrassment, racial inequality had become a national malady."[2] When racial inequalities reached the national agenda, the support of other elements of the New Deal coalition—especially white, urban, working-class voters—began to totter, and the generation-long hegemony of the Democrats first staggered, then stumbled.

The Republicans were the beneficiaries as the Democrats faltered. Building on the anger and alienation in white America discovered by George Wallace, but not succeeding until they crafted softer, more oblique approaches to appealing to whites' racial reactions, the Republicans rode the white backlash to major electoral victories, if not secure majority status. Using a more populist style so long pervasive in the South, Republican politicians, especially Ronald Reagan, managed to pry many voters in the lower half of the socioeconomic scale away from their traditional Democratic moorings and to convince them that their best interests lay with the more conservative party. In other words, the Republicans used many working-class voters' social and racial concerns to weld them to a party that had previously appealed to more upper-status adherents. Social movements of the 1960s, especially the civil rights and women's movements and efforts to help the poor, unleashed many changes that threatened social stability, including established racial and gender hierarchies. Many Americans, occupying the great middle between the haves and have-nots, now began to feel closer to the haves on the basis of social status than they did to the have-nots, their traditional partners in the New Deal coalition, on the basis of common economic interests. The economic crisis of the 1970s and the failure of New Deal economics to respond effectively reinforced this migration away from dependable Democratic voting habits and into the Republican column, no matter how tentatively. Democrats, too, were forced to give new attention to social concerns, first by welcoming social change, and later by reaffirming "traditional family values" in an effort to inoculate themselves against conservative discontent. This emphasis, as well as the failure of old economic formulas, hastened the rise of neoliberalism, which focused

more on an economics of growth and turned a near-blind eye to issues of distribution. As was typical in "ole-timey" Southern politics, in the process of shoring up traditional racial and gender hierarchies, trends toward steeper economic inequalities were reinforced, especially in the 1980s, and the class divide continued to deepen in the 1990s.

Removing the segregationist stigma from Southern politics ironically opened the door to advancing the influence of Southern politicians in both parties. Within the Republican party, Southern conservatives figured prominently in the triumph of the conservative movement that won the presidency with Reagan in 1980 and Congress with Newt Gingrich in 1994. Among the Democrats, Southern moderates helped pioneer the shift to the New Democrat leadership that emerged in the party's center in the 1990s and won the presidency with Bill Clinton in 1992. Partly because of the new influence of Southern politicians, but more as a consequence of how issues of class, race, and gender have interacted with partisan politics in the last political generation, the South has liberalized while the nation has moved sharply to the right. This dual movement in contradictory directions has left region and nation comprehensively aligned. In chapter 3, we traced how the South evolved to its new political position. In this chapter, we trace the migration of American politics as the nation has, in some respects, rejoined the South.

New Deal Demise

The Democratic party dominated American politics during the middle third of the twentieth century. In response to the Great Depression, ushered in by the stock market crash of 1929, voters elected Franklin Delano Roosevelt president in 1932. Promising the American public a New Deal, FDR launched numerous initiatives to aid the millions trapped in dire economic straits. If New Deal programs did not cure the depressed economic conditions,[3] they brought sufficient relief to prove extraordinarily popular with the voters, who overwhelmingly reelected Roosevelt to four terms in office and returned reliable Democratic majorities in Congress to pass his proposals.

The New Deal was not a consistent set of initiatives but a hodgepodge of experiments in governmental activism. Some were designed

to relieve symptoms: the shorter-lived programs such as the Civilian Conservation Corps and Public Works Administration aimed at putting the unemployed back to work. Other regulatory programs, such as the Bank Regulatory Act, the National Industrial Recovery Act, and the Agricultural Adjustment Act, sought to alleviate the perceived chaotic conditions in industry and agriculture that some believed had triggered the depression. Some New Deal initiatives sought to correct more fundamental flaws or imbalances in American society in order to lay foundations for longer-term economic health. The Social Security Act, designed to insure income for those unable to work because of old age or incapacity, and the National Labor Relations Act, intended to restore industrial peace and stability by balancing the overweening power of employers with the organized voice of workers, are examples of more sweeping New Deal reforms.

The coalition that supported the New Deal was a broad "majority of minorities," including groups that had suffered most and were least able to cope with the plague of economic depression: the poor, union members, Jews, Catholics, African Americans, and Southerners.[4] The working class, hit hardest by the industrial downturn, and their organized expression, trade unions, provided the core support for the Democrats. Urban voters, especially Northern ethnic Americans whose support was often organized by urban political machines, were another component of New Deal politics. African Americans, whose loyalties traditionally had resided with the party of Lincoln, also experienced extreme deprivation during the economic cataclysm, and they increasingly switched their allegiance to the Democrats. This shift became more important as blacks migrated from the depressed conditions of the South into the urban areas of large Northern industrial states rich in electoral college votes.

The other pillar of the New Deal was the South, but this component of the New Deal coalition was somewhat shaky. Although Southern voters supported FDR at unprecedented levels, the strange electoral system of the Solid South often produced representatives more beholden to the Southern planter elite than to the majority of have-not voters. This anomaly resulted in mixed Southern support for New Deal programs in Congress, with Southern congressional representatives ranging from positions to the left of the New Deal (e.g., Huey Long of Louisiana and Hugo Black of Alabama), to consistent

Roosevelt loyalists (e.g., Maury Maverick and Lyndon Johnson of Texas), to staunch opponents of the New Deal and all it stood for (e.g., Senators Carter Glass and Harry F. Byrd of Virginia and Josiah Bailey of North Carolina). At the least, the strong contingent of Solid South politicians within Roosevelt's Democratic coalition ensured that New Deal programs would not disturb the peculiar hierarchical racial and class system of the South.[5] For example, the Agricultural Adjustment Act was shaped to give relief to farm owners without any assurance that the benefits would trickle down to the sharecropping tenants of Southern plantations. An alternative experiment in agricultural relief, the Farm Security Administration, sought to promote farm and home ownership by encouraging an American land reform program, but the agency met with fierce opposition from Southern politicians. Its budgets and programs were crippled, and as the public's attention was diverted to war, both hot and cold, the agency was abolished in 1946.[6]

As World War II loomed larger in Europe and the Pacific, Roosevelt gradually curbed relief and reform efforts at home to assume the posture of "Dr. Win-the-War." With the return of prosperity and peace in the late 1940s, the Democratic party became the "normal" majority party,[7] and the era of social tensions and conflict settled into a time of relative harmony, partly attributable to a de facto social compact implicitly entered into by capital, labor, and government. In essence, American business accepted a limited welfare state, government's active role in the economy, and the right of workers to organize into unions to bargain collectively for higher wages and benefits and better working conditions. Unions, for their part, recognized capital's right to manage businesses and determine investments in a private-enterprise economy. In return, government restricted its role to maintaining business conditions aimed at achieving prosperity and to alleviating some of the more egregious social costs of a market economy.

Looking back on the "long 1940s" from the vantage point of the present, observers can now detect developments that halted the forward motion of the New Deal toward an American version of social democracy, as well as generating some of the fissures that would eventually crack the New Deal coalition wide open. Among the contributing factors that smoothed the radical edges from New Deal politics and laid the foundation for an "end of ideology" were a postwar prosperity that precluded a return to the more sweeping initiatives of the New Deal;

the social accord among capital, labor, and government; the Cold War obsession with stopping communism and ferreting out domestic radicalism; the first tentative steps toward civil rights for African Americans; and the beginning of the long, slow decline of American labor, stemming in no small measure from the failure of Operation Dixie to organize Southern workers into unions. Larger political economy issues of social organization and the structures of wealth and power in the country were reduced to matters of technical economics. The movements that had fueled the politics of the New Deal began to behave more like interest groups, with, for example, the labor movement narrowing its focus to winning better wages and benefits for its members. As Ira Katznelson put it, "in the 1940s, economics replaced political economics, and pluralism supplanted the politics of class." With the inclusion of a civil rights plank in the 1948 Democratic platform and Truman's desegregation of the armed forces, questions of race began to create tension within the New Deal coalition as the Democrats moved from "omission to the inclusion of race."[8] Although much less visible at the time, the political fallout occasioned the first of two "mini-realignments" away from the New Deal political order, according to David Lawrence.[9] It is instructive to note that this first mini-realignment in the 1940s, like the more visible and sizable shake-up of the New Deal party system in the 1960s, was marked by the revolt of Southern Democrats and independent presidential campaigns by Southerners (Strom Thurmond on the States' Rights or Dixiecrat ticket in 1948, and George Wallace leading his American Independent party in 1968).

Dating the fruition of the "end of ideology" a bit later, Godfrey Hodgson, in his illuminating history of postwar American politics through Watergate, claims that by the late 1950s and early 1960s, a "liberal consensus" had crystallized in this country. Despite the label "liberal," the consensus was actually centrist. It reflected the disappearance of both left and right political forces in the Cold War with communism, which shaped politics after World War II. The left was tagged with doubts about its loyalty and association with radical anti-capitalism, while the right was discredited by the excesses of McCarthyism.[10] The center dominated politics, and elites of both parties backed active government policies to ensure prosperity at home and security abroad. Intervening in the economy, the so-called New

Economics used Keynesian fiscal and monetary tools to guard against the recurrence of depression and to smooth out the boom-and-bust cycles of capitalism, guaranteeing growth with stability. Socially, the government intervened with policies to aid those unable to reap the rewards of the market economy. Internationally, the United States intervened around the world to contain the threat of communism and to protect American interests.[11]

Hodgson argues that this "liberal consensus" rested on nearly universally shared assumptions that simply turned out to be wrong. In foreign policy, the assumption of unquestioned American power was based on the unique position the United States occupied as World War II ended. The United States had grown in strength during the fight against fascism, but its allies as well as its former enemies were exhausted by the struggle. This temporary hegemony could not last, but while it did, the power vacuum tempted American policy makers to overreach, resulting in the no-win commitment in Vietnam. Domestic intervention rested on a similar complacency about American society and an unquestioned acceptance of our institutions as fundamentally sound. Any flaws were considered residual, easily remedied by using money and social science expertise to implement government programs that supposedly would solve social problems, much like solutions to industrial problems are engineered. The central government institution in this liberal "welfare-warfare state" was a strong presidency.[12]

Hodgson traces how this liberal consensus first succumbed to crisis, then fragmented and polarized in the 1960s and 1970s, leading eventually to the constitutional crisis of Watergate. In foreign policy, the Vietnam War exploded the myth that the United States could control events around the world and that it could wage war abroad without paying the price in damages to American society and democracy at home. On the home front, the Kennedy assassination first signaled crisis, but it was the metamorphosis of the Southern civil rights movement into Northern urban unrest that killed the liberal consensus for active government domestically. With Watts, Detroit, and the cores of hundreds of other American cities smoldering in the wake of violent disturbances, it was hard to imagine that the problems of racism and inequality were merely residual or peculiar to the backward South. While Jim Crow legal segregation was unique to the South, racism was

revealed as a widespread and deep flaw in American society, one not easily amenable to solution by simple, cheap social engineering.

Simultaneous with the foundering of liberal foreign and social policies on the shoals of resistance in Vietnam and Northern ghettos, Keynesian economics seemed to lose its magical powers to regulate capitalism as the economy entered a period of transformation. The change was essentially a restructuring from a national to a global economy, as former allies and enemies became economic competitors and as communication and transportation innovations facilitated capital mobility. One long wave of capitalism, initiated with the crisis of the depression in the late 1920s, seemed to have run its course, opening the door to a new cycle. The novel problems of this latest economic cycle required a new set of social and political as well as economic institutions, updated "social structures of accumulation," to make economic growth and accumulation possible. The social compact between capital and labor was breached, and the "era of social reform" had run its course. If the South had earlier resisted the interventionist bent of New Deal programs, now many constituencies questioned the premises of liberal government, as domestic and international problems proved impervious to government solutions. New Deal Democracy had dominated American politics and policy for a generation, including the Solid South as an integral if anomalous part of its political order. Now this New Deal social infrastructure and policies of active government at home and abroad, the hegemonic force for a political generation, began to crumble.[13]

The Roots of Reaganism

The so-called Reagan Revolution had deep roots. The rise of the Republican party nationally from its decidedly secondary position in the New Deal era, as well as the rise of the right wing within the Republican party, was a long time coming. Barry Goldwater's 1964 run for the presidency set the stage. Goldwaterites rejected the "me too" moderation of Eisenhower Republicanism, which had accepted the basic outline of New Deal activism and merely claimed that Republicans could manage government policies more efficiently and economically. The Arizona senator's capture of the Republican presidential nomi-

nation offered "a choice, not an echo" and signaled the defeat of the party's pragmatic, Eastern wing by an emerging ideological, conservative movement. Goldwater also made a play to capture the Democrats' most reliable bastion, the Solid South. He voted against the Civil Rights Act of 1964, arguing that its mandate to desegregate public accommodations infringed on private property rights. At the 1964 Republican convention, in the context of extensive violence perpetrated against civil rights activists during the Freedom Summer of 1964, Goldwater used his acceptance speech to declare that "extremism in the defense of liberty is no vice . . . moderation in the pursuit of justice is no virtue!" The ploy paid off, although at the time it seemed to have worked too well. Goldwater was trounced by Lyndon Johnson, winning the electoral votes of only six states, including his home state of Arizona. In a complete reversal of long-standing voting patterns, however, the other five states for Goldwater were the Deep South states: South Carolina, Georgia, Alabama, Mississippi, and Louisiana. Moreover, within the Southern states, voting patterns were reversed as the black belts, the very core of the solidly Democratic South, disproportionately led the voting for Goldwater.[14]

In 1968, Richard Nixon squeaked by Hubert Humphrey 44 to 43 percent in a three-way contest in which third-party candidate George Wallace, governor of Alabama and a staunch segregationist, garnered 13 percent of the votes nationally. The Southern states almost universally deserted the Democrats, with the Deep South going for Wallace, but enough Peripheral South states voted for Nixon to thwart Wallace's ambition to play power broker by denying either major party candidate a majority and throwing the election into the House of Representatives. In office, Nixon set about to expand his entree into the no-longer-Solid South. Nixon's "Southern strategy" was designed to win over Southern conservatives and to eliminate Wallace as the balance of power nationally in 1972. Nixon, a Californian from the moderate wing of the party and vice-president under Eisenhower, pursued a range of policies intended to cement the Wallace constituency to his reelection efforts. Although disguising its moves,[15] the Nixon administration braked progress on civil rights enforcement and tilted social policy to the right. In a complex mixture of policy and rhetoric, Nixon's advocacy of "law and order" was overtly aimed at countering rising crime rates, but set against a backdrop of civil

rights and antiwar protests, the slogan tapped into the silent majority's fear of disorder and change. He denounced "forced busing" without renouncing the goal of school desegregation, despite the fact that his own law-and-order Supreme Court appointees voted to require busing in Charlotte in a unanimous opinion authored by his first nominee, Chief Justice Warren Burger. He criticized welfare as subverting the work ethic, although he introduced the Family Assistance Plan, a welfare reform that amounted to a guaranteed income. He railed against quotas, even though his own administration had forced quotas on union apprenticeships in the Philadelphia plan. The common denominator underlying these seemingly contradictory moves was Nixon's attempt to send an encoded message, especially but not exclusively aimed at Southern whites, that the Republican party had now replaced the Democrats as the defender of white interests. This strategy seemed to achieve success in 1972, as Nixon defeated Democratic challenger George McGovern by 59 to 41 percent, winning roughly the equivalent of the combined Nixon and Wallace totals in 1968.[16]

Watergate intervened to derail Nixon's plans to build a new conservative majority. After a brief interlude, however, the conservative movement regrouped. Ronald Reagan made a bold but futile attempt to unseat incumbent but unelected President Gerald Ford in 1976, but the thunder out of California when that state passed Proposition 13 in 1978 was the most audible announcement of the revived movement's gathering strength.[17] President Jimmy Carter, a fiscally conservative, managerial-minded, moderate Southern Democrat when elected over Ford in 1976, led the Democratic Congress in a defensive swing to more conservative positions in the late 1970s. These policy shifts foreshadowed many initiatives that the Reagan administration would introduce in more extreme measure, for example, tax cuts tilted toward upper-income groups, a regressive increase in payroll taxes to fund Social Security, deregulation of several industries, and a revised energy program relying on incentives to producers rather than on conservation. After the Soviet invasion of Afghanistan and revolutions in several third-world countries, the Carter administration soft-peddled its original emphasis on human rights and returned to a harder anticommunist line in foreign policy, including a dramatic increase in defense expenditures.[18]

Revolt of the Reagan Democrats

None of these stratagems was sufficient to stem the conservative tide that burst on the national scene fully with Ronald Reagan's victory in 1980. Besides being perceived as weak on foreign policy, especially after Iranian students seized fifty-three hostages at the American embassy in Tehran, Carter's inept management of the economy proved to be his nemesis. Carter had the misfortune to reside in the White House when the globalization of the economy began to hit home hard. Having stood almost alone as the dominant force in the world economy after World War II, the United States now faced stringent competition in world markets with the revival of our former allies and enemies. The American share of world gross national product (GNP) declined from 40 to 23 percent in the two decades between 1950 and 1970, while the country's portion of world trade fell from 20 to 11 percent. American productivity rates lagged from their impressive postwar levels, and after doubling in the decades after World War II, the real incomes of Americans began to stagnate and even decline. Carter's "politics of austerity" offered no relief for hard-pressed Americans. Although he had reduced budget deficits from $66 billion in 1976 to $27.7 billion in 1979, Carter had not fulfilled his promise to balance the budget by the end of his term. More seriously, after OPEC's second oil embargo in 1979, inflation raced to unprecedented levels, reaching 12.4 percent in the year of the presidential election. Perhaps even more damaging to the president's reelection prospects, the tight-money policy pursued by Paul Volcker, chair of the Federal Reserve Bank, yielded a 7 percent unemployment rate and negative growth for the economy for 1980, with the GNP shrinking by $39 billion and real per capita income falling from $4,503 to $4,435. The Democrats, associated since Roosevelt with expansive economic policies and prosperity, defaulted, yielding the economic initiative to the Republicans, who could now claim to be the progressive party of change.[19]

After winning 50.7 percent of the vote in a three-way contest against Carter and moderate Republican John Anderson, Reagan used his early days in office to redirect the policies of the country. Although social issues such as abortion and school prayer had played an important role in the campaign, the administration focused its energies on economic measures.[20] In reducing taxes while astronomically raising

spending for the military, deregulating industries, and reducing spending for the poor, Reagan crafted a basic policy framework for years to come. Reagan's Economic Recovery Tax Act of 1981 cut top tax rates on higher incomes and reduced estate and capital gains taxes; corporations received $150 billion in tax relief over the next five years. During that time, the whole package cost the government an estimated $600 billion in lost tax revenues. Meantime, the Omnibus Budget and Reconciliation Act of 1981 cut $140 billion from federal spending through fiscal year 1985, with employment, education, public housing, and social welfare programs for the poor taking the biggest hits. Combined with beefed-up defense spending of $1.6 trillion in five years, these fiscal policies produced annual deficits of over $200 billion by 1983. The tight monetary policies of the Federal Reserve initially wrung inflation out of the economy at the price of a severe recession and high unemployment in the early 1980s. The "military Keynesianism" of huge deficits fueled by defense spending, however, stimulated the economy sufficiently to spur a return to economic growth and to ensure not only Reagan's reelection in 1984 but also the election of Vice-President George Bush as his successor in 1988.

Democratic party elites, traumatized by electoral defeat and mesmerized by the conservative ideological offensive, proved unable to counter the conservative diagnosis of America's economic ills: that economic growth was faltering for lack of private investment. They could not effectively oppose the Reagan administration's proposed prescription: policies that reduced the public sector and redistributed wealth to the rich in the hope that they would save and invest more, the fruits of which were supposed to trickle down to average citizens. The Democrats, although pleading for more compassion and moderation from Reagan, yielded the high ground to the president's initiatives and contented themselves with fighting rearguard actions.[21] Despite Democratic majorities in the House during the entire Reagan era and in the Senate for the last Congress, Democratic defectors to Reagan, led by Southern "boll weevils," provided crucial support for administration proposals. Phil Gramm, then a Democratic representative from Texas, even led the fight for Reagan's crucial 1981 budget revisions.

Reagan did more than reengineer New Deal economic policies into a new, conservative supply-side package. He also recast the racial dialogue in the nation. Reagan preached what Thomas and Mary Edsall

call conservative or populist egalitarianism. Proponents of this perspective deplore racial discrimination but also view it as a thing of the past. Imagining that the worst forms of prejudice have been stamped out, they perceive the current opportunity structure to be a more or less level playing field for all. Any further attempts to aid minorities or eradicate residual inequalities are considered unnecessary at best, favoritism or "reverse discrimination" at worst. Believing the barriers to individual achievement to be a thing of the past, conservative egalitarians can feel complacent about their condemnation of racism while simultaneously opposing any remedies with real teeth. Through the combination of rhetoric and policy redirections, Reagan led the construction of what Michael Omi and Howard Winant call a new racial formation in the nation.[22]

Although materially aiding corporations and the wealthy, many of the administration's pseudopopulist stances were designed to appeal to critical swing voting blocks, especially the so-called Reagan Democrats: white, urban, ethnic European, often Catholic working-class voters and white Southerners. Both groups had once been pillars of the New Deal coalition. Both now found Republicanism appealing, particularly on so-called social issues. Although these groups historically favored government programs and economic measures advocated by the Democrats, in a time of rapid change and perceived social disintegration, Republicans successfully wooed their votes on the basis of morality, patriotism, and race.[23] Sharing a deep-abiding populism that inclined them toward traditional values against cultural modernism, these groups' positions on "the new politics of old values" strained their relations with the more liberal Democratic party.[24]

The Edsalls argue that four issues—rights, reform, race, and taxes—deprived the Democrats of the support of these traditionally New Deal constituencies in the 1980s. Under Democratic leadership, the federal government instituted a "rights revolution" that extended legal protections to, "among others, criminal defendants, women, the poor, non-European ethnic minorities, students, homosexuals, prisoners, the handicapped, and the mentally ill." Rights-oriented reforms guaranteed women, minorities, and youth representation at the Democratic convention. To many Reagan Democrats, these reforms smacked of special privileges or, worse, undermined traditional authority, such as by "coddling criminals." Moreover, the emphasis on rights for

"exotic minorities" seemed to come at the expense of neglecting the traditional bread-and-butter economic issues that had sustained the New Deal coalition since the Great Depression. To some populist-minded voters, Democratic liberals had shifted their stance to protecting "the one against the many—not the many against the powerful."[25]

The Reagan Democrats' perception that liberal Democrats had abandoned their economic interests was not entirely illusory. Subtle policy changes since the 1960s had undermined the popularity of tax-and-spend policies, once the key to Democratic majorities but now transformed into a political epithet in the rhetoric of Reaganism. On the spending side of the equation, New Deal welfare programs such as Social Security had generally been "universal," aimed at a broad middle-class constituency. Almost all Americans were covered, and most could reasonably expect to benefit from these measures' protections. Lyndon Johnson's Great Society programs, in contrast, were primarily "means-tested." Programs such as Medicaid, Head Start, and Job Corps were targeted to the poor. Although it was not explicitly targeted for racial minorities, Johnson intended his War on Poverty to correct the neglect of race by many New Deal programs, measures that consequently failed to correct the scourges of poverty and racism while lifting the nation out of the depression. These Great Society programs, however, lacked the broad constituency of more universal policies and did not win the political support enjoyed by older Democratic policies among the working and middle classes.[26]

On the tax side, shifts in the tax burden from corporate to individual income taxes, from income taxes to payroll taxes, and from progressive to flatter tax rates all undermined the willingness of less wealthy Americans to pay for government programs. In particular, inflation meant that taxpayers paid income taxes at higher rates because of "bracket creep," even though their larger incomes reflected nominal rather than real gains. In 1953, the median family paid income taxes at an 11.8 percent rate. In 1976, as the economy was stagnating and real incomes slipping, the average family was paying at a rate of 20.2 percent. These developments meant that Democratic constituencies were picking up an increasing share of the tax tab at a time when they perceived decreasing stakes in the programs being funded by their tax dollars. In other words, Democrats open to Reagan's appeal often felt that the Democratic party had moved from "tax-

ing the few for the benefit of the many" to "taxing the many on behalf of the few."[27] The party had flunked the cardinal lesson in politics: "rewarding and protecting its own constituents."[28]

According to the Edsalls, however, race was the most potent solvent in dissolving the Democratic coalition. The Democrats' advance of the civil rights agenda and the Republicans' skillful exploitation of the white backlash caused some Reagan Democrats to view Democratic messages through a "racial filter." Even economic issues that had traditionally favored the Democrats now came to be tarred with a racial brush. In the lexicon of Reaganism, seemingly neutral economic terms such as "groups," "big government," "taxes," and "special interests" assumed coded, racial overtones. The consequences played havoc with the once-broad Democratic coalition that had included North and South, white and black:

> Just as race was used, between 1880 and 1964, by the planter-textile-banking elite of the South to rupture class solidarity at the bottom of the income ladder, and to maintain control of the region's economic and political systems, race as a national issue over the past twenty-five years has broken the Democratic New Deal "bottom-up" coalition—a coalition dependent on substantial support from all voters, white and black, at or below the median income. The fracturing of the Democrats' "bottom-up" coalition permitted, in turn, those at the top of the "top-down" conservative coalition to encourage and to nurture, in the 1980s, what may well have been the most accelerated upwards redistribution of income in the nation's history.[29]

The 1988 election provided the most stunning proof of this analysis. Republican George Bush defeated "bloodless liberal" Michael Dukakis partly by riding the coattails of the Reagan recovery. The campaign, however, saw some of the most blatant use of racist coding ever. Under the guidance of South Carolina's Lee Atwater, the Bush campaign capitalized on a series of television advertisements aired by a conservative political action committee featuring Willie Horton, a black convicted murderer who had raped and assaulted a white couple while on furlough from a Massachusetts prison during Dukakis's term as governor.[30] Adding patriotism to the mix after the U.S. victory in the Persian Gulf War in 1991, Bush seemed unassailable in his bid for reelection.

We're All Southern Democrats Now

By the early 1990s, then, political scientist Byron Shafer could plausibly speak of a new political order in the United States: "Republicans capture the presidency without even threatening to capture Congress." Shafer argued that this state of affairs resulted less from shifts on traditional social welfare and economic issues than from the advent of new divisions of foreign policy and cultural issues. The presidency, being uniquely the lead actor in international relations and a bully pulpit, as Teddy Roosevelt had noted, for the symbolic politics of culture, was a prime target for Republicans, who preached nationalism and traditional values. Members of Congress, in contrast, generally used that arena to push pragmatic programs guarding the social welfare and economic prosperity of their constituents, giving the mildly activist Democrats the upper hand in that forum. This political division of labor between Republican presidents and Democratic Congresses, Shafer maintained, reflected a majority predisposition to conservatism in foreign policy and cultural issues but a continuing commitment to at least moderate activism on economic issues.

While this crosscutting of traditional New Deal issue stances might seem to be a strange new development in recent American politics, Shafer noted that it had a precursor: "For there was, throughout, one party faction actually embodying these larger national preferences, a faction moderately supportive of social welfare but concerned about paying its bills, a faction reliably supportive of international activism but concerned about ensuring success, a faction deeply traditionalistic on cultural values in a world where economic development was putting inevitable stresses on them. . . . It was, of course, the southern Democrats." Ironically, this faction appeared to be in steep decline just when the nation seemed to be adopting its ideology, but as Shafer explained, "if the rest of the nation now finds itself in the same position that southern voters once did—preferring cautious liberals on social welfare, cautious conservatives on cultural values—then there is no real basis for such a 'faction' to exist. We are all southern Democrats now."[31]

A slightly different, although not incompatible, explanation for our split-level political order builds on findings about American public opinion that date back to the 1960s but still retain their pertinence.

Analyzing survey results, Lloyd Free and Hadley Cantril concluded that Americans' political beliefs varied by the level of abstraction at which questions were posed. In the abstract, Americans tend to be conservatives, agreeing to statements such as the government is too big, taxes are too high, government programs are wasteful and should be cut back, or there are too many government regulations. When asked more concrete, pragmatic questions about government programs, however, most Americans support programs to help the poor and support health and education, regulations to protect the environment and public safety, and the taxes necessary to pay for such programs. In Free and Cantril's terms, we are ideological conservatives but operational liberals, a belief system that might be viewed as slightly schizophrenic.[32] These contradictory views help explain why, during the conservative upsurge of the late 1960s through the early 1990s, a more thoroughgoing rout of Democrats in lower offices did not accompany the tendency to elect Republican presidents. Instead, we have elected more conservative presidents, an office that functions on a more symbolic plane and deals with more ideologically charged issues, while simultaneously electing more operationally liberal Congresses and state politicians, whose work often deals with the pragmatic nitty-gritty details of operating government programs.

Of course, the two-tiered political order Shafer described flip-flopped in the mid-1990s, as most of the decade witnessed a pragmatic, centrist, Democratic president arrayed against an extremely ideologically conservative Republican Congress. This turn of events is not inconsistent with Free and Cantril's interpretation of public opinion pulled simultaneously in two directions. President Bush seemed invincible as long as foreign policy and cultural and ideological issues were salient, but when the economy stagnated in the early 1990s, the electorate had more pragmatic economic issues on its mind. Democrats, who had moved toward more traditionalist stances during the 1970s and 1980s, had positioned themselves to diffuse social and cultural issues. Students of voting behavior found a rise in retrospective rather than prospective voting. Voters tended to cast their ballots on the basis of past performance, a more pragmatic test, rather than future promise, which rests more on ideological vision. Carter suffered the retribution of the voters for his failure to tame inflation and for presiding over an election-year recession. Reagan benefited in 1984, as did Bush in 1988,

from the recovery from the early 1980s recession, but when the economy deteriorated again in the early 1990s, it was the Democrats who benefited and Bush who paid the price.[33]

The return of a Democrat to the White House did not presage an era of revitalized liberalism. The Reagan Revolution may have run its course by the early 1990s, but Reagan's successes ensured that when Democrats did regain the reins of power, they inherited a government defunded and delegitimated by the legacies of the Reagan-Bush era. Budget deficits in particular hampered new initiatives.[34] More importantly, the Democrats capitulated to the conservative agenda of balanced budgets and less government. Early in his first term, well before he faced a Republican Congress and negotiated a balanced budget deal with them, President Clinton complained to staffers: "Where are the Democrats? We are all Eisenhower Republicans. We are Eisenhower Republicans here and we are fighting Reagan Republicans. We stand for lower deficits and free trade and the bond market."[35]

After the Republican capture of Congress in 1994, Clinton eased even further to the right, announcing in his 1996 State of the Union Address that "the era of big government is over."[36] While this rhetoric positioned him as a centrist for the November election, it also signaled the repudiation of the political prescription that had worked to elect Democrats from Roosevelt through Johnson. "Tax and spend" had been a formula for providing government that won the allegiance of most Middle Americans, and deficit financing had given the economy the necessary Keynesian stimulation to ensure a growing economy and widespread prosperity. In the post-Reagan era, such policies served only to stigmatize their proponents. Edsall notes that if the Democratic party was the energy-generating sun of the New Deal party system and the Republicans were the light-reflecting moon, that relationship is now reversed.[37] The Republican party is the new Energizer Bunny of American politics.

By the 1990s, the old structure of national politics had fractured. The New Deal had evolved first into a centrist "liberal consensus," which in turn had been shattered by the traumatic events of the 1960s and 1970s. The result was ideological fragmentation with numerous neoideologies (e.g., neoliberalism, neoconservatism, and the New Right) contending for acceptance. The contest between the two parties was increasingly fought on terrain that looked very different from

the older political order, with issues of race and cultural values occupying a central position. Even when economic issues predominated, they were cast in very different terms from the partisan axis of the New Deal regime.

The nation's politics increasingly resembled Southern politics in this transition phase. For one thing, Southern groups, along with the Northern, urban, white, ethnic working class, were the critical swing groups who played large roles in determining election outcomes. Second, the conservative political agenda associated with traditional Southern Democrats reigned in each party.[38] Third, the partisan competition at the national level was remarkably well aligned with the electoral terrain of the contemporary South. Arguably, this congruence of partisan contests reflected the outcomes of various factional struggles that were occurring within each party.[39] By the 1990s, the internal factional configurations within the two parties produced a partisan lineup remarkably similar to the lines along which parties in the South now vie for political support.

The Republicans Reborn

Since World War II, the Republicans have been the more unified party, although some tension existed between stalwart (or Main Street) and liberal (or Wall Street) Republicans.[40] Ike and his vice-president Richard Nixon forged a potent amalgam that combined stalwart stances on domestic issues with militant anticommunist foreign policy.[41] The advent of "Southern" Republicanism in the Southeast and Southwest launched the New Right conservative movement, which displaced the liberal wing and laid the basis for party factionalism in recent decades.

Shifting success at the polls has attended this emergence of a New Republican Right. On a policy plane as well, the party agenda has been dominated by the ideology espoused by this "thunder on the right," sounding from the Southern regions of the United States.[42] One way to gauge this connection is to note that former Alabama governor George Wallace pioneered many of the themes that sustained the conservative movement that first gained a toehold in the Nixon administration and assumed power with Reagan in 1980. In his biography of Wallace, historian Dan Carter argues that Wallace discovered the constituency of

angry, alienated voters that Nixon would seek to claim as his own base—the "silent majority." Wallace's forays into the North in the 1964 presidential primaries, where he rolled up impressive vote tallies in such presumably liberal states as Wisconsin, Indiana, and Maryland, demonstrated the existence of a vein of resentment among urban ethnic workers that conservative Republicans could also mine to their advantage. Having narrowly defeated Hubert Humphrey in a three-way race in 1968, Nixon understood that he had to appeal to the Wallace voters to cement a second term in 1972. Two groups were particularly receptive: Southern Democrats, repelled by the directions taken by the national Democrats under LBJ's Great Society programs and its championing of civil rights; and traditionally Democratic Northern, mainly working-class white ethnics, disenchanted with the party's perceived elitism embodied in its emphasis on civil rights and civil liberties and neglect of bread-and-butter economic programs.[43] The Nixon administration shaped its rhetoric and policy to appeal to these Democratic deserters. The strategy included backing away from the GOP's traditional pro–civil rights stand and the commitment of the executive branch to strict enforcement of civil rights laws.[44] Although the electoral victories went to Nixon, he shaped his Southern strategy to respond to the forgotten "little people" to whom George Wallace appealed. As Carter noted, "When George Wallace had played his fiddle, the President of the United States had danced Jim Crow."[45]

Wallace's influence, however, extended well beyond the civil rights backlash and antibusing, antiprotester rhetoric of the Nixon administration. Wallace discovered, and did much to foster, the antigovernment sentiment in Middle America that fueled the Reagan Revolution of the 1980s and proved to be Reagan's most lasting legacy for the 1990s and beyond. Wallace tapped into the anti-Establishment mood of the 1960s but gave it a decidedly right-wing populist spin. When he argued that the federal government should stay out of local affairs, it was a fairly transparent ploy to perpetuate the white supremacy favored by his local constituency. Yet his attack on Washington and the "liberal Establishment" encompassed much more than merely a defense of the "Southern way of life." Sensing the moral unease of many in the midst of changing social mores, he attacked intellectuals as "snobs who don't know the difference between smut and great literature." He chided the efforts of the federal government to spawn pro-

grams to solve social problems, saying that the bureaucrats lacked even the common sense to "park their bicycles straight." That other pillar of the Establishment, the "liberal media," also suffered from his scathing attacks. His shrewd understanding of how the media's own rules of newsworthiness and objectivity could be used against them and for politicians' own political purposes guided such media-savvy conservatives as Spiro Agnew, Ronald Reagan, and Newt Gingrich.[46]

Although Wallace's rhetoric was too crass to achieve respectability, it had its impact in the declining faith of Americans in Establishment institutions, especially the federal government. Michael Lind contends that "today's Republican anti-intellectualism is the gift of George Wallace to the GOP. Dan Quayle may talk about 'cultural elites,' but everyone knows he means 'pointy-heads.' "[47] As a measure of this anti-Establishment alienation, Carter observes that whereas in 1964, 80 percent of Americans thought that the national government could be trusted to do the right thing most or all of the time, by the 1990s, the number of Americans trusting their government in Washington had been cut to a mere 20 percent. Americans increasingly doubted the national government's ability to solve problems. The middle and upper-middle classes deserted the public spaces of the cities and fled to suburbs, where they sought to avoid the social problems of a grossly unequal society, and abandoned the public sphere's services and programs for private market solutions. Seizing on this loss of faith in politics, Republicans have ridden the "message of antipower" into the halls of power.[48]

Carter notes the "flight into nostalgia" that occurred in Russia and the social turmoil that accompanied the collapse of communism, a transition that unleashed the scourges of nationalism, racism, and religious fundamentalism. In the social turmoil of the 1960s and 1970s, Wallace tapped into a similar yearning for tradition, authority, and stability. Wallace "recognized the political capital to be made in a society shaken by social upheaval and economic uncertainty," and by appealing to these same forces in American society, he moved "the politics of rage . . . from the fringes of our society to center stage."[49] Wallace never got to the promised land; like Moses, he remained on the outskirts, felled by a would-be assassin's bullet, while others seized his themes and marched into national prominence. Although Wallace never renounced his membership in the Democratic party, Republican

conservatives used his formula to transform the "politics of rage" into electoral victories. In the process, Reagan, Gingrich, and others on the Republican Right transformed the Republican party from a party of moderate to libertarian conservatism into a party dominated by the social conservatism of the New Right.[50]

Social upheaval and economic uncertainty have historically been conditions for revolt by the have-nots of this country. Wallace's populist style appealed to the anger and frustration of many Americans who had traditionally turned to the federal government and Democratic party for security in tough times. But, like Southern demagogues of old, Wallace substituted nationalism, racism, and religious fundamentalism for popular economic and social programs. Unlike his Southern demagogic predecessors, however, Wallace perfected this formula on a national scale. He was not just whistling Dixie when he claimed, "Alabama has not joined the nation, the nation has joined Alabama."[51]

William Greider notes that contemporary conservative politics takes its cue from the familiar Southern formula:

> Uniting alienated voters into political coalition with the most powerful economic interests has a distinctly old-fashioned flavor of southern demagoguery, since the strategy requires the party to agitate the latent emotional resentments and turn them into marketable political traits. The raw materials for this are drawn from enduring social aggravations—wounds of race, class and religion, even sex.[52]

The "populism" pioneered by Wallace and adopted by 1980s and 1990s conservatives lacked substance beyond its public relations function to disguise the real impact of the policies implemented by the conservative movement—a massive redistribution of wealth to the upper class. In effect, Wallace discovered the tag lines that transformed traditional populism from a program of "soak the rich" to a "rancid populism" that could be used to "cloak the rich."[53]

The Democrats Reinvented

If the former governor of Alabama pioneered the path to a rebirth of the Republican party as a party of social conservatism, the former gov-

ernor of Arkansas has led the reincarnation of the Democratic party as the "New Democrats." The Democrats, however, remain deeply divided, agreeing on little besides being Democrats.[54] Disunity, of course, is not new to the Democratic party. Many decades ago, Will Rogers quipped, "I am not a member of any organized party—I'm a Democrat."[55]

The tenuous unity mustered by the previous New Deal coalition splintered on the shoals of the Vietnam War and the social and cultural upheavals of the 1960s. Nicol Rae argues that the party splintered into four factions: the regulars, the New Left and minorities, the neoliberals, and the Southern Democrats.[56] In 1968, the old New Dealers, or regular Democrats, could control the Chicago convention only by countenancing a "police riot" to suppress the forces in the streets outside the hall clamoring for change. In 1972, the New Left and minority forces captured the party under new rules, only to suffer electoral disaster behind their nominee, George McGovern. Ironically, the party won the presidency in 1976 under Jimmy Carter, a Southerner but perhaps more accurately viewed as almost apolitical, an outsider who in some ways represented none of the Democratic factions. Carter's disdain of politics, as well as just the plain bad luck to be the incumbent when the oil crisis hit home, the economy crashed, the third world ignited in revolution, and hostages were seized in Iran, ensured that his term would not set the pattern for Democratic revival, at least not immediately. Instead, it served as the prelude to the Reagan Revolution and twelve years of conservative ascendancy.

Democrats struggled for almost three decades from the breakup of the New Deal coalition in the 1960s until the Clinton victories of the 1990s to find a way to put the humpty-dumpty Democratic factions back together again. The party regulars retained much of the New Deal substance and flavor, holding to the liberal faith in active government to help the disadvantaged, a strong defense posture, and internationalist foreign policy, but also advocating protectionist trade policies and traditional cultural values. The traditional regular base, however, rooted in the white, mostly Northern, urban, and ethnic working class, was shrinking as manufacturing jobs disappeared. Their traditional values led to conflicts with other Democratic constituencies, such as the New Left and minorities, and exposed them to wooing by the Republicans.[57] In the contest for these regulars' votes,

Reagan swamped Walter Mondale, the last regular Democrat nominated for president.

The New Left and minority faction retained faith in interventionist government to aid the disadvantaged. The programs closest to their hearts, however, were aimed less at the working class per se, as the older New Deal economic policies had been, and more at oppressed groups, especially minorities and women. Their distrust of U.S. foreign policy and opposition to interventionist military policies also brought them into conflict with the regulars, as did their "modernist" cultural values, such as defense of abortion rights and opposition to school prayer.[58] Although George McGovern carried this faction's banner to capture the nomination in 1972, he could not unite bitterly divided Democrats in the general election, even against arch-foe Richard Nixon. Although Jesse Jackson has based a couple of races for the party's nomination on this faction's backing, it has not managed, except locally, to dislodge the neoliberalism that has dominated Democratic politics for over two decades.

Neoliberalism, pioneered by the "Big Chill" politics of Gary Hart and Jerry Brown, favored more centrist policies, backing away from the Keynesian welfare state of old liberalism, which this faction found flabby and inefficient. Although favoring civil rights and women's equality, neoliberal Democrats tended to view these traditional Democratic constituencies, along with labor, as "special interests." Rather than the "something for everyone" approach of "interest-group liberalism," neoliberals advocated a lean and mean government to match the lean and mean economy they considered necessary to survive in the new global competition. Although they retained the liberal faith in activist government to enhance the national interest, neoliberals equated the interest of the nation with the interest of American business. In the new world economy, neoliberals believed, America's economy and Americans' welfare could be protected only if American corporations were strengthened to enable them to compete successfully against foreign corporations. This goal required reinventing government to reduce the drag of social programs, which represented tax costs to corporations, and to support corporations through pro-business policies. The more intellectual neoliberals referred openly to the active government programs needed as "industrial policy," but most neoliberal politicians avoided the term because of its overtones of government planning.[59]

Neoliberalism's main political problem has been finding a constituency. Its emphasis on planning and government activism frightened business leaders, who are more comfortable with the Republican rhetoric of free enterprise, even if the neoliberal program is actually pro-business.[60] The nonideological "pragmatic idealism" of neoliberalism, best exemplified by 1988 Democratic nominee Michael Dukakis, has found increasing resonance among the upper-middle-class suburbanites, the well educated, and professionals—those whom Robert Reich characterizes as "symbolic analysts"—who constitute a growing segment of the new information-based economy.[61] The old working-class and minority constituencies of the Democrats, however, recognize the pro-business slant and sense neoliberalism to be essentially "Reaganism with a human face."[62]

Southern Democrats remain the party's most conservative constituency, favoring free trade (except for those Southern-based industries that need either protection, such as, textiles, or subsidies, such as oil and agriculture). They remain conservative on cultural issues and favor a strong defense posture and interventionist foreign policy. These positions on economic issues make Southern Democrats close to neoliberals, but on cultural issues and foreign policy, they remain to the right of the other factions. On civil rights, however, the influence of enfranchised African American voters has registered, as Southern Democrats have executed a U-turn and now favor civil rights at the same levels as the most liberal wings of the party. The declining privileges of seniority and the undermining of committee chairs' powers in Congress deprived Southern Democrats of much of their power base. Along with increasing competition from Republican challengers, the congressional reforms of the 1970s hastened the decline of this faction and facilitated their submergence into neoliberalism.[63]

For decades after the collapse of the old New Deal formula, the Democrats floundered in search of a strategy to piece these factions together into a winning combination. After the McGovern debacle, most presidential candidates have tended to represent the neoliberal faction, with the exception of party regular Walter Mondale. The usual explanation is that the presidential nominating rules, with their heavy reliance on primaries, tilt toward the New Left and minority faction and the neoliberals. In 1988, Southern Democratic politicos launched a much-hyped Super Tuesday plan; by scheduling a critical mass of Southern state primaries for the same day, they hoped to maximize

the region's influence and force the nomination of a "moderate." This scheme failed to pan out, because Iowa and New Hampshire retain their importance in establishing momentum, and the Southern primary electorate is no longer monolithic. The regulars and Southerners fared better in Congress, where, before 1994, politics was less ideological, revolving more around constituency service. The same was true at the state and local levels, although neoliberals and the New Left and minorities were gaining in the North, and Rae detected a growth of neoliberalism even in the South.[64]

In the early 1990s, the Democrats appeared close to a winning formula, at least for the moment, and ironically, the lesson seemed to come from the South, where the party was losing its stranglehold on electoral politics. In the wake of Democratic electoral defeats in 1984, a group of moderate, mostly Southern and Sun Belt politicians founded the Democratic Leadership Council (DLC) in March 1985. These politicians' concerns included not just Mondale's resounding defeat by Reagan but also local losses further down the ticket, such as Jim Hunt's loss to Jesse Helms for the North Carolina Senate seat that year. The DLC's avowed purpose was to rescue the party from "liberal fundamentalism," but the organization had a dual mission from its inception. Some DLC members, themselves ideologically within the party's liberal mainstream, wanted the DLC to provide a forum for elected Democratic officials to appear temperamentally moderate and to position the party more in the middle of the political road in the voters' minds. Other members, however, desired a more substantive role for the DLC, hoping to develop messages that would move the Democrats back to the ideological center of the policy spectrum. The centrist, policy-oriented faction won out after Dukakis's 1988 defeat by Bush in an election that saw liberalism stigmatized as the unmentionable "L-word." In June 1989, the DLC created the Progressive Policy Institute as a formally separate but politically affiliated think tank, and the DLC itself took on more movement characteristics.[65]

As the DLC took its policy turn, however, new strains arose, especially between the more moderate-conservative strain exemplified by Senators Sam Nunn of Georgia and Chuck Robb of Virginia versus the more adventurous "New Democrats" led by Clinton and Gore, who wanted to "reinvent" the party. During Bill Clinton's term as DLC chair, the latter were successful in seizing the initiative, symbolized

by the renaming of the DLC newsletter from the *Mainstream Democrat* to the *New Democrat* in 1990. Accused by more liberal Democrats of being "shadow Republicans" or "Democrats for the Leisure Class," the DLC actually moved closer to the neoliberal faction of the party. The New Democratic program of the DLC retained faith in a traditional tenet of liberalism, advocating a "new formula for activist government," but it called for a reinvented government that would be less bureaucratic and more flexible and responsive. It favored public spending conceived of as social investments rather than as "government handouts," for example, spending on education, health, job training, and a national service program. Although it endorsed traditional progressive policies such as environmental protection, handgun regulation, legalized abortion, family leave, and minimum wages, the New Democrats were altogether closer to business than to labor.[66]

The success of the DLC became apparent in the 1992 election. Governor Bill Clinton of Arkansas, a founding although not originally active DLC member, used his early 1990s role as DLC chair to launch his drive for the presidency. He chose as his running mate fellow DLC member and New Democrat Al Gore, senator from Tennessee. The New Democratic ideas embodied in the DLC's "New Choice" programmatic statement formed the basis for the Democrat's 1992 platform, "A New Covenant with the American People." The platform was organized around themes drawn from the New Democrats: opportunity, responsibility, community, and national security. Jon Hale's analysis of the two documents reveals substantial similarities. Thirty-seven of the fifty-one specific subheadings in the party platform matched items in the DLC's New Choice agenda, and none of the party planks contradicted the DLC program. The 1996 Democratic campaign likewise reflected a script authored by the DLC.[67]

In 1992, the Democrats seemed to have at long last stumbled across the secret of success: they united neoliberal policies with candidates drawn from the South. Oddly enough, this formula bore a striking affinity with the prescription used by Southern "night and day" coalitions to attain victories in the face of rising Republicanism below the Mason-Dixon line. If successful Southern candidacies required political savvy and ties to the local electorate, in Clinton and Gore the national Democrats appeared to have found politicians, unlike bloodless Northern neoliberals such as Dukakis and Tsongas, with sufficient

campaign smarts and local moorings to avoid alienating the mass of Southern and regular Democrats needed to win the presidency. If Southern politicians had almost perfected the "segregated campaign," Clinton proved adept at campaign tactics that appealed separately to diverse Democratic constituencies. He could appeal to New Left youth by appearing on MTV and to minorities by speaking at the NAACP, while reassuring Southern and working-class whites by denouncing Sista Souljah and keeping the Reverend Jesse Jackson at arm's length. Just as winning "night and day" coalition leaders learned that economic issues must remain central to winning campaigns, while downplaying race and social issues, the Clinton team managed to keep the focus of the 1992 campaign on economic issues ("it's the economy, stupid") and off divisive culture battles (abortion, affairs, affirmative action, and draft dodging, to name a few failed Bush broadsides). Most important, like the Southern "modernizers," the New Democrats' approach to economics abandoned the New Deal's emphasis on working-class, distributive, bubble-up policies in favor of a pro-business, pro-growth, trickle-down activism.

By the 1990s, partisan competition at the national level was remarkably well aligned with the matchup in the South: neoliberal-modernizer Democrats, if they could recruit capable candidates and focus campaign issues on corporate-led growth that would filter down as jobs and prosperity for all, could hold together diverse coalitions of voters to defeat Republican New Right–traditionalists who advocated pro-market policies favoring the wealthy while appealing for votes mainly on traditional social and cultural values. Ironically, the national Democrats embraced the winning formula at the very time when the prescription seemed to be weak medicine in the South, in the face of the spreading epidemic of relentlessly advancing Republicanism.

New Democracy: Government Southern Style

Winning elections is not governing. Governing with a "night and day" coalition has proved tricky for Southern Democrats, and the New Democrats have had trouble retaining support from the diverse wings of the party. The Clinton administration, despite enjoying Democratic majorities in both houses of Congress when it assumed office, found

the going tough. Failure to produce viable solutions to divisive issues such as gays in the military, tax breaks for the middle class, balanced budgets, and a health reform proposal that would simultaneously save money and extend access exacerbated tensions between conservative and liberal Democrats in Congress. The Democrats, who had made gains in relative cohesion in 1992, had squandered this advantage by 1994. Furthermore, Clinton alienated many Southern and regular Democrats; by June 1993, 49 percent of the public perceived him as a liberal, up from 38 percent in September 1992, and the percentage perceiving him as a moderate had eroded from 37 to 31 percent. After Clinton's maneuverings to achieve consensus during his first few months in office, many who had voted for him thought that he appeared less "New" than slippery. The disastrous drubbing the Democrats took at the midterm congressional elections in 1994 signaled the public's discontent with the failure of New Democracy to translate itself from a campaign posture to a public philosophy for governing the nation.[68]

The Republican congressional rout in 1994, sustained in 1996, cast doubts on the viability of the Southern-neoliberal synthesis. Although Clinton was reelected in 1996, that victory may have been a short-term exception, reflecting the Republican overreaching under Speaker Newt Gingrich in the great budget battles of 1995 and the lack of appeal of the seventy-five-year-old Republican challenger Bob Dole. Even Clinton's 1992 success might be dismissed as a fluke; Clinton probably won the Democratic nomination only because stronger potential nominees refused to challenge Bush, whose post–Gulf War approval ratings made the incumbent seem invincible. Clinton's squeaker of a victory over Bush probably hinged on the timing of a severe preelection economic recession. Jimmy Carter, who could be seen as a forerunner of the Southern-neoliberal combination, won his 1976 election in equally unusual circumstances, when the national Democrats were torn apart by post-Vietnam recriminations and the Republicans were discredited by Watergate. His presidency, however, stands as a monument to the difficulty of translating the neoliberal-modernizer prescription into a governing coalition.

To govern successfully, the Democrats must find solutions to two problems that have perplexed them since their rout by Ronald Reagan in the 1980s. First, Democrats face a dilemma of "identity politics"—how to address divisive issues of race, ethnicity, gender, and culture

without destroying their "majority of minorities" coalition on the one hand, and without alienating their working-class base on the other. In particular, the issue of affirmative action strains Democratic credibility. The Clinton administration's "mend it, don't end it" approach helps ease the tension but leaves the issue available for more ideologically consistent Republicans to exploit. A second, related Democratic dilemma is how to protect their working- and middle-class constituency from economic dislocations occasioned by globalization. The sustained economic growth and prosperity during the Clinton administration has bought time for more permanent solutions, but the growing gap between rich and poor has excluded many in the working and lower classes from enjoying the fruits of the 1990s boom. It seems unlikely that the Democrats could jettison their traditional class base and win by pitching their wares exclusively to those prospering in the new global economy. Yet the Democrats' dependence on corporate campaign donations as well as union political action committees and working-class votes makes them hesitant to commit to a more bottom-up approach to economic policy. Instead, they temporize.[69]

Still, this Southern-neoliberal formula has managed to cling, however precariously, to power in the White House, just as it has managed to patch together winning, if rickety, combinations in Southern elections. For these successes, Democrats may owe as much to Republicans as to their own exertions. The Gingrich-engineered Republican takeover of Congress proved to have its own fatal flaws as a governing formula. Deluded by his own overblown rhetoric and prodded by his more extreme adherents—the freshmen members elected in the 1994 sweep—Gingrich and his fellow Republicans overreached themselves by forcing the showdowns with Clinton that temporarily shut down the government in 1995 and 1996.[70] With most of the public pinning blame on the "Gingrichistas" for the closures, Clinton cruised smoothly to reelection, but the 1996 congressional contest was a standoff.

The Republicans' ultimately unsuccessful efforts to remove Clinton by impeachment and the backlash they suffered at the polls in 1998 suggest that although New Democracy is not a surefire winner, neither have the post-Reagan Republicans identified a dependable counterstrategy. The ascendancy of the New Right within party circles has alienated many more moderate, traditional stalwarts. Indeed,

evidence from voting patterns in 1996 and 1998 indicates that growing Republican strength in the South, which in turn has produced augmented Southern hegemony within the party, may be driving out Republican loyalists in historically Republican strongholds, particularly in the Northeast. At the very least, heightened factionalism has sharpened the divisions within the Republican party.[71]

Commentators have argued that parties in Congress are helped rather than hindered by being diverse, pragmatic, and even ideologically unfocused.[72] A factionalized party representing multiple political tendencies may be better able to serve the sheer diversity of interests in the nation than a more ideologically cohesive but narrower party. But without the guidance of a consistent vision, the party holding the White House will be unable to provide decisive leadership and can appear to succumb to deadlock and drift. Ironically, by the late 1990s, the more ideological American political party, the Republicans, held a majority, however slight, in Congress, while the less ideological Democrats, however embattled, were ensconced in the White House. The new, inverted electoral order seemed unsteady indeed.

Electoral fortunes are dependent not simply on the short-term maneuverings of candidates and campaigns. It is conceivable that the fluctuating electoral shifts of recent years merely register the tremors of a deeper shift in the fault lines of American politics. If the country as a whole, led by the emerging South, is undergoing a Republican realignment, the New Democratic formula is likely to prove a holding strategy at best. Conversely, if the country has entered a period of more fluid, candidate-centered politics, both Southern and national politics may see a series of contests between neoliberal-modernizer New Democrats and more conservative New Right–traditionalist Republicans. Whether candidates actually hail from the South, the lineup is likely to appear distinctly "Southern."[73]

5 / *Realignment Versus Dealignment*
Hunting Where the Ducks Are

Democrats Derailed

The dual convergence traced in chapters 3 and 4 ended the uniqueness of Southern politics and the isolation of the region. Southern politicians now play prominent roles on the national scene, and the issues driving politics in the South do not differ sharply from public choices facing other parts of the country. What the authors of a recent survey of Georgia politics suggest about that state could just as accurately be said about the region as a harbinger of national political trends: "What is, and what will be, happening in Georgia politics as the last decade of the twentieth century ends is as good a predictor as any of the course of American politics—not just southern politics—in the early years of the twenty-first."[1] Yet if we turn from tracing how the South and the nation arrived at their present positions to contemplating the future of regional and national politics, we need to consider longer-term and deeper forces that shape electoral politics. Whether the South has permanently left behind the dismal politics of the once Solid South or whether it will continue to be plagued by at least some of the pathologies associated with that system, albeit expressed in novel ways, depends not solely on developments in the region but also on the larger national forces that structure our party system. Likewise, the future of American politics will be indelibly marked by the changes that continue to remake Southern politics as part of the larger forces driving national political developments.

This chapter focuses on an overarching and open question faced by observers of American politics as they try to understand these developments: whether our party system has undergone, or is currently undergoing, a major realignment. The purpose here is merely to outline

some of the major positions and issues, not to answer definitively the hugely complex question of whether American politics is experiencing a transition to a new party system. Even this brief foray into that territory may seem like a detour from the main path of this book's argument, but the realignment question provides some crucial grounding for analyzing whether national politics is tending to resemble the electoral structures of the Solid South. On the one hand, if American politics is merely in the throes of a major, but temporary, realignment, the problems with current American parties, participation, and issue contestation (discussed in chapter 6) may simply be short-lived symptoms of that transition. On the other hand, if the changes taking place in current American politics represent a longer-term and more dramatic dealignment rather than merely cyclical fluctuations, the structural problems noted in chapter 6 and the symptoms of political pathology they produce (described in chapter 7) will almost surely prove to be more enduring features of our national political life. Thus, getting an orientation to the layout of realignment versus dealignment debates should help judge the permanence of the problems plaguing our political structures explored in later chapters.

The outcomes of electoral contests are shaped not only by immediate factors such as candidates and campaign events but also by longer-term factors that structure party systems. The American party system has shown great continuity since the early years of the Republic. Two major parties historically have enjoyed a "duopoly," relegating third parties to relative insignificance as they competed for majority status.[2] Although neither major party is completely shut out from electoral victories, one party generally enjoys a distinct advantage as the nationally dominant majority party. The minority party can win elections where it is strongest, even capturing the presidency on occasion when short-term forces such as scandals, wars, or economic downturns work to its advantage, but the lopsided distribution of partisan loyalties ensures that over the long haul the playing field is not level. Normal voting patterns remain relatively fixed, guaranteeing a predictable electoral dominance to the majority party and stability to the system during that era.[3]

Periodically, however, dramatic transformations have produced such sweeping changes that analysts detect a succession of different party systems rather than a single American party system. These

successive party systems have varied in their majority parties, coalition alignments, modes of competition, and types of party organizations, as well as the salient issues on which elections turned. Walter Dean Burnham charts six party systems across American history, beginning with the founding of elitist American parties during the first days of the Republic. The Jacksonian revolution swept in a second, democratized system. During the Civil War era, a third system witnessed the birth of the Republican party, which came to dominate national politics even as the Democratic party consolidated its grip on the South. In the 1890s, with the challenge of populism defeated in the South and West, the fourth "system of 1896" produced a sectional party system based on low turnout and a business-friendly Republican elite firmly in control of the national government. From the Civil War until the 1930s, Grover Cleveland and Woodrow Wilson were the only Democrats elected president.

After seven decades of Republican dominance under the two post–Civil War party systems, the Great Depression ushered in a fifth party system that witnessed a generation of Democratic party hegemony. Democrats held the presidency from 1932 until 1968, with the exception of Eisenhower's two terms from 1953 to 1961. They also controlled Congress, except for the 1946 and 1952 elections. Besides being indisputably the majority party, the Democrats enjoyed the loyalty of most voters, who thought of themselves as Democrats. The most visible issues of the era reflected the Democrats' policy agenda: government management of the economy and provision of social welfare measures. Although other demographics continued to influence Americans' political choices, social class constituted the primary basis for partisan cleavage. The fifth, New Deal party system, in short, constituted a "stable political order."[4]

Beginning in the mid-1960s, at about the time another cyclical realignment was due, the Democrats began to experience difficulty winning the presidency. Since Richard Nixon won the presidency in a three-way contest with Hubert Humphrey and George Wallace in 1968, some observers have claimed that the party system is experiencing another long-term shift, this time away from New Deal Democracy toward Republican ascendance. The 1972 Nixon landslide seemed to confirm this interpretation, but Watergate intervened to thwart the expected Republican realignment. Still, between 1964 and

1992, the only Democrat to be elected president was Jimmy Carter. Other commentators thought that the overdue realignment was merely delayed until the Reagan Revolution of the 1980s. As the Reagan-Bush era stretched into twelve years of Republican administrations, it began to appear that the Republicans had a "lock" on the electoral college and the White House.[5] Although Bill Clinton recaptured the presidency for the Democrats twice in the 1990s, the significance of these victories was unclear: were they temporary flukes or harbingers of an emerging trend?

Unfortunately, political science does not offer a clear answer, but rather provides several competing interpretations of the American party system in the last decades of the twentieth century. On the one hand, some interpret the loss of a predictable Democratic majority in American politics as the latest in a series of realignments, a sea change ushering in a sixth party system. A realignment occurs when a durable shift in the partisan loyalties of large groups of the public takes place. Realignments can be either "secular," caused by gradual shifts in the makeup of the electorate, or "critical," ushered in by dramatic and tumultuous shifts in partisan voting and loyalties.[6]

Most analysts have focused on the cyclical patterns discovered by theories of critical realignment. Beginning with the stable political order that emerges from the previous critical election, a party system initially exhibits equilibrium, as issues, voters' preferences, and party government are in harmony. The New Deal, with its activist government to ensure economic prosperity and its coalition of party loyalists that guaranteed it majorities at most levels of government, illustrates the equilibrium phase of the party system cycle for the first two decades after the 1932 election of Roosevelt. Although party systems usually exhibit stable patterns for several decades, roughly every political generation, seismic dislocations reshape the party system for the next period. As Burnham has written, "In the United States all elections are equal, but some are decidedly more equal than others."[7]

As David Lawrence describes Burnham's version of realignment theory, "the increase over time in incongruity between citizens' partisan loyalties and the political system's underlying social and economic realities ma[k]e realignment a natural, inevitable, and regular aspect of American political life." With the passage of time, the memory of the crucial issues behind the party alignment fade, and a new

generation comes to political consciousness. New issues arise that cut across the older partisan alignments, giving rise to disputes within parties about the correct policy and political responses, as well as providing platforms for the birth of new third parties. The second half of the approximately forty-year realigning cycle is thus a period of "disaggregation," as issues and policies no longer match comfortably with opinions and partisan identifications. When novel polarizing issues pit the parties against each other along new fault lines, massive shifts in votes and loyalties can produce new coalitions and a new majority party. For example, foreign and defense policies, race, and the declining effectiveness of the New Deal welfare state contributed to the demise of New Deal Democracy. This disaggregating stage ends when the realigning crisis resolves itself into a distinctly new, stable political order based on durable party loyalties formed during the critical election that upended the old order.[8]

Reality, however, has been recalcitrant, failing to fit neatly into realignment theory's predicted patterns. The old New Deal alignment has deteriorated and, in most respects, seems to have been relegated, as Reagan said of communism, to the dustbin of history. The expected full-fledged realignment, however, should have produced reliable Republican majorities supported by stable partisans voting regularly for GOP policies over the long haul. Although Republicans have enjoyed an advantage in presidential elections since the 1960s, other parts of the puzzle are notably missing. To cite only the most salient discordant data, Democrats managed to extend their control of Congress until 1994, with the exception of Republican control of the Senate during the height of the Reagan years (1981–1987). By the time the Republicans finally won majorities in both houses of Congress after 1994, they had lost the presidency to Bill Clinton. The failure of the "full realignment package" has spawned several alternative interpretations of what has followed in the wake of New Deal Democracy.[9]

The most divergent rival interpretation argues that the American party system has been undergoing a dealignment rather than a realignment.[10] A dealignment would mean "a decline in the centrality of parties to citizen political orientations and behavior."[11] A dealignment would not necessarily or even likely entail the complete disappearance of political parties. Rather, under the dealignment scenario, the role played by parties would be drastically drained of content or reduced in significance. Presumably, citizens' ties to parties would be

weakened, or the importance of partisanship would somehow pale in comparison to other factors in influencing political attitudes or actions.[12] For example, electoral contests might be organized around individual candidates rather than party tickets, and voters would obtain more of their information about issues and candidacies from the media than from party sources. The resulting dealigned politics, with voters "failing to identify with either party, switching allegiance from election to election, and even splitting their tickets on one election ballot," would produce discrete contests for separate offices. The resulting volatile outcomes would reflect the lack of any predictably stable party majority governing the country on a fairly regular basis for an appreciable period of time.[13]

Which scenario, realignment or dealignment, best captures the reality of contemporary American politics? Unfortunately, assessments of the many types of data that might answer the question differ, and the evidence itself seems to point in different directions. The voluminous scholarly literature on realignment and dealignment does not offer definitive explanations. Many authors have interpreted recent developments as a realignment, but the variety of labels given to the perceived realignment—"regional, rolling, hollow, major, minor, creeping, step, non-critical, top-down, incomplete, no majority, post-industrial, evangelical, southern, and policy"—graphically conveys the different interpretations put forward by students of the subject.[14] Other authors even reject the usefulness of realignment as a concept for understanding political eras in American politics. Yet others contend that whatever its usefulness in the past, dealignment, not realignment, best characterizes recent developments on the political scene. The hotly contested concepts of realignment and dealignment can be seen as playing a somewhat analogous role to the disputed natural science concept of global warming. Global warming, although not accepted by all scientists, provides an intellectual glue for linking and explaining widely disparate observations of temperature variations, climate changes, polar ice cap thinning, and crop failures, suggesting that these apparently unconnected phenomena are not mere random deviations but instead are encompassed in one overarching development. Similarly, the political science notions of realignment and dealignment provide different interpretations for observed changes in political behavior, such as party identification, electoral outcomes, congressional voting patterns, salient policy issues, and public opinion. Realignment theory could

imply that many of the variations observed in recent years are merely temporary discontinuities resulting from the disruptions of the realignment process, but that these deviations will become the new norm once a realigned party system is in place. The dealignment interpretation, in contrast, implies that the old patterns are more or less permanently in flux, that instability and incoherence are the norms of the new party system that is replacing the older partisan alignment.

There is simply too much research, and too little agreement, to survey the vast outpouring of writing on this topic, much less to settle definitively the question of transformations in the American party system. Instead, the goal of the following sections is more modest: to examine three possible interpretations of recent changes in our party system in order to estimate the likelihood that the structural convergence between Southern and national politics is permanent. The first possibility considered is that a realignment has occurred, even if it only roughly approximates the classic version of a critical realignment. Second, a split-level realignment in the South may have been matched nationally by divided government, perhaps a more or less regular partisan division of labor between a Republican presidency and a Democratic Congress. Finally, and most likely, American electoral competition may have moved into a sixth party system that is seriously dealigned in salient respects.

In surveying these three scenarios, it is well to remember that the Solid South was an essential support in shoring up Democratic hegemony during the New Deal system, and the desertion of the South after the mid-1960s was pivotal in undermining Democratic presidential aspirations in the most recent period.[15] The question of whether the South has shifted solidly to Republicanism thus takes on crucial significance in determining whether a realignment of national politics has occurred. The course of American politics, in turn, will influence the fate of party candidacies and coalitions for at least a political generation.

Waiting for the Republican Realignment

One possible way of interpreting the gap between the theory of realignment and the observable facts of contemporary American politics is

to suggest that the theory is correct in its broad outlines, but that the reality is messier than any neat theory can capture. One problem may be, ironically, that we have too many facts. Public opinion polling has come of age since the last undisputed realignment of the 1930s, giving political scientists a wealth of information about voter sentiments that is lacking when studying historical realignments. Also, a cottage industry has developed, with historians and social scientists devoting their careers to studying public opinion, voting, and change in party systems.[16] The result has been more sophisticated conceptualizations of party system transformation, but also the development of a plethora of information, much of which does not fit comfortably with any single interpretation of current trends.

Party identification, for example, seems to be central to assessing the progress of possible realignment, defined as a shift in long-term party loyalties.[17] During the "steady state" period of 1952–1964, Democrats enjoyed a decided advantage among the public, with 45 to 52 percent identifying with the Democrats, compared with roughly 24 to 30 percent considering themselves Republicans. If so-called closet partisans, people who call themselves independent but admit to leaning toward one party, are added to strong and weak identifiers, the Democrats typically held an absolute majority ranging from 51 to 61 percent. In the tumultuous 1964–1974 era, spanning the desegregation of the Jim Crow South, the Vietnam War, and Watergate, however, Democratic defections dramatically reduced that party's electoral advantage. In the 1970s, declining partisan identification seemed to plateau. Democratic identification hovered around 40 percent; independent identification seemed to be the main beneficiary of Democratic decline, as Republican self-identification remained around 23 percent. When partisan loyalties began to shift again during the Reagan era, it appeared that the Republicans might have achieved a stunning switch in voter loyalties, with some surveys reporting dramatic gains in Republican identification. For example, by 1988, Republicans could claim 28 percent of the electorate, approaching the Democratic level of 35 percent.[18] After the Persian Gulf War in 1991, Republicans even outnumbered Democrats by 37 to 30 percent.[19] Following the recession in the early 1990s and the disillusionment with many Reagan-Bush policies, however, these changes in partisanship seemed to lack staying power. Although polls showed considerable variability, in the

mid-1990s, Democrats still held a slight edge—36 percent of the public identified with them, over 33 percent for the GOP in 1996, leaving almost another third who identified with neither party.[20] If anything, the long decade of prosperity under the Clinton administration increased the share of Democratic identifiers (57 percent of those who identified with any party in the fall of 1999), although this advantage was not as large as levels of consumer confidence and presidential popularity would have predicted.[21]

If patterns of party identification at the national level constitute clearer evidence of the decline of Democratic ascendancy than of its expected displacement by a new Republican majority, there have been significant shifts among population segments that constitute the respective party coalitions. African Americans migrated decisively into the Democratic camp after the 1960 election, while the proportion of Democrats who were working class fell from between 65 and 70 percent in 1960 to about 55 percent in 1992.[22] Among white Southerners, the drop in Democratic identification was precipitous, plummeting from 73.4 percent in 1952 to 51.3 percent in 1976. Between 1976–1978 and 1992–1994, Alan Abramowitz and Kyle Saunders estimate that Democratic support (including party identifiers and Democratic-leaning independents) fell from 58 to 49 percent among whites nationally, but among Southern whites, the drop was from 64 to 48 percent.[23] The most pronounced shift in loyalties has been among Southern white males, three out of ten of whom have switched party allegiance. In effect, Southern whites have moved from being one of the political pillars of the Democratic party to being less supportive than non-Southern whites, a shift that Warren Miller judges to be "a realignment of massive proportions" for the region.[24] Exit polls in the 1996 election, however, found that the Democrats still retained a slight edge in identification in the South, with 40 percent of all Southerners identifying as Democrats, 37 percent as Republicans, and 23 percent as independents.[25]

Nationally, under any scenario, the Democrats seem to have lost their huge advantage in partisan loyalties among the electorate. But the Republicans have not been able to consolidate this decline into a reliable partisan advantage. Roughly one-third of the voters are generally predisposed toward the GOP, but this figure differs little from the number of self-declared independents in the contemporary elec-

torate. William Keefe argues that the growth of independents, from one-fifth of the electorate in 1940 to one-third in the 1970s and 1980s, has been the most important change in identification. The growth in independent identification could, of course, indicate the advent of a dealigned, less stable party system with more possibilities of electoral flux.[26] Wilson Carey McWilliams argues that partisan loyalties have become more ambiguous and that Americans are thinking more third-party thoughts. Michael Lind calls independents "a de facto third party of floating, alienated voters." Alternatively, if the process of shifting loyalties is a traumatic one that requires time for readjustment, perhaps independence is merely a halfway house for Democrats in their trek to Republicanism. This process could even hold true for younger citizens who come from disproportionately Democratic households but who may eventually form Republican ties.[27]

Declining numbers of party identifiers is only one way that parties may be losing their foothold in the electorate, as opposed to merely realigning their bases. Not only do fewer citizens identify with the traditional two parties, but among party identifiers, partisan loyalty may be less central to their political world than previously. Miller argues that partisan loyalty remains stable, showing that the correlation between partisan identification and presidential choice was as strong in 1988 as it was in 1952. For voting below the presidential level, however, the influence of identification has slipped substantially. Ticket splitting has also increased dramatically, from about 26 to 31 percent in the steady-state 1950s to about 60 percent by 1974.[28] Everett Carll Ladd found that even those who consistently rate themselves as partisans do not vote the party line; instead, about 60 percent of both groups report that they typically split their tickets.[29] Using multiple measures of ticket splitting, Martin Wattenberg found that while the percentage identifying with a party fell from 75 in 1952 to 61 in 1992, the percentages voting for a presidential candidate of one party and a congressional candidate of another roughly tripled in that same period. Wattenberg concludes that "strength of party identification no longer has the depth of meaning it once did."[30]

Other studies challenge the strength of the relationship between identification and other aspects of political behavior. Harold Stanley, for example, found that among white Southerners of both Republican and Democratic persuasions, the relative number of comments about

parties versus mentions of candidates has reversed itself, now one-sidedly favoring frequent candidate comments; this finding is in line with claims of a more candidate-centered politics. After surveying various indicators of the strength of partisan identification, William Mayer concluded that "for all the twists and turns in these data, the general trend is immediately clear: party loyalties and allegiances, however conceptualized and measured, are weaker today than they were in the days of Harry Truman and Dwight Eisenhower."[31]

The shifting sands of partisan loyalties seem to correlate with a long-term change in voting behavior that has affected the foundations of electoral competition. At least in the South, election results register impressive gains in officeholding by Republicans. The Republican contingent elected to the U.S. Senate grew from none of twenty-two seats for the eleven Southern states in 1960 to ten in 1980, but stood at only seven after the 1986 Democratic successes in Southern Senate races. In the 1990s, however, Republican victories were impressive; the number of GOP Southern senators grew to ten in 1992, thirteen in 1994, and fifteen in 1996. This growth was matched in the U.S. House of Representatives. In 1960, there were only seven Southern Republican representatives in the House, a mere 6.6 percent of the region's delegation. This proportion had grown to 25.5 percent by 1970 but stagnated in the 30 percent range until the 1990s, reaching only 33 percent by the beginning of that decade. After the 1990 reapportionment, however, the Republican share jumped to 38.4 percent after the 1992 elections, to 51.2 percent after 1994, and crept up to 56.8 percent after 1996. By the 105th Congress elected in 1996, Texas and Virginia were the only Southern states with majority Democratic House delegations.[32] The backlash of public opinion against the impeachment of President Clinton stalled Republican gains in the 1998 congressional elections. Republicans dropped a seat in North Carolina to control 14 of the region's 22 Senate seats, and they retained 71 of 125 seats (56.8 percent) in the House, picking up one seat in North Carolina but losing their one-seat majority in Mississippi's delegation.[33]

Republican congressional victories were paralleled by Republican successes in gubernatorial campaigns. Between 1962 and 1978, Republicans won 19 percent of the region's governorships, a figure that reached 30 percent in the 1980s. After the 1996 elections, Republican governors led eight of the eleven Southern states, but by 2000, the pendulum had

Republican Gains in National Offices in the South

	PRESIDENT (Electoral Votes)			U.S. SENATE (Members)		U.S. HOUSE (Members)	
	Democrat	Republican	Other	Democrat	Republican	Democrat	Republican
1952	71	57		22	0	99	7
	55%	45%		100%	0%	93%	7%
1956	61	67		22	0	99	7
	48%	52%		100%	0%	93%	7%
1960	81	33	14	22	0	99	7
	63%	26%	11%	100%	0%	93%	7%
1964	81	47		20	2	90	16
	63%	37%		91%	9%	85%	15%
1968	25	57	46	18	4	80	26
	20%	45%	35%	82%	18%	75%	25%
1972*	0	129	1	14	7	74	34
	0%	99%	1%	64%	32%	69%	31%
1976*	118	12		16	5	81	27
	91%	9%		73%	23%	75%	25%
1980*	12	118		11	10	69	39
	9%	91%		50%	45%	64%	36%
1984	0	138		12	10	73	43
	0%	100%		55%	45%	63%	37%
1988	0	138		15	7	77	39
	0%	100%		68%	32%	66%	34%
1992	39	108		12	10	77	48
	27%	73%		55%	45%	62%	38%
1996	51	96		7	15	54	71
	35%	65%		32%	68%	43%	57%

Source: *America Votes*, 23 vols. (Washington, D.C.: Congressional Quarterly, 1956–1998).
*Senate totals are less than 100 percent because Harry Byrd, Jr., of Virginia left the Democratic party to become an independent.

Republican Gains in State Offices in the South

	GOVERNOR		STATE SENATE		STATE HOUSE	
	Democrat	Republican	Democrat	Republican	Democrat	Republican
1952	11 100%	0 0%	439 98%	11 2%	1293 97%	49 3%
1956	11 100%	0 0%	436 97%	14 3%	1288 96%	51 4%
1960	11 100%	0 0%	438 97%	12 3%	1292 96%	48 4%
1964	11 100%	0 0%	435 95%	23 5%	1271 95%	72 5%
1968	9 82%	2 18%	403 87%	61 13%	1161 87%	178 13%
1972	8 73%	3 27%	389 85%	66 15%	1088 83%	221 17%
1976	9 82%	2 18%	411 91%	42 9%	1168 89%	147 11%
1980	6 55%	5 45%	389 85%	66 15%	1079 82%	235 18%
1984	9 82%	2 18%	378 83%	75 17%	1019 77%	297 23%
1988	6 55%	5 45%	352 77%	104 23%	960 73%	356 27%
1992	8 73%	3 27%	316 70%	136 30%	903 69%	414 31%
1996	3 27%	8 73%	266 58%	191 42%	783 59%	538 41%

Sources: *The Book of the States,* 5 vols. (Lexington, Ky.: Council of State Governments, 1972–1998); *Statistical Abstract of the United States* (Washington, D.C.: Bureau of the Census, 1952–1999).

swung back toward the Democrats, who recaptured governorships in South Carolina, Alabama, and Mississippi while yielding the governor's mansion of Arkansas to the Republicans. Although Republicans lagged in Southern state legislatures, the trend toward growth in GOP representatives was unmistakable. In 1976, Republicans held only 12.2 percent of the state legislative seats in the region. By 1995, the Republican share had risen to 39.5 percent. By the century's end, Republicans controlled just over 40 percent of Southern legislative seats and held majorities in the Florida legislature, the lower houses in North and South Carolina, and the senates of Texas and Virginia.[34]

If the realigning trends in voting are observable in the South, electoral results are more difficult to interpret for the nation as a whole. In retrospect, the New Deal's reliable Democratic majorities in presidential, congressional, and state voting seem to have expired in the mid-1960s. A pattern of divided government under Republican presidents and Democratic Congresses replaced stable majority Democratic government by the 1970s. This configuration has flip-flopped in the 1990s, with the Democratic Clinton administration facing what appears to be a fairly entrenched majority of Republicans in Congress. A Democratic backlash in the Northeast in 1996, however, has somewhat offset the movement of the South toward Republican congressional delegations.[35]

If we are indeed experiencing a realignment, supporting evidence should appear at the level of elite behavior as well as among the mass public. One indicator of realignment might be party switching by public officials, as leaders seek to align themselves on the issues and to reconstruct viable constituencies among potential supporters. As early as the 1960s, some conservative Southern Democrats converted to the GOP (e.g., South Carolina senator Strom Thurmond), and Northern liberal Republicans followed the opposite path to the Democrats (e.g., former New York mayor John Lindsey). The 1980s saw a continuation of the trend, but at the same rather slow pace. For example, Texas senator Phil Gramm led the battle for the Reagan budget as a Democratic representative before bailing out to the Republicans. Considering the shift to the right in the national political climate following the so-called Reagan Revolution, however, the stream of party switchers was only a trickle. After the 1994 capture of the House by the Gingrich-led Republicans, the trend seemed to pick up steam again, at least

among Southern legislators. In 1995, the GOP picked up five seats from the South through party switching; Nathan Deal of Georgia and Billy Tauzin of Louisiana are examples of Democratic representatives who defected to the Republican majority. A similar trend occurred in some Southern state governments. In Georgia, for example, at least fifteen elected officeholders switched affiliations between 1994 and 1996, including the state's highly visible attorney general Michael Bowers.[36] Perhaps Clinton's appointment of former Maine senator William Cohen to be secretary of defense and the nomination, albeit unsuccessful, of former governor of Massachusetts William Weld as ambassador to Mexico portend a countertrend of party switching by Northeastern Republican moderates. In 1999, Republican Representative Michael Forbes of New York switched to the Democrats, prompting his entire staff to resign.[37]

Candidate recruitment, at least in the South, hints at the potential for realigned party prospects. Whereas once many conservative white males seeking office ran as Democrats, despite ideological affinities with the Republican party, now they increasingly run as Republicans. Democratic aspirants increasingly look like the voter base of that party—disproportionately African American and female. While the demographic diversity of tickets may be a boon to Democratic fortunes, the desertion by white male candidates tends to hasten the flight of white male voters to the GOP. Furthermore, the party's loss of its monopoly over lower public office as the tried-and-true stepping-stone to a political career undercuts one of the traditional Democratic advantages that has for decades forestalled Republican successes in regional politics, perpetuating the split-level realignment. Increasingly, Republicans are now able to field candidates for higher office who have served in lower-level posts. Electoral success feeds on electoral success, hastening the penetration of realignment further down the ballot.[38]

Although partisanship seems to be loosening its grip on the public, among politicians, partisan feuding has reached unprecedented levels. Congressional voting patterns reflect pronounced partisan divisions. One sign of party differences is the decline of the "Conservative Coalition," a term coined by the *Congressional Quarterly* to describe an informal alliance of Republicans and Southern Democrats in furtherance of conservative policy. The Conservative Coalition is defined as a majority of Republicans along with a majority of Southern Demo-

crats opposing a majority of non-Southern Democrats. From its formation in the 1930s through the 1980s, the Coalition enjoyed great success in blocking Democratic initiatives on civil rights, education, and labor and in passing the agendas of Republican presidents, appearing on nearly one-third of congressional roll calls a quarter of a century ago. By 1997, it appeared on only 8.6 percent of the roll-call votes, and in 1999, the *Congressional Quarterly* decided that the Conservative Coalition was too insignificant to warrant reporting its infrequent appearance.[39]

Party-line voting in Congress is also more frequent. Majorities of each party opposed each other on 41 percent of the roll calls in the House in 1955, 44 percent in 1956; in the Senate, partisans splits occurred 30 percent of the time in 1955, 53 percent in 1956. By 1995, a peak year for party-line voting, there were opposing party majorities on 73 percent of the votes in the House and 69 percent in the Senate. In 1996, those percentages declined, as they often do in election years, but only to 56 percent in the House and 62 percent in the Senate. By the late 1990s, there had been a slight decline in partisanship in the House, but party voting held steady in the Senate.[40] Members of Congress were also becoming more loyal when the parties confronted each other on legislation. In 1962, congressional Republicans voted with the majority of their party on an average of 68 percent of the party-unity votes; Democrats matched that loyalty, averaging 69 percent. By 1998, Republicans in both the House and the Senate averaged 86 percent party-unity scores, while Democrats scored 87 percent in the Senate and 82 percent in the House.[41] Such ideological distance between the parties and cohesion within them led to comments about the "parliamentarization" of Congress, reflecting the higher degree of partisan cohesion in most democratic parliaments compared with the fluid partisanship that historically characterized Congress. Moreover, by all accounts, the tone of partisan rancor has been much sharper in recent years, especially after the Republican capture of Congress in 1994. The bitter partisanship even drove some senior members of Congress into retirement as they decried the decline of comity and the loss of bipartisan collegiality in the 1990s legislature.[42]

The heightened party loyalty rested on a foundation of greater ideological compatibility within each party and ideological distance between the parties. Compared with 1971, when 84 percent of Republicans in

Congress were rated clearly or mostly conservative and 50 percent of Democratic members were rated mostly or clearly liberal, in 1993, the Republicans, of whom 97 percent were conservatives, faced off against the Democrats, of whom 76 percent were liberals.[43] After the Gingrich-engineered Republican Revolution of 1994, with its Speaker-dominated party government and the Contract with America as the centerpiece of its legislative agenda, partisan ideological distance in Congress was even greater. In 1995, House Democrats averaged 83 on the Americans for Democratic Action's 100-point liberalism scale, versus 7 for House Republicans, compared with scores of 52 and 23, respectively, in 1970.[44] By the 1990s, Southern Democratic representatives' party loyalty records, which had dropped precipitously in the 1960s and 1970s, approached the levels of Republicans and other Democrats.[45]

Cataclysmic social crises and dramatic shifts in public policies to respond to these critical issues have accompanied previous realignments. The public's opinions on issues and on the parties' abilities to handle salient issues presumably also shifted in the aftermath of these traumatic events. In the 1960s, the displacement of familiar New Deal issues of economic prosperity by civil rights and other racial and social issues produced great dissension in both party coalitions. Kevin Phillips, in what might be considered a duck-hunting manual for the ducks that Barry Goldwater proposed to hunt (Southern white votes for the GOP), suggested a Southern strategy to take advantage of Southern white disenchantment with Democratic advocacy of civil rights.[46] Simultaneously, the debacle of U.S. involvement in Vietnam shattered the post–World War II bipartisan anticommunist consensus and led to sharp disagreements over foreign and defense policies. New Politics lifestyle issues compounded the so-called social issues to cut across older lines of cleavage based more squarely on class. To some extent, no doubt, a "policy realignment" has occurred as these newer issues displaced New Deal economic disputes and produced gaping divisions within the New Deal constituencies, helping to explain the high rate of defection among Democratic voters.[47] New issues dividing the electorate, however, are not sufficient to produce realignments. The divisions must be deep, the parties must adopt different positions in response to critical issues, and the public must respond positively to these party platforms.[48] The evidence is mixed, at best, that any of these issues or partisan responses

have so affected the public's perceptions of the parties that loyalties have permanently shifted.

Ladd has proclaimed a realignment to a postindustrial party system. He suggests that this shift has been driven by a philosophical realignment that tilted public opinion in a decidedly conservative direction. He argues that public opinion is profoundly skeptical of government, yielding a conservative stance on most issues. Michael Barone supports such a claim, contending that "we are in a Tocquevillian era, in which the basic leaning of the society is toward decentralization, devolution, markets, choice and individual liberty. This is a vivid contrast with the America of the 1930s through 1970s, which leaned toward centralization, bureaucratization, regulation and deference to supposed experts. This Tocquevillian America naturally tends to favor Republicans." One should be cautious about accepting such sweeping claims about the ideology of American voters, however. Ladd's references are to sociocultural questions or issues of fiscal responsibility, that is, issues that tend to produce more conservative responses than questions about the government's role in ensuring economic prosperity and domestic security. While terms such as *centralization, bureaucracy,* and *government regulation* doubtless rub raw nerves with the public, Americans' opinions on concrete programs remain more complex. The findings of Free and Cantril long ago still retain their validity. Americans are conservative at the abstract level of political slogans, but they often simultaneously support active government at the level of specific programs. As Free and Cantril put it, Americans are ideological conservatives but operational liberals.[49]

Wattenberg has presented powerful evidence of a "disconnect" between partisanship and public opinion. He discovered that the group that responds "no preference" when asked about party identification is different from classic independents. Rather than representing disdain for party labels, these no-preference responses "result from a decrease in the salience of parties as attitudinal objects," according to Wattenberg. They exhibit, in other words, more indifference than independence or dissatisfaction. Ironically, at a time when partisan differences among politicians are at a peak, the public's images of the parties seem to be losing their edge. Although the public does see differences between the parties in their stances on social problems, the percentage who believe that one party or the other would be better at solving those problems has been shrinking. Wattenberg argues that the public is not

so much negative, or alienated, as it is neutral. Moreover, surveys using "feeling thermometers" to tap party images show that both positive and negative feelings toward parties have declined and that both parties have lost some of the positive images that once sustained them. Having lost much of their salience to plebiscitary presidents, candidate-centered campaigns, and mass media, parties have simply been displaced from the center of many voters' screens.[50]

These findings hold true for Southerners as well as for the national electorate. Stanley found that Southern perceptions of issue differences between the parties rose significantly in the 1980s. In 1952, only slightly more than one-third of Southern white Democrats and Republicans saw general party differences. This proportion rose but remained stable between 40 and 49 percent during the 1960s and 1970s. In the 1980s, however, the perception of party differences jumped to 67 percent for Democrats and 72 percent for Republicans. Moreover, almost two-thirds of Republicans remained disposed to see their party as better able to handle the most important problems, while such partisan policy confidence among white Southern Democrats fell from 44 percent in 1960 to 33 percent in 1984. In contrast, "thermometer readings" measuring the intensity of voters' feelings toward parties and candidates reveal little change in white Southern Democratic and Republican feelings toward the parties but more intense polarization in feelings about their respective presidential candidates. Such results suggest candidate rather than party voting, a finding supported by the decline of straight-ticket voting.[51]

If the evidence is less than overwhelming that a classic critical realignment has occurred, not everyone is prepared to abandon the concept altogether. Lawrence, for one, claims that there have been two mini-realignments since World War II, at least at the presidential level. In the late 1940s, increasing affluence, the looming shadow of the Cold War, and the Democrats' first tentative steps toward adopting a civil rights agenda produced cracks in the Democratic coalition. Beginning in the late 1960s, the Democrats' image of being ultraliberal on the decade's hot-button issues—racial, social, defense, and lifestyle issues—as well as the economic malaise of the Carter years, resulted in further Democratic defections. The first mini-realignment signaled the transition from dependable Democratic dominance to a pattern of partisan balance. The later mini-realignment yielded a party system in which

Republicans enjoy predominance, at least in presidential contests. Lawrence concludes that even though the path was not that of a critical realignment, the end result is not markedly dissimilar.[52]

Rolling to Regional Realignment?

Others are more skeptical that developments in recent decades deserve to be called a realignment. At best, they see a partial realignment, or a realignment stuck in midstream. Such a split-level, bifurcated, two-tiered, rolling, even creeping realignment has produced a generation of divided government in Washington and indecisive outcomes in many states, including some in the South. The issue is whether this pattern reflects a viable, long-term steady state or merely a prolonged transition period during which the realignment of presidential politics seeps down through the capillaries of the political system. The evidence at the national level points more to dissatisfaction with incumbents and politicians in general than a transfer of loyalties to the GOP. In the South, the Democrats' loss of many of the region's white voters has sounded the death knell of the solidly Democratic party system, but the Republicans have not been able to consolidate their appeal to their new voters with anything like the strength of loyalty that the old yellow-dog Democrats displayed. Partisan loyalties seem tenuous and still somewhat fluid throughout the nation, and neither leaders nor issues have yet emerged to solidify new patterns of partisan competition.

The very concept of realignment has come under fire in academic circles in recent years, with some theorists rejecting the theory in toto while others merely suggest that its fundamental tenets should be rethought. Joel Silbey thinks the essential logic of realignment theory can be salvaged, but only if fit into a larger framework of electoral eras that include a prepartisan era before 1838 and a postpartisan era encompassing our own times.[53] Ladd, for example, questions whether realignments follow the idealized pattern of a single critical election characterized by crisis, intense issues, sharply inflated turnout, clear party choice, and decisive victory by a new party majority coalition. Stanley Watson builds on the work of Edward Carmines and James Stimson to develop an issue evolution model. In this approach, rather

than critical elections at decisive junctures in shifting patterns of partisan loyalties, there are critical moments in the evolution of issue stances when " 'a mass polarization along [a] new line of issue cleavage' manifests itself." Although the shift is not fully realized at the time of the election, as in the model of critical elections, a critical moment recognizes a process of dynamic evolution as significant numbers of voters become aware of differences between the parties on salient issues, sparking a corresponding shift in party identification among the electorate. Watson argues that such a critical moment occurred in the 1984 election, occasioning not a realignment but a sizable tilt toward Republicanism in the South.[54]

Even Peter Nardulli, a defender of the concept of critical realignment, suggests that it should be understood as a process that plays itself out primarily at the subnational level rather than as the dramatic national event often portrayed in historical accounts. Key himself spoke of "secular realignments." James Sundquist's account of the Democratic realignment that spawned the New Deal party system demonstrated that although the shock waves were dramatic at the presidential level in 1932, the ripples were still making themselves felt further down the ticket decades later. Even into the 1950s, local politics was slowly being brought into alignment with national voting patterns as incumbent retirements, new recruits, and voter sentiments and habits were adjusting themselves to the no-longer-new national partisan structures. Given this more nuanced portrait of realignment below the highly visible national level, it is not implausible that the South and other areas are still feeling the aftershocks of the post-1968 Democratic demise at the presidential level. As the last remnants of the New Deal generation retire from the political scene, new possibilities open for a differently aligned structure of partisan competition.[55]

A New (Solidly Republican) Solid South?

What kind of new pattern will emerge? One possibility is that the white voters of the South have deserted the Democrats for the Republican party, probably in retaliation for the national Democrats' championing of civil rights. This explanation would make sense in terms

of historical continuity. After all, the very reason for the creation of the solidly Democratic South was the defense of white supremacy. Recently, there has developed a lively scholarly debate over the sources of the growth of Republican voting. The prevailing view of scholars of Southern politics is to discount the importance of purely racial issues in defining Southern partisanship, stressing instead the importance of economic and more general ideological opinions.[56] The reasons for rising Republicanism identified in an analysis of Mississippi politics can be generalized to the region. Stephen Shaffer and his coauthors argue that Republican victories become self-reinforcing, making Republican identification socially respectable as well as undermining the image of the Democrats as the "natural governing party" of the South. Republican successes breed more success by expanding the candidate pool, through recruitment of ambitious new politicians to the GOP and through party switching by Democratic officeholders. Ironically, Democratic victories can also work for Republicans by raising the visibility of national trends and personalities, subverting the attempts of Southern Democratic politicians to distance themselves from their national party's liberal image.[57]

In contrast, Watson argues that the 1984 election was a critical moment in the rise of Republicanism in the South precisely because it represented a critical moment in the evolution of the race issue. Between the 1980 election of Ronald Reagan and his reelection bid in 1984, Southern voters came to perceive a clear gap between the two parties' approaches to civil rights. This issue evolution, according to Watson, is responsible for the growth of Republican partisanship among Southern whites in the mid-1980s. In a case study of the 1995 Louisiana gubernatorial race, John Kuzenski and Michael Corbello likewise confirm that race rather than economics played the critical role in determining votes.[58]

If Southern whites are fleeing the Democratic party based on traditional attitudes on race, there is at least the prospect that the region could become as solidly Republican as it once was Democratic, with the Republican party serving as the new "haven for racist white voters."[59] If this massive realignment occurred, many of the evils of the old Solid South system might well persist, and V. O. Key's portrait of one-party politics might depict a literal image of the region's future as well. David Rohde, however, cautions against this perhaps precipitous

conclusion. He points out that political differences among regions are declining. He also notes that Republican gains are not irreversible and that forces outside the control of political actors do not predetermine partisan shifts. The rhetoric and actions of political leaders of all stripes influence voter decisions and opinion preferences.[60]

Despite the Republican domination of Southern presidential votes, Democrats have remained remarkably successful at retaining offices below the presidency. James Glaser argues that even if there is a realignment in progress, past realignments have filtered down to subnational levels in much less time than is evident in the growth of Southern Republicanism. Southern Democrats have continued to win congressional seats in districts carried by Republican presidential candidates, even without the obvious advantages of incumbency. Studying open-seat contests won by Democrats in the 1980s, he outlines winning strategies employed by Democrats. One ploy was to emphasize populist economic appeals, reinforcing the image of the Democrats as siding with the "little people" versus the "country club" Republicans. Democratic aspirants could use resentment issues other than race to define in-group versus out-group bonds with Southern voters. Examples that Glaser cites include foreign trade and aid and the threat of drugs. While stressing economic and resentment, and sometimes even class, issues, the Democrats were often able to defuse racial issues by surgically targeting their black and white constituencies with more or less separate campaigns, for example, by "narrowcasting" their more liberal messages on black radio, a tactic made possible by the still largely segregated reality of American life. More generally, Democratic candidates highlighted bread-and-butter constituency service issues rather than the ideological issues favored by their GOP opponents. Finally, the Democrats tried to localize and particularize ("parochialize") congressional contests, talking about local concerns and claiming independence from their national party and its leadership. Conversely, Republicans often invited national "stars" to appear in their districts and linked themselves to national conservative causes and policies in efforts to bolster their local campaigns. As a corollary, Democratic candidates reaffirmed their deep local roots against the often shallow district ties of Republicans.[61]

Although Southern Democrats managed to retain many state and local as well as congressional offices through these strategies for some

two decades after the disintegration of the Democratic presidential coalition, by the mid-1990s, these tactics proved less effective, and Southern Democrats were more beleaguered than ever. Part of the brilliance of the Contract with America as a Republican congressional campaign strategy was that it served to nationalize the 1994 election, resulting in sizable gains for Republicans. Ironically, part of the Democrats' problem was precisely their success in electing a Democrat—a Southerner, no less—to the White House. Clinton's very visibility made it increasingly impossible to insulate local Democratic candidates from national political tides.[62]

Further stress on the biracial Democratic coalition may be triggered by the ascension of African American and women candidates within the party. Keith Reeves contends that "black aspirants cannot compete equally or effectively in electoral jurisdictions comprised overwhelmingly of white voters because of the continued vigor of racial prejudice and discrimination."[63] Context is crucial, however, and the prospects for biracial coalitions may be less bleak where African Americans and other minorities constitute a significant portion of the electorate.[64] One hopeful example of the prospects for healthy party competition is the fate of African American incumbents in majority white districts in the 1996 congressional elections. Five of six were reelected, and the sixth yielded his seat in a bid for statewide office.[65] In Georgia, the redistricting in 1992 to comply with the Voting Rights Act produced two majority minority "access districts" and one "influence district" with a heavy concentration of black voters. African American Democrats won in all three districts, but when the redistricting plan was challenged by white plaintiffs, the Supreme Court struck it down in *Miller v. Johnson*.[66] A panel of federal judges redrew the congressional district lines, leaving Representative John Lewis's Atlanta district as the only majority black district in the state. In 1996, despite the history of racially polarized voting in the state and dire predictions of "bleaching" the state's congressional delegation, both Cynthia McKinney in the Fourth District and Sanford Bishop in the Second District retained their seats by comfortable margins in these majority white districts. In winning reelection, these minority candidates used different strategies: Bishop ran toward the center as a moderate who had served local interests, while McKinney remained on the ideological left, emphasizing her ties to liberal groups such as women, labor, gay rights advocates,

and environmentalists. Both, however, drew a significant portion of the white vote, as well as solid support among black constituents. Although these elections may say more about the power of incumbency in contemporary elections than the demise of racially polarized voting, they offer some hope that enough whites might vote on a nonracial basis to support a competitive two-party system in the South well into the next century.[67]

Democrats are not alone in experiencing trouble maintaining viable coalitions. The rise of the religious right has alienated more moderate and libertarian-leaning Republicans across the South as well as across the United States. The Christian Coalition controls the Republican party in eight of eleven Southern states, and nationally, 29 percent of the Republican votes in 1994 came from evangelical Christians.[68] As Southerners have risen to prominence in the leadership of the Republican party nationally, and as the religious right has flexed its muscle in Republican circles, a twofold, overlapping reaction has occurred as Northerners and social moderates feel less and less comfortable in the GOP. Even in the South, Republican social moderates fare better in general elections than do candidates identified with the Christian right, whose extreme positions on morality drive away middle-of-the-roaders and economic conservatives who would otherwise back GOP candidates. The GOP's dilemma, however, is that these same social moderates have trouble winning their party's nominations.[69] Republican experience confirms an observation that Key made about American party politics: factional conflict intensifies as a party's prospects of victory increase. Thus, while the rise of Republicanism may be somewhat self-reinforcing, the party's success also has self-limiting aspects.[70]

The fluctuating fortunes of the parties nationally has combined with the resiliency of Southern state and local Democratic politicos to sustain viable Democratic "staying power" in the South.[71] Although the majority of white voters have cast their lot with the Republicans in most elections, both the continuing high levels of independent identification and the frequency of ticket splitting weigh against the levels of partisan loyalty and consistent party voting necessary to produce a solidly Republican South. Along with the addition of African American voters to the rolls in roughly the same proportion as whites, enough white Southerners have remained willing to vote for Demo-

cratic candidates to support competitive politics in many areas and Democratic victories in many races. A recent thorough survey of politics in each of the Southern states concludes that "the biracial Democratic coalition is very much alive today."[72]

Rather than a lopsided realignment reminiscent of the Solid South, then, a second possibility might be a revitalized party system with realigned parties but healthy party competition. Ladd maintains that although the postindustrial philosophical realignment has arrived "swiftly and decisively," the corresponding partisan realignment has not. Instead, Ladd argues, well after the new pattern began emerging in the 1960s, a kind of "partisan parity" has remained. In discussing the 1996 election, Ladd details the latest electoral results that portend continued close competition, with no party enjoying clear or secure majority status. He concludes that while past party systems were characterized by one dominant party and an obviously secondary minority party, this latest postindustrial system will not exhibit such "sun" and "moon" parties, because the electorate is too loosely tied to either party to support such a stable model.[73]

Realignment (Not Delayed But) Derailed?

These unstable attachments suggest a third possibility beyond a realignment, however messy, or an incomplete split-level realignment tarrying midway through the process. Ladd's description of "an electorate remarkably unanchored in partisan terms" might suggest a realigned party system characterized not merely by close partisan competition but also by unstable and shallow competition.[74] In other words, the current alignment differs from previous alignments not only by lacking parties that are securely slotted in majority and minority roles but also by having parties that are less firmly anchored in the electorate than parties in past systems. It might be instructive to say that the party system has been realigned into a new system that is characterized by traits that resemble dealigned politics. As William Schneider suggested years ago, we seem to have realigned into a dealigned party system.[75]

Burnham has argued that there was a critical realignment in the 1968–1972 period, but that the sixth party system that emerged from

that upheaval was a candidate-centered politics of the "permanent campaign." Proclaiming an end of the partisan era, Burnham foresees this "postpartisan" system as exhibiting remarkable staying power, even while it is characterized by flux and discontinuity.[76] In fact, this latest political order has inverted the norm, with a dealigned system appearing to be the durable rather than transitory state of American politics.[77]

Such a "hollow realignment," even "nonalignment," represents yet another step in the "onward march of party decomposition" toward a politics marked by continuing volatility.[78] Flourishing third-party activity, epitomized by Ross Perot's two bids for the presidency, but replicated at local levels by numerous minor parties; withering partisan attachments; weak social group alignments; and, above all, extremely low voter turnout all betoken a political alignment unlikely to be characterized by the stability of previous party systems more deeply rooted in the electorate.[79] Even Lawrence, who argues that two mini-realignments have produced Republican dominance at the presidential level, suggests that Democratic adjustments to appear more centrist on social issues after the early 1970s and the rise of retrospective voting on presidential performance after the 1980s have limited the Republican edge in contests for the White House. Moreover, Lawrence characterizes the overall party system as marked by a "discontinuity" between the pattern of presidential and subpresidential politics.[80]

Oddly enough, a "collapse of continuity"[81] resulting from a realignment into a permanent campaign system dominated by highly competitive yet vacuous parties could produce a party system with a strong family resemblance to the one-party Solid South. As Burnham presciently observed in 1969,

> If one assumes that the end result of a long-term trend toward electoral disaggregation is the complete elimination of political parties as foci that shape voting behavior, then the possibility of critical realignment would, by definition, be eliminated as well. Every election would be dominated by TV packaging, candidate charisma, real or manufactured, and short-term, ad hoc influences. Every election, therefore, would have become deviating or realigning by definition, and American national politics would come to resemble the formless gubernatorial primaries that V. O. Key described in his classic *Southern Politics*.[82]

Shaffer and Johnson claim that "both processes of realignment and dealignment characterize the contemporary South."[83] Once again, the South serves as a bellwether for national political trends. If this "dealigned realignment" is accurate, despite the closeness of the competition between the parties on national, state, and local levels, the nature of that competition may not produce the desirable results that Key thought partisan competition promised. If parties are weak and unstable, and if the quality of party competition is low enough, there may not be a meaningful difference between the superficial and essentially meaningless competition of unrepresentative parties and the distortions of dealigned politics that critics fear. With unattached parties and dealigned politics, the deformities that Key observed in the traditional South may begin to sound disturbingly familiar again.

6 / Politics
America's Number One Problem

The More Things Change

Since the 1990s, American society has seemed somewhat schizophrenic, and politics has taken on a remoteness from reality that defies comprehension. A huge gap separates individual lives, the sphere of the everyday, workaday world where ordinary people plan and lead their lives, and the nation's social, economic, and political institutions. Our lack of social cohesion may indicate that we as a people are increasingly unconnected to one another; maybe we really do "bowl alone" more these days, as Robert Putnam suggested in a metaphor designed to capture the growing phenomenon of social isolation experienced by many Americans.[1] Perhaps we are not so much isolated as increasingly connected to our larger social institutions through the unmediated mass media rather than through community social groups such as churches, clubs, neighborhoods, and extended families. Perhaps, however, there are specifically political explanations for why American politics seems so removed from the experienced realities of our lives.

The 1990s supplied Americans with plenty of reasons to feel satisfied, even smug, about their governing institutions, which after all had arguably scored extraordinary successes after the tumultuous 1960s and 1970s and lackluster 1980s. Most notably, the Cold War ended, and we won, although "peacekeeping missions" continue to needle the isolationist mood of Americans, and traditional trouble spots such as the Middle East appear as unsettled as ever. China also looms large on the horizon, but perhaps as much a potential economic rival as a military threat. The nation seems to have turned some invisible corner in the global economic competition, however. After years of lagging Japan,

Germany, and Western Europe, the U.S. economy hums along on the fast track, while globalization has dealt harsher blows to these allies and sometimes bitter rivals. Worries about competition from the dynamic "Asian tigers" have been replaced with concern about "Asian crises." At home, unemployment is lower than it has been in decades, while inflation continues to be low and the stock market soars to unprecedented heights. Even the signs of social decay that had so troubled Americans in the 1970s and 1980s, such as rising welfare rolls, divorce rates, and crime statistics, are leveling off or abating, although perhaps more because of changing demographics and economic fortunes than due to any policy successes.

Nonetheless, many Americans feel alienated from their social, and especially political, institutions.[2] Maybe this sense of estrangement reflects lives increasingly focused on the trials and tribulations of daily life. Studies documented that Americans are working longer hours, for example, just to keep up with their customary standard of living.[3] Maybe, however, this remoteness is more than preoccupation outside the public sphere; perhaps it is disenchantment with the leaders and institutions by which we might address our problems collectively. Rather than expecting leadership from public officials, Americans increasingly greet all proposals with diffuse skepticism. Neither party, as we have seen, commands great loyalty. Incumbent political leaders are reelected more from a base of low expectations than from satisfaction. In 1996, for instance, the best reason many people saw for reelecting Bill Clinton was so that he could restrain the ideologues in Congress led by Speaker Newt Gingrich. Many of these same voters, however, split their tickets, hedging their bets by electing a Republican Congress to thwart any liberal plans a second Clinton administration might harbor.[4] When the resulting session of the 105th Congress spent much of its time and energy holding hearings and exchanging charges of campaign finance corruption and violations of sexual ethics, leading to impeachment of the president, the American public was turned off, and it basically tuned out the Beltway politics that seemed so irrelevant to Main Street.

Despite the public placidity of the 1990s, what W. Lance Bennett calls a "governing crisis" is simmering just below the surface.[5] Major problems such as the effects of a traumatic economic restructuring and global economic forces; threats to job security and the quality of

work; creeping inequalities of income, wealth, and life chances; deteriorating public services and vastly unequal private services; and dire environmental and resource crises looming on the horizon are uncorrected and even unaddressed by political institutions that do not or cannot respond to public needs. Our electoral institutions are more and more disconnected with and irrelevant to the problems plaguing ordinary Americans. Although surely not the whole explanation, part of the answer lies in the largely unnoticed development that the dual convergence of Southern and national politics spawned a politics with more than a few qualities characteristic of the traditional Solid South system.

A realigned party system with many dealigned traits has weakened the party competition that benefited most average Americans during the New Deal era. Now parties are much less responsive and responsible. Participation in politics has declined precipitously. Although the kinds of barriers that kept most Southerners on the sidelines in the Solid South have been outlawed or otherwise removed, the shrinking American electorate provides only a narrow base to support political institutions that are supposed to solve broad public problems. And last but certainly not least, the politics of broad class coalitions that constituted the core of the New Deal foundered on the reefs of racial and ethnic divisiveness, although the new racialized politics is surely more subtle than the raw politics of the explicitly white supremacist Solid South. No one would be foolish enough to suggest that contemporary U.S. politics exactly mirrors the pre-1950 politics of Dixie. But many of the transformations of the last decades, both of the South and of the nation, have produced trends that result in certain structural similarities—weak party competition, a narrow electorate, and racialized politics—that, if unchecked, augur poorly for the prospects for American democracy.

The Party's Over: The M^3 System

The result of the dual convergence of the South and the rest of the country is a party system characterized by very close competition between the two parties at both the national and state levels. It might seem absurd on its face, therefore, to suggest any similarity between

contemporary, closely competitive party politics and the politics of the one-party Solid South. Remember, however, that Key's analysis revealed that the essence of one-party politics in the traditional South was not the domination of one party organization to the monopolization of all competition; rather, one party meant, in effect, no party.[6] There was in truth a plethora of electoral competition, but it was among candidates and loose factions and lacked the stabilizing and organizing influence of party organizations. It was, in other words, not the lack of competition per se that was the problem, but rather the nature of electoral competition without parties. Today, despite sharp partisan competition, the nature and quality of that competition are problematic. To the extent that our current parties are weakly tied to the electorate and do not provide the organizing impetus to our electoral contests, the comparison to partyless Southern politics is not so far-fetched.

Has the role of parties in our politics diminished to the point of changing the nature of American electoral politics? Some critics argue that American political parties, always weak by European standards, have indeed suffered a precipitous decline in recent decades that drastically undermines their ability to play crucial functions in a mass democracy. Political science texts differ in the exact list of functions that parties are expected to perform, but these party roles generally include recruiting and supporting candidates, assembling and articulating interests, formulating policy and coordinating the fragmented institutions of American government, and educating (or propagandizing) the public on political issues.[7] In a word, parties are a linking mechanism between the public and its leaders in a mass democracy. To the extent that parties decline, can other institutions take their place in linking citizens and elites? Can alternative connections be as effective and democratic as parties?

Bennett maintains that the governing crisis in this country results largely because the place of political parties has been usurped by money, marketing, and media—an M[3] system. Although the two major parties continue to exist, and nowadays they contest elections with ferocious intensity and impressively close results, the real impetus in elections is not the hollowed out party shells but rather campaign finance committees, professional advertising and public relations experts, and the formally detached, objective bystanders, the

mass media. These major new actors in electoral politics, none of them democratically structured or accountable to the public, shape current elections in ways that undermine the linkage function of political parties.[8]

Money, of course, is not a recent arrival in American politics—it has been called, after all, the mother's milk of politics. Lately, however, campaign finance has seemed more like the crack cocaine of American politics. Scandals associated with Watergate exposed the corrupting influence of large campaign contributions to public view, leading to the Campaign Reform Act of 1972. Unfortunately, the problems were not corrected, and the money trails just found different paths into the political arena. In 1976, the Supreme Court struck down the spending-limit side of the reform equation in *Buckley v. Valeo*, ruling expenditure limits an abridgment of freedom of speech (finding, in essence, that money talks). Several innovative practices allow campaign contributors to erode the law's contribution limits. As if $1,000 limits on giving to each candidate were not unrestrictive enough, political action committees circumvent these limits by bundling contributions from like-minded donors into substantial chunks of campaign cash. Supposedly independent committees can legally expend unlimited amounts as long as they maintain the charade of not explicitly coordinating their expenditures with the candidates. The amount of supposedly independent spending doubled from the 1992 to 1996 elections. So-called soft money given to state party organizations or national parties for "party-building" activities (e.g., voter registration or mobilization not directly tied to any particular campaign) is entirely uncapped. The net result is millions of dollars beyond the official limits spent on elections in ways that basically escape public regulation and accountability.[9]

The level of spending on campaigns continues to rise sharply. The 1996 elections cost the two major parties $2.2 billion, the most expensive elections in history. The median price of a 1996 Senate campaign was $3.5 million, up from $2.7 million in 1994; in the House, the median campaign cost rose from $348,287 in 1994 to $559,807 two years later. Spending can be sharply steeper in hotly contested races. The 1996 challenge of cookie magnate Michael Cole to Speaker of the House Newt Gingrich drew combined expenditures of over $7.1 million for a single compact suburban house district.[10] The increased

spending has been accompanied by a significant shift in giving to the more conservative party. In the 1980s, the Democrats managed to leverage control of Congress to shake down sizable campaign gifts from normally conservative corporate interests. By 1996, however, the alignment of ideology and incumbency in the majority-Republican Congress proved a lethal combination for the Democrats and probably undermined their ability to wrest back control of Congress, even as they readily retained the White House. In 1996, the Republican share of business contributions increased from 49 to 63 percent, and among ideological groups, the Republicans increased their share from 33 to 51 percent of the gifts. Even among unions, the Republicans doubled their percentage from 4 to 8 percent.[11]

Of course, money did not inevitably mean victory, but it did not hurt either. In fact, candidates who spend more generally win nine out of ten races. Although unsurprising, this correlation fails to capture the full impact of money on campaigns. Large donors want to buy access and influence with their contributions, so they give to likely winners. Because incumbents enjoy a multitude of advantages, officeholders are the surer bet, making them more attractive recipients. Incumbents' privileged access to large donors, in turn, reinforces their already impressive advantages in a vicious circle that works to stifle innovation and insulate officeholders from electoral challenge and from the public. The need to raise big bucks to finance credible campaigns serves as a threshold, weeding out candidates without lots of money or entree to the wealthy. In an "investment theory of elections"—a who-pays-the-piper-calls-the-tune theory—the need for money to run for office makes candidates dependent on large donors and less accountable to political parties and, through the mechanism of party competition, to the public.[12]

The consequences of this dependence on big money have numerous effects on our politics. If recipients are concentrated disproportionately among incumbent officeholders, donors are found disproportionately among the wealthy. The Center for Responsive Politics estimates that less than 1 percent of the population now supplies roughly 80 percent of all political contributions.[13] Not only is the range of possible candidates limited to those acceptable to donors with money to invest, but the range of ideas raised by candidates is correspondingly circumscribed. One recent study of the new high-tech,

high-cost politics found that wealthy interest groups are able to speak more effectively and have their voices heard above the din in the public dialogue. This capacity "changes the nature of the policy debates and allows those who control the narrative, in both public and private arenas, to determine the policy."[14] The frantic pursuit of campaign donations fragments our politics, as every politician is forced to turn entrepreneur and spend huge amounts of time fund-raising. By the late 1990s, estimates suggest that from one-third to one-half of legislators' time is devoted to seeking campaign contributions and that senators need to raise $3,000 a day during their six-year terms to amass sufficiently sizable war chests to withstand electoral challenges.[15] The need to please donors also contributes to the atomizing of Congress as the committee system, as well as individual members' time and energy, is devoted to serving the financial stakes of special interests. As Darrell West and Burdett Loomis conclude: "Simply put, we argue that in a world of information overload, moneyed interests will be able to construct narratives more clearly and effectively than other groups or organizations. To be sure, political parties, populist voices, and public-interest groups all work to convey their perspectives. All continue to have some real success in shaping the policy agenda. In the end, however, none of these voices can sing with the specificity, direction, and forcefulness of private interests that purchase a clear, coherent, and often-repeated message."[16]

The increased levels of campaign contributions are, not surprisingly, related to the rising costs of campaigns. Part of the problem is the professionalization of electoral contests. Professional management is usurping the volunteer and partisan people-power of traditional campaigns. The major cost factor is television ads, which now devour the largest chunk of campaign expenditures. We are, in effect, moving from a labor-intense form of politics to capital-intense politics, as candidates seek to contact potential voters not through the linkage of people organized into parties but through impersonal technological channels. As direct advertising replaces partisan linkages between candidates and the electorate, the ties between campaign slogan and governance are also attenuated. TV ads make it possible to sell candidates like soap, based more on image than on substance. As early as Joe McGinniss's 1968 exposé of the Nixon media manipulations, it became clear that message can be separated from political reality by slick advertising.

The science of surveying allows the pulse of the public to be constantly monitored by public opinion polls, deliberative polls, push polls (actually deceptive propagandizing disguised as phone polls), and exit polls. Focus groups, more closely resembling college psychology labs than democratic assemblies of citizens, enable campaign professionals to explore popular fears and predispositions in even more depth and to use the knowledge gleaned to shape a campaign "message" that echoes, however hollowly, what the public thinks it wants to hear. Like product developers, then, professional public relations experts can create the political "product" to satisfy the public's cravings. The difference between product development and campaigns, however, is that businesses often develop new products to market to popular tastes, while politicians generally limit their offerings to new images. As stagecraft increasingly replaces statecraft, campaigns are becoming more devoid of substance, and our elections have less and less to do with the stuff of governing. In addition, professionals manage individual campaigns in isolation from other races, further undermining parties as democratic instruments of collective governance. "Hyperdemocracy" is the result of a "loop that links voters to pollsters, poll results to television ads and commentary, and television ads and commentary back to voters." This hyperdemocracy ironically leaves voters further estranged from professional politicians than ever.[17]

Some observers dissent from the thesis that modern parties are weaker than in the past. Xandra Kayden, for example, has argued that the party organizations, led by the Republican National Committee but with the Democrats in hot pursuit, have boosted their technical capacities to raise money, to appeal to donors and voters directly, and to communicate campaign messages to the electorate through sophisticated public relations ploys. She argues that this increasing technical strength entails a strong corresponding trend toward centralization, as national party organizations are in positions to dictate which local parties and candidates receive aid from the richer national arsenals. She does note, however, that these more sophisticated national party organizations are dominated by cool technicians and professionals, not the old partisan pols and ideological true believers. The criteria for party aid, then, are likely to be technical competence and the odds of winning, not partisan loyalty or ideological alignment with party programs.[18] The widely publicized marriage of Democratic professional

James Carville and Republican campaign consultant Mary Matalin, shortly after they served as top hired guns in the 1992 campaigns of Bill Clinton and George Bush, respectively, exemplifies just how content-free modern professionalized politics has become. For example, Dick Morris, the president's top political adviser for the 1996 election until felled by a sex scandal, had built his reputation as a winning political operative by managing successful campaigns for conservative Republicans, including Southern senators Trent Lott and Phil Gramm.

The advent of the "permanent campaign" furthers the tendencies toward candidate-centered politics, in which incumbents enjoy almost overwhelming advantages. Successful candidates now use public office as a base for the next election. They put pollsters on the public payroll and use their offices for fund-raising and as platforms for incessant public relations campaigns. Bill Clinton even salvaged his flagging standing in the polls in 1994 by hiring a well-known Republican operative, David Gergen, to stem the hemorrhaging caused by his failed health care initiative. Members of Congress use the franking privilege and extensive in-house public relations facilities to generate newsletters, polls, and press releases to the folks back home. Of course, the constituent services functions of Congress, the individual casework and pork barreling for the district, can be seen as simply a nonpartisan form of the old-fashioned patronage and preferments of political machines.

Mass media's influence has done more than anything to increase campaign costs and to induce the use of professional campaign management. Increasingly, voters rely on television for news, and most find this source to be the most reliable. Even more startling, 44 percent of Americans report that they get their political information from talk radio.[19] Voters say that they rely heavily on broadcast sources in making their voting decisions.[20] As the influence of broadcast journalism especially has risen, politicians have invented strategies for controlling the information relayed by the media. No one, of course, could match the Reagan press strategy. Following the advice of a brain trust of media managers, the Reagan White House focused news about the administration around a unified "line of the day" and ensured the unitary status of this exclusive emphasis by coordinating statements and suppressing leaks that might detract from the day's focus. The line was developed by extensive polling and marketing analysis to create

a constant feedback loop to evaluate the effectiveness of press management. The presidential handlers retained the initiative in the press wars by refusing to engage the media except on favorable terrain, such as the scripted presidential speech. The White House even took advantage of presidential trip departures to dangle irresistible photo opportunities before the image-hungry media, while Reagan's difficulty in hearing against the backdrop of helicopter noise conveniently drowned out reporters' questions, thereby avoiding spontaneous presidential statements. Naturally, it did not hurt that the president was an experienced (if not very accomplished) actor, but once the Reagan White House had blazed the trail, other presidents have been able to follow similar strategems.[21]

The press, of course, has played into the politicians' hands in the game of manipulation. Its own rules of the game, especially its definition of "objectivity" as neutral reportage, have allowed politicians to manipulate the press, which dutifully broadcasts staged "pseudo-events" and misinformation. Ironically, even when the media criticized these techniques of campaign manipulation and misleading campaign spots, the additional airplay may have enhanced, rather than deflated, their impact.[22]

The worst consequence of the mass media, however, has little to do with the political or ideological content of their coverage. Most studies find that the overt content of media coverage of elections is not highly biased in partisan terms, and even if it were, there is little evidence of effect on the public. In fact, there is good reason to believe that increasingly skeptical and media-savvy audiences are highly resistant to overt media manipulation.[23] The most troubling impact of the mass media on American politics is more functional than substantive: the way media cover politics is more significant than what they say about it.

For one thing, politics is an ever-shrinking portion of the "news." Nightly network news focuses to a growing degree on items believed to be relevant and reassuring to the audience, such as health or consumer issues, matters of personal finance, innovative technologies, and the weather. What passes for news is often the bizarre or merely trivial instead of the information necessary for us to govern ourselves. More Americans watched the Los Angeles Police Department chase O. J. Simpson in his infamous white Blazer than voted for president in

1996.[24] Even the political news is spoon-fed through the happy-talk format to reassure the audience that the events reported on the "Eyewitness News" are not threatening to the viewers. Jarol Manheim has labeled this "eyewitless" approach to news "journalism as group therapy." National newscasts, coached by "news doctors" who advise media on marketing and profitability and downsized to reduce personnel costs, have followed local broadcasts along this path.[25]

One result is that political leaders less frequently speak for themselves. The average length of sound bites in political campaigns decreased from 42.3 seconds in 1968 to 9.8 seconds in 1988.[26] The content of what the media have to say about campaigns has fixated on the horse-race angle, focusing not on the substantive differences between candidates and their respective platforms but rather on the Who's winning? question. From 1988 to 1992, horse-race coverage of the election on the nightly news rose from 27 to 35 percent, with attention to tracking polls accounting for another 33 percent of airtime. Meanwhile, policy coverage fell from 40 to 33 percent of the news. This strategic framing is marked by its concentration on winning and losing, often reported in the language of wars, games, or competition. Performance, style, and perceptions dominate story content; tellingly, politicians are often billed as actors, journalists are cited as critics, and the public is reduced to the passive part of the audience.[27] Even more insidious, this strategic perspective now permeates coverage of policy issues as well as elections. For example, much of the reporting on Clinton's health care reform initiatives was devoted not to explaining their complex provisions or alternative plans but rather to the political motivations behind various proposals and the strategic feasibility of those plans. The reduction of policy making to merely a continuation of the campaign horse race is another aspect of the harnessing of governance to the permanent campaign.

The functional impact of this type of media coverage is to entertain but not enlighten the audience. Media treat viewers as consumers of information to be amused, rather than as citizens who require information to make decisions about their own governance. Whether the cause of this trend is the increasing squeeze of profits or the criteria for defining news, the effect is to vitiate a prerequisite of democracy—an informed electorate. The American public is not treated as a public at all, but rather as spectators who merely make up the audience

of politics. As Neil Postman puts it, the real media threat to democracy is not the Orwellian fear of *1984*, in which the content of politics is controlled by Big Brother in a technologically sophisticated totalitarianism. Instead, the more relevant threat is a Huxleian "brave new world" in which we are so busy being entertained that we have not the time, information, nor motivation to govern ourselves.[28]

Mass media's effects on our political campaigns are as pervasive as they are perverse. The "hype, hoopla, and negativity" of modern media campaigns echo the stump styles of Southern politicians, only now tailored for the "cool" medium of television. If spellbinding oratory and the ability to mouth memorable catchphrases were the hallmarks of successful campaigners in the old Solid South, the new criterion of candidate viability is being telegenic. One consultant-turned-professor has suggested that instead of asking whether we trust a political leader with the awesome responsibility of "the bomb," we now subject politicians to the "clicker test": do we click the remote whenever their faces appear on the TV screen?[29] The trivializing effects on campaigns are not limited to the election season (which, in the case of presidential politics, now extends at least a full two years before voting day), because "campaigning is governing is campaigning." As Thomas Mann and Norman Ornstein point out, campaigning is swallowing the governing process, which undermines good government, because "campaigning seems increasingly antithetical to governing." The cost of the "endless election" is also paid in public cynicism and disengagement.[30] As government and policy become ever more remote from public influence, the people get scintillating sound bites and gripping visuals, but the substance of popular control is diluted. Like the barbecues and one-liners of the Talmadges of old, electioneering media-style may make for "a dern good show," but democracy it is not.

The consequences of mass-media politics are myriad and perverse. In the first place, mass-media politics has contributed to the decline of parties and the rise of candidate-centered campaigns. Candidates are tempted to run away from their parties' less popular platform planks to avoid being linked to the voters' images of the parties. More generally, candidates operate as independent political entrepreneurs, "stand[ing] above their parties rather than with them."[31] This atomistic style is reflected in public perceptions. A recent study found that the most important campaign themes in Senate elections across the

country were candidates and that "campaign rhetoric often has little to do with substantive policy issues." Despite the glut of information in the media, the study found voters to be confused and poorly informed. Only 35 percent of the voters could accurately identify the most-discussed issue in their state's Senate campaign. More startlingly, the voters were less informed in those elections in which more money was spent on the race.[32] In reviewing a study of the media's effects, Robert Entman concludes that "according to Patterson, the media's professional norms, commercial imperatives, and cognitive limitations create a limited and distorted portrayal of politics that discourages informed citizenship. The media appear ill suited to carry out the screening and selection functions once performed by a healthier party system."[33] Mass media fail to provide the glue that could link the public to its leadership.

Worse than the failure to inform and the tendency to personalize politics, the media actually misinform the public. The Dalager study of Senate races found 39 percent of the voters uninformed about the most important campaign issues, but a full 26 percent were misinformed, with more misinformed voters residing in states where campaign spending was greater.[34] A recent study of perceptions of President Clinton brilliantly captures the distorting effects of media on public opinion. The survey, conducted in February 1998, during the early phase of the Monica Lewinsky scandal, discovered that people were remarkably well informed about the specifics of that affair. Nearly two-thirds could correctly answer five of the six detailed questions about the scandal. People were less knowledgeable about Clinton's policy stances, however, even in the president's sixth year in office. Only two in five could correctly identify more than three of nine positions Clinton had taken on major policy issues. The survey also found strong evidence that besides leaving the public uninformed on policy, the media misinform the public on issues. Respondents were actually fairly accurate in their perceptions of Clinton's policy stances on issues on which the president had taken a liberal position. But the majority tended to incorrectly identify the president's positions when he adhered to more conservative positions, such as backing welfare reform, deregulating the telecommunications industry, and refusing to back an anti–land mine treaty. The authors conclude that the media's tendency to label politicians and to frame issues simplistically

as merely conflict between liberals and conservatives actually misinforms the public about important issues.[35]

Beyond misinforming, this simplistic, strategic framing fosters, instead of "healthy skepticism," a "corrosive cynicism" and disillusionment with our political leaders and institutions.[36] In a no-win trap, "politicians are almost continually derided for failing to tell the whole truth, yet they are trashed for naivete and incompetence when they do so, because that shows they do not know how to win. The public is told that essentially all politicians are dissembling, opportunistic hypocrites, yet it is scolded for not knowing or caring enough to vote."[37] Unlike parties as instruments of political mobilization, mass media demobilize the electorate, with all too familiar effects on political participation.

The Gaping Hole in the Body Politic

A second characteristic that the contemporary American polity shares with the traditional Southern system is a narrow electoral base. In 1996, a mere 49 percent of the eligible population of the United States voted, the smallest turnout since 1924 and the second lowest in the history of mass democratic politics in this country. Since its post–World War II peak of 62.8 percent in 1960, turnout in presidential elections has sharply declined. In 1992, 55 percent of the potential electorate voted in the three-way race among Clinton, Bush, and Perot, but the contest among Clinton, Dole, and Perot in 1996 attracted less than half of those eligible to vote. Not surprisingly, congressional midterm elections attract even fewer voters. Voting fell from 48.2 percent in 1966 to about 36 percent in 1998. Without the stimulation of party competition, the typical turnout for intraparty nominating primaries is only about 10 percent of those eligible.[38] Nonvoters have, in effect, become "our abiding third party," and if their abstention counted as votes, they would be by far the majority party.[39]

In the traditional one-party South, disenfranchisement was based on various legal barriers, as well as on many extralegal obstacles to voting by African Americans, women, and the poor. In contrast, today, many legal barriers to voting have been removed in the South and nationally. As a result, the regional gap in turnout has almost closed:

in 1960, the turnout rate was a mere 40 percent in the South, versus 70 percent in the rest of the nation. By 1996, however, 46 percent of Southerners voted, compared with only 50 percent of non-Southerners.[40] Unfortunately, the disparity is closing less because of rising participation in the South than because of a national decline in voting. Even the requirement for registration, which many critics allege creates a subtle barrier to voting, was alleviated by the passage and implementation of the Motor Voter Act of 1993, allowing for registration at more convenient times and locations. Although the act led to the registration of about 14 million new potential voters from 1994 to 1996, the actual turnouts in 1994 and 1996 were disappointingly small.[41] Clearly, factors other than formal barriers were deterring the public from voting.

During the twentieth century, the United States has had markedly lower participation in elections than comparable European democracies, leading to endless speculation and disputes over the causes and consequences of this unique feature of our politics. Some theories suggest that Americans do not vote because they are satisfied, on the seemingly self-evident premise that they would take the minimal time and effort to vote if they were not. These explanations are contradicted by the correlation between trends toward nonvoting and increasing alienation among the public, as well as by data on who abstains from voting. The less educated, lower income, and minority groups who vote less often are exactly the groups one would sensibly expect to be least satisfied with American society and government. Other theories correlate individual traits, such as less education, lower income, and less prestigious occupations, with nonvoting ignoring historical data that demonstrate that voting has declined from typical turnouts of 90 percent in the nineteenth century to today's abysmal rates of under 50 percent, even as education and income levels have risen. These individualistic explanations also fail to take account of comparative data showing that voting levels abroad, which run 20 to 40 percent higher than in this country, do not vary by class in many other democracies.

Instead of implausible explanations focusing on individual characteristics, it is more fruitful to explore the ways in which political institutions and social structures fail to encourage, or even discourage, voting in contemporary America. One attitudinal trait of individuals

that seems to be tellingly connected with institutions is political efficacy: Americans who feel politically ineffective, who believe that their votes will not make a difference, tend not to vote.[42] This relationship may reflect aspects of our political institutions, such as lack of competitiveness. Unit voting in the electoral college, for example, rewards all of a state's electoral votes to the winner of even a bare plurality of that state's poplar votes. Unless the presidential race is close, there is little realistic incentive to vote in state-based presidential contests where the outcomes are foregone conclusions, because slightly improving the losing candidate's showing will not affect the allocation of the electoral votes. The nature of the competition may be as important as its closeness, and several features of politics discussed earlier may inhibit voters from believing that professionalized, heavily financed, media politics will be responsive to their interests.[43] The potential electorate, for example, might quite realistically assume that politicians are more likely to be beholden to campaign contributors than to average voters. Polls, to take another example, foretell the outcome of many races with sufficient accuracy to reduce voting in many contests to mere rituals of citizen duty.

Perhaps the most interesting response of the public to the rise of media politics is the alienation registered in response to negative campaigning. Although initial claims were that negative ads worked, leading to the defeat of many candidates in early success stories of sleazy campaigns, the longer-run effect of such negative appeals is to turn off the voters, who increasingly tune out in droves. Stephen Ansolabehere and Shanto Iyengar conducted experiments that demonstrated that negative ads reduced the propensity to vote. Despite finding that negative ads were no less informative than other campaign ads and that their effectiveness in manipulating votes was checked by partisan predispositions, the researchers discovered that the intent to vote fell 5 percent in experiments where citizens were exposed to attack ads instead of more positive campaign messages. They also found that turnout was actually 4 percent lower in the 1992 Senate races where attack ads predominated. They estimate that an additional 6.4 million citizens would have voted in those elections had the tone been more positive. Maybe the public is not prevented by overt barriers, as in the Old South, but a politics flooded with "anti-political speech" may be erecting invisible obstacles to public engagement.[44] Ironically, in an

era of candidate-centered elections, the public seems to feel less connection with the candidates than ever.

This public disconnect from politics may reflect a larger trend of isolation in American society. Robert Putnam suggests that Americans are less likely to belong to and participate in organizations than in the past. This decline in organized group life, he claims, has led to a loss of "social capital," in the sense that organization represents a kind of collective social resource in much the same way that money and machinery represent economic capital and that education and skills constitute individual human capital. Putnam's thesis has been hotly disputed, and it is not at all clear that Americans are actually joining fewer organizations; perhaps their participation is merely taking different forms and is devoted to different types of organization. Still, modern advocacy groups differ from traditional membership associations in their failure to encourage genuine participation. These "mail order groups" or "associations without members" do not link citizens to the civic sphere.[45] Moreover, the decline of trade unions and the shrinking of local party organizations are notable, in that these were the two most overtly political mass organizations in America. With the precipitous drop in union membership from over one-third to barely over one-tenth of the private workforce, and with local party committees increasingly bypassed by professionalized campaigns, the organizations that traditionally played the greatest role in mobilizing the public for elections have almost disappeared from the current scene. It is especially noteworthy that these organizations are precisely the ones that in other countries, and in the past here, concentrated their efforts on involving the poor and working classes in politics.

Steven Rosenstone and John Hansen examined the mobilization efforts of parties, candidates, and movements, primarily the civil rights movement. They found that mobilization does affect the likelihood to participate, not so much by affecting people's perceptions or opinions as by overcoming some of the costs of participation, such as furnishing information, transportation, or aid with registration, and by providing social contacts that are, in essence, benefits of participating. Their study concludes that focusing on individual characteristics to explain the puzzling decline in participation since 1960 misses at least half the story. In fact, enfeebled mobilization accounts for 54 percent of the decrease in participation over the last three decades. Partisan

mobilization declined: "As campaigns abandoned the labor-intensive canvassing methods of the 1960s for the money-intensive media strategies of the 1980s, they contacted fewer and fewer Americans." Incumbency in particular undercut the intensity of competition, and extensive primaries spread campaign resources thin. Last, social movement activity dissipated. Rather than merely blaming the public for its apathy, Rosenstone and Hansen's analysis points to the significance of American institutions' and leaders' failure to mobilize voters:

> The decline of electoral mobilization from the 1960s to the 1980s, our simulation indicates, produced 8.7 percent of the 15.9 "real" decline in voter turnout over the same three decades. . . . People vote because they have the resources to bear the costs and because they have the interests and identities to appreciate the benefits. But people also turn out to vote substantially because somebody helps them or asks them to participate. The actions of parties, campaigns, and social movements mobilize public involvement in American elections. The "blame" for declining voter turnout, accordingly, rests as much on political leaders as on citizens themselves.[46]

The net effect of falling participation has been to create a "hole" in the American electorate. With both parties aiming their appeals at more affluent voters, and with the Democrats adopting a strategy that attempts to match the Republicans' lead in the "air wars and arms race in data," the net effect has been, according to Robert Dreyfuss, to transform GOTV (get out the vote) efforts into an SOTV (stamp out the vote) demobilization.[47] Rather than push potential voters out of the political arena, as in the Old South, modern American political institutions, and especially our contemporary parties, simply fail to pull them into the civic realm.

Moreover, the decline in turnout accelerates as one proceeds down the socioeconomic scale. Thus, the missing voters create an "ideological and partisan skew in the electorate." In 1996, for example, a poll of likely voters found that Clinton led Dole by 9 percent, but among registered but likely nonvoters, his lead was a whopping 37 percent. The likely voters also split evenly among Republican and Democratic congressional candidates, but the likely nonvoters favored Democrats by 18 percent.[48] The missing voters, moreover, reflect both feelings of political inefficacy on the part of individual

voters and unresponsiveness on the part of political institutions, especially parties. In a vicious circle, parties and politicians have recognized that upscale voters are the ones that count, because they are more likely to cast votes; accordingly, they have skewed platforms and public policy toward the upper ends of the social scale.[49] Likewise, feeling powerless to affect the direction of American society, the disenfranchised have been plagued by a pathology of powerlessness. In the absence of institutions to mobilize the politically inefficacious, nonvoters have scaled back their demands and expectations and decided that there is nothing much at stake for them in the increasingly vacuous politics of middle- and upper-class consensus, creating a self-fulfilling prophecy.[50] The result is, paradoxically, a politics open to all but one in which the socially disadvantaged feel as out of place as they would in an upscale country club, leaving politics today, as in the old Solid South, increasingly the private preserve of the well-off.

Politely Winking at Racism

The third leg of the Solid South was a racist political system designed to maintain white supremacy. The rest of the nation has never adopted the South's overt racism, and the peculiar Southern Jim Crow system was soundly defeated by the civil rights movement and by the corresponding revolution in respectability in Southern politics. Since the 1960s, there has nonetheless been a trend in national politics toward more racialized appeals that has had the effect, whether intended or not, of perpetuating white privilege and blocking progress for African Americans and other minorities.

It would be naive to suggest that American politics has ever been without racial overtones. Even during the heyday of the New Deal, the price of political support from the Solid South wing of the Democratic party was a kind of color-blindness to policies that helped all the poor, but generally the white poor more. With the expansion and availability of urban black votes in the wake of the depression, the national Democrats felt increasing pressure to respond to African American needs. Beginning with Harry Truman and continuing under Adlai Stevenson and John Kennedy, the national party led by Demo-

cratic presidents and aspirants tried to balance black demands for progress with white Southerners' vested interests in the status quo. It was up to Lyndon Johnson, however, to decisively cut the knot in favor of programs explicitly designed to aid minorities and the poor. Although clearly the right thing to do from moral and policy perspectives, the political fallout of the Great Society was to open a crack in the traditional Democratic coalition that contained both Southern white segregationists and Northern African Americans.[51]

The Republicans were not slow in exploiting the opened rift. Beginning with Barry Goldwater's vote against the 1964 Civil Rights Act, the conservative wing of the party determined to go hunting "where the ducks were." Nixon launched the Southern strategy in 1968, a move reflected in the rightward tilt of his civil rights policies in his first administration. *The Emerging Republican Majority* by Kevin Phillips provided the duck-hunting manual. Phillips advised Republicans to seek out conservative votes, ignoring the votes of liberals and newly enfranchised African Americans. Although Republicans should appear more "moderate" than Goldwater, the identification of the Democratic party with African Americans would result in "political apartheid" as disaffected whites deserted to the Republicans. Phillips foresaw that this white backlash was not limited to the South. Finally, he advised Republicans to encourage rather than resist voting rights legislation, recognizing that gains in black votes would be more than offset by the countermobilization of white voters.[52] As Chandler Davidson suggests, "*The Emerging Republican Majority* was, in brief, a handbook for Republicans on how to capitalize on—and how to encourage—racial polarization along party lines without appearing to be racists 'in the Deep South vein.' "[53] Although interrupted by Watergate and the more moderate and "Northern" Gerald Ford, the Southern strategy, without the moniker, returned with a vengeance with Ronald Reagan.

The secret to the demolition of the New Deal coalition was not overt race baiting but rather so-called wedge issues. As Thomas Byrne Edsall and Mary Edsall argue, the Republicans have used voter resentment over "race, rights, and taxes" to divide the Democrats and win over key constituencies. Particularly critical has been the desertion of two groups of so-called Reagan Democrats—largely Northern, urban, ethnic, working-class whites and Southern whites, especially males.

Although some of the Republican appeal is undoubtedly economic, the most effective wedge issues have been social and cultural issues that involve a moral dimension and rarely are overtly racial. For example, abortion seems to involve religious beliefs to a far greater degree than racial attitudes. School prayer appears to be another moral issue devoid of racial overtones. Many of these issues, however, such as drugs, crime, gun control, welfare, sexual promiscuity, and immigration, relate to a generalized sense of social breakdown that in turn is rooted in a commitment to a society firmly anchored in racial and gender hierarchies.[54] And when linked to widespread racial stereotypes of African Americans as less moral, diligent, and disciplined than whites, these issues take on a more sinister racial hue.[55]

Arguably, the rise of the culture wars (announced by Pat Buchanan in his keynote address to the 1992 Republican convention) has more to do with the success of right-wing ideology than with racism. Conservative ideology, with its emphasis on individualism and a reduced role for government, as well as the high value placed on stability, would naturally lead adherents to favor the social status quo, including the current hierarchy of racially distributed privileges and deprivations, and to oppose government-sponsored programs designed to equalize social hierarchies. The Edsalls discovered a populist or conservative egalitarianism that favors equal opportunity in principle while opposing all realistic remedies for existing inequalities. Likewise, Newt Gingrich's Conservative Opportunity Society and the Contract with America touted opportunity and blamed government for interfering with Americans' freedom to exploit the nation's ripe opportunities for social mobility, but they deplored government efforts to build platforms that could provide a floor for equalizing opportunity for all. All these views are consistent with the larger worldview of conservatism that sees government as the source of, not the solution to, most social problems and urges individual efforts to overcome any distinctions and disadvantages remaining in today's society.[56]

Conversely, there is a clear racial coating that adheres to many conservative appeals. "Welfare mess" and "crime" and "drugs" are often little more than code words—in essence, rhetorical winks—that hint in unspoken ways that race is the root of the problem. Martin Gilens has argued that attitudes toward welfare reform are racially coded. The

backlash against affirmative action reflects white male resentment of having to compete with minorities and women on a more level playing field, as well as a sense of violation of the traditionally individualistic rules of advancement by "merit." James Glaser contends that the term "liberal" has come to mean "pro-black," helping to explain why, by the late 1980s, it had become the dreaded "L-word."[57] Even something as seemingly nonracial as school prayer can disguise a concern for a perceived breakdown of discipline in public schools ordered by courts to desegregate. Indeed, the mobilization of the religious right can be dated from the reaction of fundamentalist churches to an Internal Revenue Service ruling denying tax exemption for private religious schools that practiced racial discrimination.[58]

Politically, what is profoundly significant is that racism, though less pervasive on the left, plays havoc with the liberal coalition much more so than with conservative politics. Recent research by Paul Sniderman and Edward Carmines found a slight correlation between political conservatism and racial prejudice, and "racial prejudice is more common on the political right." Still, the authors conclude that prejudice is "very far from a dominating factor in contemporary politics of race" and that the "new politics of race" has strained liberalism and the Democratic coalition for two decades. Although only about one out of four liberals, as opposed to one out of three conservatives, exhibits great prejudice against African Americans, the political import of their prejudice differs markedly.

> In terms of general principles conservatives start out on the right and wind up on the right on racial issues, regardless of how they feel toward blacks. By contrast, liberals start out on the left, but where they wind up on racial issues depends very much on how they feel toward blacks. . . . If they are racially prejudiced, they break ranks and go over to the right. . . . In short, on issues of race, the right tends to hold together; the left tends to splinter apart.[59]

Increasingly, racial issues play the same role in American politics today that they once did in traditional Southern politics. Conservatives, by raising the specter of race, divide the potential majority of ordinary citizens along racial lines, making a class coalition, and indeed majority rule, untenable. As Robert Huckfeldt and Carol Kohfeld describe the current situation, "race serves as the wedge that

fractures the lower class Democratic coalition and is thus responsible for increased levels of volatility in electoral politics."[60]

There is a profound irony here: this rise of racial politics has occurred during a period when polls document measurable and significant progress in terms of individual racial attitudes. Of course, some of that individual racial liberalization may be nothing more than hypocrisy, or at least a hesitancy to advance racist answers that are no longer accepted as "polite." In a deeper sense, however, the problem stems not from individual racism at all but rather from a set of institutions, and leadership, willing to mobilize racism in the pursuit of political advantage.[61] Michael Omi and Howard Winant maintain that, in effect, the racial components of political issues have been socially, or politically, constructed.[62] The net effect of such racial reconstructions of politics has been to divert white, especially lower- and working-class white, attention from the economic dimension of issues and to racialize public policies in ways that frustrate minorities' progress toward full equality in American life.[63]

Until the mid-1960s, the two major parties were relatively alike on backing civil rights, and voting patterns among blacks and whites reflected this lack of profound partisan racial differences. With the advent of the Southern strategy, however, the conservative wing of the Republican party succeeded in putting race on the agenda in ways that split the Democrats and attracted many former Democratic voters on the basis of barely covert racial appeals, while driving away minority voters. The Democrats floundered, unable to devise a successful counterstrategy. To a great extent, the "New Democratic" strategy originated by the Democratic Leadership Council and successfully practiced by the Clinton administration is more a capitulation than a counterstrategy. It answers the Republicans with a weak "we too" position and leaves racial politics and racialized policies, most notably welfare "reform," unchallenged.

In the long run, such racialized politics augurs poorly for the Democrats and for their class-based constituencies. As Huckfeldt and Kohfeld demonstrate, race has to a large extent replaced class as the great divide of American electoral politics. The lower middle and working classes have been tempted on the basis of racial solidarity to forgo class solidarity with the poor and to cast their lot with the upper middle classes and the wealthy. In doing so, they have had to settle for

crumbs "trickling down" from the upper-crust table as public policy was redirected to the right in the 1980s and beyond. The result, in contemporary America as in the Old South, has been to shore up economic hierarchy even as racial hierarchy is maintained. As Huckfeldt and Kohfeld conclude, "this racial structuring of politics is fundamentally at odds with democratic politics, and it bodes poorly for the future of democracy in America."[64]

The Semi-Southern People

At first blush, it seems a far stretch to compare politics in contemporary America to politics in the Solid South during the first half of this century. On the face of things, so much seems to have changed since Dixie was led by demagogues in a political system that made a mockery of democracy. True, many current leaders of both parties hail from the South, but Newt Gingrich and Bill Clinton seem a far cry from the likes of Gene Talmadge and "Cotton Ed" Smith (a demagogic senator from South Carolina). The one-party system has vanished even in the heart of Dixie, replaced by a party system that is more competitive regionally and nationally than any in decades. Specifically Southern barriers to voting fell with the Voting Rights Act of 1965; the extension of this act to other parts of the nation, a constitutional amendment lowering the voting age, and the passage of the Motor Voter Act have further removed legal obstacles. And today, the raw race baiting of Solid South politics would be intolerable in any section of the nation.

In fact, at one level, it is impossible not to agree with Alexander Lamis's reflections on the findings of his team of political scientists and journalists who researched Southern politics in the 1990s. He concludes this encyclopedic and authoritative study by noting how far the South has traveled on the road of self-transformation:

> Fifty years later, no one can deny that Key's hope for a "brawling, fighting, arguing, contentious" democratic South has been realized in the current, competitive two-party system firmly in place throughout Dixie in the 1990s, a system that does provide the "means for the organization and expression of competing viewpoints on public policy" and that can—given intelligent and imaginative leaders—cope with the South's problems.[65]

At a deeper level, however, Key looked beneath the brawling, fighting, arguing, and contending of electoral politics to ask "who governs and in whose interests the government is run."[66] Beneath the surface of noisy party competition for the votes of almost all adults without blatant racist appeals, similarities persist that may portend festering problems not unlike the infirmities of the Solid South not only for contemporary Southern politics but also for national democracy.

The rise of the South's influence in national politics has contributed to, but not caused, the evolving structural deformities that weaken our contemporary democracy. Instead, the factors involved are multitudinous and their paths of causation complex.[67] Moreover, the resulting structural defects are not the same as in the Solid South, but they are similar. Although the two major parties closely contest most elections, the nature of that partisan competition has been undermined by the rise of the M^3 system. Massive amounts of money from private contributors, professional management of technocratic campaigns, and a mass media that entertains audiences but does not inform citizens threaten to sever the democratic moorings of political institutions in the popular electorate. Despite the absence of legal barriers, the levels of popular participation in American politics, already low in comparison with other democracies, have continued to decline since 1960, reflecting the unattractiveness of political participation for large segments of the public. Finally, although overtly racist appeals are rare, racially coded wedge themes have polarized the electorate, splitting the New Deal coalition and halting much of the progress toward racial equality. The resulting competition among governing elites reinforces an emerging political economy stacked in favor of the interests of elites.

Arguably, American political parties are stronger than ever. In some aspects, they even approach the model of responsible parties that V. O. Key used as his implicit standard for condemning one-party politics in the South. Republicans and, to a lesser but real extent, Democrats as well have strengthened their national organizations as they have become more competent, professional, open, and centralized. Party leadership, especially in the House, is stronger after the Republican Revolution of 1994, more programmatic and more capable of discipline, although the excesses of the Gingrich leadership eroded some of the centralization erected in those initial innovations. The parties

offer distinct and relatively coherent packages of policies, and they compete vigorously and closely. Party labels better match ideological affinities since most conservative Southerners have exited the more liberal Democratic party and allied with the more ideologically compatible Republicans.

Other elements of the responsible party model, however, are notably absent.[68] Most obviously, close competition has resulted in divided control of government, making it virtually impossible for the public to pin responsibility for government on any one set of leaders. What was once an anomaly, split party control of the presidency and Congress, has now become the norm. Whereas divided control occurred for only eight years between 1886 and 1954, since 1968, the same party has controlled the presidency and both houses of Congress for only six years.[69] Split control has also permeated state governments. The percentage of states with unified party control of the governorship and legislature declined from 85 percent in 1947 to 40 percent in 1993. Without unified party control, the policy-making process often suffers the paralysis of gridlock, and the public cannot readily discern whose policies to blame or praise for governmental failures or successes. Without being able to punish or reward leaders with votes, the political system lacks accountability.[70]

Moreover, the current competition between the parties is inadequate both in substance and in style to qualify as the healthy competition necessary for a responsible party system. Today's parties often ignore matters of greatest concern to ordinary Americans; for example, the failure of either party to protect popular majorities from the ravages of economic changes in the transition to globalization and the information economy has reinforced the demobilization of the electorate.[71] When issues are addressed, the parties' stances may not offer the public what it wants. For example, E. J. Dionne has argued that "why Americans hate politics" is because liberals have demeaned most Americans' values while conservatives have short-changed their interests, leaving voters with only "false choices."[72] Not only is the content of current competition lacking, but the manner in which the parties compete today is pathological. Benjamin Ginsberg and Martin Shefter note that elite competition by means of RIP (revelation, investigation, and prosecution) has resulted in more intense political struggles at the top while leaving the mass public only marginally involved.

"During the political struggles of the past decades, politicians sought to undermine the institution associated with their foes, disgrace one another on national television, force their competitors to resign from office, and, in a number of cases, send their opponents to prison. Remarkably, one tactic that has not been so widely used is the mobilization of the electorate."[73] Besides this politics of "collision," Burnham points out that the deadlock of divided government requires periodic "transpolitical" deals to solve problems, such as Social Security financing or the savings and loan bailout. Such a politics of "collision and collusion" cannot competently resolve public problems, and, in a self-fulfilling prophecy, it produces mass disillusionment with politics itself.[74]

Unlike in the old Solid South, significant numbers of potential voters are not pushed out of politics by steep barriers to participation, but neither are citizens today pulled into the fray of public affairs. The ever-shrinking electorate feels disconnected to its leaders and their parties, trapped in a political system that is not user-friendly.[75] Political leadership appears to be floating in air, unrooted in a public that seems remote from all political appeals. The major parties are becoming "parties of officeholders," with little organic connection to the public.[76] A recent poll found that only 23 percent of Americans agreed that "the two-party system works fairly well."[77] Meanwhile, the public acts less and less like a public at all. There is a literal as well as figurative decline of "public spaces," where significant discussion and debate of common issues could occur. Although public attention has focused on the distance between society and a so-called underclass of urban ghetto poor, the "evacuation of the public realm" also leaves Americans of the middle classes increasingly isolated.[78] In what former secretary of labor Robert Reich has termed "the secession of the successful," increasing numbers of the well-off are turning to privatized services and living in the social apartheid of gated communities.[79] It might not be too much of a stretch to suggest that we are approaching a "democracy without citizens."[80]

Without resorting to blatant racism, the Republicans have found a winning formula in the "rancid populism"[81] of the Southern strategy. Coded cultural rhetoric has broken the bonds of loyalty of many former Democrats, although the GOP has not consolidated the allegiances of the newly free-floating voters. Meanwhile, the insipid "New Demo-

cratic" strategy of party moderates has merely stemmed the hemorrhaging to the Republicans. It has failed miserably to rebuild the traditional party base. Neoliberalism seems unlikely to succeed in forming a new, more business-based Democratic constituency as long as business remains enamored with the market-oriented Republicans, and the corporatism of the neoliberals continues to repel the party's traditional constituencies among labor, civil rights, and women's groups.

Instead of a responsible party system that Key dreamed of, William Mayer suggests that we have fashioned a "semi-responsible" party system. In this model, the parties are more ideologically distinct but less accountable to voters for their actions.[82] Instead of producing the benefits of a responsible party model, this semiresponsible party system yields, in some ways, the worst of both worlds: fiercer and nastier political competition, but political infighting based on less and less connection to the citizens and the public interest.

Declining Democracy

We are entering a "post-electoral era" in which parties in the electorate are decaying and being replaced by politician-centered parties in elections.[83] Critical decisions will still have to be made on the major issues facing the country, even if government seems removed from daily life and most citizens have tuned out Washington. For example, the economic restructuring in response to the globalization of the economy presents the nation with choices about the fundamental direction of economic policy. These choices have profound implications for our democracy because they will affect not just who bears the burdens and reaps the benefits of economic restructuring but also who will get to decide such important political questions.[84] While parties and other organizations linking the public to political decision makers have atrophied, elites have become more active in the shaping of public policy, as indicated by the tripling of lobbyists in Washington from 4,000 in 1977 to more than 14,500 in 1991.[85]

As our examination of traditional Southern politics showed, without strong electoral institutions to connect political decisions to the masses of voters, politics will tend to lack the coherence, continuity, and accountability that can make political decisions responsible, and

responsive, to the public. We are far from the severity of the political malformations of that old-time Solid South, but the trends of parties displaced by money, marketing, and media, a shrinking electorate, and a racialized politics threatens the long-term viability of American democracy. The undermining of democratic politics occurs at a critical juncture, when many social and economic problems need the attention of American government in ways that are responsive to the desires and interests of the American public. Purely economic institutions such as corporations and private social organizations such as charities cannot solve the problems facing the country on a sufficient scale or in a democratic manner that protects the interests of all our citizens. Because of the disarray of our electoral structures, it remains an open question whether our political institutions can address these problems in a way that will solve them democratically. As in the Solid South of old, today in the United States, politics is our number one problem.

7 / Southern Symptoms:

The Haunting Specter of V. O. Key

The Southern Side of Democracy

A striking irony characterized American politics in the late twentieth century. With the collapse of communism and heartening movements for democratization around the world, democracy seemed universally triumphant. Yet Americans seemed less content with their democracy at home than ever before. Once smug and a bit complacent about their own institutions, Americans viewed the dominant threats to their security as originating abroad. Now that America's leadership in the world seemed secure, Americans' fear of disintegration was lodged closer to home, in their own government, indeed, in their own neighborhoods.[1]

American democracy has often held itself out as a model for the rest of the world to emulate. Until recently, however, Southern politics often exhibited traits associated in American minds with third-world politics. Someone even suggested that South America begins at the Mason-Dixon line. The South that V. O. Key observed was in many respects a sort of "underdeveloped" country, exhibiting numerous traits that seemed outlandishly out of place in an "advanced" democracy. Key even explicitly compared the situation of the black-belt planter elites with that of colonizers who could not tolerate the development of democracy if they wished to maintain their privileged position and their exploitation of the indigenous majority.[2] Recent decades have seen the South rejoin the nation, economically as well as politically. Not only do Southern living standards and lifestyles approximate the rest of the country's, but also the distinctive, "colorful" politics of the traditional South has all but disappeared. Southerners, both natives and newcomers, can join in a shared sense of relief that the backward poli-

tics and clownish characters that once both bemused and appalled the nation, as well as many enlightened Southerners, mercifully seem to have been vanquished into the mists of distant memories.

Yet the nation that the South has at last rejoined politically as well as constitutionally is suffering from a crisis of confidence in its public institutions. Today there are growing fears that all is not well in the heartland of democracy. There are telltale signs of political decay that, unless corrective steps are taken, augur ill for the future of American democracy. To suggest to Americans, who have been accustomed to thinking of the nation as the world's greatest democracy, that our public life is developing the symptoms of some "Southern disease" rather than evolving toward a "more perfect union" assaults our sense of progress and faith in the future. Nevertheless, the portents of trouble seem strangely reminiscent of the traits of traditional Southern politics in their irrationality and lack of substantive democracy.

In chapter 6 we saw that although there are salient differences, like Southern politics of old, current American electoral institutions also exhibit tendencies toward less healthy partisanship, dramatically declining participation, and racialized issues that could undermine the democratic nature of our politics. To the extent that current American politics exhibits structural similarities to the Solid South, we should expect to see the same sorts of symptoms that so troubled the South during the first half of the twentieth century. V. O. Key argued that because Southern politics lacked strong, responsive parties, was based on a narrow electorate, and was designed to perpetuate white supremacy, Southern electoral institutions lacked the coherence, continuity, and accountability that could make Southern politics rational and democratic. Specifically, the maladies of the Solid South included elections that ignored or blurred issues; weak, elitist, and even demagogic leaders; a proclivity to avoid problems and coast along with the status quo; rampant corruption and policy making by deals; voters who were confused and apathetic; an appallingly narrow electoral base, including low turnout among even those lucky enough to be enfranchised; a resulting tilt toward the elites, while the have-not majority got taken for a ride; and a tendency to centralize decision making in the federal system in the face of Southern state default. But do the weaknesses and trends in contemporary American politics produce symptoms today similar to the deformities attributed by Key to the politics of the old Solid South?

The Sound and Fury of Issueless Politics

A chronic complaint against the old one-party Solid South system was its failure, despite a plethora of office-seeking candidates, to present the voters with alternatives on issues. Today's closely competitive parties should afford voters choices on alternative public policies and thus governmental accountability, but this expectation hinges on the quality as well as the degree of competition. Our elections have become increasingly fractious, contentious, noisy, even nasty, but that has not guaranteed sensible debate on issues of moment to the public. Detached politician-centered parties competing for a diminished electorate in racialized politics fail to present meaningful choices on public policy to the electorate.[3]

One problem undermining serious consideration of issues is simply the lack of information on policy stands by parties and candidates. Although studies find that platforms do matter and that the planks on issues do indicate the policies likely to be enacted if that party is victorious,[4] there is not much evidence that policy stances get through to the voters in a candidate-centered politics in which parties no longer offer a simple and reliable guide to voters' choices. In an electoral system in which most voters receive their news from television and most coverage centers on the horse-race aspects of elections, the public's information on issues is fairly sparse. The thin issue content of contemporary presidential contests was neatly captured by a campaign incident when third-party candidate Barry Commoner ran for president in 1980. Reflecting the media's obsession with strategy and winning, a reporter asked Commoner: "Are you running on the issues, or are you a serious candidate?" With media attention diverted, parties have taken advantage of the lapse to curtail the length and specificity of platforms that could potentially be millstones in a politics of image over substance.

Republican "Lite"

Without programmatic parties to hold leaders accountable for policies, professionally managed media politics offers prime opportunities to blur issues. Democrat Bill Clinton drew from Republican reservoirs to recruit professionals such as Dick Morris and David Gergen to help sell

the "New Democrat" image. Morris's post-1994 strategy of triangulation called for Clinton to position himself in the center between congressional Democrats and Republicans.[5] This shift to the right worked so well that in the 1996 presidential campaign, Republican nominee Bob Dole complained with some justification that President Clinton was stealing all his issues, leading Dole to charge that the "Commander in Thief" was committing political larceny.[6] Indeed, the New Democrat strategy of centrist politics really amounts to a deliberate blurring of the differences between the two parties as a means of winning elections. The result of the successful implementation of this strategy by President Clinton produced the first Democratic president to win reelection to a second full term since Franklin Roosevelt, but the cost has been high in terms of yielding ground on distinctly Democratic approaches to public policy. Newt Gingrich reportedly complained that Clinton was the "best Republican candidate that Democrats ever nominated."[7] Examples of Clinton's "Republicanism" are legion. Clinton's second administration witnessed significant concessions to Republican positions on deficit reduction in the balanced budget agreement of 1997, reforms to rein in the Internal Revenue Service, fast-track approval for trade treaties, most-favored-nation status for China (which candidate Clinton had opposed), and refusal to sign the anti–land mine treaty. These moves merely followed the administration's pattern during its first term of conceding much to Republican positions on significant social issues: the scaling back on admitting gays into the military to accept a "don't ask, don't tell" policy; the sponsoring of the Omnibus Anti-Crime Act of 1993, with its significantly conservative provisions; the "mend it, don't end it" approach to affirmative action; and the centrist, technocratic approach to health care reform, which was followed by even more incremental and conservative approaches after the failure of this major initiative during Clinton's first term. Clinton passed the North American Free Trade Agreement (NAFTA) in cooperation with the Republican Congress over the objections of minority Democrats. NAFTA, in fact, had serious costs to the Clinton administration in terms of building a reliable Democratic coalition to pass other presidential proposals, such as health care reforms.[8]

The abandonment of traditional Democratic approaches led a frustrated liberal Democratic Representative Barney Frank to quip that he had sent a letter addressed to "Democratic President in the White

House" but that it had been returned marked "Addressee Unknown."[9] Although the Democratic stances were not as hard-line conservative as the Republican positions, Democrats tended to follow the Republican lead in basic policy directions, merely moderating the pace and purity of the GOP's approach. Wilson Carey McWilliams characterizes Clinton's as a "third way" presidency, noting that the president poached on the Republicans' more ideological turf on abstract themes such as a balanced budget, smaller government, devolution to the states, and welfare reform, while sticking to "operational liberal" programs such as Social Security, education, and the environment. Although defending abortion rights, Clinton conceded significant ground on social issues, too, such as gay marriage, school prayer, and even school uniforms. Historian Bruce Schulman argues that Clinton's historic role has been to domesticate and, in the process, enact Gingrich-style Republicanism, in effect, consolidating the Reagan Revolution of the 1980s. Although Clinton's "amalgam of bold words and small gestures" helped earn him the nickname Slick Willie, the trend toward a vague centrism with ill-defined party differences is certainly not limited to Bill Clinton's political persona, as exemplified by German chancellor Gerhardt Schoeder and British prime minister Tony Blair (nicknamed Tony Blur by critics), both admirers of Clinton's style.[10] Nonetheless, it is noteworthy that the two Democrats who provided the major impetus driving the formerly liberal party to the center were Clinton and Carter, both Southerners. Their respective governorships of Southern, one-party-tilted states foreshadowed the courses of their presidencies, and both politicians brought to the White House personal experience operating in candidate-centered, weak-party, interest-group-dominated environments. With the 2000 presidential race touted as a contest between the "pragmatic idealism" of Al Gore and the "compassionate conservatism" of George W. Bush, Jr., with neither slogan firmly attached to any concrete policies, Southern-style issue avoidance appears to have become a permanent feature of our national political landscape.

The clearest example of Clinton's move to co-opt Republican policy positions, however, was his capitulation on welfare reform. The Personal Responsibility Act of 1996 was severely criticized by traditionally Democratic constituencies as overly harsh on the poor, especially children, and occasioned several resignations by political

appointees in the administration.[11] Welfare reform illustrates the importance in contemporary politics of valence issues, emotionally charged issues that elicit affirmation of "commonsense" hegemonic beliefs or prejudices. Rather than evoking genuinely different approaches to solving such problems, much of the competition is designed to position the party or candidate symbolically as most solidly on the side of the issue favored by the dominant consensus. The resulting herd mentality stampedes politicians of all stripes into ignoring the complex realities and intractable trade-offs, and the expensive support measures, that transforming a welfare system into a workfare system would truly entail. Instead, the temptation is to pile on, to pander to pervasive myths and racist stereotypes of welfare queens, and to posture in order to appear "tough" on welfare cheats or "hard" on crime and drugs.[12] One typical consequence of emphasizing valence issues is the resort to symbolic solutions. Symbolic politics aims not to solve problems so much as to reassure the public that something is being done about their concerns, thus rendering citizens quiescent. While the masses are fed symbols, elites are freed to reap the more tangible rewards of politics.[13] The Republican mantra of "God, guns, and gays," for example, has kept the public's attention diverted from tax and spending cuts slanted in favor of the rich that have effected a massive redistribution of wealth to the upper classes. As Christopher Hitchens recently observed, "the essence of American politics is the manipulation of populism by elitism."[14]

A secondary effect of the preeminence of valence issues is the encouragement of extreme stances that may be emotionally satisfying but unrealistic. Sound-bite politics clearly works against complicated solutions to complex problems.[15] Parties have traditionally moderated their programs and restrained their candidates in order to broaden their appeal; the decline of parties goes far to explain the rise of extremists, exemplified by the Gingrich clique of right-wing Republicans in Congress. The related issues of crime and drugs illustrate how extremism can drive out realism in policy making. The war on drugs has filled the nation's jails, while mandatory sentences have boosted prison construction as a major growth industry and clogged the federal courts with drug prosecutions. Astronomical disparities in penalties between powder and crack cocaine offenses have fallen hardest on African Americans and minorities. The U.S. Bureau of Justice

Statistics now estimates that over one in four African American males will enter the penal system in their lifetimes.[16] Even the Old South's notorious chain gangs did not rival such a pervasive system of coercion in the maintenance of a racial hierarchy.

None of this is to say that no differences exist between the parties, and certainly even shallow, insubstantial two-party competition is vastly superior to the one-partyism of the Old South.[17] If the competing parties fail to present the voters with viable choices on the significant issues of the day, however, in a very real sense, democracy has been diminished. Two-partyism in these circumstances takes on more the appearance than the reality of democracy. When Tweedledee and Tweedledum (or tweedledummer) parties compete without offering meaningful choices to the voters, we do not need a third party so much as we need a second party (as populist radio personality Jim Hightower opined).

Personality Politics in the Postpartisan Era

Although traditionally the South's politicians attained an embarrassing notoriety, Key laid the blame squarely on the Solid South's political institutions rather than on pathological personalities or political culture. As the nation has drifted toward weaker parties, a diminished electorate, and a racialized politics, the quality of its political leadership has suffered a corresponding degeneration.

A politics focused not on the issues but on the personality of politicians is the most obvious symptom of the shifting nature of leadership. Generally, the Republicans—who, like elites everywhere, manage to be more discreet about their indiscretions—have dwelt most vocally on the so-called character issue. The Democrats, however, have often felt too hard-pressed to grapple with the issues and at times have sought to transform elections into popular referendums on leadership qualities. For example, Dukakis, watching his early lead evaporate, tried to make 1988 a referendum on "competence, not ideology." And antipathy to Newt Gingrich's "radical" leadership in the House proved to be the Democrat's most potent electoral elixir in 1996. Institutional developments reinforce the preponderance of personality politics. Bruce Miroff has contended that in modern American politics, the

president monopolizes public space. Rather than rational discourse about issues, the public spectacle of the present-day presidency is a drama watched passively by the public. With active citizens reduced to mere spectators, we can vicariously participate in politics by cheering or hissing, but there is little of genuine debate and decision on policy for the citizenry to observe, much less participate in.[18]

Of course, the nature of modern campaigning in the M³ system of money, marketing, and media has boosted this tendency to substitute the appearance of character for the substance of issues. Candidates, after all, are much more susceptible to visual presentation than are complex issues. The post-Watergate media ethics that allowed for more reporting of personal peccadilloes has also, ironically, diverted press and public attention from issues and processes to people in politics.[19] The 1990s tendency for the more respectable mainstream media to be willing to follow the lead of the tabloids in ferreting out scandal, or the scent of scandal, has furthered this trend.

Not surprisingly, just as in the Old South, in formless politics with no well-defined issues and a gaggle of candidates, name recognition proves to be a decisive electoral resource. This recognition may be achieved a number of ways, most frequently by saturating the airways with expensive advertisements for the candidate. This method, of course, puts a premium on money to pay for ads. Incumbents, who already enjoy an advantage in name recognition, have a decisive edge when it comes to raising funds, largely because donors wish to favor likely winners and understand that the game is stacked in favor of current officeholders. In the 1998 elections, House incumbents in almost two-thirds of the contested elections held fund-raising advantages of at least ten to one over opponents. To maintain such odds, politicians have to engage in the incessant pursuit of donors. Even presidents are not exempt from the chase, being forced to spend major portions of their time fund-raising. In pre–election day 1996, President Clinton attended 237 fund-raisers to garner $120 million for Democratic electoral coffers.[20]

Such "full-throttle fund-raising" not only diverts leaders' time from governmental duties but also makes leaders dependent on big donors. Wealthy candidates who bankroll their own campaigns might appear to be an exception to the problem that "who pays the piper calls the tune," but the price in terms of the segment of the public able to run

for office is astronomical. Nonetheless, increasing numbers of the rich have used their own money to seek, and often to win, office. In a politics where name recognition is the key to being taken seriously, Ross Perot and Steve Forbes can use their millions to launch serious runs for the presidency, and seats in Congress and governorships are increasingly contested by such "mediagenic millionaires" as Jay Rockefeller, Guy Millner, and Michael Huffington.[21]

High-visibility occupations can serve as a surrogate for campaign spending in propelling a candidate's name before the public. The nation's leadership posts are held with increasing frequency by those whose previous careers exposed them to the media limelight. The transformation of Jesse "The Body" Ventura, pro wrestler, to Jesse "The Mind" Ventura, governor of Minnesota, is just one of the latest and most striking examples. Others include astronauts (John Glenn), war heroes (John McCain, Bob Kerrey, John Kerry), professional athletes (Jack Kemp, J. W. Watt, Steve Largent, Bill Bradley), entertainers (the late Sonny Bono), actors (Fred Thompson, Ben Jones of *Dukes of Hazard* fame, Fred Gandy of *Loveboat*, not to mention Ronald Reagan), and media careers (Jesse Helms, a former TV announcer, as hard as that is to believe).[22] Of course, these candidates are aided by experience handling publicity and the media. The example of actor Ronald Reagan immediately leaps to mind, but in the 2000 election, the trend reached absurd heights as talk-show host Jerry Springer contemplated a run for the U.S. Senate and Hollywood "hunk" Warren Beatty made serious noises about a race for the White House. Although less prominent at the national than at the state and local level, political families provide instant name recognition also. The Kennedys (Ted, Patrick, Joseph, Jr., and Kathleen Townsend), the Bushes (George Herbert Walker, Sr., George W., Jr., and Jeb), the Doles (Bob and Elizabeth), and the Rockefellers (Jay and Nelson) provide examples of family names that are real assets in attaining visibility in chaotic politics. In fact, among the House members of the 106th Congress were Udall cousins Mark and Tom, the sons of Udall bothers Morris and Stewart, who both served in the House.[23] The apogee of familial politics may have been reached in 1998 when the sons of Hubert Humphrey, Walter Mondale, and Orville Freeman contested the Democratic nomination for Minnesota governor in a primary dubbed the "My Three Sons" race.[24] The 2000 presidential election pitted Al Gore, son of a longtime

Tennessee senator, against George W. Bush, Jr., son of the ex-president, who is himself the son of a U.S. senator. This presidential contest might seem to be an extreme example, but in fact, every Republican presidential ticket since 1976 has included either a Bush or a Dole (a line that can be stretched back to 1948, excepting the insurgent Goldwater ticket of 1964, if Nixon's name is included).

Not that candidate character and charisma are unimportant. But when personality carries such weight, almost displacing stances on policies, how can voter choice represent self-governance in any meaningful manner? The ultimate danger, of course, as Key understood all too well, is that all the attention to personality actually elevates the worst types of personalities to political leadership. Demagogic political leadership is the natural corollary of extremism on the issues. In electoral contests in which there are no real issues or differences among candidates on the issues are blurred by copycatting and symbolic affirmations of the obvious, name recognition is the name of the game. Extreme personalities, whether buffoons or more sinister demagogues, stand out in the crowd of candidates. The imminent temptation to demagoguery is thus overwhelming without the longer-term restraining influences of political institutions such as parties. Modern-day demagogues may not bear much immediate resemblance to their brethren of old, because the "hot" stump style of yore has been largely displaced by the influence of that "cool" medium, television. The yawning gulf between words and deeds so characteristic of contemporary political leadership, however, betokens a separation of style and substance not unlike the fist-pounding pseudopopulists that so often deceived Southern electorates.

The rise of Newt Gingrich to national prominence brought the threat of demagogic leadership to public consciousness in the 1990s, but numerous other congressional representatives fit the bill as well. Perennial presidential candidate Patrick Buchanan should also give pause to those who smugly think that "it can't happen here."[25] Buchanan's 1992 "culture wars" challenge to Bush helped topple a sitting president. In 1996, Buchanan rode the issue of downsizing in a serious bid for the Republican nomination, despite the seeming left-wing slant of the issue and his reputation situating him on the far right of the American political spectrum. Although the "cool" television styles of Ronald Reagan and Bill Clinton certainly did not fit the mold

of old-time "hot" extremists, the divergence between image and substance of these two "Teflon" presidents suggests a type of demagoguery tailored for the age of TV, a sort of "what you see is what you don't get" style of leadership for a virtual politics in the (non)information era.

Dogs That Sleep, Don't Bark

According to Key, a politics of vacuous issues and fatuous leadership reinforced a propensity to inertia, a tendency to let sleeping dogs lie rather than anticipating and addressing challenges frontally. In such circumstances, the status quo, for good or ill, enjoys a great advantage, and problems get solved, if at all, obliquely by tiny incremental steps. Changes or novel approaches die by default, as decisions get made without alternatives being raised. Peter Bachrach and Morton Baratz coined the term "non-decisions" to describe this process of making a decision by, in effect, never raising the issue. Nondecisions result in a false consensus, as big issues that might challenge dominant institutions and groups are smothered under the weight of a pervasive status quo.[26]

Ironically, the increased volatility of candidate-centered politics serves to disguise the underlying built-in inertia. Without the longer-term leadership of parties, candidates tend to be poll driven, "free to craft their own individual appeals tailored specifically to the pressing (as well as trivial) issues of the day."[27] The flurry of activity makes it appear that the nation is suffering from "hyperdemocracy," a hyper-responsiveness to popular desires.[28] Polls fluctuate widely and dramatically, reflecting to a great extent the shallow and transitory nature of media coverage. The effect is not unlike Key's "echo chamber," wherein the public merely responds passively to the choices it is offered.[29]

Below the surface of hyperactivity, however, the deeper democratic problem is paralysis, or "demosclerosis."[30] Despite promises to rid the country of the gridlock emanating from the Bush administration–Democratic Congress confrontation, Clinton's team and the Democratic congressional leadership proved unable to unlock the logjam stifling the policy-making process. The lack of responsiveness was best

illustrated by the fate of health care reform in the first Clinton administration, which was blocked without even a vote being taken, despite the fact that it was backed by a Democratic president working with a Democratic majority in both houses of Congress.[31] Sarah Binder has statistically measured gridlock in Washington, defining it as the portion of significant issues (those addressed at least four times in a congressional term) left in limbo at the close of each Congress. She found that despite fluctuation, "gridlock has trended upward since 1947 and has been, on average, 25 points higher in the 1990s than it was in the 1940s."[32] As Walter Dean Burnham foresaw, by the late 1990s, we witnessed "a particularly virulent politics of deadlock," with the country appearing "practically ungovernable" at times, as partisan infighting reached heights of unprecedented fury in the impeachment imbroglio. Although the charges and countercharges flew fast and furious in a "politics by other means," the choices and changes presented to the voters were actually minimal.[33]

Since the mid-1970s, one of the most serious issues challenging American policies and institutions has been the economic transformation wrought by the globalization of the world's economy. The shift from a national to an international economy and the accompanying transition from a manufacturing to a service and information economy are producing profound changes in the nation, comparable to the transformation from a regional agrarian economy to a national manufacturing and commercial economy that provided the backdrop for the Solid South era. Indeed, it is likely that this underlying shift spells the doom of the American version of the welfare state and the New Deal political alignment that developed and supported it. Although there has been much clichéd discussion of "globalization," this problem was placed on the political agenda only after a decade or more in which the issue was disguised as one of "too much government," as Reaganites dominated the political dialogue with their diagnosis that "government is the problem, not the solution." Even in the new millennium, because political and business leaders treat it as a natural and inevitable process rather than engaging in debate about it, globalization is something of a buzzword that often forecloses questioning of current economic arrangements and stifles searches for solutions to social problems.[34]

Thus, the most significant issue facing American society in the

last quarter of the twentieth century remained something of a non-issue. Yet the impact of globalization and the attendant economic restructuring was huge, often causing devastating disruptions to families' lives as American employees found themselves "competing in a global hiring hall" against international workers who sometimes earned only pennies per hour.[35] The *New York Times* study on downsizing found that 43 million jobs had been abolished since 1979. The manufacturing sector was hardest hit, losing 8 million jobs in a similar time frame. Although manufacturing output rose by 13 percent from 1979 to 1992, employment in industry fell by 15 percent. One-third of all households reported that a family member had lost a job, and almost one-fourth of the workforce faced job loss every year. Even though the economy generated a net increase of 23 million jobs during this period, and unemployment was reduced to its lowest rate since 1973 under the second Clinton administration, other effects of downsizing persisted. One consequence was pervasive insecurity among employees, a fear of rocking the boat, which might explain the failure of wages to rise even as the unemployment rate dipped. Another consequence of restructuring was the shift of employment to the service sector. The failure of many workers' replacement jobs to match the salaries and benefits of their lost jobs was another explanation for stagnating average incomes in this era.[36] Many Americans tried to cope with these hardships by working longer hours. Juliet Schor estimated that Americans were working on average one month more each year by 1987 than they had been in 1969. Some commentators speculated that the longer hours were taking a toll on American family and community life.[37]

Despite the significance of the issue for personal and political life, globalization has generally been treated by political elites and the media as a natural force, not an issue calling for a policy response. By letting sleeping dogs lie, a suffocating consensus emerged that deregulation, open trade, liberalization of financial markets, and reduced government services were the only sensible responses to the global economy. Despite a "boom of busts" by the late 1990s, as free-market economies in various third-world countries tottered, any attempt to oppose this "Washington consensus" with a "Main Street alternative" by restraining market forces was labeled futile at best, positively backward at worst.[38] For example, opponents of free trade were roundly

condemned as protectionist neanderthals who would isolate the American economy and wall off American consumers from international products and markets. Keeping alternative responses off the political agenda, elites defined the issue as progress versus reaction, agilely dodging the issue of how the necessary transformations should be guided and how the inevitable costs and benefits of economic restructuring should be allocated.

To be sure, there were ideological and partisan differences among elites. In the 1970s and 1980s, however, the conservative Republican resurgence managed to dominate the political dialogue with the rhetoric of sacrifice and belt-tightening. Reaganomics as an economic program, with its deregulation, tax cuts, spending cuts, and shift from domestic to military spending, was essentially a formula for redistributing wealth upward. The logic of this supply-side economics was that more savings by the wealthy would lead to more investment and hence more jobs and income for all. Democratic liberals opposed the severity of these trickle-down policies, urging compassion, while accepting their fundamental logic. With the Clinton administration in the 1990s, the Democrats offered a slightly more neoliberal alternative to the pure market response, but it was a program that remained within the confines of corporate capitalism. The neoliberal response espoused a more activist government approach, one in which policies encourage and assist American corporations to compete, for instance, by favorable tax policies, state credit, subsidies for research and development, worker education and training, and other supports for business. Although liberal in the sense of advocating government activism, neoliberalism shares with laissez-faire Reaganomics a strong, if not quite so blind, faith in the efficacy and benevolence of market forces and a tendency to equate the interest of corporations with the interest of the nation.[39]

Although the Southern strategy in politics was widely discussed, less noted was this "Dixification" of America's economic policies. Numerous critics decried the response of American business to the global squeeze as the low road to economic competitiveness, but few noted that this approach was the traditionally Southern strategy for economic development. Stephen Cummings observes that the economic policies of George Wallace's Alabama prefigured the conservative turn in national economics. "Lower taxes on the rich, higher

regressive taxes on the poor, increased debt, and expanded services for the middle class and the corporate elite while ignoring lower incomes, foreshadowed the policies of the Reagan administration and the Contract with American in the 1980s and 1990s."[40] Southernomics prefigured Reaganomics as surely as the pseudopopulist demagoguery of Southern politicians on social issues provided models for the rancid populism of the contemporary New Right. The economic low road traveled by Southern economies began to be followed by national businesses and government, as they implemented cost cutting in order to meet the challenge of foreign competition. Corporations lowered wage bills by busting unions and downsizing long-term employees and by automating and exporting jobs. They sought to reduce other costs of doing business by lobbying for lower taxes, less government spending, deregulation, and a scaling back of environmental and health and safety standards. In addition to corporations and Washington, Northern state governments began to ape the Southern "low-wage, low-benefit, low-tax approach to economic development."[41] In an initiative strikingly reminiscent of Southern schemes to lure Yankee business investment, as well as of third-world free-trade zones, National Public Radio spots advertised eleven Michigan tax-free "Renaissance zones" conferring special benefits and exemptions for corporate takers. This "Southern" approach might have aided business, but the costs to communities, families, and individual employees were tremendous: a depersonalization of the workplace, denationalization of the economy, and disintegration of communities.[42]

Other options were available, but they were rarely discussed outside of academic and intellectual circles. For example, some economists advocated a return to more bubble-up policies of prosperity through demand stimulation. According to this scenario, redistributing wealth downward and ensuring widespread prosperity for all Americans would not only produce a more just society but would also stimulate the economy and lead to a return to economic vigor. Other alternatives, from the more cautious traditional option of budget balancing to the more radical program of worker ownership and economic democracy, might have been pursued.[43] These proposals, however, never appeared on the political agenda and were never granted serious consideration. The cost of the unimaginative stagnation of "consensus" politics was captured by Jonathan Schell:

The electoral system, instead of offering new ideas suitable to the time, devotes the amazing new instruments of the information age to discovering what the public already believes and offering that. And even these offers are not honest, because only their benefits and not their costs are advertised at election time. The procedure is a formula for stagnation. When, as at present, change is swift, deep, and fundamental, the gap between political practice and the world becomes dangerously wide. Then events race out ahead of thought and word, which stumble blindly behind in a world they cannot apprehend.[44]

A Fistful of Dollars: Crooks, Kin, and Corruption

Key accused the Solid South of being peculiarly corrupt. A politics of disconnected parties, elite participation, and neglect of economic issues in favor of distracting racism and culture wars is a politics prone to corruption, both in the narrow and broader senses. Using a narrow definition of corruption, scandals flourish in the climate of ignored issues, suppressed policies, and demagogic leadership. Such an atmosphere also corrupts politics in the larger sense that decision making for the public good tends to degenerate into deal making among self-interested elites.[45]

American politics in recent years has witnessed no shortage of scandal, whether political, financial, or sexual. Early in the decade, respected senators became ensnared in the savings and loan fiasco, rating Senate censure for their role in helping Charles Keating elude governmental regulations. By the mid-1990s, the two most powerful politicians in the nation, the president and the Speaker of the House, were both enmeshed in controversy over their political ethics. Gingrich was fined $300,000 for violating House ethics rules. Clinton, in addition to accusations and lawsuits about his sexual conduct and his personal financial affairs, fell prey to charges of corruption based on his extraordinary fund-raising efforts in the 1996 race. By decade's end, unprecedented scandal tainted both parties, as an elected president was impeached for the first time. Although Clinton was not found guilty of impeachment charges and retained the presidency, he remained personally tainted, destined to be the butt of countless late-night comedians' jokes. As the impeachment effort backfired, the fallout in-

directly forced top Republican leaders Gingrich and Robert Livingston from office.[46]

Financial scandals as well as breaches of sexual ethics were rampant in the politics of the 1980s and 1990s. Numerous high-ranking Reagan appointees resigned, and several were prosecuted for abuse of office, a trend exacerbated by many Reagan administrators' ideological opposition to the regulations they were charged with administering and by their close ties to regulated industries. The Bush administration saw the collapse of the savings and loan industry, largely because of lax government regulation and cozy relations between regulators and the regulated, and a half-trillion-dollar bailout. Although there were surprisingly few recriminations, probably because both parties were implicated, favors done for one savings and loan mogul resulted in the tainting of at least five U.S. senators, including some of the most distinguished members of that body. As the majority in Congress, Democrats were disproportionately implicated in that scandal, as well as several others involving legislators, including Abscam, the House banking scandal, and the resignations of Speaker of the House Jim Wright and majority leader Tony Coehlo. As majority control changed hands in the 1990s, this balance shifted. Bruce Shapiro reported that of the members of Congress voting on Clinton's impeachment, no fewer than thirty had "confessed, been convicted of or been credibly documented as violating laws or Congressional ethics rules," and twenty-three of the "Dirty Thirty" were Republicans.[47] Although corruption convictions have not been frequent, several Clinton appointees have been prosecuted or had special prosecutors investigate them, including former secretary of agriculture Michael Espy, late secretary of commerce Ron Brown, and Secretary of the Interior Bruce Babbitt.

No one really knows whether there is more corruption in American politics lately or whether scandals are simply more readily unearthed and reported. Some argue that Watergate tightened ethical standards in government and that the institutionalization of independent counsels created the means and motives for "the criminalizing of politics."[48] Others point to the more sweeping post-Watergate journalistic notions of what constitutes legitimate news, as reporters no longer respect the private conduct of politicians as off-limits.[49] Ginsberg and Shefter, however, see scandal as a means of waging elite political conflict in a postelectoral era. They suggest that in an era of close

and bitter partisan competition that has resulted in divided government, elections do not bestow a mandate to rule. Instead, indecisive elections leave competing partisan elites entrenched in different branches, levels, and agencies of government, from which they continue the partisan battle between elections. From these ramparts of power, partisan elites rarely seek to mobilize the electorate as traditional party leaders did, because elections produce neither clear-cut results nor party control in this era of irresponsible party government. Instead, elites attempt to undermine the institutional base of their rivals, often resorting to scandalmongering to discredit either opposing institutions or officeholders. Ginsberg and Shefter thus lay the blame for the corruption, if not the criminalization, of American politics on the atrophying of mechanisms of electoral accountability.[50]

As Dennis Thompson points out in his discussion of the Keating Five, the nature of the corruption is neither purely personal nor a simple "everyone does it" phenomenon. Instead, it reflects flaws in the political system as well as personal failings of politicians, individually or collectively. Thompson coins the term "mediated corruption" to describe the phenomenon, which differs from the simple corruption of direct quid pro quo. Mediated corruption involves (1) a public official who gains, (2) a private party who benefits, and (3) an improper connection between the gain and benefit. Thompson observes that "mediated corruption is not new, but it is newly prospering. It thrives in the world of large, multinational financial institutions that increasingly interact, in closed and complex ways, with governments."[51] Without the offsetting influences of strong linking mechanisms such as parties in an M^3, candidate-centered, money-driven politics, the influence of private interests increasingly overwhelms the representation of the public good.[52]

Morris Fiorini has argued that the very foundation of the public policy system in this country is self-interest rather than the public interest. Politicians back programs that "bring home the bacon" to their constituents, with little or no thought as to cost or a larger conception of the national interest. The resulting "iron triangles" of congressional politicians, especially interested committee members, bureaucrats with programs to push, and self-interested clienteles, create closed systems of privilege that are highly resistant to challenge and change. Although some pluralist political scientists maintain that the public

interest emerged from the clash of private interests, Ted Lowi persuasively demonstrates that the public interest was "factored out" of this
system he called "interest group liberalism." Newer and pervasive
issue networks may be broader than iron triangles, but interested
groups rely on their vast resources to frame messages that drown out
competing prescriptions and shape policies in their self-interest.[53] At
the very least, former generations of Americans, more imbued with
the spirit of "republicanism," would have been appalled at relying on
a naive faith that the common good would blindly emerge as an acci-
dental by-product of the pursuit of private interest. Our democracy's
founders would have worried that a politics without "virtue" (i.e., concern for the common good of the Republic) would be primed to produce not citizens and a "commonwealth" but corruption in its
broadest sense.[54]

Dazed and Confused

Not surprisingly, a bankrupt politics of sideshow issues and elusive
leadership that ignores the burning social needs of the day is not a politics that inspires citizens to action. Key thought that voters were confused by the muddle of multifactionalism and tended to drop out of
politics in numbers even beyond the masses of legally disenfranchised
nonvoters.[55] Since the 1960s and the decline of New Deal politics,
American politics has witnessed a comparable disillusionment of
American voters. While formal barriers to participation have fallen
one by one, citizens have, ironically perhaps, become increasingly
angry and absent.[56] Voting for president in 1996 was the lowest since
1924, and the turnout in the congressional elections of 1998 was the
lowest level since 1818 outside the South.[57] Access to the vote may be
readily available, but actual voting rates are abysmally low.

   Part of the problem is sheer confusion. Parties simplify the voters'
information-gathering task by reducing the voters' choices. Strong parties also link a platform, or bundle of specific policies, and a team of
aspiring leaders promising to implement these proposals with a constituency of the public that finds the party's approach attractive. Without these links, voters are faced with a multitude of candidates whose
connections to particular policies are tenuous at best. No wonder that

political knowledge among the American public is abysmally low. One survey revealed that two-thirds of the respondents could not name their U.S. representative, 54 percent could not identify either of their U.S. senators, and a considerable majority believed that foreign aid was more costly than Medicare.[58] Despite the media attention given to the Republicans' 1994 Contract with America and the frequency with which pundits assumed that the contract was central to the Republican recapture of Congress that year, 71 percent of Americans polled had never heard of the contract.[59] Rather than blame the public, however, we should acknowledge what Key recognized long ago: a disorganized politics produces a confused public. Our national politics no longer presents clear or sensible alternatives to the public, which, in its frustration, either lashes out at politicians or sits out politics altogether.

A prime example is the 1993 Clinton health care reform proposals. The ignominious defeat of the president's plan resulted in a backlash that catapulted Republicans into majority control of the Congress in 1994. Part of the public's response hinged on negative reaction to the perceived lack of choice in the White House plan, a theme harped on in much of the media discussion and ads. The public missed the point that for most Americans, the Clinton health initiative actually would have expanded, not contracted, choice in health services.[60] Theda Skocpol has documented that most voters were initially in favor of a plan like the one the president championed but did not recognize that these provisions were included in the Clinton plan. When asked about "the Clinton plan" in a survey, many rejected the plan identified only as Clinton's proposal, even though they actually favored the provisions included in this plan when presented with them minus the Clinton label.[61]

Part of the fault, no doubt, is directly attributable to the mass media, which increasingly entertain rather than inform and treat their audiences as consumers, not citizens.[62] At the height of the 1998 campaign, political ads during newscasts outnumbered political news stories by four to one. Of course, a for-profit media would not emphasize "infotainment" if there was not a ready market for it, and defenders of the media often claim that mass media, although admittedly lowbrow, merely reflect what the public wants. Despite the appearance of choice between types of media and media outlets, this contention blames the victim by ignoring the very real and awesome power of the mass media

and their isolation from public control while blaming the audience for media content. The growing concentration of corporate ownership and the containment of media competition within an entertainment format mean that citizens are helpless, despite polls indicating that large numbers want more substantive content, to force media to cover policy-relevant news and refrain from obsessing on scandal, strategy, and the sensational.[63]

A particularly poignant example of the public frustration with mass-media coverage was reported by Richard Fox, a political scientist at Union College. During the height of the Monica Lewinsky scandal, while the eyes of the press were trained on the impeachment trial of President Clinton, Jesse Jackson spoke at Union. Jackson's speech, reports Fox, focused on "the dilapidated condition of inner city public schools, the high number of children living in poverty and the expanding prison population," and "he noted that the civil rights movement is now stalled along economic, not racial, lines. One thing Mr. Jackson did not dwell on was the impeachment trial of President Clinton." Members of the press present for the talk, who got first crack at querying the speaker, asked six questions, ranging from Jackson's opinions on the Lewinsky affair to his presidential ambitions to his prediction about the upcoming Super Bowl. When the students' turn came, they asked about the problems Jackson had addressed in his talk and the prospects for fixing them. The highlight came, however, when a student noted: "You just gave a very powerful and moving speech, and the press asked you only about the scandal in Washington. What does that say to you?" Fox reports that "the hall erupted in the loudest applause of the evening."[64]

Still, high ratings for sensational stories might indicate some support for the notion that what we say is not actually what we do when it comes to media. Is it not true that audiences prefer the "sensational goo" of "sex-crime-celebrity stories"? Joshua Gamson argues that infotainment treats information as play, and that play occurs most readily when the consequences are small. He believes that the heart of the infotainment phenomenon is the disturbing possibility that the public believes that politics lacks important consequences, that alternative outcomes no longer matter, and that Americans cannot meaningfully affect public life. This being the case, significant and trustworthy information, "public-service news," is irrelevant. Gamson concludes

that today, a shrunken sense of political efficacy makes possible the unsurprising conversion of news into infotainment.[65] Without a renewed sense of political consequence, we can only expect television news to continue on its happy, profitable march toward the trivial and sensational.

Confusion and disenchantment take their toll at the voting booth. Tom DeLuca notes that apathy has two faces and argues that rather than simply indicating individual disinterest in politics, our incredible shrinking electorate reflects a political system that has failed to protect the interests of the American public at a time when significant restructuring of society and the economy is producing many losers as well as winners.[66] It seems plausible to recognize that the exit of large numbers of the neediest Americans from political engagement represents a "silent vote of no confidence" in contemporary politics.[67]

To Have and Have Not

Politics may not exclusively be about who gets what, when, and how, as Harold Lasswell once suggested, but it definitely has that dimension. If so, who can be surprised if those very groups that participate less in politics end up with the short end of the public policy stick?[68] In Key's day, that meant the have-nots. Of course, in a South that Franklin Roosevelt described as "the nation's number one economic problem," the have-nots encompassed the vast majority of Southerners, black and white. The region seriously lagged the nation in average income; in 1929, the South's per capita income was only 53 percent of the national figure. Today that gap is almost closed, with Southern per capita income standing at 92 percent of the national level. Although poverty crept upward after the 1960s as Washington abandoned the War (actually a skirmish) on Poverty, most Americans, North and South, are surely not have-nots.[69] If we read Key, however, as speaking about the vast majority who have significantly less than the wealthy elites, how have the majority of middle class and poor—we might label them the have-lesses—fared as American politics has increasingly assumed the traits of traditional Southern politics?

In the years after World War II, an implicit tripartite social accord among capital, labor, and government laid the groundwork for un-

precedented economic growth and a sharing of prosperity among wide segments of the public. Management tolerated unions, at least in the core industries that had organized after the Wagner Act ensured workers the right to bargain collectively. Unions, for their part, accepted management's prerogative to control work and direct production. They also moderated their wage demands to match productivity gains and implicitly assumed a part in disciplining labor for efficiency. Both business and unions accepted an expanded role for government in regulating industries and in pursuing macroeconomic policies to manage the economy and smooth the boom-bust cycles of capitalism.[70]

Regardless of whether America's much-vaunted equality of opportunity has been real or mostly mythical, there can be no doubt that this social compact yielded expanding opportunity and prosperity that pulled many Americans out of the ranks of the have-nots. Between 1947 and 1973, median family income doubled, from $20,102 to $40,979. Moreover, the poorest 20 percent and the middle 20 percent of households saw their income grow faster than that of the richest quintile (116 and 111 percent, respectively, versus 99 percent).[71] But if Americans were growing together in the years after World War II, in the last decades of the twentieth century, they were drifting apart. With the globalization of the economy, the postwar social compact began to disintegrate as spiraling inflation, declining profits, and stiffer international competition motivated capital to declare war on labor and to launch a political offensive for more corporate-friendly government policies. The inevitable result was that by the 1980s, the trend was decidedly toward more inequality, as Reaganomics redistributed income up the socioeconomic scale. From 1979 to 1998, the richest 20 percent of Americans enjoyed a 38 percent jump in income, while the middle quintile's income grew by only 8 percent and the poorest one-fifth actually lost by 5 percent. The income of the richest 1 percent vaulted by 64 percent.[72] The resulting distributions of income and wealth have become more highly skewed toward the haves. In 1989, the upper fifth of American households received 55.5 percent of the national income, while the bottom fifth received only 3.1 percent. By 1994, the richest million American households received 140 times more income than the poorest million.[73] The Clinton prosperity of the 1990s failed to reverse this trend. From 1990 through 1999, workers' pay rose an average of 28 percent (with much

of the increase being gobbled up by the 22.5 percent inflation for this period), while top corporate executives' pay rose a whopping 481 percent.[74] In 1989, the United States had 66 billionaires and 31.5 million people living in poverty. At the end of the prosperous 1990s, there were 268 billionaires and 34.5 million poor in this country.[75] Not only is this disparity in income growing at a quickening pace, but "the inequality of income in the United States is also greater than the inequality in any other populous industrialized country."[76]

As recently as 1974, the average American corporate chief executive officer received $35 in salary for every $1 earned by the average worker in manufacturing. By 1990, that ratio had risen to a multiple of $85 to $1, but by 1999, the multiple had skyrocketed to an astonishing 475 executive dollars for every worker dollar earned. Meanwhile, comparable ratios in Japan and Germany were only 16 and 21 to 1, respectively.[77] Although some Americans are reaping the benefits from the recent transformations of the economy, many more are falling behind, and the gap in the middle is expanding. As Robert Kuttner observes, "in this economy you are either king of the road or you are the road kill."[78]

Michael Hout persuasively refutes various "myths" that purport to explain and justify the outrageous levels of income inequality characterizing America, including the need for flexibility and productivity, the supposed lag in worker productivity, differences in natural abilities, and our inability to address problems of inequality. Instead, he blames the growth in inequality on the diversion of economic gains to profits, stock prices, and executive compensation. He claims that this massive redistribution upward reflects "the politics of the 1970s and 1980s [that] wrought changes in schools, colleges, and workplaces that gave employers and managers unprecedented power while disenfranchising parents, workers, and others who used to share power."[79]

The distribution of wealth was even more distorted in favor of the wealthy than the distribution of income, and the tilt toward the rich has grown much steeper in recent years. William Berman maintains that as a result of Reaganomics, anywhere from $120 billion to $160 billion annually was transferred to the wealthiest 5 percent of Americans during the 1980s.[80] Data from the Federal Reserve Survey of Consumer Finances analyzed by economist Edward Wolff reveal that "since the 1970s, the top 1 percent of households have doubled their

share of the national wealth at the expense of everyone else." By 1997, the richest 1 percent of the population held 40 percent of the nation's household wealth. This top 1 percent owns more wealth than the entire bottom 95 percent of all Americans.[81] In fact, Bill Gates's net worth of $46 billion in 1998 was larger than the combined wealth of the bottom 40 percent of American households, who together held only $37.8 billion if their cars were excluded.[82]

Despite an increase in working time, until recently, average income has stagnated since the unraveling of the political economy put in place by the New Deal and Great Society. The post–World War II generation saw average real standards of living double in its lifetime, but since the mid-1970s, real inflation-adjusted incomes have remained essentially flat. American families have maintained living standards by putting in more hours at work, mainly by having female family members enter the workforce. Even with the return to lower unemployment under the Clinton regime, average incomes were only beginning to rise gradually in the latter half of the 1990s. Although median household income reached a historic high of $38,885 in 1998, that partly reflected longer hours of work and more family members working. Workers earning $25,000 in 1998 would have made about $1,060 more in 1973, adjusting for inflation. Had pay kept pace with the 46.5 percent gain in productivity during this period, the average full-time worker's paycheck would have been $12,438 more.[83]

The have-lesses of America lose out in countless other ways. The number of Americans without health insurance climbed from 13.6 percent, or 33.4 million people, in 1989 to 16.3 percent of the population, or 44.2 million people, in 1998. A poll found that half surveyed had savings of less than $3,000, and 20 percent had zero or negative net worth (up from 10 percent in 1962).[84] Millions of hardworking Americans are only one illness away from financial catastrophe. American employees are not guaranteed five or six weeks of vacation, as workers in many European countries enjoy. Although the Family and Medical Leave Act finally signed into law in 1993 protects employees' right to take time off to care for newborns or sick relatives, the law covers only a bare majority of employees, and the leaves can last a maximum of only twelve weeks. Most critically, they are unpaid. By contrast, Sweden's employees are entitled to one year's leave during which they are paid at 90 percent of their salary, which can be extended for six more months

at a reduced (30 percent) salary. Only about half of American workers are entitled to company pensions. Home ownership, which historically was high in this country, is declining. Occupational health and safety are weakly protected, and employees enjoy few rights at work. Outside the workplace, environmental living standards are only loosely protected.[85] Meanwhile, the burden of government has fallen more heavily on the middle class, as "tax reform" has given breaks to the wealthy and lowered the tax rates of the top brackets. Taxes have also been shifted from corporations to individuals. Individuals now pay 73 percent of the cost of government revenues, as opposed to 44 percent fifty years ago; corporations have managed to reduce their contributions from 33 to 15 percent. Restoring the corporate share would produce enough revenue to fund a 60 percent reduction for most taxpayers.[86]

America is not an economically underdeveloped country, although it has an unusually high poverty rate among industrial democracies, especially among children (almost 25 percent of American children live in poverty, as opposed to the 4 percent or so typical of European democracies). Nor does the contemporary United States approach even the South of Key's era, where economic dependency and the ravages of the Great Depression produced a have-not majority. But recent trends have seen the fortunes of the most numerous American middle class, the have-lesses, decline.[87] Despite the media hype about the soaring stock market and the Clinton administration's justifiable pride in lower unemployment rates, the "new" economy was not as kind to ordinary Americans as it was to the upper and upper middle classes. A recent exhaustive study of economic indicators gave the "new" economy decidedly mixed reviews from the perspective of its impact on the have-less majority:

> Unfortunately for working Americans, the 1990s have been, in many ways, an extension of the 1980s. Income and wage inequality have increased (though at a slower rate), families are working longer for less, wealth has become even more concentrated, and poverty has not fallen much in response to overall economic growth.
>
> And the 1990s have introduced some new living standards problems: an increase in job insecurity, the decline of wages for white-collar and entry-level, college-educated workers, wage stagnation for middle-wage females, and, at least through 1996, worse income growth for the typical family.[88]

In an increasingly global economy, the measures protecting the security of the majority of Americans achieved by the New Deal have slowly but steadily been eroded, in the workplace and on the law books. Once moderately organized, with over one-third of workers belonging to unions, the American workforce is now among the least unionized, with the private workforce approaching 10 percent union, the lowest level since the Great Depression. Whereas many employees could once anticipate lifetime careers with the same company, loyalty increasingly counts for little as countless workers, up to high levels of management, are downsized. Companies that once limited outsourcing to peripheral tasks now resort to hiring (usually lower pay, lower benefit) "outside contractors" for even central functions. An increasing number of Americans (one estimate is now up to 30 percent of the workforce) have no stable, full-time work at all but instead find themselves stuck in the insecure world of contingent work (part-time, temporary, or subcontracted jobs), usually without the benefits and protections of longer-term jobs and careers.[89] Without protective policies, the force of global competition from countries where pay is a mere fraction of American wages seems destined to drive American wages lower and exacerbate job insecurity.[90] American standards would have to deteriorate much further to reach third-world conditions, but the many workers who feel betrayed by recent changes can identify with the authors whose work describing globalization's impact on the American economy is entitled "The Judas Economy."[91]

Just as the old Solid South reliably responded to the interests of the planter and industrial elites while ignoring the plight of the majority have-nots, so the current trends toward enervated party competition, a diminished electorate, and the disappearance of economic issues augur well for America's corporate elites. Meanwhile, many average Americans, like the have-nots of old, fume, stew, and cast about for scapegoats but find few political avenues to relieve their frustrations. Although more Americans now perceive significant differences between the parties, fewer think that these differences matter in terms of solving problems effectively.[92] In short, we are approaching once again a system deplored by V. O. Key, where politics was simultaneously irrational and undemocratic; instead of solving the problems of the vast majority of the public, government serves the interests of the wealthy few.

An Excess of Democracy?

Although Key did not say so in so many words, what the totality of traits of the Solid South really amounts to is the astounding proposition that politics in a major region of the United States, the Democratic South, was not democratic at all. Likewise, an examination of the symptoms of current American politics has to raise concerns about the health of democracy in this country today.

Democracy, "government of the people, by the people, and for the people," according to Lincoln, involves a system of policy making based on popular sovereignty under conditions of liberty and equality. These elements are being eroded in the transition to a new, post–New Deal American political economy. Conditions of equality are being undermined, as the have-lesses seem to have less and less. Popular sovereignty rests on shaky ground when political competition does not float clear alternatives on meaningful issues to the whole citizenry and when "votes count but resources decide."[93] And can liberty be secure when governmental policies increasingly flaunt the interests of the vast majority? Perhaps understandably, civil liberties have not seemed more "at risk" in recent times than in the 1980s, when the Reagan regime undertook what amounted to a vast redistribution of wealth from the many to the few. Or perhaps, rather than an Orwellian suppression of freedom *1984*-style, the real threat is a Huxleian brave new world where we are so constantly amused that we forget that we are also being governed, not governing ourselves.

One significant aspect of democracy is the issue of decentralization versus centralization. There is no simple equation of democracy and decentralization. As Grant McConnell has demonstrated, decentralization can lead to rule by local elites and suppression and exploitation of minorities. The current decentralization of welfare policy fits that bill.[94] Relatively unnoticed among current political debates, however, have been less visible but more significant tendencies to centralize policy making in ways that deny any realistic possibilities for popular participation in self-governance. Examples include proposals to centralize nuclear power, environmental regulations, and "tort reform," the last being a series of Republican-sponsored measures to make it more difficult for consumers to recover for injuries at the hands of manufacturers.[95] Even bleaker from the point of view of pop-

ular participation are recent treaties that threaten national sovereignty over trade, as the World Trade Organization assumes power over many trade disputes, with implications for domestic policy such as labor and environmental standards. The proposed Multilateral Agreement on Investment would prohibit signatories from impeding the flow of capital, whether money or production facilities, and in the process severely restrict the range of domestic policies available to protect national populations. Pessimists have questioned whether any social reforms will be viable in the face of unrelenting global competition to lure investment by maintaining a "favorable business climate."[96]

The changing global landscape seems to present an inhospitable climate for democracy. Benjamin Barber has noticed the paradoxical simultaneous trends toward centralization and decentralization, for the world appears to be both "coming together and falling apart" at the same time. The thrust of world market forces, which Barber labels "McWorld," is toward homogenization, while the counterreaction to seek refuge from market imperatives in close-knit communities—termed, perhaps unfortunately, "Jihad" by Barber—fragments the globe into numerous, often conflicting groups. Democratic theorist Barber's main point is that neither tendency is auspicious for the future of democracy. Both the market and closed communities represent the triumph of anarchy, forces beyond the control of self-governing peoples. He notes that democratic institutions have historically been national and worries that democracy may not survive the demise of the nation-state, overridden by international markets and torn apart from within by warring factions.[97]

If control by the citizenry is undermined, how will social control be maintained? Bertram Gross presented a bleak prognosis for the future of democracy in the United States, a future he labeled "friendly fascism." Gross worried not about jackbooted Nazis so much as about the preservation of the veneer of democratic processes while the substance was drained by elite domination. Although the rise of hate crimes, militias, and neo-Nazis should give us pause, Gross is undoubtedly correct in suggesting that the greatest danger stems from the reduction of institutions that once had democratic functions to the mere trappings of popular sovereignty.[98] Such were the institutions of the old Solid South, with elections and all the trimmings, but all distorted to maintain behind-the-scenes control by powerful elites.

Will American parties, campaigns, and elections be emptied of all but the appearance of democracy in order to disguise increasing elite control? Will American elites strip the content of democratic institutions to protect their interests in the socioeconomic restructuring currently under way? Writing in 1975, at the dawn of the transition from the New Deal to the current political economy, Samuel Huntington deplored the effects of widespread participation on public policies in the 1960s; in particular, he feared the overloading of the political system and the undermining of its authority. He asserted that popular participation undermined the governability of the country: "The apparent vitality of democracy in the 1960's raises questions about the governability of democracy in the 1970's." He worried about the ability of leaders to govern, because the democratic ethos of the times had raised "questions about the legitimacy of hierarchy, coercion, discipline, secrecy, and deception—all of which are, in some measure, inescapable attributes of the process of government." Huntington was adamant in his belief that the best cure for the ills of democracy was not more democracy. Instead, he boldly asserted, the United States was suffering from "an excess of democracy." His suggested solution was fewer participants and fewer democratic arenas.[99]

It is difficult to know whether Huntington's call for a retrenchment from democracy, made clearly and publicly in a respected, elite policy journal, had a significant impact in its own right, or whether Huntington's jeremiad merely reflected the shared diagnosis of a wider elite audience. In any case, since the mid-1970s, many democratic procedural reforms have been rolled back. Antireforms include the revision of the Democratic party's nominating rules, the abandonment of the party's short-lived midterm issues convention, the gutting of CIA and FBI oversight regulations, the curtailing of the Freedom of Information Act, the circumventing of campaign finance reforms, the weakening of congressional budget reforms, the ignoring of the War Powers Act, the Supreme Court's chiseling away at individual rights in the name of law and order, and congressional reforms that undermined party cohesion. These procedural reforms were accompanied by policy positions reflecting less substantively egalitarian stances as well, such as the defense shift under Reagan, the near-abandonment of national commitment to integration, the gradual erosion of abortion rights, and the curtailing of the welfare state. This retrenchment, serv-

ing to strengthen the hands of elites at the expense of popular rule, may not amount to fascism even in its "friendly" variant, but it represents movement away from democratic ideals. Our current politics, "while democratic in form, is more and more oligarchic in content."[100] Maybe the American political system, although preserving the facade of democracy, could better be termed "semidemocratic," "quasi-democratic," or "neodemocratic."[101]

No Globalization without Representation?

The institutions of the Solid South were constructed at the turn of the twentieth century after a decade of populist political rebellions during the transition from an agricultural to an industrial society. They were designed, and served effectively for many decades, to maintain elite domination on the big questions of the day that impinged on the elites' interests, all the while presenting the surface illusion of democracy in a nation whose politics was framed by a democratic constitution and ideals. The costs were high, including racism and sexism, the neglect of the interests of the most numerous classes, and the inability to respond effectively to the public interest of the region in solving its problems of poverty, illiteracy, poor health, decent jobs, and economic development. Ultimately, however, the biggest loser was democracy itself, the capacity for citizens to govern themselves.

In another transitional era, after a surge of democratic participation dating from the New Deal and culminating in a decade of popular insurgence in the 1960s, the institutions of American political economy are being reshaped in ways that threaten public responsibility and popular participation. As in the Solid South of the past, racist and sexist backlashes threaten progress toward a more egalitarian society. While the wealthy reap the lion's share of the benefits and the more prosperous professions fare well, average Americans tread water or clutch desperately for moorings in the sea change sweeping the nation's social structure and the world's economy. Despite being nominally majoritarian, the public and private governing institutions of the nation seem better geared toward protecting the interests of the corporate ruling class than the public interest during the political economic restructuring accompanying globalization. American democracy itself seems

drained of much of its past vitality and present potential, not ravaged perhaps, but definitely diminished.

Not all the signs point one way, and the symptoms detailed here are merely talismanic of possible trends that may not come to fruition. There is, however, cause for genuine concern. As we enter a new century, the Solid South so poignantly described by V. O. Key at midcentury should serve as a reminder that appearances of formally free institutions can be misleading and that elections, by themselves, do not a democracy make.[102]

8 / *Southern Horizons*

The South of the Future and the South as Future

Southern Vistas

Dramatic changes in the South in recent decades, especially economic development, the civil rights movement, and the rise of a viable Republican party, have narrowed the gap between the South and the nation. More than one hundred years after the region formally rejoined the Union, the South at last seemed realistically and thoroughly reintegrated into the life of the nation. At the same time, deep changes, especially the eclipse of the New Deal and the shift toward racial and cultural politics, have altered the national landscape. The United States that the South rejoined is very different politically from the nation that the region resisted for so long. The same flaws that bedeviled traditional Southern politics increasingly characterize national politics: detached, irresponsible parties, a shrunken electorate, and a focus on race and social issues to the detriment of economic issues. Certainly American politics after the year 2000 will not mirror Southern politics before 1950, but today's national politics does display some of that old Southern "distinctiveness": blurred or insignificant issues, manipulative leadership, nondecisions on critical new challenges, disenchanted citizens, pervasive political corruption, and outcomes that favor elites at the expense of ordinary Americans. In some ways, then, the Solid South with its perversions of democracy stands as a warning to the nation that without nurturing the roots of democratic institutions, the substance of democracy can be lost even while the trappings of democracy are retained.

* * *

Of, by, and for the People?

As Yogi Berra once observed with his usual astuteness, "it's tough to make predictions, especially about the future."[1] Although disturbing trends signal the possibility of our democracy evolving in a regressive direction, there are numerous reasons to hope that American democracy will not "head south" anytime soon. Foremost would be (1) a misfit in the analogy developed here between Southern politics of the past and current national trends, (2) certain countertrends that might take our politics today in a different direction; and (3) the possibility of citizens' choices and actions that will strengthen our democracy. In my opinion, the last is by far the most promising source of hope for reinvigorating American democracy.

First, as discussed in chapter 6, although recent developments in national politics are cause for concern, the analogy between Solid South and contemporary politics is admittedly not a perfect one. American parties today are keenly competitive, no matter how vapid the quality of that competition. The American public enjoys more participation rights today than at any point in the Republic's history, even though it does not feel engaged enough with politics to employ them. And racialized politics may taint many current issues and divert the electorate from many other problems, but the current climate is far improved from the raw racism of the Jim Crow South.[2] Still, as I concluded in chapter 6, there is genuine cause for concern that our electoral system is evolving into a "semiresponsible" party system that falls sadly short of the vibrant democracy promised by American ideals and aspirations.

Second, there are certain trends in American politics and institutional development that could augur more, not less, democracy on our national horizon. These countertrends are shaping national institutions in ways that differentiate them from the comparable structures in historical Southern politics and create openings for a more vital democratic politics on the national scene. Foremost among these countertrends are the popular and powerful presidency, a diverse and independent mass media, and a pluralistic and informative electoral finance system.[3] All these factors present possibilities for institutionalizing a politically aware public and an accountability of leaders to protect the public's interests. In my opinion, however, each is fundamentally flawed in ways that limit its democratic potential.

The modern American presidency is a far more powerful, visible, and accountable office than was the traditional Southern governorship. Presidents undergo constant media scrutiny, enjoy access to the public's attention, and have political resources that make it feasible for them to enact the programs that they promise to the public. Having a more central position in the governmental and political system, and being dependent on public approval not just for reelection but also for the popularity that is a president's main political coin, the American presidency might be expected to be a potent instrument of democracy.[4]

Several facets of the modern presidency, however, conspire to limit the democratic content of this office. In the first place, the extraordinarily high expectations vested by Americans in their presidents constitute an almost surefire formula for failure. Thomas Cronin found that the "textbook presidency" that emerged from popular and scholarly images of the office entailed several dangers for democratic government by concentrating vastly inflated expectations—and accompanying responsibilities and powers—in an office that assumed "imperial" dimensions culminating in Watergate.[5] Despite some deflation of the "imperial presidency" in the wake of the failure in Vietnam and Nixon's resignation, Theodore Lowi argues that the plebiscitary presidency observable today is entirely consistent with these earlier versions of a strong president identified with a strong state, responsible and empowered to do whatever he deems necessary to maintain sovereignty and order, domestic and foreign.[6]

One danger of inflated expectations is a tendency for presidents to overreach themselves, both by attempting too much and by sidestepping constitutional processes. The president is still seen as the "engine" of government, and "it seems perfectly normal for millions upon millions of Americans to concentrate their hopes and fears directly and personally upon him."[7] In an otherwise frustrating machinery of checks and balances, better designed to protect citizens from harmful government actions than to enable government to act to remedy social ills, the president provides the source of dynamism and innovation in American policy making. With high expectations riding on their performance, presidents are tempted to circumvent cumbersome legal procedures and "just do it." As one presidential aide candidly admitted, "Everyone believes in democracy until he gets to the White House and

then you begin to believe in dictatorship, because it's so hard to get things done."[8]

Nor are other politicians, foreign as well as domestic, the only other actors who frustrate presidents in their quests to live up to the high expectations of the voters. Economic performance is most likely to seal the fate of incumbent presidents, yet beyond the budgetary powers shared with the bureaucracy and Congress, the most direct economic instruments are lodged in the hands of the independent Federal Reserve Bank and of private investors and corporate magnates. No president can afford to risk a "capital strike" by undermining business confidence and willingness to invest. When the Clinton team considered taxing the richest 2 percent of Americans in order to afford middle-class tax relief, Robert Rubin, a multimillionaire investment banker who was then presidential economic adviser, later secretary of treasury, advised against the populism of the campaign for fear of offending the wealthy: "Look, they're running the economy and they make the decisions about the economy. And so if you attack them, you wind up hurting the economy and wind up hurting the president."[9] In a historical study of presidential leadership, Stephen Skowronek concludes that presidents typically are so hemmed in by political checks that they are unable to fulfill public expectations. Only in those rare instances when political realignments allow them to break free of past constraints are presidents able to provide decisive leadership and to achieve dramatic new departures.[10] Disillusionment is another almost inevitable consequence of overinflated expectations. Presidential popularity typically follows a "reverse J curve" of presidential approval scores over their terms in office. Beginning with initially high approval ratings based on campaign promises and optimistic expectations, presidents tend to lose popularity as the frustrations and inevitable failures of their terms accumulate. Approval usually rises slightly in the last months in office as the next election approaches. Perhaps the public now begins to measure incumbent presidents against flesh-and-blood opponents, real humans with feet of clay, instead of judging them against the idealized expectations of the textbook presidency.[11]

Yet another problem with a plebiscitary presidency that concentrates the public's political aspirations directly and solely in the highest office is the stunted role for other political actors. In particular,

citizens are reduced to mere spectators cheering on their champion as he fights on their behalf. "Most of us are unnecessarily and unduly mesmerized and perhaps made less effective citizens by our quasi-religious fixation toward the presidency," Cronin asserts. The cost of a "personal presidency" may be our personal power as sovereign citizens in a democracy.[12]

The final temptation of a plebiscitary president, so dependent on unrealistic public expectations, is manipulation of public opinion. As Lowi notes, "the President is the Wizard of Oz. Appearances become everything." Pollsters and media consultants take up permanent residence in the White House as governing blends seamlessly with perpetual campaigning. The personal president exists symbiotically with television, because "television is the central nervous system of the modern plebiscitary presidency," enabling the president to go over the heads of Congress and other political actors, over the heads of the press even, directly to the people. But the process is dynamic, and the office itself is a "Tar Baby," as Lowi notes. "As presidential success advances arithmetically, public expectations advance geometrically." The attempt to escape disillusionment and deflation loops back into efforts of manipulation and overreaching: "The desperate search is no longer for the good life but for the most effective presentation of appearances. This is a pathology because it escalates the rhetoric at home, ratcheting expectations upward notch by notch, and fuels adventurism abroad, in a world where the cost of failure can be annihilation."[13]

If the modern president is unlikely to fulfill the role of tribune of the people, perhaps the national media are better positioned in contemporary America to play a democratic role than was the press in the traditional Solid South. After all, the nation's media are more diverse, more powerful, more independent, and more politics-focused than the media in the various states, including especially Southern states pre-1950.[14] It seems plausible that the media could serve as the "fourth branch of government" in American democracy, checking the power of a plebiscitary president, raising important issues and facilitating public deliberation, and guarding the public interest and people's liberties by subjecting government and politicians to the scrutiny of the press.

We have seen in chapter 6 that the media do not suffice as a substitute for political parties in linking the public to their leaders and government. A number of developments are transforming mass media

into even more "uncertain guardians" of our democracy. Although American media are privately owned, their independence from government, especially from the modern presidency on which they rely for drama and images, can be easily overstated. Although the media can sometime be attack dogs in hotly contested political situations, in the face of elite consensus, the media are more likely to be reduced to lap dogs.[15] Bartholomew Sparrow suggests that rather than a fourth branch of government, the media may be more fruitfully conceived of as a fourth corner in the iron triangle of policy making.[16] Moreover, the diversity of the media should not be overestimated. Although clearly there is a growing number of types of media as well as media outlets, "there is strikingly little variation among the news media on salient political issues, as many scholars have already found."[17] Part of the problem is the trend toward mergers and acquisitions, as exemplified by the recent conglomeration of Turner–Time-Warner–AOL. The more fundamental problem, however, is the corporate ownership of mass media and the shared outlook among elites, public and private.[18]

As the press morphs into mass media, the real challenge for corporate news bureaus is "not to stay in business—it is to stay in journalism."[19] The pursuit of profits has produced a consumer-driven journalism that slights policy and politics for self-help information, celebrities, and entertainment. One study found that from 1977 to 1997 in select national newspapers, newsmagazines, and TV news broadcasts, the number of stories about government dropped from one in three to one in five, while the number of stories about celebrities tripled, from one in fifty to one in fourteen. A 1996 poll found that fully one-fourth of the voters learned about that year's presidential race through Jay Leno, David Letterman, and so on.[20] We may be literally as well as metaphorically "amusing ourselves to death." Beyond the effects of commercialization, Neil Postman claims that we are experiencing a cultural conversion reflecting the pivotal position of television as the contemporary channel of communication, arguing that the medium inherently shapes, and limits, the message. Television, he writes, "speaks in only one persistent voice—the voice of entertainment," and that blaring noise is "transforming our culture into one vast arena for show business." Postman worries that "as typography moves to the periphery of our culture and television takes its place at the center, the seriousness, clarity and, above all, value of

public discourse dangerously declines." If, as Bernard Cohen once observed, the media do not tell us what to think but rather tell us what to think about, what the public thinks about is increasingly trivia rather than real news.[21]

If mass media cannot be counted on to sustain an informed democratic citizenry, some might argue that soaring levels of campaign spending may actually play a healthy role in filling the gap in the public's political knowledge. We might ponder whether we spend enough on elections, given that Americans spent about four times the amount on health and beauty aids that they spent on electing public officials in 1992. We spent more on frozen waffles than the presidential candidates spent, and Philip Morris alone spent as much selling its cigarettes as all of our political campaigns spent.[22] More spending on campaigns just might produce a more informed public. In the old Solid South, the narrowness of the political base and the homogeneity of elite interests ensured that candidates were too strictly beholden to "the big boys," the Southern species of "fat cats." Candidates not in the pocket of the monied interests had to resort to antics or demagoguery to get the voters' attention and cut themselves out of the crowd of candidates. Especially to the extent that campaign funds come from diverse sources and candidates remain competitive in their ability to attract and spend money to support their rival messages, more rather than less campaign spending may be healthy for a vibrant pluralistic democracy.

Several caveats cloud this rosy view of contemporary campaign finance. First, there is some question whether selling candidates like soap or cigarettes produces a public discourse with sufficient content to inform citizens. A study of 1988 U.S. Senate races found that campaign rhetoric had little to do with the substance of policy issues and may have simply confused the voters; astoundingly, voters were more likely to know about the key issues the less the campaigns spent.[23] Second, even if campaign funds come from diverse sources and are available to competing candidates, the necessity to raise astronomical sums of money serves as a threshold that severely limits the opportunity to seek office to the tiny percentage of people who have access to substantial wealth. Besides, money is not widely available and accessible to candidates and other political actors to contend on a level playing field. Darrell West and Burdett Loomis remind us of Schattsneider's

classic critique of pluralism, a theory of American politics that relies on competing elites to define alternative choices for the public and to harness government by elites to the public interest. "The definition of alternatives is the supreme instrument of power," said Schattsneider, but the struggle is not a fair one. "The flaw in the pluralist heaven is that the heavenly chorus sings with an upper-class accent." West and Loomis's study of contemporary politics forces them to conclude that even with the proliferation of interests and media and messages, "the paradox of the contemporary period is that Schattschneider's heavenly chorus sings with more of an upper-class accent than ever before. Large, well-funded interests are crowding out consumer groups, public-interest groups, political parties, and even broad-based social movements."[24]

Pluralist democracy (a multiplicity of power centers and contending elites) is, unfortunately, not enough to guarantee self-government unless fortified with a more vital democratic pluralism (flatter social and economic hierarchies and more robust participation).[25] Although trends toward pluralism and visibility among national institutions work to counter possible evolution toward the draining of democratic substance from our politics, we cannot comfortably assume that passively relying on these remote developments will safeguard the future promise of democracy. A surer solution is to rely on ourselves to choose a different path. The demise of democracy is not foreordained; it is perhaps not even likely, if we citizens take action.

A Tale of Two Souths

Even assuming that a passive projection of current trends would indicate that the American future is "Southern" in some sense, which "South" foretells our fate? The history of the South is not a single story, after all, despite the region's stereotyped image. Its history is not exclusively an unrelieved tale of elite misrule, prejudice and oppression, and popular defeat. Before the Solid South system, there were moments when elements of the South led the nation toward democracy. Before the era of the Civil War and Solid South, the region provided much of the country's political leadership. Many of the Republic's founders, of course, were Southern. Revolutionary leaders such as Patrick Henry, George Mason, and Thomas Jefferson con-

tributed much to the break with monarchy, the institutionalization
of civil liberties, and the democratization of postrevolutionary government.[26] Coming at the end of the Solid South era, and in large measure responsible for its defeat, the civil rights movement still serves
as a model for reformers interested in revitalizing American democracy. Although we must be careful about which aspects of the Southern tradition we choose to learn from, the South represents more than
the negative portent of partyless, elitist, and racist politics.[27] There
are populist and progressive Southern stories as well, if we choose to
listen to these more positive narratives.

The contradictory currents of Southern politics are embodied in the
person of Tom Watson, the Georgia political rebel whose life spanned
two Southern traditions. In the 1890s, Watson was a young Populist,
a friend of the common people, black and white alike. He won a seat
in Congress and ran for vice-president on the People party's populist
reform ticket. As an old man, embittered by the defeat of the Populist
insurrection, he spread venom and hatred throughout the state, using
his newspaper to stir up racial and religious prejudice. Rejoining the
dominant Democratic party, he was elected U.S. senator in the same
Solid South system he had fought against as a young man. The story
of the populist Tom Watson reminds us that a "Southern" future
might be more instead of less democratic, depending on our actions in
the present.[28]

A More Participatory Democracy

Populism, as the root word suggests, had many elements of popular,
participatory democracy.[29] Popular self-government cannot rest solely
on elite competition. V. O. Key himself suggested that "we believe in
a brawling, fighting, arguing, contentious democracy, not because it
promotes good government but because it insures popular government
. . . [and] popular government redounds to the good of all."[30] Genuine
popular self-rule cannot be realized by unaccountable leaders competing in electoral shadowboxing contests while the citizenry remains
unengaged and inattentive. To reinvigorate America's heritage of popular, "small-d" democracy, we must find ways to reform our political
institutions so that they will be more open to widespread participation

and a truly public dialogue. Advocates of reform have no trouble enumerating long lists of prescriptions that could be tried to make American politics more genuinely democratic. The specific proposals change with the concrete circumstances, and there is probably no one quick fix or magic bullet that will suffice. Several proposals, however, recur frequently enough to suggest their centrality in any democratization program.

Campaign finance is an obvious target for reform, given the astronomical rise in the prevalence and influence of money in American politics. Reformers are not united in the types of campaign financing reforms advocated. They disagree about the particular mix of disclosure, contribution and expenditure limits, and public financing that would be most efficacious. In principle, the ideal reform would foster campaign speech widely and recognize the inevitable role of money in elections, while realistically ensuring access to the electorate for the widest possible range of campaigners and curbing the inordinate influence of those with access to big bucks. Given the truth of the adage that "who pays the piper calls the tune," public financing would be money well invested. Maine and Vermont recently passed campaign reform acts that could be signposts toward significant reform. Both provide state money to finance campaigns that qualify by demonstrating substantial public support through raising small amounts from a number of donors. They limit spending by candidates who accept state financing, and Maine even provides some matching funds to help publicly financed candidates keep pace with higher-spending privately funded opponents. Both impose contribution limits and disclosure requirements. Vermont also "caps campaign expenditures, bans soft money, and regulates political advertising and independent expenditures." In the words of one Maine reformer, "the public is ready not just for tinkering but for a complete overhaul of our campaign finance system. It's not just that voters are disgusted, it's a hope for something better, for the kind of democracy that they want their kids to grow up in."[31]

Electoral experiments should be continued in an effort to make voting easier for citizens, especially those in the bottom half of the socioeconomic scale. "Motor voter" laws should be defended, and states should be encouraged to continue to ease voter registration requirements. Different and more convenient methods of balloting should

also be explored. Among others, Oregon's experiments in mail ballots demonstrate encouraging levels of increased participation. Allowing parties to cross-nominate candidates on so-called fusion ballots would allow voters to endorse candidates from major parties running simultaneously on minor-party tickets without "wasting" their votes on hopeless third-party campaigns. Most states currently prohibit fusion ballots. These laws were generally enacted around the turn of the last century, part of the arsenal of "reforms" used to rig the rules to defeat the Populist challenge. Although the Supreme Court recently ruled that state laws banning fusion ballots are not unconstitutional, nothing prevents states from allowing fusion ballots, as ten states, including New York, now do. By expanding the range of party options available to the electorate, it is likely that more issues could be raised, options clarified, and participation correspondingly expanded.[32]

A More Deliberative Democracy

If participation was the buzzword of the 1960s, by the 1990s, democratic theorists were increasingly aware that the quality as well as the quantity of popular participation is a critical issue for a revitalized democracy. Experience with the politics of abortion has amply demonstrated that participation per se cannot satisfactorily resolve issues if participants are merely shouting past each other.

Hence, there has developed in recent years vigorous defenses of deliberation in politics. Some of these works are quite philosophical and abstract, but they make the point that dialogue is the lifeblood of democracy. If discussion and debate are informed, free, and lively, voting actually takes a backseat in democratic decision making. Other thinkers have clarified the conditions for deliberation in democratic politics, including publicity, reciprocity, and accountability. Translating these philosophical positions into legal doctrine, Cass Sunstein has suggested that the goal of the framers in creating the four cornerstones of our Constitution—checks and balances, federalism, individual rights, and judicial review—was to establish the foundations of a deliberative democracy. Sunstein advocates a method of constitutional interpretation that he calls the impartiality principle: in a deliberative "republic of reasons," legitimate government requires there to be reasons

intelligible to differently minded people justifying policy in terms of a public interest beyond the mere self-interest of interest-group pluralism. Political scientist James Fishkin has attempted to implement these philosophical insights politically by sponsoring "deliberative opinion polls." These innovations bring together a representative sample of people to hear issues debated before being asked to state their opinions on the issues. Fishkin claims that these forums of informed citizens, as a kind of national caucus, represent what public opinion would be on issues if formed under authentically deliberative conditions.[33]

The mass media are absolutely essential for a more deliberative politics. W. Lance Bennett criticizes the media's approach to news as unhelpful to a democratic polity. A combination of economic and organizational structures as well as professional norms conspires to produce news coverage that focuses on crises, dramatizes stories, tends to personalize the drama as a struggle between good and bad individuals, and finally normalizes the ending by reassuring the audience that ultimately all is well. A democratic citizenry needs the kind of news coverage that provides adequate information for self-governance. Such coverage would report on conditions and states of affairs, as well as on events. It would be analytic, not simply dramatic, and it would describe the workings of institutions as well as individuals. Last, democratic news would be critical in the broadest sense of assessing and indicating options; it would not simply alarm and then symbolically reassure an ultimately quiescent public.[34]

The many suggestions for restructuring the delivery of news in ways that would better support democratic deliberation include limiting conglomeration and cross-ownership of media outlets; expanding public access to mass media; increasing the length of sound bites in the news; limiting the use of thirty-second campaign spots; requiring broadcasters to provide candidates with longer time slots; sponsoring more and better formatted candidate debates; strengthening the independence of, and adequately funding, public broadcasting; better educating the journalism profession; and modifying the journalism profession's norms, especially its "horse-race" mentality. The point of all these specific proposals is to suggest ways that the media could treat the audience as a public, not merely as consumers to be sold entertainment. To act as a public and govern ourselves, we need the media to present us with information, analysis, and alternatives.

"Democracy means the power to choose, and choice is an illusion without information."[35]

A More Responsible Democracy

Expanded turnout requires institutions that mobilize the electorate. Potential voters need reasons to turn out to vote. Political parties, so critical to Key's analysis, must be revitalized to be more open and responsible. One way to do this might be to foster—through less restrictive ballot access, among other ways—third-party competition. Minor-party activity is currently swelling, with significant initiatives being launched by the Reform party, the Concord Coalition, the Greens, the New party, and the Labor party, to name just some. Third parties in this country historically have had dismal records in winning government offices directly, but they have enjoyed a healthy influence on the major parties by spurring them to get back in touch with popular constituencies.[36]

Calls for more responsible parties are not new. Over the years, a number of specific suggestions have been proposed to strengthen American parties and their role in politics. For example, proponents have suggested midterm issues conventions,[37] institutionalization of a means to vote no confidence in the president, linked terms for presidents and congressional representatives, a stronger role for national party conventions, and more party control over nominations. What these reforms share is a desire for more responsible parties, parties that are more open internally, that contest elections on the basis of competing issue positions, and that are then held accountable for their performance on these issues once their candidates are in office.[38]

To be fully realized, a responsible party system may require multiple parties to present numerous options on issues of public policy. Lowi argues that while reformers have been correct in their attraction to enhanced party responsibility, they have been wrong to link that goal to a reinvigorated two-party system. He deflates numerous myths supporting the two-party system, arguing that third parties offer a viable route to party responsibility and increased popular control of government.[39] Several electoral reforms would probably break the duopoly of two-party ascendancy; for example, proportional representation would

give incentive for smaller parties to retain their organizational independence by accurately translating voter preferences into legislative seats.[40] At a minimum, party responsibility in this country requires a Democratic party with backbone. That backbone must be supplied by a broad progressive coalition.

The long-standing nature of these reform proposals for more responsible parties and the fact that some progress has been made in both opening the parties up, especially in the form of presidential primaries, and strengthening the technical capacities of parties suggest that perhaps these innovations are not entirely effective in achieving their goals. Some critics claim that the goals of making parties both more participatory and more issue oriented may even be mutually contradictory. Many advocates of strong parties suggest that the same reforms that opened up the presidential nomination process in the 1970s contributed to the splintering and debilitating of the parties in the current candidate-centered era.[41] The main conclusion to be drawn from the limits of these reforms, however, is that responsible parties are not likely to be attained solely by tinkering with the structures of the parties themselves.

A More Popular Democracy

Politically, reform requires the formation of a popular coalition. In essence, the conservative movement has transformed the Republican party into at least a semiresponsible party. Contrary to the claims of critics of the responsible party model, the clear issue stances of the Republicans have brought the party more than its share of electoral successes, first during the Reagan-Bush era and most recently with the 1994 congressional sweep of conservative Republicans with their Contract with America. The conservative movement, especially its Christian right component, has opened up the party and entered it in numbers sufficient to ensure that it will remain true to its right-tilting agenda, despite electoral pressures to "sell out" and seek votes in the ideological middle by softening its stands on issues.[42] Progressives, in contrast, have failed to capture a sufficient hold on the Democratic party to prevent it from muddying its issue positions in the shameless pursuit of electoral victories at any price.

To win power on a par with the right, progressive groups must search for common ground on which to coalesce. Although progressive single-issue groups have attained a measure of influence operating independently of one another, what they have not achieved since the New Deal era is governing power. Part of these groups' shortcomings has been an intellectual failure. Here, the left could take a lesson from the right, which in recent years has put major stress on a politics of ideas. By generously funding and adroitly manipulating think tanks and foundations, conservatives have managed to modify America's societal agenda in a conservative direction.[43]

Successful coalition building also requires addressing the issues of racism and sexism and various other forms of social oppression, such as heterosexism, without succumbing to the fragmenting influences of identity politics.[44] In other words, groups on the left need to learn to honor our important and legitimate differences while recognizing and valuing our commonalties as well. In a society rapidly polarizing by class, that means that class cannot be paid mere lip service in discussions of race, gender, and class. It also means that issues of political economy promise a broad platform on which to contest political power.

This prescription for a progressive politics cannot mean ignoring or avoiding issues of racism, sexism, and other forms of discrimination. For better or worse, "the locus of racial conflict is no longer restricted to the South."[45] The "practical convergence" of the regions means that issues of inequality and discrimination are now national quandaries. Paul Sniderman and Edward Carmines have demonstrated that although there are fewer racists on the political left than on the right, racial prejudice presents a more formidable barrier to a liberal agenda than to conservatism. Conservatives share a common opposition to government action to redress inequality; whether their beliefs rest on ideology or prejudice, they are able to unite around rallying cries for "small government." Liberals generally favor government activism to counteract social and market inequalities, but prejudiced liberals who would otherwise approve of egalitarian programs are deterred from supporting programs they perceive as aiding minorities, depriving the liberal coalition of badly needed backing. Race thus reinforces conservatism but divides liberalism.[46]

Sniderman and Carmines advocate that liberals frame their programs in "color-blind" terms to win the support of prejudiced as well

as more tolerant liberals. The term "color-blind" is an unfortunate label for the approach they advocate, however, since many who use this term, as the authors recognize, aim not to affirm a broader egalitarian ideal but to "put out of sight the divisive ideal of racial justice." Actually, Sniderman and Carmines favor policies that "reach beyond race," in the sense of being "color inclusive" rather than color-blind. Their research indicates that proposals framed in universal rather than group-specific terms win broader support, because prejudiced liberals do not so much oppose programs targeted at minorities as they disapprove of race-based programs that would exclude deserving whites. Based on their findings, Sniderman and Carmines call for "a politics centered on the needs of those most in need. It is not to argue for a politics in which race is irrelevant, but in favor of one in which race is relevant so far as it is a gauge of need. Above all, it is to call for a politics which, because it is organized around moral principles that apply regardless of race, can be brought to bear with special force on the issue of race."[47]

Whether policies that "reach beyond race" are merely color-blind in the sense of being self-delusional—seeing society through rose-colored classes and avoiding the harsh realities of race in America—or have the potential to address particular group problems in the context of more universal approaches depends not only on who is being assisted but also on how the program is implemented and why the assistance is justified. Whatever the specifics of a progressive program, Michael Goldfield has demonstrated that race cannot be ignored in American politics, indeed, that the interplay of race and class has shaped American history at its critical junctures.[48] Goldfield decries prescriptions that pessimistically give up on white people, especially workers, as hopelessly prejudiced or that try to ignore or disguise racial issues. In a position that seems to contradict Sniderman and Carmines, Goldfield advocates placing racial equality at the top of a progressive agenda. Yet the way in which he frames this progressive stance is not entirely incompatible with Sniderman and Carmines's "reaching beyond race." Goldfield criticizes the individualistic liberal perspective that racism is merely a matter of personal immorality or ignorance. He gives examples from history of alternative progressive or left approaches that link the battle for racial equality with struggles against broader inegalitarian structural features of American society

and political economy. He thus advocates a movement that would include, centrally, demands for racial justice, but not to the exclusion of calls for a more equal and just society for all.[49]

This last point resonates with the requirements of a more deliberative democracy. Progressives need to highlight concerns that speak to their particular interests but simultaneously address the public interest, because politics is not only about who gets what, when, and how but also about who should get what, when, and how. This congruence of group and common interest must be plausible if it is to meet the test of constitutionality in a "republic of reasons" and win the support of the large segment of public opinion that approves of policies justified by universalism.[50] Revitalized democracy itself is one such genuine interest that progressives share with the general public.

A More Organized Democracy

Democracy cannot be sustained in the purely political sphere. As America's philosopher of democracy John Dewey recognized, democracy must be a way of life, and that requires a thoroughly democratic society.[51] In a capitalist democracy, power flows from either money or numbers. Experience has shown that sheer numbers, unless organized, are ineffective counterweights to money. In the political realm, parties help organize popular power, but democratic parties must rest on an organized society, and that foundation has been crumbling recently in the United States.

In contrast to the Democratic party in this country, for instance, the Swedish Social Democratic party (SAP) has a long history of advancing progressive social legislation, sometimes even in the face of electoral adversity. The key to this historic stance has been the relationship of the party to the Swedish labor movement, especially the largest blue-collar union federation, the Landsorganisationen. Labor, in effect, represents the electoral engine that drives the SAP, giving unions an inordinate amount of influence in shaping party doctrine and platforms. Because Swedish workers are highly organized, with over 90 percent belonging to unions, employee interests are effectively represented in the party and faithfully translated into policies in the interests of the vast majority of Swedish workers. Swedish employers

have organized in reaction, and the result is that Swedish voters are presented with clearly defined and divergent programs from which to choose a government.[52]

Currently, the right is far better organized than the left. Religious right churches and parareligious organizations such as the Christian Coalition, talk radio, business organizations, the right-to-life movement, racist and paramilitary organizations, and single-issue groups such as the National Rifle Association have given conservatives in general and the Republican party in particular a strong base in civil society.[53] By contrast, the potentially broadest progressive popular organizations, unions, are terribly weak and are locked in a subservient relationship with the Democratic party. Unions now represent a minuscule portion of American workers and are politically less potent than at any point in recent history. Although unions represent the core of the Democratic constituency and its chief source of volunteers and campaign funding, they are, in effect, captive partners to Democratic politicians, who often accept their electoral aid and then turn their backs at critical junctures, secure in the knowledge that labor has nowhere else to go.[54] In falling from a high of about one-third of the workforce being organized to slightly over one-tenth union membership, the nation has assumed the traditional Southern stance of an unorganized workforce. As the historical exceptionalism of the anti-union South has been enveloped in a national crusade against labor, ironically, the South, long the soft underbelly of the labor movement, is now the most fertile field for union organizing.[55]

The most likely source of democratic renewal in America today is a revitalized labor movement. Under new leadership dedicated to more vigorous organizing and more independent politics, unions are showing new signs of life. Organizing victories, especially in the health care, textile, and custodial services industries, give hope that increased resources devoted to organizing and new, more creative strategies are beginning to reap benefits, especially in organizing the lower-paid workers who have lacked voice in the economic transformation under way. More vital unions, however, will require innovative organizational forms. Most obviously, unions that can serve as a foundation for democracy must be internally democratic themselves. Movements for union democracy in many major American unions, as well as stirrings among the rank and file, augur well for more participatory

unions. Unions will have to discover new ways of representing their members' interests, especially in an economy that is rapidly moving further away from a manufacturing and toward a service and information economy. New forms of adversarial bargaining and labor-management cooperation need to be invented to cope with the burdens placed on employees by new systems of "lean production," as well as to empower American workers and businesses to compete in the global economy.

To attract new members from a broader base and to fulfill their mission to speak for all sorts of employees in America, unions need to move away from their traditional, quite hierarchical and conservative, business unionism and embrace a more social unionism. The success of Justice for Janitors campaigns in several major cities shows the potential for organizing when unions reinvent themselves, overcoming their recent legacy of being narrow interest groups designed to serve dues-paying members and instead becoming broader social movements, rooted in the community, aiming to obtain representation and justice for working people more generally.[56] Another example of efforts bearing fruit when unions reach out to other community groups is the Union Cities program to reactivate urban labor councils. The case of the Atlanta Labor Council under the leadership of Stewart Acuff is instructive of innovative thinking and practices in the labor movement. Forming a tight alliance with community groups, the council used a variety of strategies, ranging from orthodox (e.g., providing campaign support for friendly politicians and lobbying government and business decision makers) to highly imaginative and daring tactics (e.g., protest and even civil disobedience) to make sure that the 1996 Olympic Games in Atlanta would not trample the interests of workers and the community.[57]

Beyond reaching out to local community groups, the labor movement must discover ways of organizing and cooperating across borders if it is to check the unrestrained power of transnational corporations in our globalized world. The participation of labor in the anti–World Trade Organization demonstrations in Seattle in the fall of 1999 illustrates just how far labor has come in its willingness to reach out and form coalitions with activist groups it often spurned as too radical just a few years ago. The images of union members and environmentalists marching together under banners proclaiming "Teamsters and Turtles

United" indicate a growing recognition that, whatever the immediate, short-term conflicts between jobs and protecting nature, in the long run, workers and the environment must be protected together, or they will be ravaged separately. The anti-sweatshop movement that is newly reactivating many college campuses is another prime example of the labor movement, working in tandem with students and community activists, thinking globally and acting locally.

In the meantime, many employees will not be organized into unions; yet for all employees, a voice at work is a strong component of empowerment and a vital training ground for democratic citizenship. Surveys show that American workers are interested in having more say in their workplaces, but they are pessimistic about their employers' willingness to allow them real influence in managerial decisions. Employers, too, have been moving rapidly to implement more participative management, employee involvement, and teamwork. Since the early 1990s, business has clamored for reform of labor laws to legalize employee involvement programs, many of which run afoul of current labor law as constituting, in essence, company-dominated sham labor organizations. Businesses and their Republican allies in recent Congresses have pushed the TEAM (Teamwork for Employees and Managers) Act, which would legalize employee involvement committees and teams, even if they are dominated by employers. Paul Weiler has suggested that unorganized employees, who lack unions to represent their rights and interests, are the ones whose voices need protection from employer domination under reformed labor laws. He proposes that rather than merely trusting employers to "empower" their workers on the company's terms, legislation is needed to ensure the rights of all employees to participate in workplace decisions freely and with a guaranteed voice.[58]

Other forms of organization are necessary if society is to be thoroughly democratized. The social uprisings that toppled the Soviet empire as well as democratic theorists have focused attention on the critical role of civil society—those institutions and practices that exist in the civil space between the market and the state—in sustaining a healthy democracy. If American civil society is in disarray, the causes must be diagnosed and remedies designed, but revitalizing American civil society is no small order. Doubtless it would require the invention of new forms of participation, as well as the retrieval of some

older traditions, in numerous social spaces, or "third places," as they have been termed. Cooperatives and worker ownership are two existing forms that might be expanded. Neighborhood organizations have been a source of genuine citizen participation and power at various periods. In *Retrieving Democracy*, Philip Green suggests numerous modifications to institutions and policies that could overcome the steep hierarchies eviscerating democracy today. In particular, he advocates abolishing the strict social divisions of labor that inhibit many groups from full social participation. For example, lifelong access to education would help individuals navigate between various social roles and aid mobility.[59]

The basic point is that "small-d" democrats must look beyond the political realm of voting and parties, where Key focused most of his attention, if they are to revive genuine democracy today. Benjamin Barber points to an enriched civil society as the best hope for taming the blind forces of "McWorld," the global market forces, and "Jihad," the close-knit conflicting communities, that are eroding the bases of democracy in our contemporary world. Only a strong civil society can redeem the concepts of citizenship and the public and restore the substance of self-governance to democratic forms. The realm of factories and offices, schools, churches, and homes must nourish the roots of democratic life if we expect to see political democracy thrive in the future.[60]

Which Future Beckons?

South and North seem more thoroughly reunited than at any time since the Civil War. In the process, the South has made tremendous progress, socially, economically, and politically, and has now taken its place as one of the nation's leading regions. In many respects, the South that had so long been the backwater of the country today serves as a pacesetter for the nation. In the meantime, the demise of the New Deal alignment has changed the nature of party competition nationally, gutting American politics of much of the policy substance and popular character it once had. The America that the South is now in step with, if not actually leading, is evolving a politics eerily reminiscent of the Solid South politics that the South itself has left behind,

at least in its literal form. As national political structures tend to resemble the worst aspects of traditional Southern politics, the country is increasingly plagued with symptoms produced by those political maladies. Until it develops democratic institutions that can make parties more responsible, entice more people to participate, and focus on genuine issues rather than racially encoded rhetoric, it will still lack the essential characteristics of rationality and genuine democracy that Key anticipated that two-party competition would bring.

We must take a cue from the experiences of the Solid South system if we are to avoid the perverse consequences of such chaotic politics that responded so faithfully to the interests of the elites, yet so shamefully neglected the most basic needs of common citizens. If we want to salvage the best qualities of American democracy for ourselves, in every region and nationally, we must build democratic institutions, practices, and policies that are more popular and participatory, that encourage more democratic deliberation, and that foster a more organized and autonomous public capable of self-governance. If we fail to heed the lessons of the Solid South of the past, in the future, politics may indeed be our number one problem, but it will assuredly drag along a whole host of other ills in its wake.

Notes

Introduction

1. David E. Sturrock, review of *The Disappearing South*, ed. Robert P. Steed, Laurence W. Moreland, and Tod A. Baker, *Journal of Politics* 53, no. 1 (February 1991): 240.

2. David S. Cecelski and Timothy B. Tyson, *Democracy Betrayed: The Wilmington Race Riot of 1989 and Its Legacy* (Chapel Hill: University of North Carolina Press, 1998), 6.

3. Lakoff and Johnson have analyzed the pervasive and powerful role that metaphors play in all levels of our thinking, from the most mundane and routine to much more intellectual conceptualization. George Lakoff and Mark Johnson, *Metaphors We Live By* (Chicago: University of Chicago Press, 1980).

4. Larry J. Griffin, "Why Was the South a Problem to America?" in *The South as an American Problem*, ed. Larry J. Griffin and Don H. Doyle (Athens: University of Georgia Press, 1995), 14; Larry J. Griffin, "Southern Distinctiveness, Yet Again: Or, Why America Still Needs the South," *Southern Cultures* (forthcoming).

5. Griffin argues that many problems identified as uniquely Southern are actually American problems. For example, on racism, he quotes Malcolm X, who once remarked: "As far as I am concerned, Mississippi is anywhere south of the Canadian border." Nonetheless, Griffin contends that this projection of American social problems onto the South represents more than mere scapegoating. The process of creating the South as "an American counterpoint" has served important functions in constructing the very idea of the nation. Griffin, "Why Was the South a Problem," 23, 28.

6. Griffin, "Southern Distinctiveness, Yet Again." In the conclusion, I note that alongside the undemocratic, dominant Solid South exists a populist and progressive Southern strand as democratic in its heritage as any in the country.

7. Larry Griffin, "Southern Distinctiveness, Yet Again," is not alone in noting the contested nature of metaphors. Even Lakoff and Johnson, who argue for the centrality of metaphors in our lives and thought, suggest that metaphors can hide aspects of reality. They contend that political and economic metaphors "matter more, because they constrain our lives. A metaphor in a political or economic system, by virtue of what it hides, can lead to human degradation." Lakoff and Johnson, *Metaphors We Live By*, 236.

8. Frederick Wirt, *"We Ain't What We Was"*: *Civil Rights in the New South* (Durham, N.C.: Duke University Press, 1998).

1. Dixie Déjà Vu

1. Following the lead of the foremost analyst of Southern politics, V. O. Key, Jr., I define the South here as the eleven states that seceded to form the Confederacy: South Carolina, Georgia, Alabama, Mississippi, Louisiana, Virginia, North Carolina, Florida, Tennessee, Arkansas, and Texas. V. O. Key, Jr., *Southern Politics in State and Nation* (New York: Vintage, 1949), 10.

2. Although Bush was a Connecticut transplant, he migrated to Texas early in his adult life and was elected to Congress from there.

3. Joseph A. Aistrup, *The Southern Strategy Revisited* (Lexington: University Press of Kentucky, 1996), 47. See also Kurt Ritter, "Ronald Reagan's 1960s Southern Rhethoric: Courting Conservatives for the GOP," *Southern Communication Journal* 64 (summer 1999): 333–45. Ritter analyzes how Reagan moved from apocalyptic rhetoric to more optimistic restoration and reform jeremiads to broaden his appeal beyond the alienated followers of Barry Goldwater and George Wallace. He also presented a more affable persona than Goldwater and avoided the overt racism of Wallace, enabling him to reach a wider constituency without losing the Southern segregationist backers of these two earlier presidential candidates. As one South Carolinian exclaimed upon hearing Reagan speak in Columbia in 1967, "Reagan is the real Goldwater. He's the man we were looking for in 1964" (ibid., 343).

4. Gerald Pomper, "The Presidential Election," in *The Election of 1992: Reports and Interpretations*, ed. Gerald M. Pomper et al. (Chatham, N.J.: Chatham House, 1993), 134.

5. Walter Dean Burnham, "Bill Clinton: Riding the Tiger," in *The Election of 1996: Reports and Interpretations*, ed. Gerald M. Pomper et al. (Chatham, N.J.: Chatham House, 1997), 4.

6. Michael Lind, in "Southern Coup," *New Republic*, 19 June 1995, 20–29, was one of the first commentators to notice the ascendance of Southern leaders. See also Terrel L. Rhodes, *Republicans in the South: Voting for the State House, Voting for the White House* (Westport, Conn.: Praeger, 2000).

7. Daniel J. Parks notes that Yale political scientist David Mayhew concurs that a shift of power from the Speaker to majority whip Delay has transpired in the post-Gingrich era. Daniel J. Parks, "Partisan Voting Holds Steady," *Congressional Quarterly Weekly*, 11 December 1999, 3. Retrieved 22 June 2000 from the World Wide Web: *http://libraryip.cq.com*.

8. Harold W. Stanley, "The South and the 1996 Presidential Election: Republican Gains Among Democratic Wins," in *The 1996 Presidential Elections in the South: Southern Party Systems in the 1990s*, ed. Laurence W. Moreland and Robert P. Steed (Westport, Conn.: Praeger, 1997), 238.

9. Of course, if George Bush is considered a Texan, the country has already seen an all-Southern presidential election in the Bush-Clinton contest of 1992. Nor was the Southern influence limited to candidates from below the Mason-Dixon line. Some observers noted a resemblence between John McCain's bid for the Republi-

can presidential nomination in 2000 and Jimmy Carter's style in the primaries of 1976. Both candidates ran in the wake of presidential scandals and offered populist messages, along with promises of nobler character in the White House. Mark Sherman, "McCain Sounding a Lot Like Carter on the Campaign Trail," *Atlanta Journal/Constitution*, 13 February 2000, B4.

10. Gary Orfield, "The Growth of Segregation: African Americans, Latinos, and Unequal Education," in *Dismantling Desegregation: The Quiet Reversal of* Brown v. Board of Education, ed. Gary Orfield, Susan E. Eaton, and the Harvard Project on School Desegregation (New York: New Press, 1996), 26, 48.

11. The "traditional" or "Old" South of the past referred to here and elsewhere in this book is the one-party Democratic "Solid South." This political system was constructed around the turn of the twentieth century and dominated Southern politics and policy making until the 1960s and 1970s. This Solid South is described more fully in chapter 2.

12. David Stoesz, *Small Change: Domestic Policy Under the Clinton Presidency* (White Plains, N.Y.: Longman, 1996).

13. Neal R. Pierce, "Two Million: Couldn't We Do Better?" *San Diego Union-Tribune*, 7 February 2000, B6, retrieved 23 April 2000 from the World Wide Web: *http://web.lexis-nexis.com/universe*; Duncan Campbell, "Anger Grows as the US Jails Its Two Millionth Inmate, 25 Percent of World's Prison Population," *Guardian*, 15 February 2000, 3, retrieved 23 April 2000, from the World Wide Web: *http://web.lexis-nexis.com/universe*; Michael J. Sniffen, "Justice Department Reports Rate of Growth in Prison Population; Is Lowest Since 1979," *Buffalo News*, 16 August 1999, 3A, retrieved 23 April 2000 from the World Wide Web: *http://web.lexis-nexis.com/universe*; Peter Slevin, "Growth in Prison Population Slows," *Washington Post*, 20 April 2000, A34, retrieved 23 April 2000 from the World Wide Web: *http://web.lexis-nexis.com/universe*; and Manning Marable, "America: Toward a Police State?" BRC-NEWS (on-line), retrieved 9 April 2000 from the World Wide Web.

A statistic cited by Pierce, "Two Million," highlights the discrimination that pervades the criminal justice system: "African Americans represent about 13 percent of the nation's population and 15 percent of its drug users, but about 50 percent of prison inmates in an era when drug offenses have been the driving force in prison expansion." Several caveats should be noted. First, much of the incarcerated population is in state prisons. Second, the rate of growth of the prison population has slowed. Third, some contend that the higher number of inmates accounted for the reduction in crime experienced in the late 1990s. Critics challenge this claim about the effectiveness of incarceration, noting that "crime rates, before and after the prison buildup, were about the same" (Pierce, "Two Million") and suggest that other factors, such as full employment and demographic changes, were more significant.

14. Stoesz, *Small Change*, 202–3.

15. Theda Skocpol, *Boomerang: Health Care Reform and the Turn Against Government* (New York: W. W. Norton, 1997).

16. William C. Berman, *America's Right Turn: From Nixon to Clinton*, 2d ed. (Baltimore: Johns Hopkins University Press, 1998), 165.

17. Stephen D. Cummings, *The Dixification of America: The American Odyssey into the Conservative Economic Trap* (Westport, Conn.: Praeger, 1998).

18. Richard K. Scher, *Politics in the New South: Republicanism, Race, and Leadership in the Twentieth Century*, 2d ed. (Armonk, N.Y.: M. E. Sharpe, 1997), 274.

19. Randall Kennedy, "Is He a Soul Man? On Black Support for Clinton," *American Prospect*, March–April 1999, 30.

20. Berman, *America's Right Turn*, 178.

21. W. J. Cash, *The Mind of the South* (New York: Random House, 1941); Leroy Percy, *Latterns on the Levee: Recollections of a Planter's Son* (New York: Alfred A. Knopf, 1941).

22. Abramson notes that although Clinton and Starr share some similarities of background, their experiences growing up shaped very different men. Clinton, whose mother was a devotee of racetracks and jazz clubs, loved rock and roll and played the saxophone. Starr, a minister's son, was raised in a house where swearing and alcohol were forbidden; his hobby in junior high was polishing shoes. While Clinton emulated John Kennedy and William Fulbright, the liberal senator from Arkansas, Starr was inspired by Richard Nixon. Clinton attended George Washington, Yale, and Oxford Universities; Starr attended Harding College in Searcy, Arkansas, "the academic seat of America's radical right," and wore a coat and tie when he transferred to George Washington University in the late 1960s. Neither served in Vietnam, but Starr supported the war that Clinton protested. One Clinton friend characterized Starr's interminable investigations of the president's ethics "a culture war about the 60's." Jill Abramson, "Baby Boomers, and There the Likeness Ceases," *New York Times*, 16 February 1998, retrieved 2 June 1998 from the World Wide Web: *http://web.lexis-nexis.com/universe*. The sharp differences between these two people born into the same regional culture should serve as a reminder that the South is not homogeneous and that there are, in reality, many "Souths" from which to choose, a point reiterated in the concluding chapter.

23. "Comic opera" was V. O. Key's characterization of the nation's view of traditional Southern politics. Key, *Southern Politics*, 3.

24. Peter Applebome argues that "Dixie rising" encompasses a position of leadership not only politically but also culturally, economically, and socially. Peter Applebome, *Dixie Rising: How the South Is Shaping American Values, Politics and Culture* (New York: Random House, 1996). On economics, see Kirkpatrick Sale, *Power Shift: The Rise of the Southern Rim and Its Challenge to the Eastern Establishment* (New York: Random House, 1975); and Larry Sawyers and William K. Tabb, *Sunbelt/Snowbelt: Urban Development and Regional Restructuring* (New York: Oxford University Press, 1984).

25. *Congress and the Nation*, vol. 9: *1993-1996* (Washington, D.C.: Congressional Quarterly Press, 1998), 1182.

26. David Galef, "The South Has Risen Again. Everywhere," *New York Times*, 19 October 1997, retrieved 2 June 1998 from the World Wide Web: *http://web.lexis-nexis.com/universe*.

27. Gil Klein, "Southerners Take Helm of Nation's Cultural Agencies," *Tampa Tribune*, 14 February 1998, 6, retrieved 2 June 1998 from the World Wide Web: *http://web.lexis-nexis.com/universe*. Klein reported that one Iowa National Endowment of the Humanities official reacted to the appointments by e-mailing colleagues, "Reckon I better dust off ma boot. . . . I'd be pleased to hear from y'all

on Southern themes that might appeal to Iowans. How about 'South Finally Wins Cold War'?"

28. A million-dollar reward offered by *Hustler* magazine publisher Larry Flynt for details of sexual misconduct by Republican members of Congress elicited enough dirt to ensure that all the mud slung during the impeachment proceedings did not stick to the White House.

29. Howard Fineman, "Virtuecrats," *Newsweek*, 13 June 1994, 30–36; John Shelton Reed, *The Enduring South* (Chapel Hill: University of North Carolina Press, 1972), 50. See also Andrew Sullivan, "Giving Conservatism a Bad Name," *Seattle Post-Intelligencer*, 22 November 1998, G1, G3. Sullivan argues that American neo-conservatism is being redefined from a philosophy of limits into an ideology of neo-Puritanism by thinkers dubbed the "theo-conservatives." Obsessed with a perceived breakdown of traditional morals dating from the 1960s, conservative thinkers such as William Kristol, Robert Bork, and David Frumm are animated by issues of personal morality, especially abortion, homosexuality, and adultery. Sullivan links this "remoralization" of conservatism with the Right's vendetta against Bill Clinton and the effort to impeach him "not for illegality but for immorality." According to Sullivan, "So Clinton, arguably the most conservative Democratic president since Harry S. Truman, becomes for these conservatives the apex of '60's liberalism. The fact that he balanced the budget, signed welfare-reform legislation, has shredded many civil liberties in the war against terrorism, is in favor of the death penalty and signed the Defense of Marriage Act is immaterial to his conservative enemies. For the model of cultural collapse to work, Clinton must represent its nadir" (ibid., G3).

30. Sue Tolleson-Rinehart, "Can the Flower of Southern Womanhood Bloom in the Garden of Southern Politics?" *Southern Cultures* 4, no. 1 (April 1998): 82. I am grateful to my daughter, Molly Cochran, for pointing out the connection between current calls for old-fashioned values and traditional Southern culture with its reinforcement of hierarchical institutions. She also drew the Fineman article to my attention.

31. Daniel Elazar, *American Federalism* (New York: Thomas Y. Crowell, 1966).

32. Lind, "Southern Coup," 23, 29. Lind recalls that in *The Mind of the South,* the pained native analyst of Southern culture W. J. Cash characterized the Southern ideal of a homogeneous community as "a place where dissent and variety are completely suppressed . . . where men become virtual replicas of one another." Lind also quotes Thomas Jefferson's comparison of regional political culture: "In the North they are cool, sober, laborious, independent, jealous of their own liberties and just to those of others." Southerners, by contrast, are "fiery, voluptuary, indolent, unsteady, zealous for their own liberties, but trampling on those of others" (ibid., 29).

33. Applebome, *Dixie Rising,* 16; emphasis added. Jefferson Davis may not be chief justice, but in the summer of 1999, controversy surfaced because the current chief justice, William Rehnquist, persisted in leading judges and lawyers in singing "Dixie" at his annual songfests during American Bar Association meetings, despite strenuous objections from some that the song carried overtones of slavery and the Confederacy. Bill Rankin, "Black Lawyers Urge Rehnquist to Ditch Tune," *Atlanta Journal/Constitution,* 11 August 1999, 3A, retrieved 12 June 2000 from the World Wide Web: *http://web.lexis-nexis.com/universe.*

34. This list could be dramatically expanded by adding issues of foreign policy to our domestic dilemmas, for example, issues of defense expenditures and the wisdom of building missile defense systems, trade restrictions and the compromising of national sovereighty with international associations such as the World Trade Organization, proper peacekeeping roles and interventions in a world awash with ethnic cleansings, population policies, aid policies, immigration policies, and many more. Readers need not agree with my list of problems and priorities, much less with my views about how to resolve them. As I discuss more fully in the introduction, my central concern here is with the political processes by which we attempt to address these issues, not the substantive policies that I believe we should pursue. Readers with widely divergent political opinions may nonetheless agree that, in a democracy, the public's will should guide our choice of policies. It is the efficacy and responsiveness of our evolving political structures in ensuring this democratic process that concern me in this analysis.

35. James A. Mackay, former congressional representative and longtime political activist from Georgia, wrote these words in the preface of *Who Runs Georgia?* a previously unpublished study of Georgia politics written in the late 1940s. He wrote the remark after reflecting on the similarities between the daily news in 1998 and the contents of the fifty-year-old manuscript. Calvin Kytle and James A. Mackay, *Who Runs Georgia?* (Athens: University of Georgia Press, 1998), xxvi–xxvii.

36. Key, *Southern Politics*, 4.

37. The low esteem assigned to politics seems especially prevalent among the young. An annual survey of first-year college students in 1998 revealed that a paltry 27 percent believed that following political affairs was an important life goal, less than half the number so affirming in 1966. Only 14 percent discussed politics frequently, a decline from 30 percent in 1968. Robert Greene, "Political Fires Burn Low on Campuses, Poll Finds," *Atlanta Jounal/Constitution*, 12 January 1998, A6.

38. Wilson Carey McWilliams, "The Meaning of the Election," in *The Election of 1996: Reports and Interpretations*, ed. Gerald M. Pomper et al. (Chatham, N.J.: Chatham House, 1997), 241, 245.

39. Ronald Reagan, "First Inaugural Address" (delivered in Washington, D.C., 20 January 1981), retrieved 27 June 2000 from the World Wide Web: *wysiwyg:// 166/http://www.bartleby.com/124/pres61.html.*

40. See, however, E. J. Dionne's intriguing argument that far from capitulating to the Right, Clinton's tactical retreats actually shifted the political debate toward a more progressive agenda. E. J. Dionne, Jr., "Why Americans Hate Politics: A Reprise," *Brookings Review* 18, no. 1 (winter 2000): 8–11, retrieved 28 January 2000 from the World Wide Web: *http://www.brookings.edu/press/REVIEW/winter 2000/dionne.htm.*

41. I am, of course, making a distinction between the Democratic party (capitalized) and principles of popular self-governance, or small-d democracy.

42. Ira Katznelson, "Reversing Southern Republicanism," in *The New Majority: Toward a Popular Progressive Politics*, ed. Stanley Greenberg and Theda Skocpol (New Haven, Conn.: Yale University Press, 1997), 238.

43. Walter Dean Burnham, "The End of American Party Politics," *Society* 35, no. 2 (1998): 72, originally published in *Society* (1969), retrieved 9 June 1998 from the World Wide Web: *http://venuse.galib.uga.edu.*

44. William Faulkner, *Requiem for a Nun* (New York: Random House, 1951), 92.

2. Politics in the Land of Cotton

1. V. O. Key, Jr., *Southern Politics in State and Nation* (New York: Vintage, 1949), 10.

2. T. Harry Williams, *Huey Long* (New York: Bantam Books, 1969).

3. William Anderson, *The Wild Man from Sugar Creek: The Political Career of Eugene Talmadge* (Baton Rouge: Louisiana State University Press, 1975), 60.

4. Dan T. Carter, *The Politics of Rage: George Wallace, the Origins of the New Conservatism, and the Transformation of American Politics* (New York: Simon and Schuster, 1995), 108.

5. Fitzhugh Brundage, *Under Sentence of Death: Lynching in the South* (Chapel Hill: University of North Carolina Press, 1997).

6. Joseph L. Bernd, *Grassroots Politics in Georgia* (Atlanta: Emory Research Committee, 1960).

7. Quoted in Frank Freidel, *F.D.R. and the South* (Baton Rouge: Louisiana State University Press, 1965), 99.

8. Richard K. Scher, *Politics in the New South: Republicanism, Race, and Leadership in the Twentieth Century*, 2d ed. (Armonk, N.Y.: M. E. Sharpe, 1997), 45–56.

9. Key, *Southern Politics*, 3.

10. Ibid., 4. I am grateful to Fitz Brundage for this formulation of the characteristics identified by Key as central to the Solid South system.

11. Williams, *Huey Long*, 433, 436, argues that Long was not a demagogue who simply sought power for himself but was a mass leader who benefited his followers.

12. Walter Dean Burnham, "Critical Realignment: Dead or Alive?" in *The End of Realignment? Interpreting American Electoral Eras*, ed. Byron E. Shafer (Madison: University of Wisconsin Press, 1991), 133.

13. J. Morgan Kousser, *The Shaping of Southern Politics: Suffrage Restriction and the Establishment of the One-Party South, 1880–1910* (New Haven, Conn.: Yale University Press, 1974), 240; C. Vann Woodward, *Origins of the New South, 1877–1913* (Baton Rouge: Louisiana State University Press, 1951), ch. 12. Southern states employed an impressive array of techniques to disenfranchise African Americans and to narrow their electorates. The poll tax hit hardest at the poor, especially where it was cumulative, which meant that citizens could not vote until back as well as current poll taxes were paid. Treating the Democratic party as if it were a private political club, the all-white primary prevented African Americans from participating in nominating elections that were tantamount to victory, given the certainty of Democratic victories in general elections. Registration requirements presented further opportunities to discriminate against unwanted potential voters. Literacy tests could be a barrier to poor whites as well as African Americans and could easily be administered arbitrarily. Six African American Ph.D.s were ruled illiterate in Alabama, for example (Harrell R. Rodgers, Jr., and Charles S. Bullock III, *Law and Social Change: Civil Rights Laws and Their Consequences* [New York: McGraw-Hill, 1972], 21). A requirement to interpret clauses of the state constitution could be manipulated by election officials, who presented would-be registrants with unbelievably arcane or simple passages, depending on the whim of the official. A good character test provided yet another option for subjective judgment by election officials. Trivial errors in filling out registration documents also provided ample opportunity for discrimination. If all these formal barriers were

insufficient to block participation, intimidation—physical as well as economic—could be used to prevent African Americans from exercising their legal rights. This ensemble of disenfranchisement techniques proved terribly effective. In Louisiana, for example, 130,334 African Americans were registered to vote in 1896. By 1904, only 1,342 remained on the voter rolls, and in the South at large, only 5 percent of eligible African Americans were registered in 1940 (ibid., 17, 25).

The South was also more hostile than other regions to the participation of women (Sue Tolleson-Rinehart, "Can the Flower of Southern Womanhood Bloom in the Garden of Southern Politics?" *Southern Cultures* 4, no. 1 [April 1998]: 78–87). Only four of the eleven Southern states ratified the Nineteenth Amendment extending suffrage to women (Ruth Anne Thompson, review of *Southern Strategies: Southern Women and the Woman Suffrage Question*, by Elna C. Green, H-Net Reviews in the Humanities and Social Sciences, retrieved 20 April 1999 from the World Wide Web: *http://www.h-net.msu.edu/reviews*).

Not surprisingly, the size of the Southern electorate was minuscule, although Key stresses that this diminution results from one-partyism as well as from disenfranchisement. Turnout in gubernatorial elections from 1920 to 1946 ranged from 42.8 percent in North Carolina to 11.6 percent of the eligible population of Virginia. These rates were one-half to one-fifth the comparable turnout of Northern states. Voting for other offices, including president and U.S. senators, was even lower in the South (Key, *Southern Politics*, ch. 23).

14. C. Vann Woodward, *The Strange Career of Jim Crow*, 2d ed. (New York: Oxford University Press, 1966).

15. Key, *Southern Politics*, 9, 5; Frances Fox Piven and Richard A. Cloward, *Why Americans Don't Vote* (New York: Pantheon Books, 1989), 72.

16. Walter Dean Burnham, *The Current Crisis in American Politics* (New York: Oxford University Press, 1982), 263.

17. Key, *Southern Politics*, 9.

18. Ibid., 527, 299; Walter Dean Burnham, "V. O. Key, Jr., and the Study of Political Parties," in *V. O. Key, Jr., and the Study of American Politics*, ed. Milton C. Cummings, Jr. (Washington, D.C.: American Political Science Association, 1988), 6.

19. In an extremely insightful and useful essay, David Mayhew presents Key's analysis of one-party politics in a series of twenty propositions linking party systems with the conduct of politics and government. David R. Mayhew, "Why Did V. O. Key Draw Back from His 'Have Nots' Claim?" in Cummings, *Key and Study of American Politics*, 24–38.

20. Ibid., 8.

21. Key, *Southern Politics*, 17–18, 212; Allan P. Sindler, "Bifactional Rivalry as an Alternative to Two Party Competition in Louisiana," *American Political Science Review* 49, no. 3 (September 1955): 641–62.

22. Joseph L. Bernd, "Georgia: Static and Dynamic," in *The Changing Politics of the South*, ed. William C. Havard (Baton Rouge: Louisiana State University Press, 1972), 294–365; Key, *Southern Politics*, 301.

23. Scher, *Politics in the New South* (1997), 92–93; Anderson, *Wild Man from Sugar Creek*.

24. Key, *Southern Politics*, 655, 507.

25. Ibid., 304.

26. Carter, *Politics of Rage*, 95–96, 109.

27. Key, *Southern Politics*, 304. As few as 10 percent of Southern governors may have been demagogues, according to Scher, *Politics in the New South* (1997), 318. Their influence, however, especially on the region's image, was disproportionate to their numbers.

28. Robert Sherrill, *Gothic Politics in the Deep South* (New York: Ballantine, 1969), 161.

29. Key, *Southern Politics*, 304–5.

30. The number of father-son combinations in North Carolina politics is stunning. Kerr Scott was governor from 1948 to 1952. Son Robert was governor from 1968 to 1972. Melvin Broughton, Jr., son of World War II governor Melvin Broughton, lost the gubernatorial race in 1968 to Bob Scott. Pat Taylor, lieutenant governor under Bob Scott, was the son of a former lieutenant governor. Luther Hodges served as governor from 1956 to 1960. Luther, Jr., was defeated for a senate seat in 1978. I. Beverly Lake was a segregationist candidate for governor in 1960 and 1964. His son, I. Beverly Lake, Jr., was the Republican gubernatorial candidate in 1980.

31. Key, *Southern Politics*, 310; Peter Bachrach and Morton S. Baratz, *Power and Poverty* (New York: Oxford University Press, 1970), 43.

32. Earl Black and Merle Black, *Politics and Society in the South* (Cambridge, Mass.: Harvard University Press, 1987), 8.

33. Key, *Southern Politics*, 305.

34. Ibid.

35. Ibid., 303.

36. Ibid., 307–8.

37. Ibid., 308.

38. Although democracy is one of the most complex and contested concepts in political thought, Lincoln's Gettysburg address, endorsing the ideal of "government of, by, and for the people," is a simple but eloquent formulation of the complex concept of democracy. The stirring words of the Declaration of Independence identify equality, liberty, and popular sovereignty as the central components of democracy: "We hold these truths to be self-evident; that all men are created equal; that they are endowed by their Creator with certain unalienable rights; that among these are life, liberty, and the pursuit of happiness; that, to secure these rights, governments are instituted among men, deriving their just powers from the consent of the governed."

39. On the issue of religion, especially fundamentalism, the South again exhibits the most exceptional aspects of American exceptionalism. Eighty-six percent of Southerners believe the Devil is real, compared with 52 percent of non-Southerners. John Shelton Reed, *The Enduring South* (Chapel Hill: University of North Carolina Press, 1972), 60.

40. Seymour Martin Lipset, *American Exceptionalism: A Double-Edged Sword* (New York: W. W. Norton, 1996), 61–62; Jill Quadagno, *The Color of Welfare: How Racism Undermined the War on Poverty* (New York: Oxford University Press, 1994), 189–96; Michael Goldfield, *The Color of Politics* (New York: New Press, 1997), 19.

The major exception to the usual inattention to the South is Ira Katznelson, whose current work stresses the significance of "race and region" to American political development right up to the present (Ira Katznelson, "The Southern Origins of Our Times," paper presented at the Center for the History of Business, Technology, and Society, Hagley Museum and Library, Wilmington, Del., 10 December 1998, 42). Katznelson argues that the centrality of "the South and its racial civilization" in American politics, especially its entrenched power in Congress, both "produced—by shaping, facilitating, and permitting—the New Deal" and helps explain "the Southern origins of our times" (ibid., 7, 37).

Many theorists of exceptionalism at least mention the South's prominence in the country's distinctiveness but do not stress the region's unique role. Quadagno is rare in her emphasis on the South as a cause of U.S. exceptionalism, but this stress stems mostly from her focus on the "racial fault line" in American politics. She pays less attention to the specific peculiarities and effects of the Solid South political system (Quadagno, *Color of Welfare*, 6).

41. Kelly D. Patterson, *Political Parties and the Maintenance of Liberal Democracy* (New York: Columbia University Press, 1996), 30.

42. Burnham, "Critical Realignment," 112–13.

43. Key, *Southern Politics*, 528; Michael Goldfield, *The Decline of Organized Labor in the United States* (Chicago: University of Chicago Press, 1987); James Atleson, "Law and Union Power," *Buffalo Law Review* 42 (1994): 463; Timothy J. Minchin, *What Do We Need a Union For?* (Chapel Hill: University of North Carolina Press, 1997).

44. Katznelson, "Southern Origins," argues that the failure of unions to organize the South prevented labor from assuming an integral role as a political class in the United States, unlike the pivotal role played by labor in European social democracies. Instead of social corporatism, labor was reduced to the role of one interest group among many.

45. The Great Depression in the 1930s and the aftermath of World War II in the 1940s brought to power working-class-based labor and socialist parties in many industrialized democracies. Social democratic governments initiated or extended welfare-state programs such as health, retirement, and unemployment insurance to protect workers against the vagaries of market capitalism. The New Deal in some ways played the function of a social democratic party, enacting many programs that offer ordinary Americans protections they might not be able to afford to purchase privately (John D. Stephens, *The Transition from Capitalism to Socialism* [Urbana: University of Illinois Press, 1986]). While European social democratic parties rested on urban, working-class constituencies, however, the Democratic party depended not only on this base for support but also on the Solid South, dominated by agrarian planter elites. This element inevitably placed a drag on the development of welfare-state programs. For instance, Social Security initially did not cover domestic or agricultural workers (Quadagno, *Color of Welfare*, 21).

46. Quadagno, *Color of Welfare*, 9–10.

47. Lipset, *American Exceptionalism*, 72; Theda Skocpol, *The Missing Middle: Working Families and the Future of American Social Policy* (New York: W. W. Norton, 2000).

48. Katznelson, "Southern Origins," 38; Brigitta Loesche-Scheller, *Reparations*

to Poverty: Domestic Policy in America Ten Years After the Great Society (Bern: Peter Lang, 1995).

49. Katznelson, "Southern Origins," 39, 7, 40, details the contributions of the South to the creation of America's "Janus-like liberal state" as a "financial, interest-group, national security hybrid." He notes the oddity of this institution. Domestic policy making is characterized by minimal macromanagement and interest-group liberalism, as opposed to planning and corporatist representation. Meanwhile, in the national security arena, the U.S. military constitutes "the world's largest planning instrument," and defense industries and their unions are incorporated into the policy process on a quasi-corporatist basis.

3. Dual Convergence

1. V. O. Key, Jr., *Southern Politics in State and Nation* (New York: Vintage, 1949); Jack Bloom, *Class, Race, and the Civil Rights Movement* (Bloomington: Indiana University Press, 1987); Chandler Davidson, *Race and Class in Texas Politics* (Princeton, N.J.: Princeton University Press, 1990); James Loewen, *The Mississippi Chinese: Between Black and White,* 2d ed. (Prospect Heights, Ill.: Waveland Press, 1988).

2. This subhead is taken from the title of a prescient book by John Edgerton, *The Americanization of Dixie: The Southernization of America* (New York: Harper's Magazine Press, 1974). This section relies heavily on the analysis of Earl Black and Merle Black, *Politics and Society in the South* (Cambridge, Mass.: Harvard University Press, 1987), updating their statistics where appropriate.

3. Black and Black, *Politics and Society,* 13; *State of the South 1998* (Chapel Hill, N.C.: MDC, 1998), 13.

4. Surveys rate Southern locales among the places with the highest quality of life. In a survey by *Money* magazine, for example, 39 of the 100 best communities were Southern ("Best Places 1997," *Money,* July 1997, 140–41).

5. Black and Black, *Politics and Society,* 13. Southern states continue to range rather widely in the percentage of African Americans in their populations. The Census Bureau estimated that in 1998, African Americans made up more than a quarter of the population of all five Deep South states (see note 14), ranging from 36 percent in Mississippi to 26 percent in Alabama. The six Rim South states all had African American populations in greater proportions than did the nation as a whole (12.7 percent), except for Texas (12.3 percent). U.S. Census Bureau, "Population Estimates for States by Race and Hispanic Origin: July 1, 1998," published 15 September 1999, *http://www.census.gov/popuation/estimates/state/srh/srhus98.txt.*

6. *New York Times, Downsizing of America* (New York: Times Books, 1996), 4; *State of the South 1998,* 13; "Education and Progress in the South" (Atlanta: Southern Regional Education Board, 1998), quoting the *Economist,* retrieved 18 June 1998 from the World Wide Web: *http://www.sreb.org/temp/1998.html.*

7. Black and Black, *Politics and Society,* 34–35; *State of the South 1998,* 18–20. The 1990 census showed a wide variation in the percentage of urban residents among Southern states' populations. Florida (85 percent) and Texas (80 percent) continued to be more urban than the nation (75 percent). Virginia, Louisiana, Georgia,

Tennessee, and Alabama ranged from 60 to 70 percent urban, while South Carolina, Arkansas, and North Carolina fell in the 50 to 55 percent range. Only Mississippi (47 percent) was more rural than urban. U.S. Census, *1990 Census of Population and Housing, Population and Housing Unit Counts* (1990 CPH-2), retrieved 27 June 2000 from the World Wide Web: *http://web.lexis-nexis.com/statuniverse*.

8. Black and Black, *Politics and Society*, 20; Bloom, *Class, Race, and Civil Rights*; Clarence Stone, *Urban Regimes: Governing Atlanta, 1946–1988* (Lawrence: University Press of Kansas, 1989). One often overlooked factor in the industrialization and economic development of the South is the advent of air-conditioning. Although the first air-conditioning was installed in 1902, as late as 1960, only 18.2 percent of Southern homes were air-conditioned. By 1970, that figure had jumped to 50.1 percent, and by 1980, 73.2 percent of homes in the South were air-conditioned. Not only did air-conditioning facilitate industrial development, it also contributed to better health for the region's population, increased urbanization, and declining out-migration. Raymond Arsenault, "The End of the Long Hot Summer: Air Conditioning and Southern Culture," *Journal of Southern History* 50 (1984): 597.

9. *State of the South 1998*, 24, 25; Black and Black, *Politics and Society*, 26, 48, 70.

10. Black and Black, *Politics and Society*, 57. The Blacks' analysis demonstrates that the increases in working-class and middle-class occupations had a significant racial dimension. While a majority of whites held middle-class jobs in 1980, less than a third of blacks did. The growth in working-class jobs was occurring primarily among African Americans, remaining level among whites. Moreover, gender had important impacts. For one thing, the workforce became proportionately whiter as large numbers of white women joined the paid labor force, constituting only 14 percent of employed Southerners in 1940 but 34 percent in 1980 (ibid., 54).

11. "Education and Progress in the South."

12. Ibid.

13. James H. Kuklinski, Michael D. Cobb, and Martin Gilens, "Racial Attitudes and the 'New South,'" *Journal of Politics* 59, no. 2 (May 1997): 325. There is, however, some question whether these responses to pollsters reflect real attitudinal changes or merely the new social climate that makes overt and raw racism "politically incorrect." Although they reported only minor differences on survey items tapping racial opinions, using unobtrusive measures of racial attitudes, Kuklinski, Cobb, and Gilens found that racial prejudice is still much more prevalent in the South than in the rest of the nation. Interestingly, much of this racism is concentrated among Southern males (ibid., 345, 340). In studies of attitudes in two Mississippi cities, Von Bakanic, "I'm Not Prejudiced, but . . . : A Deeper Look at Racial Attitudes," *Sociological Inquiry* 65, no. 1 (February 1995): 67–86, also found subtler forms of racism and a continuing divergence between whites and blacks on race relations. Distinguishing old-fashioned from new value-stereotyping racism, Simo V. Virtanen and Leonie Huddy, "Old-Fashioned Racism and New Forms of Racial Prejudice," *Journal of Politics* 60, no. 2 (May 1998): 327, found that although it affects old-fashioned racism, Southern socialization has no impact on the new racism. They conclude that "this difference in the determinants of old-fashioned racism and value stereotypes thus suggests a possible shift from a regional to a class-based prejudice as negative stereotypes surface among blue-collar workers" (ibid., 329). On Southern defensiveness and localism, see W. J. Cash, *The Mind of*

the South (New York: Random House, 1941); Black and Black, *Politics and Society;* and John Shelton Reed, *The Enduring South* (Chapel Hill: University of North Carolina Press, 1972).

14. The Deep South states are South Carolina, Georgia, Alabama, Mississippi, and Louisiana. Peripheral or Rim South states are Virginia, North Carolina, Florida, Tennessee, Arkansas, and Texas. For an analysis of differences between these two groups of states, see Terrel L. Rhodes, *Republicans in the South: Voting for the State House, Voting for the White House* (Westport, Conn.: Praeger, 2000), 13.

15. Key, *Southern Politics,* 7, 10.

16. Ibid., 116; William Anderson, *The Wild Man from Sugar Creek: The Political Career of Eugene Talmadge* (Baton Rouge: Louisiana State University Press, 1975), 42–43.

17. Richard K. Scher, *Politics in the New South: Republicanism, Race, and Leadership in the Twentieth Century,* 2d ed. (Armonk, N.Y.: M. E. Sharpe, 1997), 92–93.

18. Calvin Kytle and James A. Mackay, *Who Runs Georgia?* (Athens: University of Georgia Press, 1998), 272. Anderson, *Wild Man From Sugar Creek,* strongly implies that Talmadge had fascist overtones. Gene personally had some affinity for the European fascists of his day, expressing admiration for Mussolini and reading Hitler's *Mein Kampf* seven times. There are also many points of similarities between the ideologies and constituencies of fascism and Talmadgism. Both political tendencies supplied order and consolation in decaying social systems and plied a trade in virulent racism.

19. Key, *Southern Politics,* 108–10, 127; Kytle and Mackay, *Who Runs Georgia?* 272.

20. Key, *Southern Politics,* 217, 224, 228.

21. Ibid., 205, 211.

22. Ibid., 206.

23. Joseph L. Bernd, "Georgia: Static and Dynamic," in *The Changing Politics of the South,* ed. Willaim C. Havard (Baton Rouge: Louisiana State University Press, 1972), 331, 303, 315, 319.

24. Jack Bass and Walter DeVries, *The Transformation of Southern Politics* (New York: New American Library, 1977), 138.

25. Bernd, "Georgia: Static and Dynamic," 308.

26. Bruce Galphin, *The Riddle of Lester Maddox* (Atlanta: Camelot, 1968).

27. Alexander P. Lamis, *The Two-Party South,* 2d ed. (New York: Oxford University Press, 1988), 96.

28. Preston W. Edsall and J. Oliver Williams, "North Carolina: Bipartisan Paradox," in *The Changing Politics of the South,* ed. William C. Havard (Baton Rouge: Louisiana State University Press, 1972), 369.

29. Ibid., 370–71, 377–82.

30. Ibid., 382–87; Bass and DeVries, *Transformation of Southern Politics,* 231; *Brown v. Board of Education,* 349 U.S. 458 (1955).

31. Edsall and Williams, "North Carolina," 387–91.

32. Ibid., 421.

33. Harrell R. Rodgers, Jr., and Charles S. Bullock III, *Law and Social Change: Civil Rights Laws and Their Consequences* (New York: McGraw-Hill, 1972), 27; Chandler Davidson, "The Recent Evolution of Voting Rights Law Affecting Racial and Language Minorities," in *The Quiet Revolution in the South,* ed. Chandler

Davidson and Bernard Grofman (Princeton, N.J.: Princeton University Press, 1994); Donald R. Matthews and James W. Prothro, *Negroes and the New Southern Politics* (New York: Harcourt, Brace and World, 1966); Harold W. Stanley, *Voter Mobilization and the Politics of Race* (New York: Praeger, 1987), 97.

34. Laughlin McDonald, "Reapportionment, Racial Gerrymandering, and Georgia's Eleventh District," lecture at Agnes Scott College, Decatur, Georgia, 6 December 1994.

35. Stanley, *Voter Mobilization,* 97, 155; Laughlin McDonald, Michael Binford, and Ken Johnson, "Georgia," in Davidson and Grofman, *Quiet Revolution,* 89; William R. Keech and Michael P. Sistrom, "North Carolina," in Davidson and Grofman, *Quiet Revolution,* 161.

36. Rodgers and Bullock, *Law and Social Change,* 31; James E. Alt, "The Impact of the Voting Rights Act on Black and White Voter Registration in the South," in Davidson and Grofman, *Quiet Revolution,* 372.

37. William R. Keech, *The Impact of Negro Voting: The Role of the Vote in the Quest for Equality* (Chicago: Rand McNally, 1968); Richard K. Scher, Jon L. Mills, and John J. Hotaling, *Voting Rights and Democracy: The Law and Politics of Districting* (Chicago: Nelson-Hall, 1997), 62; Frank R. Parker, *Black Votes Count* (Chapel Hill: University of North Carolina Press, 1990); James W. Button, *Blacks and Social Change: The Impact of the Civil Rights Movement in Southern Communities* (Princeton, N.J.: Princeton University Press, 1989).

In Clarence Stone's study of the advent of black majority politics in Atlanta, he traces how the city's downtown economic elite incorporated African Americans into the governing coalition as junior partners. Stone, however, clearly delineates the limits of electoral politics in shaping the city's development and in redistributing the resources that flow from the overall progress of Atlanta. As Stone summarizes it, "votes count but resources decide" (Stone, *Urban Regimes,* 239).

38. Lisa Handley and Bernard Grofman, "The Impact of the Voting Rights Act on Minority Representation: Black Officeholding in Southern State Legislatures and Congressional Delegations," in Davidson and Grofman, *Quiet Revolution,* 345; McDonald, Binford, and Johnson, "Georgia," 89; Keech and Sistrom, "North Carolina," 165–69.

39. Stephen D. Cummings, *The Dixification of America: The American Odyssey into the Conservative Economic Trap* (Westport, Conn.: Praeger, 1998), 11.

40. Bass and DeVries, *Transformation of Southern Politics,* 144.

41. Ibid., 147.

42. Ibid., 149.

43. Philip D. Duncan and Christine C. Lawrence, *Politics in America 1996* (Washington, D.C.: Congressional Quarterly, 1995), 338; Lamis, *Two-Party South,* 101, 102. Given Republican Mattingly's success in luring votes from such Democratic constituencies as African American and metro Atlanta counties, Lamis (103) suggests that his victory might have been urban Georgia's long-delayed revenge against the rural Talmadge machine.

44. Michael Binford, "Georgia: Political Realignment or Partisan Evolution," in *The South's New Politics: Realignment and Dealignment,* ed. Robert Swansbrough and David Brodsky (Columbia: University of South Carolina Press, 1988), 185, 175. By 1996, Republican strength in the General Assembly had reached 40 percent.

The estimate for the Republican share of elected county offices was between 10 and 12 percent. Michael Binford, Tom Baxter, and David Sturrock, "Georgia: Democratic Bastion No Longer," in *Southern Politics in the 1990s*, ed. Alexander P. Lamis (Baton Rouge: Louisiana State University Press, 1999), 129, 130.

45. Lamis, *Southern Politics*, 133. An example of Barnes's tendency to ape Republican policy is his education reform package, which stresses standardized testing and "accountability" and removes tenure (actually, merely a mild form of due process protection against unjust dismissal in the Georgia public schools) from teachers. Barnes himself jocularly conceded that "85 to 90 percent of this bill is Republican dogma." Doug Cumming, "Lighthearted Barnes Delivers Serious School Message," *Atlanta Journal/Constitution*, 2 April 2000, H3.

46. Rob Christensen and Jack D. Fleer, "North Carolina: Between Helms and Hunt No Majority Emerges," in Lamis, *Southern Politics*, 95, noting that Republicans won seven of the last eight presidential elections of the twentieth century.

47. Jack D. Fleer, Roger C. Lowery, and Charles L. Prysby, "Political Change in North Carolina," in Swansbrough and Brodsky, *South's New Politics*, 94–102. Christensen and Fleer note that "Helms never wins by wide margins, but he always wins." Hunt, in contrast, is the only statewide Democrat in the 1990s to receive more than 40 percent of white votes, a figure that is the rule of thumb for the minimum needed for a Democrat to win. He carried 47 percent of the white votes in 1992 and 54 percent in 1996 (Christensen and Fleer, "North Carolina," 83, 97).

48. Thomas A. Kazee, "North Carolina: Conservatism, Traditionalism, and the GOP," in *The New Politics of the Old South*, ed. Charles S. Bullock III and Mark J. Rozell (Lanham, Md.: Rowman and Littlefield, 1998), 148; Harold W. Stanley, "The South and the 1996 Presidential Election: Republican Gains Among Democratic Wins," in *The 1996 Presidential Election in the South: Southern Party Systems in the 1990s*, ed. Laurence W. Moreland and Robert P. Steed (Westport, Conn.: Praeger, 1997), 235.

49. Walter Dean Burnham, "Critical Realignment: Dead or Alive?" in *The End of Realignment? Interpreting American Electoral Eras*, ed. Byron E. Shafer (Madison: University of Wisconsin Press, 1991), 119.

50. Robert Huckfeldt and Carol Weitzel Kohfeld, *Race and the Decline of Class in American Politics* (Urbana: University of Illinois Press, 1989), 10.

51. Lamis, *Two-Party South*, 99.

52. Bass and DeVries, *Transformation of Southern Politics*, 150; Reed, *Enduring South*, 33.

53. Joseph A. Aistrup, *The Southern Strategy Revisited* (Lexington: University Press of Kentucky, 1996).

54. James M. Glaser, *Race, Campaign Politics, and the Realignment in the South* (New Haven, Conn.: Yale University Press, 1996), 76.

55. This tendency for incumbents to concentrate on constituent services (casework and pork) to win reelection is, of course, not an exclusively Southern Democratic strategy. Morris Fiorini, *Congress: Keystone of the Washington Establishment* (New Haven, Conn.: Yale University Press, 1977), has argued that the widespread use of this strategy results in a high rate of reelection for incumbents but also a distortion of national priorities and disdain for Congress as an institution.

56. Charles S. Bullock III, "Georgia: Election Rules and Partisan Conflict," in Bullock and Rozell, *New Politics of the Old South*, 57; Charles Prysby, "North Carolina: Republican Consolidation or Democratic Resurgence," in Moreland and Steed, *The 1996 Presidential Election in the South*, 170–71. Prysby's figures are based on exit polling. Christensen and Fleer's data from 1998 show a slight overall edge for the Republicans (36 percent Republican to 32 percent Democratic identification), with a much larger independent contingent of 22 percent. They also note that in the 1990s, Republican candidates consistently attracted a majority of independent votes (Christensen and Fleer, in Lamis, "North Carolina," 97, 102).

57. Paul Luebke, *Tar Heel Politics: Myths and Realities* (Chapel Hill: University of North Carolina Press, 1990).

58. Nicol C. Rae, *Southern Democrats* (New York: Oxford University Press, 1994), 45.

4. Dual Convergence II

1. My focus in this chapter is on the growing similarities between national and Southern politics, but it could also be argued that the South is becoming less culturally distinct as well. John Shelton Reed, *The Enduring South* (Chapel Hill: University of North Carolina Press, 1972), 19, argues strongly that the South is still different, but even he seems to recognize that in the long run, the homogenizing pressures of mass media, mass culture, and travel and migration are reducing the cultural gap. Much as I argue that U.S. politics has converged toward the Southern norm as well as vice versa, Peter Applebome, *Dixie Rising: How the South Is Shaping American Values, Politics and Culture* (New York: Random House, 1996), notes that part of the closing gap is accounted for by the South's influence on the nation's culture. This point was driven home through personal experience recently. While visiting my daughter at college, we found instant grits being sold in a small-town grocery store in western Vermont.

2. Jill Quadagno, *The Color of Welfare: How Racism Undermined the War on Poverty* (New York: Oxford University Press, 1994), 4.

3. Many historians and economists now believe that the economic activity generated by the need to gear up to fight World War II, rather than the New Deal programs aimed specifically at relieving the depression, was the crucial factor in restoring prosperity to the country.

4. William C. Berman, *America's Right Turn: From Nixon to Clinton*, 2d ed. (Baltimore: Johns Hopkins University Press, 1998), 42; William G. Mayer, *The Divided Democrats* (Boulder, Colo.: Westview, 1996), 100.

5. For an analysis of the various Southern congressional factions, their motivations explaining their varying stances toward the New Deal, and an assessment of the consequences of Roosevelt's dependence on Southern legislative support, see Frank Freidel, *F.D.R. and the South* (Baton Rouge: Louisiana State University Press, 1965).

6. Sidney Baldwin, *Poverty and Politics: The Rise and Decline of the Farm Security Administration* (Chapel Hill: University of North Carolina Press, 1968), 3.

7. James McGregor Burns, *Roosevelt: The Lion and the Fox* (Orlando, Fla.: Har-

court, Brace, 1956). C. Wright Mills, *The Power Elite* (New York: Oxford University Press, 1956), argued that the experience of government-business partnership in industrial planning to win World War II convinced the American corporate elite of the benefits of an active government role in the economy. On the post–World War II social compact, see Martin Carnoy and Derek Shearer, *Economic Democracy* (Armonk, N.Y.: M. E. Sharpe, 1980).

Historically, the two dominant American political parties have not been evenly matched (Samuel Lubell, *The Future of American Politics*, 3d ed. [New York: Harper and Row, 1962], 192). Rather, during any electoral epoch, there is a distribution of long-term partisan loyalties that produces an electoral order that normally favors one of the parties. Although the minority party can still win elections on occasion, when short-term forces such as a popular candidate or a scandal temporarily offset the majority party's advantage, the norm is for the majority party to win most elections during the persistence of any particular electoral order. See Angus Campbell, Philip E. Converse, Warren E. Miller, and Donald E. Stokes, *Elections and the Political Order* (New York: John Wiley and Sons, 1966), for a discussion of the normal vote concept.

8. Ira Katznelson, "The Southern Origins of Our Time," paper presented at the Center for the History of Business, Technology, and Society, Hagley Museum and Library, Wilmington, Del., 10 December 1998; Ira Katznelson, "Was the Great Society a Lost Opportunity?" in *The Rise and Fall of the New Deal Order, 1930–1980*, ed. Simon Fraser and Gary Gerstle (Princeton, N.J.: Princeton University Press, 1989), 192, 194.

9. David G. Lawrence, *The Collapse of the Democratic Presidential Majority* (Boulder, Colo.: Westview, 1996), 7. Walter Dean Burnham, "Critical Realignment: Dead or Alive?" in *The End of Realignment? Interpreting American Electoral Eras*, ed. Byron E. Shafer (Madison: University of Wisconsin Press, 1991), 119, views the 1948–1952 period as a "midlife crisis" of the New Deal political order.

10. Godfrey Hodgson, *America in Our Time* (New York: Vintage, 1976). Joseph McCarthy was a Republican senator from Wisconsin who, in the late 1940s and early 1950s, claimed to have knowledge of communist infiltration in high government posts. Using his congressional investigative powers, McCarthy harassed and hounded individuals with leftist sympathies, violating their civil liberties and often ruining their careers. McCarthy himself was censured by the Senate in 1954.

11. Hodgson, *America in Our Time*, 76. Michael Sandel, *Democracy's Discontent: America in Search of a Public Philosophy* (Cambridge, Mass.: Harvard University Press, 1996), ch. 8, argues that the Keynesian liberalism that the New Deal later evolved into was a major departure from the older, more republican conceptions of American politics. Although republicanism has been in retreat since the nineteenth century, the decentralist and planning factions of the earlier New Deal reflected republican concerns for the economic conditions necessary for freedom, in the sense of self-governance, and for the development of citizens able to participate in their own governance—a "political economy of citizenship." Keynesian liberalism, in contrast, was value free, almost apolitical, in that it aspired to achieve prosperity and minimal fairness but evaded tough, substantive political questions by leaving decisions to individuals deemed free to voluntarily choose on their own—a "political economy of growth and distributive justice" (ibid., 250).

12. Hodgson, *America in Our Time*, 492. Richard Neustadt reflected the liberal consensus when he wrote in *Presidential Power* (New York: New American Library,1964), originally drafted for John Kennedy during the transition to his presidency as a sort of modern-day version of Machiavelli's *Prince*, that "what is good for the country is good for the president, and *vice versa*" (175).

13. Barry Bluestone and Bennett Harrison, *The Great U-Turn: Corporate Restructuring and the Polarizing of America* (New York: Basic, 1988); David M. Gordon, Richard Edwards, and Michael Reich, *Segmented Work, Divided Workers* (New York: Cambridge Univesity Press, 1982).

14. Barry Goldwater, "Acceptance Address," *Vital Speeches of the Day* 30, no. 21 (15 August 1964): 644; Bernard Cosman, *Five States for Goldwater* (University: University of Alabama Press, 1966).

15. Using released secret documents from the Nixon era, Jonathan Schell, *The Time of Illusion* (New York: Vintage, 1975), offers a fascinating account of that administration, contrasting in retrospect the public utterances and events of that time with the maneuverings of Nixon and his cronies behind the veil of secrecy imposed by the administration. Although Schell concentrates on contrasting the rhetoric with the reality of the conduct of the Vietnam War, he also lays bare a pattern of public relations that characterized Nixon's approach to domestic policy as well. The more liberal the substance of a policy, the more conservative was the rhetoric that accompanied it. For instance, the proposed Family Assistance Plan, in essence a guaranteed income, was billed as a plan to reform welfare, a forerunner of workfare. Conversely, conservative policies were disguised with liberal verbiage. The rollback of civil rights enforcement was smothered with liberal statements affirming the ideal of integration. Leon E. Panetta and Peter Gall, *Bring Us Together: The Nixon Team and the Civil Rights Retreat* (Philadelphia: Lippincott, 1971).

16. Reg Murphy and Hal Gulliver, *Southern Strategy* (New York: Charles Scribner, 1971); Joseph A. Aistrup, *Southern Strategy Revisited* (Lexington: University Press of Kentucky, 1996). Wallace entered the 1972 Democratic presidential primaries but was shot and seriously injured while campaigning that spring in Laurel Park, Maryland.

17. Proposition 13 limited the ability of California's state and local governments to spend for services and to raise revenues.

18. Stephen D. Cummings, *The Dixification of America: The American Odyssey into the Conservative Economic Trap* (Westport, Conn.: Praeger, 1998), 73.

19. Berman, *America's Right Turn*, 14, 53, 76.

20. Although he did apply an ideological litmus test to judicial nominees, beyond this attempt to stack the federal judiciary, Reagan never devoted his main energies to pushing the social agenda of the religious right. Despite token backing for such items as antiabortion and pro–school prayer amendments to the Constitution, Reagan failed to provide the strong leadership that could have energized and united proponents of these measures. Still, the symbolic opposition of the "Great Communicator" was sufficient to cement the loyalties of the religious right in spite of the lack of concrete accomplishments on social issues by the Reagan administration. Berman, *America's Right Turn*, 110.

21. After the initial onslaught in Reagan's early years, Democratic opposition

became more potent. Democrats in Congress managed to moderate administration budget cuts, and many programs slated by the Reaganauts for total elimination, such as Amtrak and Legal Services for the Poor, were saved by trench warfare in congressional committees led by Democrats but sometimes supported by moderate Republicans feeling the heat from constituents of the programs. The earned income tax credit, a version of a negative income tax, even represents a successful liberal initiative in the midst of the larger conservative currents (Jared Bernstein, "Two Cheers for the Earned Income Tax Credit," *American Prospect*, 19 June–3 July 2000, 64–67). Despite these Democratic victories, Reagan succeeded in shifting the ideas, rhetoric, and agenda of American political economy decidedly to the right, casting a shadow on government programs per se and extolling the market as the presumptive preferred solution to all social problems.

22. Thomas Byrne Edsall with Mary D. Edsall, *Chain Reaction: The Impact of Race, Rights, and Taxes on American Politics* (New York: W. W. Norton, 1992), 144; Michael Omi and Howard Winant, *Racial Formation in the United States from the 1960s to the 1980s* (New York: Routledge and Keagan Paul, 1986).

23. Edsall with Edsall, *Chain Reaction*, 4; Richard M. Scammon and Ben J. Wattenberg, *The Real Majority* (New York: Coward, McCann and Geoghegan, 1970); Benjamin Ginsberg and Martin Schefter, *Politics by Other Means*, 2d ed. (New York: W. W. Norton, 1999), 116–17; Berman, *America's Right Turn*, 43.

Lawrence, *Collapse of the Democratic Presidential Majority*, 37, 99, notes that the particular items that composed the so-called social issue have fluctuated over time. In the aftermath of the civil rights struggle, urban unrest, and Vietnam protests, race and patriotism fueled much social issue voting. By the mid-1970s, the cultural revolution of the 1960s and 1970s had placed what some researchers called the New Politics issues (sometimes referred to as cultural issues) with heavy moral components, such as the environment, lifestyle, and abortion, at the cusp of divisions in public opinion.

24. Conversely, economic differences divided them from Republican elites. Lawrence, *Collapse of Democratic Presidential Majority*, 117, demonstrates that economic issues can be disaggregated into fiscal, class, social welfare, and prosperity dimensions whose varying levels of salience shift over time, so different dimensions of economic issues may have different ramifications in various contexts. Prosperity, for example, historically worked for the Democrats, although in the 1980s, recession and subsequent recovery fueled Republican victories. By the 1990s, however, all dimensions of economics as an electoral issue coalesced to boost Clinton's presidential aspirations.

25. Edsall with Edsall, *Chain Reaction*, 4–5; Berman, *America's Right Turn*, 138.

26. Quadagno, *Color of Welfare*; Theda Skocpol, *The Missing Middle: Working Families and the Future of American Social Policy* (New York: W. W. Norton, 2000).

27. Berman, *America's Right Turn*, 79.

28. Edsall with Edsall, *Chain Reaction*, 142.

29. Berman, *America's Right Turn*, 79; Edsall with Edsall, *Chain Reaction*, 104, 142, 5–6, 175. For an account of how the Swedish Social Democrats deftly used the politics of taxing and spending to reward their political base and maintain their electoral hegemony almost uninterrupted for most of the years since 1932, see

Gosta Esping-Andersen, *Politics Against Markets: The Social Democratic Road to Power* (Princeton, N.J.: Princeton University Press, 1985).

30. Kathleen Hall Jamieson, *Dirty Politics: Deception, Distraction, and Democracy* (New York: Oxford University Press, 1992), 17–22.

31. Byron E. Shafer, "We Are All Southern Democrats Now," in *Present Discontents: American Politics in the Very Late Twentieth Century*, ed. Byron E. Shafer (Chatham, N.J.: Chatham House, 1997), 171, 178.

32. Lloyd A. Free and Hadley Cantril, *The Political Beliefs of Americans* (New York: Simon and Schuster, 1968), 51, 180.

33. Lawrence, *Collapse of Democratic Presidential Majority*, ch. 6; Martin Wattenberg, *Candidate-Centered Politics: Presidential Elections of the 1980s* (Cambridge, Mass.: Harvard Univesity Press, 1991), ch. 6.

34. Skocpol's account of the Clinton health care initiative demonstrates how fundamentally it was shaped by the budgetary constraints and political climate of the Reagan Revolution. Theda Skocpol, *Boomerang: Health Care Reform and the Turn Against Government* (New York: W. W. Norton, 1997).

35. Berman, *America's Right Turn*, 165.

36. Ibid., 179.

37. Thomas Byrne Edsall, "The Cultural Revolution of 1994," in Shafer, *Present Discontents*, 136.

38. Michael Lind, "Southern Coup," *New Republic*, 19 June 1995, 20–29; Shafer, "We Are All Southern Democrats Now"; Cummings, *Dixification of America*.

39. Nicol C. Rae, "Party Factionalism, 1946–1996," in *Partisan Approaches to Postwar American Politics*, ed. Byron E. Shafer (New York: Chatham House, 1998), 43.

40. Conservatism in America has been heir to two contradictory philosophical legacies. Classical or organic conservative thought, exemplified by English parliamentarian Edmund Burke, believes in authority, hierarchy, and strong institutions in defense of valued traditions. Antistatist or libertarian conservatism, more accurately recognized as nineteenth-century liberalism represented by English reformer John Stuart Mill, advocates individualism, maximum freedom, and minimal government in pursuit of progress (Kenneth M. Dolbeare and Linda J. Medcalf, *American Ideologies Today* [New York: Random House, 1988]). These strands of thought make uneasy bedfellows, the one favoring social regulation and the status quo, while the other backs laissez-faire and change. One way conservatives have reconciled these tendencies is to apply different standards to different areas of social life. Typically, conservatives such as Ronald Reagan lean toward authority and tradition in the social sphere, while opting for individualism and laissez-faire in the economic sphere. This combination helps explain how some conservatives can comfortably, if not altogether logically, want government to legislate morality in the bedroom and in the schoolroom but not in the boardroom (Berman, *America's Right Turn*, 120). Anticommunism has provided American conservatives in the Cold War era an even more potent method of fusing their contradictory heritages (E. J. Dionne, Jr., *Why Americans Hate Politics* [New York: Simon and Schuster, 1992], 160). Classic conservatives may oppose communism more for its threat to the traditional social order and its values, especially religion, whereas libertarian conservatives decry its assault on individual liberties, but the pressing common enemy has served to bridge more abstract philosophical divisions.

41. Rae, "Party Factionalism," 51.

42. Alan Crawford, *Thunder on the Right: The "New Right" and the Politics of Resentment* (New York: Pantheon Books, 1981); Lind, "Southern Coup."

43. Ruy A. Teixeira, "Economic Change and the Middle-Class Revolt Against the Democratic Party," in *Broken Contract: Changing Relationships Between Americans and Their Government*, ed. Stephen C. Craig (Boulder, Colo.: Westview, 1996).

44. Gary Orfield, *The Reconstruction of Southern Education* (New York: John Wiley and Sons, 1969); Panetta and Gall, *Bring Us Together*.

45. Dan T. Carter, *The Politics of Rage: George Wallace, the Origins of the New Conservatism, and the Transformation of American Politics* (New York: Simon and Schuster, 1995), 465.

46. Carter quotes Gingrich as saying that "the number one fact about the news media is they love fights. You have to give them confrontations" (ibid., 466).

47. Lind, "Southern Coup," 23, argues that "the new Republican movement has much more in common with the old Dixiecrats than with neoconservatives." He advises that "the most fruitful way to analyze and predict its course is not to read *The Public Interest* but to examine the history of state and local politics in the South," specifically Key's *Southern Politics in State and Nation*. Although obviously I find much to recommend itself in Lind's approach, the analysis here argues for a broader Southern influence beyond the Republican conservative movement to American politics generally. Also, the stress here is on shared structural characteristics rather than on culture and ideological influences.

48. William Greider, *Who Will Tell the People: The Betrayal of American Democracy* (New York: Simon and Schuster, 1992), 274.

49. Carter, *Politics of Rage*, 468.

50. Theodore J. Lowi, *The End of the Republican Era* (Normon: University of Oklahoma Press, 1995); Dolbeare and Medcalf, *American Ideologies Today;* Nicol C. Rae, *Southern Democrats* (New York: Oxford University Press, 1994).

51. Lind, "Southern Coup," 29; Cummings, *Dixification of America*, 12; Michael Kazin, *The Populist Persuasion* (New York: Basic, 1995).

52. Greider, *Who Will Tell the People*, 275.

53. Thomas Byrne Edsall, *The New Politics of Inequality* (New York: W. W. Norton, 1984); Kevin Phillips, *The Politics of Rich and Poor: Wealth and the American Electorate in the Reagan Aftermath* (New York: Random House, 1990); Greider, *Who Will Tell the People*, 275.

While using social and cultural issues such as school prayer and abortion to attract right-wing populist voters, the Reagan Republicans never really delivered on these issues. The Reagan administration was clear that economic policies were top priorities. Greider, *Who Will Tell the People*, 277, suggests that the failure to take concrete action on these issues was a deliberate ploy. By keeping these issues alive as open social wounds, even inflaming them as hot-button issues, the Republican Right could use them in election after election to rally the faithful for moral crusades in ways that practical steps to correct the perceived problems could never have done. In essence, as Edelman suggested long ago, much of the politics of social issues was symbolic, designed to give only immaterial reassurance and thereby keep the masses quiescent. Murray Edelman, *The Symbolic Uses of Politics* (Urbana: University of Illinois Press, 1964).

54. Mayer, *Divided Democrats*, 104. Tellingly, the label "New Democrat" suggests a lack of substantive promise: no New Deal (Roosevelt) or Fair Deal (Truman), not even a New Frontier (Kennedy), just New.

55. Suzy Platt, ed., *Respectfully Quoted: A Dictionary of Quotations Requested from the Congressional Research Service* (Washington, D.C.: Library of Congress, 1989), 85.

56. Rae, *Southern Democrats*, 15.

57. Ibid., 20.

58. Ibid.

59. Berman, *America's Right Turn*, 112; Dolbeare and Medcalf, *American Ideologies Today*; Theodore J. Lowi, *The End of Liberalism: Ideology, Policy, and the Crisis of Public Authority* (New York: W. W. Norton, 1969).

60. Not all business leaders rejected planning. Some recognized the inevitability of planning and perceived that the key issue was not planning versus laissez-faire market policies but what sort of planning: planning for what, in whose interest, and by whom (which, ironically, was the lifelong message of America's most prominent advocate of democratic socialism, Michael Harrington). For example, in 1980, Philip E. Benton, Jr., general manager of the Ford Motor Division, said, "Let's face it. Our system of 'laissez-faire' private enterprise has run its course. Government, industry and unions have to work together now. It's what people like me used to condemn as socialism." Richard Reeves, "Would You Buy a Car from America?" *Atlanta Journal/Constitution*, 24 October 1980.

61. Robert B. Reich, *The Work of Nations* (New York: Vintage, 1992), 177.

62. Thomas Ferguson and Joel Rogers, "Neoliberals and Democrats," *Nation*, 26 June 1982, 786.

63. Rae, *Southern Democrats*, 22; Rae, "Party Factionalism," 58.

64. Rae, *Southern Democrats*, 22, 56.

65. Ibid., 113, 114; Jon F. Hale, "The Making of the New Democrats," *Political Science Quarterly* 110 (summer 1995), retrieved from the World Wide Web: http://epn.org/psq/pashale.html.

66. Rae, *Southern Democrats*, 117, 118, 122; Hale, "Making of New Democrats."

67. Hale, "Making of New Democrats"; Theda Skocpol, "Democrats at the Crossroads," *Mother Jones*, January–February 1997, retrieved from the World Wide Web.

68. Berman, *America's Right Turn*, 165; Mayer, *Divided Democrats*, 122; David Stoesz, *Small Change: Domestic Policy Under the Clinton Presidency* (White Plains, N.Y.: Longman, 1996).

69. Berman, *America's Right Turn*, 114, 121.

70. Gingrich et al. overread the mandate that they thought the voters had given them to enact the Contract with America. In fact, one poll found that only 7 percent surveyed said that the contract made them more likely to vote Republican for Congress, 5 percent said it made them less likely to, and a whopping 71 percent had never heard of the contract. Marjorie Randon Hershey, "The Congressional Elections," in *The Election of 1996: Reports and Interpretations*, ed. Gerald M. Pomper et al. (Chatham, N.J.: Chatham House, 1997), 208.

71. Christopher Caldwell, "The Southern Captivity of the GOP," *Atlantic Monthly*, June 1998, 55–72; Rae, "Party Factionalism," 64; Lowi, *End of the Republican Era*.

72. Rae, "Party Fationalism," 69.

73. The argument developed in chapter 6 is not only that this lineup of politics is "Southern," in the sense of matching contemporary Southern partisan alignments, but also that modern candidate-centered politics, although competitive in a partisan way that the politics of the old Solid South was not, still resembles the basic traits of the older Southern political system, including, as I argue in chapter 7, its major pathologies.

5. Realignment Versus Dealignment

1. Michael Binford, Tom Baxter, and David E. Sturrock, "Georgia: Democratic Bastion No Longer," in *Southern Politics in the 1990s,* ed. Alexander P. Lamis (Baton Rouge: Louisiana State University Press, 1999), 135.

2. Paul R. Abramson, John H. Aldrich, and David W. Rohde, *Change and Continuity in the 1996 Elections* (Washington, D.C.: Congressional Quarterly, 1998), 257.

3. Partisan loyalty, defined as partisan identification, has most frequently been measured by the response to the question, "Generally speaking, do you usually think of yourself as a Republican, a Democrat, an Independent, or what?" (Michael B. MacKuen, Robert S. Erikson, and James A. Stimson, "Question Wording and Macropartisanship," *American Political Science Review* 86, no. 2 [June 1992]: 475). This question has been asked of samples of the American electorate by the Survey Research Center (later renamed the Center for Political Studies) of the University of Michigan since the early 1950s.

4. Walter Dean Burnham, "Critical Realignment? Dead or Alive?" in *The End of Realignment? Interpreting American Electoral Eras,* ed. Byron E. Shafer (Madison: University of Wisconsin Press, 1991), 117; David G. Lawrence, *The Collapse of the Democratic Presidential Majority* (Boulder, Colo.: Westview, 1996), 2.

5. Earl Black and Merle Black, *The Vital South: How Presidents Are Elected* (Cambridge, Mass.: Harvard University Press, 1992), 12.

6. Harold F. Stanley, "Southern Partisan Changes: Dealignment, Realignment or Both?" *Journal of Politics* 50, no. 1 (February 1988): 66; Lawrence, *Collapse of Democratic Presidential Majority,* 3; V. O. Key, Jr., "Secular Realignment and the Party System," *Journal of Politics* 21, no. 2 (May 1959): 198–210; V. O. Key, Jr., "A Theory of Critical Elections," *Journal of Politics* 17, no. 1 (February 1955): 3–18.

7. Burnham, "Critical Realignment," 101.

8. Lawrence, *Collapse of Democratic Presidential Majority,* 13, 3–5. Party loyalty, or identification, is often seen as the critical linchpin of realignments, linking individual voting with systemic changes in the partisan balance of power (ibid., 15). Party identification, of course, is only one factor in influencing voting decisions. Other influences include shorter-term factors such as perceptions of the candidates, the issues, and aspects of the particular election, including campaign events and discussions with friends and relatives. Party identification is a longer-term force. Research in the post–World War II era showed partisan loyalties to be shaped by group membership and historic events. For example, white Southerners tended to be Democrats and Northerners Republicans because of the Civil War, a

trauma that occurred more than a century ago. Class differentials between the parties were fixed in the Great Depression, when less wealthy Americans became attached to the Democrats because of Roosevelt's New Deal programs. Ethnic affiliations reflect the timing and experiences of different groups immigrating to this country. The most important finding of much of the early voting research was that party identification was the single most powerful influence on the voting decision, and the salient implication of this finding was that voting rested on a stable base of partisan loyalty for groups that tended to be fixed long ago and that shifted among individuals only rarely. Angus Campbell, Philip E. Converse, Warren E. Miller, and Donald E. Stokes, *Elections and the Political Order* (New York: John Wiley and Sons, 1966).

9. Lawrence, *Collapse of Democratic Presidential Majority*, 12.

10. Abramson, Aldrich, and Rohde, *Change and Continuity in 1996*, 259.

11. Stanley, "Southern Partisan Changes," 66.

12. Ibid.

13. L. Sandy Maisel, "Political Parties on the Eve of the Millennium," in *The Parties Respond*, ed. L. Sandy Maisel, 3d ed. (Boulder, Colo.: Westview, 1998), 363.

14. Donna R. Hoffman, "A Theory for All Elections? Realignment Theory and a Changing Electorate," paper presented at the annual meeting of the American Political Science Association, Atlanta, 2–5 September 1999, 1.

15. Black and Black, *Vital South*.

16. Harold F. Bass, Jr., "Background to Debate: A Reader's Guide and Bibliography," in Shafer, *End of Realignment?*

17. There has been some variation in the way pollsters have measured party identification, using slightly different wording of questions designed to tap this loyalty (MacKuen, Erikson, and Stimson, "Question Wording," 475). In addition, although partisan loyalty is primarily a long-term, stable phenomenon, there seems to be some short-term fluctuation in party identification in response to more immediate political events, at least in some measures of the concept. Paul R. Abramson and Charles W. Ostrom, "Response," *American Political Science Review* 86, no. 2 (June 1992): 483.

18. Lawrence, *Collapse of Democratic Presidential Majority*, 142; William G. Mayer, "Mass Partisanship, 1946–1996," in *Partisan Approaches to Postwar American Politics*, ed. Byron E. Shafer (New York: Chatham House, 1998), 192, 197.

19. Abramson and Ostrom, "Response," 484.

20. Gerald M. Pomper, "The Presidential Election," in *The Election of 1996: Reports and Interpretations*, ed. Gerald M. Pomper et al. (Chatham, N.J.: Chatham House, 1997), 188, 202. Estimates of partisan identification vary for a number of reasons besides timing and the inherent fluctuations across samples. Slight variations in the wording of questions may produce different responses (Abramson and Ostrom, "Response," 484; but see MacKuen, Erikson, and Stimson, "Question Wording"). Others claim that adding independent leaners to overt partisans produces more accurate results (e.g., Mayer, "Mass Partisanship,"197), but the resulting division still slightly favors the Democrats 48 percent to 41 percent in the 1992–1994 era (Alan I. Abramowitz and Kyle L. Saunders, "Party Polarization and Ideological Realignment in the U.S. Electorate, 1976–1994," in Maisel, *Parties Respond*, 135). Ladd reports that "national surveys asking about partisan identification typically find a small Democratic edge, on the order of 2–4 percentage

points. Thirty-nine percent of those interviewed by VNS [Voter News Service] on 5 November [1996] called themselves Democrats, 35 percent Republicans. There has been no significant movement in party identification distributions since 1984." This split leaves almost another third of the electorate who identify themselves as independents. Everrett Carll Ladd, "1996 Vote: The 'No Majority' Realignment Continues," *Political Science Quarterly* 112, no. 1 (1997): 10.

21. Donald Green, Bradley Palmquist, and Eric Schickler, "The Coming Democratic Realignment," *PS: Political Science and Politics* 33, no. 2 (June 2000): 199–200.

22. John H. Aldrich and Richard G. Niemi, "The Sixth American Party System: Electoral Change, 1952–1992," in *Broken Contract? Changing Relationships Between Americans and Their Government*, ed. Stephen C. Craig (Boulder, Colo.: Westview, 1996), 89–91.

23. Abramowitz and Saunders, "Party Polarization," 135.

24. Warren E. Miller, "Party Identification, Realignment, and Party Voting: Back to the Basics," *American Political Science Review* 85, no. 2 (June 1991): 562.

25. Harold F. Stanley, "The South and the 1996 Presidential Election: Republican Gains Among Democratic Wins," in *The 1996 Presidential Election in the South: Southern Party Systems in the 1990s*, ed. Laurence W. Moreland and Robert P. Steed (Wesport, Conn.: Praeger, 1997), 229.

Charles S. Bullock III and Mark J. Rozell, "Southern Politics at Century's End," in *The New Politics of the Old South*, ed. Charles S. Bullock III and Mark J. Rozell (Lanham, Md.: Rowman and Littlefield, 1998), 10, report that in 1996, Democrats still enjoyed the edge in partisan identification in most individual Southern states as well. The advantage remained overwhelming in Arkansas and Louisiana, while the Democratic tilt ranged from two to eight percentage points in five more states (Alabama, Georgia, Mississippi, North Carolina, and Tennessee). The Republicans held leads of one to four points in three states (South Carolina, Texas, and Virginia), while loyalties were tied in Florida.

26. William J. Keefe, *Parties, Politics, and Public Policy in America*, 8th ed. (Washington, D.C.: Congressional Quarterly, 1998), 197. The increase in independents is much less impressive (a mere 3 percent gain compared to a 13 percent growth) if independents who lean toward a party are counted among party identifiers (Mayer, "Mass Partisanship,"195–97). This procedure is justified, according to some analysts, because the voting propensities of leaners is closer to party identifiers than to true independents.

27. Wilson Carey McWilliams, "The Meaning of the Election," in Pomper, *Election of 1996*, 257; Michael Lind, "Southern Coup," *New Republic*, 19 June 1995, 22. Abramowitz and Saunders, "Party Polarization," 136, found 46 percent Democratic supporters (identifiers plus independent leaners) among white respondents in 1996. These same respondents, however, reported that 61 percent of their parents were Democratic supporters.

28. Miller, "Party Identification, Realignment, and Party Voting," 565; Mayer, "Mass Partisanship," 198–99, 211; Aldrich and Niemi, "Sixth American Party System," 95.

29. Ladd, " 'No Majority' Realignment," 15.

30. Martin Wattenberg, *The Decline of American Political Parties*, 4th ed. (Cambridge, Mass.: Harvard University Press, 1996), 174, 179.

31. Stanley, "Southern Partisan Changes," 82; Mayer, "Mass Partisanship," 211.

32. Marjorie Randon Hershey, "The Congressional Elections," in Pomper, *Election of 1996*, 228.

33. Terrel L. Rhodes, *Republicans in the South: Voting for the State House, Voting for the White House* (Westport, Conn.: Praeger, 2000), 41, 56.

34. Richard K. Scher, *Politics in the New South: Republicanism, Race, and Leadership in the Twentieth Century* (Armonk, N.Y.: M. E. Sharpe, 1992); John J. McGlennon, "Party Competition in Southern State Legislatures, 1976–1996: The Last Block of the Solid South Crumbles," *American Review of Politics* 17 (1996): 218; Stanley, "South and 1996 Presidential Election," 235; Richard M. Scammon, Alice V. McGillivray, and Rhodes Cook, *America Votes 23, 1998: A Handbook of Contemporary American Election Statistics* (Washington, D.C.: Congressional Quarterly, 1998); *The Book of the States: 1998–99 Edition*, vol. 32 (Lexington, Ky.: Council of State Governments, 1998), table 3.3.

35. Abramowitz and Saunders, "Party Polarization," 141–42; Christopher Caldwell, "The Southern Captivity of the GOP," *Atlantic Monthly*, June 1998, 60–62.

36. Binford, Baxter, and Sturrock, "Georgia," 129.

37. "Party Switcher's Staff Resigns en Masse," *Atlanta Journal/Constitution*, 20 July 1999. Senator Bob Smith of New Hampshire also left the Republicans, but for the U.S. Taxpayers' party rather than the Democrats. Tom Baxter, "GOP Splintering on Tax Vote Underscores Cost of Defections," *Atlanta Journal/Constitution*, 22 July 1999.

38. Merle Black, "Roundtable on the 1996 Election," presented at the annual meeting of the Southern Political Science Association, Atlanta, 7 November 1996.

39. Jonathan Weisman, "Will the Rise of 'Blue Dogs' Revive Bipartisan Right?" *Congressional Quarterly Weekly*, 21 December 1996, 3446; Lori Nitschke, "Political Trends Come Together to Diminish Coalition's Clout," *Congressional Quarterly Weekly*, 3 January 1998, 1, retrieved 24 September 1999 from the World Wide Web: *http://libraryip.cq.com*; Stephen Gettinger, "R.I.P. to a Conservative Force," *Congressional Quarterly Weekly*, 9 January 1999, 1, retrieved 22 June 2000 from the World Wide Web: *http://libraryip.cq.com*.

40. Rebecca Carr, "GOP's Election-Year Worries Cooled Partisan Rancor," *Congressional Quarterly Weekly*, 21 December 1996, 3432, 3462; Daniel J. Parks, "Partisan Voting Holds Steady," *Congressional Quarterly Weekly*, 11 December 1999, 1, retrieved 22 June 2000 from the World Wide Web: *http://libraryip.cq.com*.

41. Alan K. Ota, "Partisan Voting on the Rise," *Congressional Quarterly Weekly*, 9 January 1999, 3, retrieved 24 September 1999 from the World Wide Web: *http://libraryip.cq.com*.

42. Walter Dean Burnham, "Bill Clinton: Riding the Tiger," in Pomper, *Election of 1996*, 8; Eric Uslaner, *The Decline of Comity in Congress* (Ann Arbor: University of Michigan Press, 1993).

43. Wattenberg, *Decline of American Political Parties*, 211.

44. Burnham, "Riding the Tiger," 20.

45. Randall W. Strahan, "Partisan Officeholders, 1946–1996," in Shafer, *Partisan Approaches*, 28–30.

46. Kevin Phillips, *The Emerging Republican Majority* (Garden City, N.J.: Anchor Books, 1969).

47. Aldrich and Niemi, "Sixth American Party System," 101; Lawrence, *Collapse of Democratic Presidential Majority*, 98–99; and William G. Mayer, *The Divided Democrats* (Boulder, Colo.: Westview, 1996), 77, 153.

48. Lawrence, *Collapse of Democratic Presidential Majority*, 5.

49. Ladd, "'No Majority' Realignment," 2, 11; Michael Barone, "Advantage GOP," retrieved 1 January 1998 from the World Wide Web: *http://www.intellectualcapi tal.com*; Lloyd A. Free and Hadley Cantril, *The Political Beliefs of Americans* (New York: Simon and Schuster, 1968).

50. Wattenberg, *Decline of American Political Parties*, 48, 38, 65, 69.

51. Stanley, "Southern Partisan Changes," 80–85.

52. Lawrence, *Collapse of Democratic Presidential Majority*. Ira Katznelson, "Was the Great Society a Lost Opportunity?" in *The Rise and Fall of the New Deal Order, 1930–1980*, ed. Simon Fraser and Gary Gerstle (Princeton, N.J.: Princeton University Press, 1989), has described the decomposition of New Deal policy in the 1940s that paralleled the mini-realignment away from New Deal politics portrayed by Lawrence. It is also interesting to note the role of race and the South at both junctures in the 1940s and 1960s. The Democratic party's first tentative steps toward a civil rights plank in 1948 prodded some Southerners to walk out of the convention and back the third-party campaign of the Dixiecrats. In 1968, the independent candidacy of George Wallace profited from the disaffection of many white Southern Democrats with the national party's backing of civil rights measures.

53. Joel H. Silbey, "Beyond Realignment and Realignment Theory: American Political Eras, 1789–1989," in Shafer, *End of Realignment?* 5, 17–18.

54. Everett Carll Ladd, "Like Waiting for Godot: The Uselessness of 'Realignment' for Understanding Change in Contemporary American Politics," in Shafer, *End of Realignment?* 13; Stanley J. Watson, "Race and Alignment Reconsidered: Issues Evolution in the South Since 1972," *American Review of Politics* 17, no. 2 (summer 1996): 147–48; Edward G. Carmines and James A. Stimson, *Issue Evolution: Race and the Transformation of American Politics* (Princeton, N.J.: Princeton University Press, 1989).

55. Peter F. Nardulli, "The Concept of a Critical Realignment, Electoral Behavior, and Political Change," *American Political Science Review* 89, no. 1 (March 1995): 10–22. McWilliams, "Meaning of the Election," 258, notes that the growth in Republican strength in the South and among religious conservatives indicates that a subnational realignment is under way that will increase the influence of social conservatives in Republican councils. He cites the example of the Iowa Republican party's condemnation of the 4-H club movement for leaning toward socialism.

56. Watson, "Race and Alignment Reconsidered," 145.

57. Stephen D. Shaffer et al., "Mississippi: From Pariah to Pacesetter?" in Lamis, *Southern Politics*, 270.

58. John C. Kuzenski and Michael K. Corbello, "Racial and Economic Explanations for Republican Growth in the South: A Case Study of Attitudinal Voting in Louisiana," *American Review of Politics* 17 (summer 1996): 129–43. The 1995 race, however, pitted a white Republican, Mike Foster, against a black Democrat, Cleo Fields. This contest may not be representative of most elections because of the obvious salience of race in a campaign with candidates of different races.

59. Ibid., 130. Such a result would depend, of course, on how Southerners' attitudes on race continue to evolve. There is extensive evidence from surveys that Southerners' opinions on racial issues continue to converge with non-Southerners' views. Conversely, James H. Kuklinski, Michael D. Cobb, and Martin Gilens, "Racial Attitudes and the 'New South,'" *Journal of Politics* 59, no. 2 (May 1997): 323–49, contend that social mores make it socially unacceptable for many to state their actual views on race. Using disguised measures of racism, they found significantly more racism among Southern survey respondents. Watson, "Race and Alignment Reconsidered," uses opinions on government aid to minorities as an indirect measure of racial attitudes. None of this research gets at an even knottier issue of whether attitudes on questions such as aid to minorities reflects "polite" racism or merely a more general conservative ideology. See David O. Sears, Jim Sidanius, and Lawrence Bobo, eds., *Racialized Politics: The Debate About Racism in America* (Chicago: University of Chicago Press, 2000).

60. David W. Rohde, "The Inevitability and Solidity of the 'Republican Solid South,'" *American Review of Politics* 17 (summer 1996): 23–46.

61. James M. Glaser, *Race, Campaign Politics, and the Realignment in the South* (New Haven, Conn.: Yale University Press, 1996), 184, 121, 132, 75–76.

62. Ibid., 138–39.

63. Keith Reeves, *Voting Hopes or Fears? White Voters, Black Candidates, and Racial Politics in America* (New York: Oxford University Press, 1997), 9.

64. Glaser, *Race, Campaign Politics, and Realignment*, 31.

65. Alexander P. Lamis, "Southern Politics in the 1990s," in Lamis, *Southern Politics*, 387.

66. Richard K. Scher, Jon L. Mills, and John J. Hotaling, *Voting Rights and Democracy: The Law and Politics of Districting* (Chicago: Nelson-Hall, 1997), 90; *Miller v. Johnson*, 515 U.S. 900 (1995).

67. D. Stephen Voss, "Black Incumbents, White Districts: An Appraisal of the 1996 Congressional Elections in Georgia and Florida," paper presented at the annual meeting of the Southern Political Science Association, Atlanta, 29 October 1998; Cynthia McKinney, "A Product of the Voting Right Act," *Washington Post*, 2–8 December 1996, national weekly edition. Voss doubts the value of incumbency. He also notes that while there is good news for Democrats in the willingness of some whites to vote for black Democratic candidates, the bad news is that so few whites are willing to vote for any Democrats, white or black (Voss, "Black Incumbents," 20).

68. Lamis, "Southern Politics in the 1990s," 383; Hershey, "Congressional Elections," 222.

69. Paige Schneider, "Factionalism in the Southern Republican Party," *American Review of Politics* 19 (summer 1998): 138–41. One current example illustrates the coalition maintenance problems faced by both parties. The drive to remove the Confederate battle flag from Southern state flags and capitols is a classic wedge issue with the potential to play havoc with the fragile biracial Democratic alliance. Republicans, however, are discovering that the issue poses plenty of mischief for them as well. The party's business elite leadership, concerned about the negative image presented by the Confederate flag in efforts to attract tourism and investment, finds itself hemmed in by its recalcitrant neopopulist (or neo-Confederate)

mass electoral base. Glen T. Broach and Lee Bandy, "South Carolina: A Decade of Rapid Republican Ascent," in Lamis, *Southern Politics*, 80.

70. Christopher Caldwell, "The Southern Captivity of the GOP," *Atlantic Monthly*, June 1998, 55–72; Theodore J. Lowi, *The End of the Republican Era* (Norman: University of Oklahoma Press, 1995); Rhodes, *Republicans in the South*, 12, citing V. O. Key. Rhodes notes that after the 1992 elections, 29 percent of the Republican seats in Congress came from the East, a number equal to Southern Republican seats. After the 1996 election, however, the Southern GOP percentage had risen slightly to 31 percent, but the portion of Republican seats from the East had declined precipitously to 17 percent (ibid., 114).

71. Stephen D. Shaffer and Monica Johnson, "A New Solid South? The Drama of Partisan Realignment in the Deep South State of Mississippi," *American Review of Politics* 17, no. 2 (summer 1996): 185.

72. Lamis, "Southern Politics in the 1990s," 385. Rhodes, *Republicans in the South*, 17, confirms the assessment that the South is two-party competitive at national and state office levels, although the Democrats still hold an edge in state legislative races. Rhodes rightly calls this competition a realignment from Democratic one-partyism but notes that the demise of the Democrats, which some had predicted, has not occurred (ibid., preface).

73. Ladd, "'No Majority' Realignment," 10, 16.

74. Ibid., 14.

75. William Schneider, "Realignment: The Eternal Question," *PS: Political Science and Politics* 15, no. 3 (summer 1982): 449–57.

76. Burnham, "Critical Realignment," 107; Sidney Blumenthal, *The Permanent Campaign* (New York: Simon and Schuster, 1983).

77. Martin Wattenberg, *Candidate-Centered Politics: Presidential Elections of the 1980s* (Cambridge, Mass.: Harvard University Press, 1991), 33.

78. Ibid., 32; Warren E. Miller, "Party Identification and the Electorate of the 1990s," in Maisel, *Parties Respond*, 116; and Walter Dean Burnham, *Critical Elections and the Mainsprings of American Politics* (New York: W. W. Norton, 1970), 32. Burnham, "Critical Realignment," 116–17, discusses the existence of a "nonpartisan-channeled" realignment and suggests that such a postpartisan realignment has occurred during the last decades of the twentieth century.

79. Abramson, Aldrich, and Rohde, *Change and Continuity in 1996*, 259–60.

80. Lawrence, *Collapse of Democratic Presidential Majority*, 29.

81. Ibid., 22.

82. Walter Dean Burnham, "The End of American Party Politics," *Society* 35, no. 2 (1998: 6, first published in *Society* (1969), retrieved 9 June 1998 from the World Wide Web: *http://venuse.galib.uga.edu.*

83. Shaffer and Johnson, "New Solid South?" 189.

6. Politics: America's Number One Problem

1. Robert Putnam, "Bowling Alone: America's Declining Social Capital," *Journal of Democracy* (January 1995): 65–78.

2. In 1997, the American Political Science Association formed a Commission

on Citizenship Education to diagnose the problem of the declining commitment of Americans to their political institutions and to suggest correctives.

3. Juliet B. Schor, *The Overworked American* (New York: Basic, 1991); Barry Bluestone and Stephen Rose, "Overworked and Underemployed," *American Prospect*, March–April 1997, 58–69.

4. L. Sandy Maisel, *Parties and Elections in America: The Electoral Process*, 3d ed. (Lanham, Md.: Rowman and Littlefield, 1999), 149.

5. W. Lance Bennett, *The Governing Crisis* (New York: St. Martin's Press, 1992).

6. V. O. Key, Jr., *Southern Politics in State and Nation* (New York: Vintage, 1949), 299.

7. In many party texts, the education function is omitted. To American ears, it sounds a bit totalitarian to suggest that parties should educate the public. But even democratic institutions do influence the masses of citizens, as well as reflecting mass opinion, however badly or unself-consciously they might perform this role.

8. Bennett, *Governing Crisis*, 14.

9. *Buckley v. Valeo*, 424 U.S. 1 (1976); Darrell M. West and Burdett A. Loomis, *The Sound of Money: How Political Interests Get What They Want* (New York: W. W. Norton, 1999), 65.

10. Michael Binford, Tom Baxter, and David E. Sturrock, "Georgia: Democratic Bastion No Longer," in *Southern Politics in the 1990s*, ed. Alexander P. Lamis (Baton Rouge: Louisiana State University Press, 1999), 123.

11. Center for Responsive Politics, "The Big Picture" (15 November 1997), retrieved 31 August 2000 from the World Wide Web: *www.opensecrets.org/ newsletter/ce46/CE1115P1.html*; William Greider, *Who Will Tell the People: The Betrayal of American Democracy* (New York: Simon and Schuster, 1992).

12. Thomas Ferguson, *Golden Rule: The Investment Theory of Party Competition and the Logic of Money-Driven Political Systems* (Chicago: University of Chicago Press, 1995), 29.

13. Chuck Collins, Chris Hartman, and Holly Sklar, *Divided Decade: Economic Disparity at the Century's Turn* (Boston: United for a Fair Economy, 1999), 10, retrieved 13 March 2000 from the World Wide Web: *http://www.ufenet.org/press/ divided_decade.html*.

14. West and Loomis, *Sound of Money*, 15.

15. Bartholomew H. Sparrow, *Uncertain Guardians: The News Media as a Political Institution* (Baltimore: Johns Hopkins University Press, 1999), 41. The schemes resorted to by enterprising politicians to raise money were legion and were often an assault on the dignity of public office. The scandals surrounding the Democrats' fund-raising efforts for the 1996 election revealed that large donors were frequently invited to stay overnight at the White House, threatening to turn the Lincoln bedroom into a Motel 6 for millionaires.

16. West and Loomis, *Sound of Money*, 225–26.

17. Walter Dean Burnham, "The 1996 Elections: Drift or Mandate?" *American Prospect*, July–August 1996, 43–49, retrieved 9 June 1998 from the World Wide Web: *http://epn.org/prospect/27/27burn.html*; Joe McGinniss, *The Selling of the President 1968* (New York: Pocket Books, 1968); Bruce Miroff, Raymond Seidelman, and Todd Swanstrom, *The Democratic Debate: An Introduction to American Politics*, 2d ed. (Boston: Houghton Mifflin, 1998), 222; Robert Schumhl, *Statecraft and Stage-*

craft: American Political Life in the Age of Personality, 2d ed. (Notre Dame, Ind.: University of Notre Dame Press, 1992); Jonathan Schell, "The Uncertain Leviathan," *Atlantic,* August 1996, 3, 6, retrieved 4 June 1998 from the World Wide Web: *http://www.theatlantic.com/issues/96aug/schell/schell.htm.*

18. Xandra Kayden, "Alive and Well and Living in Washington: The American Political Parties," in *Manipulating Public Opinion,* ed. Michael Margolis and Gary A. Mauser (Pacific Grove, Calif.: Brooks/Cole, 1989), 70–94.

19. Charles W. Logan, Jr., "Getting Beyond Scarcity: A New Paradigm for Assessing the Constitutionality of Broadcast Regulation," *California Law Review* 85 (December 1997): 1720, retrieved 23 April 1998 from the World Wide Web: *http://web.lexis-nexis.com/universe.*

20. Walter DeVries and Lance Tarrance, Jr., *The Ticket Splitter* (Grand Rapids, Mich.: William B. Eerdmans, 1972).

21. Bennett, *Governing Crisis,* 33–34.

22. Theodore Glasser, "Objective Reporting Is Irresponsible," in *The Mass Media: Opposing Viewpoints,* ed. Neal Bernards (St. Paul, Minn.: Greenhaven, 1988), 28; Kathleen Hall Jamieson, *Dirty Politics: Deception, Distraction, and Democracy* (New York: Oxford University Press, 1992).

23. Thomas Patterson, *Out of Order* (New York: Vintage, 1994); Douglas Rushkoff, "Media Democracy," in *Debating Democracy,* ed. Bruce Miroff, Raymond Seidelman, and Todd Swanstrom (Boston: Houghton Mifflin, 1997), 150–59.

24. Clay Calvert, "When First Amendment Principles Collide: Negative Political Advertising and the Democratization of Democratic Self-Governance," *Loyola of Los Angeles Law Review* 30 (June 1997): 1539, retrieved 23 April 1998 from the World Wide Web: *http://web.lexis-nexis.com/universe.*

25. Jarol Manheim, "Packaging the People," in Miroff, Seidelman, and Swanstrom, *Debating Democracy,* 146; Penn Kimball, *Downsizing the News* (Baltimore: Johns Hopkins University Press, 1994).

26. Kiku Adatto, "The Incredible Shrinking Sound Bite," in *Voices of Dissent: Critical Readings in American Politics,* 2d ed., ed. William F. Grover and Joseph G. Peschek (New York: HarperCollins, 1996), 205.

27. Joseph N. Cappella and Kathleen Hall Jamieson, "News Frames, Political Cynicism, and Media Cynicism," *Annals of the American Academy of Political and Social Science* 546 (July 1996): 6, retrieved 14 May 1998 from the World Wide Web: *http://web.lexis-nexis.com/universe.*

28. Neil Postman, *Amusing Ourselves to Death: Public Discourse in the Age of Show Business* (New York: Penguin, 1985), vii. Postman's comparison of the totalitarian dysutopias portrayed by Orwell and Huxley is insightful and frighteningly relevant to contemporary cultural critique: "What Orwell feared were those who would ban books. What Huxley feared was that there would be no reason to ban a book for there would be no one who wanted to read one. Orwell feared those who would deprive us of information. Huxley feared those who would give us so much that we would be reduced to passivity and egoism. Orwell feared that the truth would be concealed from us. Huxley feared the truth would be drowned in a sea of irrelevance. Orwell feared we would become a captive culture. Huxley feared we would become a trivial culture, preoccupied with some equivalent of the feelies, the orgy porgy, and the centrifugal bumblepuppy. . . . In *1984,* Huxley added,

people are controlled by inflicting pain. In *Brave New World*, they are controlled by inflicting pleasure." Ronald K. L. Collins and David M. Skover, *The Death of Discourse* (Boulder, Colo.: Westview, 1996), have developed the implications of these insights for our conceptions of freedom of speech and press.

29. Scott Shepard, "Voters Don't Find Gore Warm and Fuzzy, Polls Show," *Atlanta Journal/Constitution*, 12 May 2000, A4, quoting Jack Pitney; Bennett, *Governing Crisis*, 14.

30. Thomas Mann and Norman Ornstein, "After the Campaign, What? Governance Questions for the 2000 Election," *Brookings Review* 18, no. 1 (winter 2000): 2–3, retrieved 28 January 2000 from the World Wide Web: *http://www.brookings. edu/press/REVIEW/winter2000/ornstein.htm*.

31. Martin Wattenberg, *The Decline of American Political Parties*, 4th ed. (Cambridge, Mass.: Harvard University Press, 1996), 81.

32. Jon K. Dalager, "Voters, Issues, and Elections: Are the Candidates' Messages Getting Through?" *Journal of Politics* 58, no. 2 (May 1996): 493, 495–96.

33. Robert M. Entman, review of *Out of Order*, by Thomas E. Patterson, *Journal of American History* 8 (1995): 1826–27, retrieved from the World Wide Web: *http://ganymede.galileo.gsu.edu*.

34. Dalager, "Voters, Issues, and Elections," 501.

35. Justin Lewis, Michael Morgan, and Sut Jhally, "Libertine or Liberal? The Real Scandal of What People Know About President Clinton," retrieved 4 April 2000 from the World Wide Web: *http://www.umass.edu/newsoffice/archive/1998/ 021098study2.html*.

36. Cappella and Jamieson, "News Frames," 2.

37. Entman, review of Patterson.

38. Wilson Carey McWilliams, "The Meaning of the Election," in *The Election of 1996: Reports and Interpretations*, ed. Gerald M. Pomper et al. (Chatham, N.J.: Chatham House, 1997), 241; Steven J. Rosenstone and John Mark Hansen, *Mobilization, Participation, and Democracy in America* (New York: Macmillan, 1993), 57; Robert L. Borosage, "Election 98: The End of the Gingrich Revolution," Campaign for America's Future, 1998 (on-line), retrieved 12 November 1998 from the World Wide Web: *http://www.ourfuture.org/tpoint/98boro.asp*; Schell, "Uncertain Leviathan," 6.

39. Jack Beatty, "The Road to a Third Party," *Atlantic Monthly*, August 1995, 3, retrieved 4 June 1998 from the World Wide Web: *http://www.theatlantic.com/ election/connection/policamp/goldenr.htm*.

40. Wattenberg, *Decline of American Political Parties*, 2; Paul R. Abramson, John H. Aldrich, and David W. Rohde, *Continuity and Change in the 1996 Elections* (Washington, D.C.: Congressional Quarterly, 1998), 75.

41. Frances Fox Piven and Richard A. Cloward, *Why Americans Don't Vote* (New York: Pantheon, 1989), stress the barrier presented by registration requirements in the United States. Unlike in most other democracies, where the government ensures registration, in this country, the entire burden of registration is placed on the citizen. In contrast, Burnham notes that in North Dakota, the only state without a personal voter registration requirement, turnout fell in every presidential election from 1960 through 1984. The abstention rate was 20 percent of eligible voters in 1960, but it had almost doubled to 36 percent by 1984. Walter Dean Burnham, "The Class Gap," in Grover and Peschek, *Voices of Dissent*, 202.

42. Rosenstone and Hansen, *Mobilization, Participation, and Democracy*, 140–41.

43. Piven and Cloward, *Why Americans Don't Vote*, xii, note the interconnections between the M^3 system and low participation. Many have suggested that the Democrats should attempt a mobilization strategy, rallying the one-half of the electorate who have not been voting by appealing to their economic self-interest. Such a strategy appears to be a potential winner for the Democrats, since many of the nonvoters seem naturally more at home with a party whose constituents are drawn disproportionately from the bottom half of the socioeconomic scale. Piven and Cloward suggest, however, that such a mobilizing strategy would threaten the party's appeal to large donors. This anticipated loss of revenue gives the wealthy, in effect, a veto over party appeals. Failing to mobilize the inert nonvoters, in turn, makes the party much more dependent on professional public relations consultants to match Republican appeals and on the sources of the funds to pay for these campaign tactics.

44. Stephen Ansolabehere and Shanto Iyengar, *Going Negative: How Attack Ads Shrink and Polarize the Electorate* (New York: Free Press, 1995); Calvert, "When First Amendment Principles Collide," 8.

45. Putnam, "Bowling Alone"; Theda Skocpol, "Associations Without Members," *American Prospect*, August 1999, 66.

46. Rosenstone and Hansen, *Mobilization, Participation, and Democracy*, 210, 213–15, 218–19.

47. Robert Dreyfuss, "The Turnout Imperative," *American Prospect*, July–August 1998, retrieved 31 August 2000 from the World Wide Web: *www.prospect.org/archives/39/39dreyfs.html*.

48. Scott Keeter, "Public Opinion and the Election," in Pomper, *Election of 1996*, 113.

49. This political truism simply reflects what E. E. Schattsneider, *The Semi-Sovereign People* (New York: Holt, Rinehart and Winston, 1960), 2, established in his political science classic—that the scope of who gets involved in politics is one critical determinant of the outcome of political decisions.

50. John Gaventa, *Power and Powerlessness: Quiescence and Rebellion in an Appalachian Valley* (Urbana: University of Illinois Press, 1982), ch. 1.

51. Rogers M. Smith, "Beyond Tocqueville, Myrdal, and Hartz: The Multiple Traditions in America," *American Political Science Review* 87, no. 3 (September 1993): 549–66; Frank Freidel, *F.D.R. and the South* (Baton Rouge: Louisiana State University Press, 1965), ch. 3; Robert Huckfeldt and Carol Weitzel Kohfeld, *Race and the Decline of Class in American Politics* (Urbana: University of Illinois Press, 1989), 5, 9. But see Jill Quadagno, *The Color of Welfare: How Racism Undermined the War on Poverty* (New York: Oxford University Press, 1994), ch. 1, on the racially discriminatory aspects of the New Deal.

52. The history of the Voting Rights Act as played out in the 1990s suggests that this tactic has had longer-term ramifications than could have been imagined in the 1960s. As the issue turned from simple access to the ballot to dilution of minority votes, the 1982 congressional amendment of the Voting Rights Act and federal court interpretations ensured that minority votes would be meaningful by requiring that election rules guarantee minorities "an equal opportunity to participate in the electoral process and to elect candidates of their choice" (Richard K. Scher, Jon L. Mills, and J. Hotaling, *Voting Rights and Democracy: The Law and*

Politics of Districting [Chicago: Nelson-Hall, 1997], 62). The Bush Justice Department enforced this standard vigorously, requiring majority minority districts wherever possible (James Everett Voyles, "Don't Cross This Line: A Comparison of the Reagan, Bush, and Clinton Departments of Justice on Majority-Minority Districts," paper presented at the annual meeting of the Southern Political Science Association, Atlanta, 4 November 1994). The effect was to "pack" black voters into a few districts where they constituted a majority but to "bleach" surrounding districts by draining them of African American voters. Politically, the net result was to cost the Democrats at least a few seats after the 1992 election. Ironically, when the Republican-dominated Supreme Court struck down many of the majority minority districts as constituting racial gerrymanders, the political fallout still seemed to benefit the GOP by inflaming white reactions against "quotas."

53. Chandler Davidson, *Race and Class in Texas Politics* (Princeton, N.J.: Princeton University Press, 1990), 232–33; Kevin Phillips, *The Emerging Republican Majority* (Garden City, N.J.: Anchor Books, 1969).

54. Thomas Byrne Edsall with Mary Edsall, *Chain Reaction: The Impact of Race, Rights, and Taxes on American Politics* (New York: W. W. Norton, 1992). See also Thomas Byrne Edsall, *The New Politics of Inequality* (New York: W. W. Norton, 1984); Richard M. Scammon and Ben J. Wattenberg, *The Real Majority* (New York: Coward, McCann and Geoghegan, 1970). Although less often noted by analysts of the demise of the New Deal coalition, sexism also played a role in the Republican backlash against the cultural revolution of the 1960s and 1970s. For example, the Edsalls note that the conservative revulsion against the Democrats was based on the perception that they were too permissive toward criminals, disorderly demonstrators, and welfare cheats at home and too weak in their opposition to communism abroad. It is striking how the masculinist concern with "softness" pervades these disparate issues (ibid., 20). See also Suzanne Mettler, *Dividing Citizens: Gender and Federalism in New Deal Public Policy* (Ithaca, N.Y.: Cornell University Press, 1998).

55. Paul M. Sniderman and Edward Carmines, *Reaching Beyond Race* (Cambridge, Mass.: Harvard University Press, 1997), 63. Many issues lacking any racial overtones on their face may have hidden racial dimensions. For example, Peter Irons, *The Courage of Their Convictions: Sixteen Americans Who Fought Their Way to the Supreme Court* (New York: Penguin, 1990), 207, notes possible connections between racism and opposition to teaching evolution: "But the evolution controversy tapped the deep roots of Southern racism: Those who called black people 'monkeys' recoiled at the notion that humans had evolved from apes. And for those Fundamentalists who mixed racism with religion, the Genesis account of creation allowed a separate origin for blacks and whites." Even the impeachment of President Clinton may be seen as having racial undercurrents, especially given the strong support of African Americans for the president in the face of attacks by a Republican leadership that was lily white and Southern to boot. "Some blacks went so far as to suggest that 'white skin notwithstanding, this is our first black President'" (Randall Kennedy, "Is He a Soul Man? On Black Support for Clinton," *American Prospect*, March–April 1999, 26, quoting Toni Morrison). If President Clinton is truly a "soul man," the impeachment proceedings could take on the cast of a political lynching.

56. Edsall with Edsall, *Chain Reaction*, 144–45.

57. Martin Gilens, "'Race Coding' and White Opposition to Welfare," *American Political Science Review* 90, no. 3 (September 1996): 593–604; James M. Glaser, *Race, Campaign Politics, and the Realignment in the South* (New Haven, Conn.: Yale University Press, 1996), 22.

58. William C. Berman, *America's Right Turn: From Nixon to Clinton*, 2d ed. (Baltimore: Johns Hopkins University Press, 1998), 62. See Edsall with Edsall, *Chain Reaction*, 214, discussing the way such seemingly neutral terms as "group," "big government," "taxes," and "special interests" became freighted with meaning by Republican political strategists, who skillfully used these terms against segments of the old New Deal coalition. West and Loomis, *Sound of Money*, 112–13, note that even the legislation passed in the Hundred Days' wake of the 1994 Republican Revolution bore names "carefully scripted" to take advantage of focus-group-tested themes. Examples include "the Personal Responsibility Act (welfare reform), the Taking Back Our Streets Act (crime), the American Dream Restoration Act (tax relief), and the Common Sense Legal Reforms Act (tort reform)."

59. Sniderman and Carmines, *Reaching Beyond Race*, 75, 73, 96–97.

60. Huckfeldt and Kohfeld, *Race and Decline of Class*, 22. Ethnocentrism colors some conservative backlash as well. To the extent that issues are now more broadly cultural than specifically racial (although I have argued that disentangling the two is nearly impossible), immigrants may play the role in national politics once played by African Americans in traditional Southern politics. As the bugaboo for white fears and the whipping boy for white resentment, especially in bad times and to groups falling behind in good times, immigrants make a tempting target on which to blame troubles. Scapegoating immigrants serves to divert attention from the real issues, structures, and groups that benefit from, and exert real power over, the tumultuous transformations remaking our social landscape. Although the analogy fits less closely, majority antipathy to progress by gays and lesbians performs similar functions.

61. Ibid., 16.

62. Michael Omi and Howard Winant, *Racial Formations in the United States from the 1960s to the 1980s* (New York: Routledge and Keagan Paul, 1986), ch. 4.

63. Another irony of the heightened racism of American politics in recent years is that it occurs simultaneously with the increased political participation by African Americans, especially in the South. Although registration rates and turnout each typically lag white rates by about 10 percent, this gap is minuscule compared with that of even a few decades ago (Terrel L. Rhodes, *Republicans in the South: Voting for the State House, Voting for the White House* [Westport, Conn.: Praeger, 2000], 112). Moreover, African Americans can and do mobilize at rates higher than whites, potentially providing the key to victory, as in the 1998 elections in Georgia. A possible explanation for this paradox lies in the concept of "electoral capture." Paul Frymer suggests that some groups have no choice but to remain loyal to one party because the opposing party is uninterested in their votes. Their own party is then free to ignore their interests, because group members' only options amount to electoral suicide: abstention or wasting their votes on the doomed challenges of third parties. The corollary of electoral capture is that party leaders pander to groups of swing voters they believe capable of determining elections (Paul

Frymer, *Uneasy Alliances: Race and Party Competition in America* [Princeton, N.J.: Princeton University Press, 1999], 8]. This situation well describes the current state of neglect of African American interests and the pursuit of Reagan Democrats by New Democratic leaders, but Frymer sees the problem embedded more deeply in our two-party system. Without the heightened racialization of current politics, however, both parties would have more incentive to seek out African American votes and less incentive to appeal to swing voters' racism.

64. Huckfeldt and Kohfeld, *Race and Decline of Class*, 191.

65. Alexander P. Lamis, "Southern Politics in the 1990s," in Lamis, *Southern Politics*, 406.

66. Key, *Southern Politics*, 4.

67. Chapter 4 discusses the role of the South and other factors in influencing the transformation of national electoral structures.

68. See Theodore J. Lowi, *The Personal President: Power Invested, Promise Unfulfilled* (Ithaca, N.Y.: Cornell University Press, 1985), 127, 131–32, for a discussion of why party regularity is not equivalent to party discipline and for an analysis of why the stronger Republican party organization and an increasingly strong Democratic party have not attained the level of responsibility sought by party reformers.

69. William G. Mayer, "Mass Partisanship, 1946–1996," in *Partisan Approaches to Postwar American Politics*, ed. Byron E. Shafer (New York: Chatham House, 1998), 214.

70. Wattenberg, *Decline of American Political Parties*, 188–89. Not only has divided party control become entrenched in American political practice, but there is also abundant evidence that the ideal of responsible party government currently lacks popular support as a governmental norm. A 1992 survey found that only 35 percent preferred unified party control, while 38 percent preferred divided control, and 25 percent were indifferent (ibid., 190). A 1996 survey found that 92 percent of the public believes in voting for the candidate, not the party, giving this antipartisan norm practically creedal status (ibid., 163). Indeed, a 1994 survey found that although 37 percent of respondents preferred a two-party system, compared with the 24 percent who endorsed third parties, a 39 percent plurality preferred candidate-centered politics (ibid., 213). Such lack of support for a responsible party system must be taken with a grain of salt. As V. O. Key observed, public opinion is in a real sense an "echo chamber," responding to choices it is offered (Warren Miller, "Party Identification and the Electorate of the 1990s," in *The Parties Respond*, ed. L. Sandy Maisel, 3d ed. [Boulder, Colo.: Westview, 1998], 123). When the public's views of the parties identify them with the current crop of politicians, with a RIP (revelation, investigation, and prosecution) type of politics of collision and collusion, and with bickering and acrimony as opposed to serious efforts to conduct the public's business, the popular antiparty sentiment is more than understandable. Benjamin Ginsberg and Martin Shefter, *Politics by Other Means*, 2d ed. (New York: W. W. Norton, 1999); L. Sandy Maisel, "The Parties on the Eve of the Millennium," in Maisel, *Parties Respond*, 370.

71. Tom DeLuca, *The Two Faces of Political Apathy* (Philadelphia: Temple University Press, 1995), 87.

72. E. J. Dionne, Jr., *Why Americans Hate Politics* (New York: Simon and Schuster, 1992), 345.

73. Ginsberg and Shefter, *Politics by Other Means*, 44.

74. Walter Dean Burnham, "Critical Realignment: Alive or Dead?" in *The End of Realignment? Interpreting American Electoral Eras*, ed. Byron E. Shafer (Madison: University of Wisconsin Press, 1991), 126.

75. Wattenberg, *Decline of American Political Parties*, 4.

76. Barbara G. Salmore and Stephen A. Salmore, *Candidates, Parties, and Campaigns: Electoral Politics in America*, 2d ed. (Washington, D.C.: Congressional Quarterly Press, 1989), 261–71.

77. "Poll Finds Desire for Third Party," *Atlanta Journal/Constitution*, 25 December 1999, C2.

78. Calvert, "When First Amendment Principles Collide," 3. On the controversial notion of an underclass, see William Julius Wilson, *When Work Disappears* (New York: Vintage, 1996); Herbert Gans, *The War Against the Poor: The Underclass and Anti-Poverty Policy* (New York: Basic, 1996); Michael B. Katz, *The Undeserving Poor* (New York: Pantheon, 1989).

79. Robert B. Reich, *The Work of Nations* (New York: Vintage, 1992), 276. By 1997, 9 million Americans were living in gated communities (Carl Boggs, *The End of Politics: Corporate Power and the Decline of the Public Sphere* [New York: Guilford, 2000], 285). A reflection of this evacuation of the public domain is the shared themes of the 2000 presidential candidates. Both George W. Bush, Jr., and Al Gore claim to be focusing on the "inner frontier" of moral values. Although understandable in the wake of the Monica Lewinsky scandal, the post-Watergate obsession with character and personal morality takes us further from an era when our politics sought to meet the challenges of a "New Frontier" or to offer Americans a "New Deal" or a "Fair Deal" by addressing shared issues of common concern. The "Virtuecrats" have nurtured these conservative tendencies by "pushing politics away from world affairs and economics into something more personal." "The New Frontier of the '90s is an inner one," according to former Republican speechwriter Peggy Noonan (Howard Fineman, "Virtuecrats," *Newsweek*, 13 June 1994, 32).

80. Bennett, *Governing Crisis*, 86, quoting Robert Entman. See also Boggs, *End of Politics*.

81. Greider, *Who Will Tell*, 275.

82. Mayer, "Mass Partisanship, 1946–1996," 215.

83. John H. Aldrich and Richard G. Niemi, "The Sixth American Party System: Electoral Change, 1952–1992," in *Broken Contract? Changing Relationships Between Americans and Their Government*, ed. Stephen C. Craig (Boulder, Colo.: Westview, 1996). Bartels has provided strong arguments and data suggesting that the trends toward declining partisanship in the electorate bottomed out in the 1970s and that since then, voters have become increasingly attached to parties (Larry M. Bartels, "Partisanship and Voting Behavior, 1952–1996," *American Journal of Political Science* 44 [January 2000]: 35–50). Whether these trends toward resumed partisan attachments continue or are offset by voter disaffection from parties may depend on whether the leadership of the parties follows the polarizing models of Reagan and Gingrich or the less partisan tacks of Clinton-Gore and the Bushes.

84. Public Agenda Foundation, *Prescription for Prosperity: Four Paths to Economic Renewal* (Dayton, Ohio: National Issues Forums Institute, 1992); Kenneth

Dolbeare, *Democracy at Risk: The Politics of Economic Renewal* (Chatham, N.J.: Chatham House, 1986).

85. Miroff, Seidelman, and Swanstrom, *Democratic Debate*, 239.

7. Southern Symptoms

1. Several commentators have noted the irony of Americans' discontent with their own democracy at the very moment of democracy's apparent triumph world-wide. For example, see E. J. Dionne, Jr., *Why Americans Hate Politics* (New York: Simon and Schuster, 1992), 9, and Michael Sandel, *Democracy's Discontent: America in Search of a Public Philosophy* (Cambridge, Mass.: Harvard University Press, 1996), 3. See Godfrey Hodgson, *America in Our Time* (New York: Vintage, 1976), to appreciate what a reversal this is from a time not so long ago when Americans were content at home and believed that all their significant problems had foreign origins.

2. V. O. Key, Jr., *Southern Politics in State and Nation* (New York: Vintage, 1949), 5.

3. John H. Aldrich and Richard G. Niemi, "The Sixth American Party System: Electoral Change, 1952–1992," in *Broken Contract? Changing Relationships Between Americans and Their Government*, ed. Stephen C. Craig (Boulder, Colo.: Westview, 1996). Mann describes the current climate of party competition this way: "American politics, at least as it is practiced in Washington, is not a pretty sight these days. In contrast to the vibrancy of the U.S. economy and society, the political arena abounds in personal animosity, bitter partisanship, pettiness, negativity, and transparent disingenuousness" (Thomas Mann, "Governance in America 2000: An Overview," *Brookings Review* 18, no. 1 [winter 2000], 4, retrieved 28 January 2000 from the World Wide Web: *http://www.brookings.edu/press/REVIEW/winter2000/mann.htm*).

4. Kelly D. Patterson, *Political Parties and the Maintenance of Liberal Democracy* (New York: Columbia University Press, 1996), 22.

5. Benjamin Ginsberg and Martin Shefter, *Politics by Other Means*, 2d ed. (New York: W. W. Norton, 1999), 77.

6. David M. Shribman, "Era of Pretty Good Feelings: The Middle Way of Bill Clinton and America's Voters," In *The Parties Respond*, ed. L. Sandy Maisel (Boulder, Colo.: Westview, 1998), 343.

7. Robert Borasage, "Is Big Government Really Dead?" *Orlando Sentinel*, 11 May 1997, retrieved 1 April 1998 from the World Wide Web: *http://www.ourfuture.orb/library/ORL5-11.asp*. Borosage argues that the hallmarks of Clinton's presidency are deficit reduction, free trade, deregulation of industry, and reinvention (cutbacks) of government—all standard Republican themes.

8. Theda Skocpol, *Boomerang: Health Care Reform and the Turn Against Government* (New York: W. W. Norton, 1997). Rather than selling out the Democratic agenda, the retreat from liberalism during Clinton's first term could be seen as an abandonment of policies that in themselves represented a leftward shift from Clinton's 1992 campaign themes. Early moves by the Clinton administration contributed to the impression of a more orthodox liberal presidency than New

Democrat Clinton had hinted at during the campaign. Some voters doubtless felt betrayed because Clinton " 'ran right but governed left' " (Ginsberg and Shefter, *Politics by Other Means*, 60). See also, Jonathan Schell, "Uncertain Leviathan," *Atlantic*, August 1996, 4. For a divergent point of view, see E. J. Dionne, Jr., "Why Americans Hate Politics: A Reprise," *Brookings Review* 18, no. 1(winter 2000): 8–11, retrieved 28 January 2000 from the World Wide Web: *http://www.brook ings.edu/press/REVIEW/winter2000/dionne.htm*. Dionne argues that Clinton's rightward moves were merely politically astute feints that took the wind out of right-wing initiatives and established a progressive agenda for the nation in the year 2000.

9. L. Sandy Maisel, "Political Parties on the Eve of the Millennium," in *The Parties Respond*, ed. L. Sandy Maisel (Boulder, Colo.: Westview, 1998), 363.

10. Wilson Carey McWilliams, "The Meaning of the Election," in *The Election of 1996: Reports and Interpretations*, ed. Gerald M. Pomper et al. (Chatham, N.J.: Chatham House, 1997), 252; Bruce Schulman, "Clinton's Reaganite Legacy," *Los Angeles Times*, 13 September 1998; Robert L. Borosage, "Democrats Face the Future," *Nation*, 2 February 1999, 3.

11. Several Clinton policy makers responsible for welfare policy not only resigned but wrote blistering attacks on the reforms. Mary Jo Bane, a widely respected academic who served as assistant secretary for children and families in the Department of Health and Human Services, wrote that "my fears about what would happen to poor children when states were no longer required to provide the modest assurances and protections we insisted on in waiver demonstrations led me to resign after President Clinton signed the welfare bill" (Mary Jo Bane, "Welfare as We Might Know It," *American Prospect*, January–February 1997, 47–53, retrieved from the World Wide Web: *http://epn.org/prospect/30/30bane.html*). Peter Edelman called the plan "The Worst Thing Bill Clinton Has Done" in the title of his *Atlantic Monthly* (March 1997) article on the administration's caving in to Republican pressures.

12. Wedge issues in particular seem especially susceptible to pandering to the public's desire for simple solutions to complex problems. Thomas Byrne Edsall with Mary D. Edsall, *Chain Reaction: The Impact of Race, Rights, and Taxes on American Politics* (New York: W. W. Norton, 1992), criticize liberals for failing to develop effective discourse that would allow alternative approaches to these issues and protect liberals from the pressure either to ignore these legitimately troubling issues or merely to copycat conservative stances.

13. Murray Edelman, *The Symbolic Uses of Politics* (Urbana: University of Illinois Press, 1964).

14. Christopher Hitchens, "His Place in History: The Triangulations of William Jefferson Clinton," *In These Times*, 30 May 1999, 10.

15. Martin Wattenberg, *The Decline of American Political Parties*, 4th ed. (Cambridge, Mass.: Harvard University Press, 1996), 144.

16. *State of the South 1998* (Chapel Hill, N.C.: MDC, 1998), 30.

17. Key himself recognized that even within one-partyism, states with persistent and somewhat organized factions had more coherent politics than multifactional free-for-alls with their "veritable melee[s] of splinter factions." Key, *Southern Politics*, 301.

18. Michael S. Dukakis, "Acceptance Speech" (delivered at the Democratic National Convention, Atlanta, 21 July 1988), in *Vital Speeches of the Day* 54, no. 21 (August 15, 1988): 643; Bruce Miroff, "Monopolizing the Public Space: The President as a Problem for Democratic Politics," in *Debating Democracy*, ed. Bruce Miroff, Ray Seidleman, and Todd Swanstrom (Boston: Houghton Mifflin, 1997).

19. Anthony Lewis, *Make No Law: The Sullivan Case and the First Amendment* (New York: Vintage, 1991), argues that the heightened standard for constitutional protection of the media in libel suits by public officials and public figures has emboldened the press to undertake more investigative reporting and to criticize government officials. Interestingly, the 1964 case that established "actual malice" as the required test for libel in these cases came out of the South. In *New York Times v. Sullivan*, 376 U.S. 254 (1964), the police commissioner of Montgomery, Alabama, sued the nation's newspaper of record for certain allegedly libelous inaccuracies in an advertisement placed in the *Times* by civil rights supporters. Lewis asserts that the suit was part of a concerted strategy to silence the national media's coverage of the civil rights movement in the South, thereby cutting off the movement from public awareness and support.

These heightened protections were important bulwarks of press freedom that may have strengthened critics of government during the Vietnam War and Watergate eras. In protecting the media against segregationists' suits, Lewis implies, the Supreme Court erected such a high standard that after Watergate the media could report on the private lives of public officials and public figures with virtual impunity from legal damages. Even if a report was defamatory and inaccurate, public plaintiffs were required to prove that the media published it with "actual malice," that is, "with knowledge that it was false or with reckless disregard of whether it was false or not" (Lewis, *Make No Law*, 147). To the extent that the *New York Times* standards have shielded the press in its pursuit of private scandal, it is an ironic outcome to a legal decision that sought to protect the "uninhibited, robust, and wide open" debate on public issues that is the lifeblood of democracy (ibid., 143).

20. Center for Responsive Politics, "Who's Paying for This Election?" (on-line), retrieved 27 October 1998 from the World Wide Web: *http://www.crp.org/whospay ing/bigpic/intro.html*. Glenn F. Bunting, "Clinton's Political Money-Gathering Unprecedented," *Atlanta Journal/Constitution*, 28 December 1997, B2. Although the headline brands Clinton's fund-raising efforts in 1996 "unprecedented," the trends in campaign finance make it likely that such commitment by political leaders to fund-raising activities is part of a long-term and universal trend, not an aberration.

21. Michael Lind, "Southern Coup," *New Republic*, 19 June 1995, 29.

22. The line between politics and entertainment is being crossed from both directions. Defeated presidential candidate Bob Dole does ads for Visa and Viagra, while other politicians such as Geraldine Ferraro and Susan Molinari parlay their name recognition and experience into media positions.

23. Charles Pope, "New Congress Is Older, More Politically Seasoned," *Congressional Quarterly Weekly*, 9 January 1999, retrieved 22 June 2000 from the World Wide Web: *http://libraryip.cq.com*.

24. Ronald Brownstein, "The Successor Generation: American Politics as a Family Business," *American Prospect*, November–December 1998, 38. Brownstein

gives myriad examples of politicians who are the children of politicians, including many examples from the U.S. House and Senate, such as Jesse Jackson, Jr., Harold Ford, Jr., Chris Dodd, and Mary Landrieu. The list can be geometrically expanded if one adds political candidates and slightly more remote relations, such as uncles, cousins, and grandparents. Brownstein recognizes that family name is only one source of extraneous advantage enjoyed by some candidates that has nothing to do with qualification for the job. Although family advantage does violate the ideal of equal opportunity to seek political office, he judges it to be a less serious deviation from democratic norms than other external advantages, such as access to money.

25. Sinclair Lewis, *It Can't Happen Here* (Garden City, N.Y.: Sun Dial, 1935), the depression-era novel about the rise of domestic dictatorship in America.

26. Key, *Southern Politics*, 310; Peter Bachrach and Morton S. Baratz, *Power and Poverty* (New York: Oxford University Press, 1970), 43.

27. Martin Wattenberg, *Candidate-Centered Politics: Presidential Elections of the 1980s* (Cambridge, Mass.: Harvard University Press, 1991), 21.

28. Anthony King, "Running Scared," *Atlantic Monthly*, January 1997, 6, retrieved 4 June 1998 from the World Wide Web: *http://www.theatlantic.com/issues/97/jan/scared/scared.htm.*

29. Wattenberg, *Candidate-Centered Politics*, 20; Warren E. Miller, "Party Identification and the Electorate of the 1990s," in Maisel, *Parties Respond*, 123.

30. Jonathan Rauch, *Demosclerosis: The Silent Killer of American Government* (New York: Times Books, 1994).

31. Darrell M. West and Burdett A. Loomis, *The Sound of Money: How Political Interests Get What They Want* (New York: W. W. Norton, 1999), 106.

32. Sarah A. Binder, "Going Nowhere: A Gridlocked Congress," *Brookings Review* 18, no. 1 (winter 2000): 16–19, retrieved 28 January 2000 from the World Wide Web: *http://www.brookings.edu/press/REVIEW/winter2000/binder1.htm.* A major cause of increased gridlock is, of course, divided partisan control of the separated branches. Another may be the rising frequency of Senate filibustering. Thomas Mann and Norman Ornstein, "After the Campaign, What? Governance Questions for the 2000 Election," *Brookings Review* 18, no. 1 (winter 2000): 44–48, observe that "the filibuster in the Senate is now routine, setting the bar at 60, not 50 votes [the number needed to cut off debate] for most key issues." Binder, "Going Nowhere," suggests that "'tit-for-tat' filibustering" between Democrats and Republicans as the Senate majority has changed hands over recent decades has compounded the problem.

33. Walter Dean Burnham, "The 1996 Elections: Drift or Mandate?" *American Prospect*, July–August 1996, 43–49, retrieved 9 June 1998 from the World Wide Web: *http//epn.org/prospect/27/27burn.html;* Ginsberg and Shefter, *Politics by Other Means.*

W. Lance Bennett, *The Governing Crisis: Media, Money, and Marketing in American Elections* (New York: St. Martin's, 1992), 161, quotes a *Wall Street Journal* 1990 election-day editorial that captures the flavor of the inertia pervading our political processes by century's end: "the American people go to the polls today, or anyway some of them will. It seems apposite to reflect on the state of their democracy, and any reflection must start with two observations: First, the palpable sentiment of the electorate is discontent with the status quo. . . . Second, the most

likely outcome of today's ballot is that nothing will change." This observation would have seemed just as apt for the "merry-go-round" politics of the old Solid South. Although the elections of the middle and late 1990s were sometimes judged to reflect voter contentment, they were equally deadlocked and might just as well have registered voters' disenchantment with the idea of using government to improve their lives.

34. McWilliams, "Meaning of the Election," 247.

35. Borosage, "Is Big Government Dead?"

36. *New York Times, Downsizing of America* (New York: Times Books, 1996), 4, 5; Holly Sklar, *Chaos or Community? Seeking Solutions, Not Scapegoats for Bad Economics* (Boston: South End, 1995), 58. The decline in manufacturing jobs continued to the end of the decade. The nation lost half a million manufacturing jobs in the last eighteen months of the 1990s. Steven Greenhouse, *New York Times*, 17 October 1999.

37. Juliet B. Schor, *The Overworked American* (New York: Basic, 1991), 29; Robert Putnam, "Bowling Alone: America's Declining Social Capital," *Journal of Democracy* (January 1995): 65–78. Other authors put a different spin on the relationship between work and leisure. Arlie Hochschild, "The Time Bind," *WorkingUSA*, July–August 1997, 21–29, argues that the traditional role of the home as a haven from trials and tribulations has been usurped by work organizations. She maintains that Americans were actually receiving more emotional and social nurturing at work than in their families by the 1990s. In contrast, Jeremy Rifkin, *The End of Work?* (New York: G. P. Putnam's Sons, 1995), predicts the "end of work" as technology rapidly replaces human labor, mental as well as manual. Overwork, then, is just one more symptom of the misallocation of increasingly scarce productive work. To Rifkin, the real issue is how to allocate the fruits of work and how to use leisure more meaningfully.

38. Thomas Palley, "Goodbye Washington Consensus, Hello Main Street Alternative" (on-line), retrieved 5 February 1999 from the World Wide Web: *http://www.fmcenter.org/fmc_superpage.asp?ID+179*.

39. Kenneth M. Dolbeare and Linda J. Medcalf, *American Ideologies Today* (New York: Random House, 1988). Critics to the left of neoliberals point out that laissez-faire is largely an illusion. Even the Reagan administration did not really take a hands-off approach to the economy. When conservative supply-side economists believed that the public was not saving enough, they proposed and passed tax legislation to treat savings more favorably. Even the more liberal economists who favored capitalism pointed out the flaws of markets. Robert Kuttner, "The Limits of Markets," *American Prospect*, March–April 1997, 28–36.

40. Stephen D. Cummings, *The Dixification of America: The American Odyssey into the Conservative Economic Trap* (Westport, Conn.: Praeger, 1998), 12.

41. Lind, "Southern Coup," 28.

42. Cummings, *Dixification of America*, 29.

43. Joel Rogers, "The Folks Who Brought You the Weekend," *WorkingUSA*, November–December 1997, 11–20; Kenneth M. Dolbeare, *Democracy at Risk: The Politics of Economic Renewal* (Chatham, N.J.: Chatham House, 1986); Public Agenda Foundation, *Prescription for Prosperity: Four Paths to Economic Renewal* (Dayton, Ohio: National Issues Forums Institute, 1992).

44. Schell, "Uncertain Leviathan," 14.

45. Burke evaluates several alternative definitions of corruption. He demonstrates that different conceptions of politics favor alternative definitions, with pluralists leaning toward a narrower quid pro quo notion while deliberative democrats conceive of corruption as unjustified influence over political actions. Thomas Burke, "The Concept of Corruption in Campaign Finance Law," *Constitutional Commentary* 14 (spring 1997), retrieved 14 May 1998 from the World Wide Web: *http://web.lexis-nexis.com/universe.*

46. Unlike Livingston, who was forced from office because of an affair of his own, Gingrich resigned over political, not sexual, failings. Later, however, news of an affair with a congressional staffer emerged during the course of Gingrich's divorce from his second wife, damaging his credibility as a top conservative strategist.

47. Bruce Shapiro, "We, the Jury," *Nation*, 12 December 1998, retrieved 27 June 2000 from the World Wide Web: *http://www.thenation.com/issue/981130/ 1130SHAP.htm.* Shapiro reports that since 1971, at least thirty-nine members of Congress have been sent to prison.

48. Anthony Lewis, "The Prosecutorial State," *American Prospect*, January–February 1999, 31.

49. The contribution of "Monicagate" to these rapidly evolving media norms was the willingness of mainstream media to follow the lead of tabloids (John Judis, "Irresponsible Elites," *American Prospect*, May–June 1998, 16). James Fallows argues that in the rush to judgment in this fast-breaking scandal, the media's editorial function failed to distinguish private information consisting of rumor, factoid, gossip, and suspicions from public information. which has both greater weight and greater potential to damage as well as to inform (James Fallows, "Rush from Judgment," *American Prospect*, March–April 1999, 18–25).

50. Ginsberg and Shefter, *Politics by Other Means*, 47. In a compatible thesis, Mark Silverstein, *Judicious Choices: The New Politics of Supreme Court Confirmations* (New York: W. W. Norton, 1994), 76, maintains that the post-1968 breakup of the New Deal coalition forced Democrats to look to an active judiciary to advance liberal causes—in the process, significantly raising the stakes in judicial appointments. The result has been increasingly acrimonious confirmation hearings for judicial nominees, reaching its zenith in the tawdry scandal surrounding the alleged sexual harassment of Anita Hill by Bush Supreme Court nominee (now justice) Clarence Thomas. Ironically, given the heightened participation in the politics of judicial nominations, Silverstein believes that the net outcome has been to strengthen the hand of upper-status social segments in the courts, because most of the groups that mobilize to influence appointments have an upper-class tilt to them.

51. Dennis F. Thompson, "Mediated Corruption: The Case of the Keating Five," *American Political Science Review* 87, no. 2 (June 1993): 369, 376.

52. Burke , "Concept of Corruption," 10, notes that convictions for campaign contribution bribery have become far more common recently.

53. Morris Fiorini, *Congress: Keystone of the Washington Establishment* (New Haven, Conn.: Yale University Press, 1977). Theodore J. Lowi, *The End of Liberalism: Ideology, Policy, and the Crisis of Public Authority* (New York: W. W. Norton, 1969), argued that interest-group liberalism undermined the New Deal from

its very inception. Even conceding the validity of this point, there is a strong case to be made that as the political mobilization of Democratic constituencies and the policy coherence of the New Deal declined, the power of iron triangles and the potency of interest-group liberalism were enhanced. More recently, West and Loomis argue that iron triangles have weakened in their ability to exclude the public from policy-making arenas. Broader issue networks or policy communities participate in framing policies on many critical issues, but the policy process is still decidedly stacked in favor of self-interested private groups with resources to peddle their messages in public policy debates (West and Loomis, *Sound of Money*, 150, 10, 15).

54. Philip Pettit, *Republicanism: A Theory of Freedom and Government* (New York: Oxford University Press, 1997).

55. Key, *Southern Politics*, 303.

56. Tolchin notes that while the anger of the American public is general, there are also "competing angers" in the sense that different people are upset by different aspects of contemporary society and politics. This situation presents an opportunity as well as responsibility for leaders "to reconcile these opposing emotions in a constructive manner" (Susan J. Tolchin, *The Angry American*, 2d ed. [Boulder, Colo.: Westview, 1999], 125). Of course, leadership (as well as popular engagement) is in scarce supply in contemporary politics.

57. Robert L. Borosage, "Democrats Face the Future: Politics After Impeachment," *Nation*, 2 February 1999, retrieved 5 February 1999 from the World Wide Web: *http://www.thenation.com/issue/990208/0208borosage.html*.

58. McWilliams, "Meaning of the Election," 257.

59. Marjorie Randon Hershey, "The Congressional Elections," in Pomper, *Election of 1996*, 208.

60. Jonathan Cohn, "Perrier in the Newsroom," *American Prospect*, spring 1995, 15–18, retrieved from the World Wide Web: *http://epn.org/prospect/21/21cohn.html*.

61. Skocpol, *Boomerang*, 98.

62. W. Lance Bennett, *News: The Politics of Illusion*, 3d ed. (White Plains, N.Y.: Longman, 1996).

63. For example, in the early stages of the 2000 presidential race, 71 percent of Americans indicated that they were not aware of news about Bush's and Gore's relative standings in the polls. As Thomas Patterson, codirector of Harvard's Vanishing Voter Project, suggested, "as fascinating as the polls are to political junkies and pundits, they are not closely followed by the vast majority of Americans" (Vanishing Voter Weekly Update [8 June 2000], available by e-mail: *vanishingvoter@ksg.harvard.edu*).

For an excellent assessment of this mirror theory of the media as merely responding to the demands of consumers, see Calvin F. Exoo, *The Politics of the Mass Media* (Minneapolis–St. Paul: West, 1994). Exoo rejects this variation of a market theory, instead arguing that the media are able to dominate and shape mass perceptions and choices because of their hegemonic position in American society. For another critique of the market theory applied to media regulation and freedom of the press, see C. Edwin Baker, "Giving the Audience What It Wants," *Ohio State Law Journal* 58 (1997): 311, retrieved 14 May 1998 from the World Wide Web: *http://web.lexis-nexis.com/universe*.

64. Richard Fox, "Audience Participation," *New York Times*, 11 February 1999.

65. Joshua Gamson, "Incredible News," *American Prospect*, fall 1994, 28–35, retrieved from the World Wide Web: *http://epn.org/prospect/19/19gams.html.*

66. Tom DeLuca, *The Two Faces of Political Apathy* (Philadelphia: Temple University Press, 1995), 55.

67. Bruce Miroff, Raymond Seidelman, and Todd Swanstrom, *The Democratic Debate: An Introduction to American Politics*, 2d ed. (Boston: Houghton Mifflin, 1998), 121.

68. Harold Lasswell, *Politics: Who Gets What, When, and How* (Cleveland, Ohio: World, 1958). E. E. Schattsneider, *The Semi-Sovereign People* (New York: Holt, Rinehart and Winston, 1960), 2, argued that one of the primary determinants of who wins and loses in politics is the scope of the conflict, that is, who gets involved in the struggle. Many of the features of the old Solid South, and an increasing number of aspects of contemporary politics, have served to limit the number of participants in politics. There is a definite skew to excluding those lower on the socioeconomic scale. As American politics becomes more exclusive, those excluded are increasingly shortchanged in American social and economic as well as political life.

69. Income statistics are from Richard K. Scher, *Politics in the New South: Republicanism, Race, and Leadership in the Twentieth Century* (Armonk, N.Y.: M. E. Sharpe, 1992), 45; and "Education and Progress" (Atlanta: Southern Regional Education Board, 1998), retrieved 18 June 1998 from the World Wide Web: *http://www.sreb.org/temp/1998.html.*
More than citizens of other nations, Americans overwhelmingly identify themselves as middle class. In 1988, only 26 percent of Americans, as opposed to 73 percent of Britons, perceived society as divided between haves and have-nots. Only 17 percent of the Americans placed themselves among the have-nots, while 37 percent of the Britons so self-identified (Seymour Martin Lipset, *American Exceptionalism: A Double-Edged Sword* [New York: W. W. Norton, 1996], 98, 83). Despite the generally upbeat mood of Americans enjoying the robust economy of the late 1990s, the proportion of Americans considering themselves have-nots rose to 24 percent in 1998 (Scott Shepard, "Mood in U.S. Upbeat, Say Results of 2 Surveys," *Atlanta Journal/Constitution*, 21 October 1998, A3).

70. Michael Eisencher, "Leadership Development and Organization: For What Kind of Union?" *Labor Studies Journal* 24, no. 2 (summer 1999): 3–21.

71. Chuck Collins, Chris Hartman, and Holly Sklar, *Divided Decade: Economic Disparity at the Century's Turn* (Boston: United for a Fair Economy, 1999), 2, retrieved 13 March 2000 from the World Wide Web: *http://www.ufenet.org/press/divided_decade.html.*

72. Ibid.

73. Michael Hout, "Inequality by Design: Myths, Data, and Politics" (on-line), retrieved 27 June 2000 from the World Wide Web: *http://epn.org.*

74. Alice Ann Love, "Workers' Pay Rises; Bosses' Surges," *Atlanta Journal/Constitution*, 30 August 1999, A3.

75. Collins, Hartman, and Sklar, *Divided Decade*, 1, 2.

76. Hout, "Inequality by Design," 2.

77. Collins, Hartman, and Sklar, *Divided Decade*, 5; Jennifer Reingold, "Exec-

utive Pay," *Business Week*, 17 April 2000, 110; Holly Sklar, *Chaos or Community? Seeking Solutions, Not Scapegoats for Bad Economics* (Boston: South End, 1995), 4–6.

78. Robert Kuttner, "The New Economy: Where Is It Taking Us?" lecture at Providence Journal–Brown University Public Affairs Conference, Providence, R.I., 12 March 1997, retrieved from the World Wide Web: *http://epn.org.* Government statistics are often calculated to highlight the brighter side of the 1990s economic recovery at the expense of the darker underside of the Clinton economy. Schwartz describes the way official unemployment and poverty statistics understate the extent of those problems (John E. Schwartz, "The Hidden Side of the Clinton Economy," *Atlantic Monthly*, October 1998, retrieved 23 October 1998 from the World Wide Web: *http://www.theatlantic.com/issues/98oct/clintec.htm*). A study for the Levy Institute by Pigeon and Wray demonstrates that despite the heartening job creation during the Clinton expansion, many have been left out. For instance, of the 11.6 million new jobs created, only 700,000 went to those without any college, and high school dropouts actually lost ground. Of the noninstitutionalized, over-twenty-five population of high school dropouts, an astounding 57 percent have dropped out of the labor force (Marc-Andre Pigeon and L. Randall Wray, "Did the Clinton Rising Tide Raise All Boats?" Public Policy Brief no. 445, Jerome Levy Institute, retrieved 11 January 1999 from the World Wide Web: *http://levy.org/docs/sumsin98.html*).

79. Hout, "Inequality by Design," 1.

80. William C. Berman, *America's Right Turn: From Nixon to Clinton*, 2d ed. (Baltimore: Johns Hopkins University Press, 1998), 106.

81. Chuck Collins, Betsy Leondar-Wright, and Holly Sklar, *Shifitng Fortunes: The Perils of the Growing American Wealth Gap* (Boston: United for a Fair Economy, 1999), 7, retrieved from the World Wide Web: *http://www.stw.org/huml/shifin_fortunes/report.html.*

82. Robert B. Reich, "My Dinner with Bill," *American Prospect*, May–June 1998, 6. By 1999, Gates's wealth had nearly doubled to $85 billion, making him worth more than the combined gross national products of eleven Caribbean and South American countries (Collins, Hartman, and Sklar, *Divided Decade*, 4). In 2000, Congress's response to the growing gap in wealth was, amazingly enough, to repeal the inheritance tax, making it even easier to transfer huge concentrations of wealth across generations. For a discussion of the mischief to democratic politics threatened by great inequalities, see Sandel, *Democracy's Discontent*, 330–33. Sandel maintains that in addition to issues of fairness and justice (a political economy of growth and distribution), democracy requires a political economy of citizenship—one that enables us to be self-governing (ibid., 250).

83. Collins, Hartman, and Sklar, *Divided Decade*, 7.

84. Ibid., 9, 3; Peter Applebome, "Where Money's a Mantra Greed's a New Creed," *New York Times*, 28 February 1999, available by e-mail: *olson@moravian.edu.*

85. Presidential Commission on the Future of Worker-Management Relations, "Fact Finding Report" (Washington, D.C: Departments of Commerce and Labor, May 1994).

86. Jack Beatty, "The Road to a Third Party," *Atlantic Monthly*, August 1995,

retrieved 4 June 1998 from the World Wide Web: *http://www.theatlantic.com/elec tion/connection/policamp/goldenr.htm.*

87. Katherine S. Newman, *Declining Fortunes* (New York: Basic, 1993).

88. Lawrence Mishel, Jared Bernstein, and John Schmitt, "Dismantling the Myth of the 'New' American Economy," *WorkingUSA*, September–October 1998, 8–25.

89. Ibid., 18.

90. Charles B. Craver, *Can Unions Survive? The Rejuvenation of the American Labor Movement* (New York: New York University Press, 1993); William Greider, "Why the Global Economy Needs Worker Rights," *WorkingUSA*, May–June 1997, 32–44.

91. William Wolman and Anne Colamosca, "The Judas Economy," *Working-USA*, September–October, 1997, 51–61.

92. Wattenberg, *Decline of American Political Parties*, 144.

93. Clarence Stone, *Urban Regimes: Governing Atlanta, 1946–1988* (Lawrence: University Press of Kansas, 1989), 239.

94. Grant McConnell, *Private Power and American Democracy* (New York: Alfred A. Knopf, 1966), ch. 4; Demetrios James Caraley, "Dismantling the Federal Safety Net: Fictions Versus Realities," *Political Science Quarterly* 111, no. 2 (summer 1996), retrieved from the World Wide Web: *http://epn.org/psq/psdism.html.*

95. West and Loomis, *Sound of Money*, 126.

96. Gary Teeple, *Globalization and the Decline of Social Reform* (Atlantic Heights, N.J.: Humanities, 1995); but see Linda Weiss, *The Myth of the Powerless State* (Ithaca, N.Y.: Cornell University Press, 1998).

97. Benjamin Barber, *Jihad vs. McWorld: How Globalism and Tribalism Are Reshaping the World* (New York: Ballantine, 1996).

98. Bertram M. Gross, *Friendly Fascism: The New Face of Power in America* (New York: M. Evans, 1980).

99. Samuel P. Huntington, "The Democratic Distemper," *Public Interest* 41 (fall 1975): 11, 24, 36–37.

100. McWilliams, "Meaning of the Election," 255.

101. Ginsberg and Shefter, *Politics by Other Means*, 46.

102. We should take to heart the words of Michel Foucault, quoting J. M. Servan: "A stupid despot may constrain his slaves with iron chains; but a true politician binds them even more strongly by the chain of their own ideas; . . . this link is all the stronger in that we do not know of what it is made and we believe it to be our own work; . . . and on the soft fibres of the brain is founded the unshakable base of the soundest of Empires" (Michel Foucault, *Discipline and Punish: The Birth of the Prison* [New York: Vintage, 1977], 102–3).

8. Southern Horizons

1. Retrieved 8 June 2000 from the World Wide Web: *http://www.slip.net/ ~hsstern/maewest/y_berra.htm.*

2. There is some evidence that the climate is improving in the nation as a whole and in the South as well. In the late 1990s and early 2000s, many elections seem to turn more on practical quality-of-life issues such as education, transportation,

environmental protection, health care, and government services than the more ideological and divisive issues of the second half of the twentieth century. Johnny Isakson, the moderate Republican who replaced Newt Gingrich in the House, captured the new mood well: "My district is still a conservative place, but the social issues of the '90's are not the fundamental foundation of people's politics anymore. We've taken care of matters like a balanced budget and welfare reform, and now people are more concerned about quality of life issues, education and transportation" (David Firestone, "Population Shifts in the Southeast Realign Politics in the Suburbs," *New York Times*, 3 June 2000, A3, 8).

3. I am grateful to Professor Richard K. Scher of the University of Florida for pointing out the existence of countertrends that work against American politics evolving in ways analogous to the Old South's politics and for suggesting several specific countertrends worth considering.

4. For a discussion of the traditional Southern governorship, as well as its more recent transformations, see Richard K. Scher, *Politics in the New South: Republicanism, Race, and Leadership in the Twentieth Century*, 2d ed. (Armonk, N.Y.: M. E. Sharpe, 1997), ch. 9. Scher finds Southern governors traditionally weak on several counts, beginning with low expectations for performance in office and an essentially caretaker conception of their role, in contrast to modern presidents, who arrive in office with high expectations and an activist agenda. Compared to the president, Southern governors were also severely limited in their formal powers, including powers of appointment, budget, staffing, tenure, and succession. Most significantly, of course, Southern governors lacked political parties as an organizational resource for leadership.

5. Thomas Cronin, "The Textbook Presidency," in *The Confused Eagle: Division and Dilemma in American Politics*, ed. Lewis Lipsitz (Boston: Allyn and Bacon, 1973), 228–50. Cronin's picture of the textbook president paints the president as the supreme activist in American politics, the architect of public policy, a change agent who should act to strengthen both his office and the government's role, and a personal and moral leader. In summary, according to the textbook definition of the president, "if only the right type of man is placed in the White House all will be well" (ibid., 237). See also Arthur M. Schlesinger, Jr., *The Imperial Presidency* (New York: Popular Library, 1974).

6. Thedore J. Lowi, *The Personal President: Power Invested, Promise Unfulfilled* (Ithaca, N.Y.: Cornell University Press, 1985), 180. Lowi describes a plebiscitary presidency as one of great scale, celebrity, centricity, and isolation. Most of all, it is a personal presidency: "an office of tremendous personal power drawn from the people—directly and through Congress and the Supreme Court—and based on the new democratic theory that the presidency with all powers is the necessary condition for governing a large, democratic nation" (ibid., 20, 112).

7. Ibid., 96.

8. Quoted in Thomas E. Cronin, *The State of the Presidency* (Boston: Little, Brown, 1975), 153.

9. Quoted in Bruce Miroff, Raymond Seidelman, and Todd Swanstrom, *The Democratic Debate: An Introduction to American Politics*, 2d ed. (Boston: Houghton Mifflin, 1998), 316.

10. Stephen Skowronek, *The Politics Presidents Make: Leadership from John*

Adams to George Bush (Cambridge, Mass.: Harvard University Press, 1993). In the twentieth century, presidents achieved dramatic policy breakthroughs rarely, with the principal surges coming under Roosevelt in 1933–1935, Johnson in 1965, and Reagan in 1981 (Miroff, Seidelman, and Swanstrom, *Democratic Debate*, 324).

11. Thomas E. Cronin, "The Presidency and Its Paradoxes," in *The Presidency Reappraised*, 2d ed., ed. Thomas E. Cronin and Rexford G. Tugwell (New York: Praeger, 1977), 81; Paul Brace and Barbara Hinckley, "The Structure of Presidential Approval: Constraints Within and Across Presidencies," *Journal of Politics* 53, no. 4 (November 1991): 996, 1007.

12. Cronin, "Textbook Presidency," 237. The disillusionment resulting from the textbook image of the president helps explain the centrality of the "character issue" in recent presidential politics, as well as the extreme vituperation of William Jefferson Clinton by the theo-conservative right and his impeachment. If presidents are "the nation's personal and moral leaders," their personal lives, even their sexual conduct, become grounds for judging their presidential performance. In extreme cases, this textbook notion that "if only the right man is placed in the White House all will be well with the world," along with the ready availability of guns in this country, may help explain the tragic penchant for presidential assassinations and attempts. To an unstable mind perceiving all to be wrong with the world, is it far-fetched to think that the blame lies with the wrong type of man in the White House and that the solution is removal of the president by any means necessary?

13. Lowi, *Personal President*, 151, 116, 20.

14. Hess notes that states have always been the "stepchild of government coverage." Part of the reason is doubtless that "only 19 of the 50 states have their capitals in their major cities." Stephen Hess, "Federalism and News: Media to Government: Drop Dead," *Brookings Review* 18, no. 1 (winter 2000): 28–31, retrieved 1 January 2000 from the World Wide Web: *http://www.brookings.edu/press/review/winter2000/hess.htm*. Southern states suffer less from this syndrome, as seven of eleven state capitals in the region are located in major cities.

15. Bartholomew H. Sparrow, *Uncertain Guardians: The News Media as a Political Institution* (Baltimore: Johns Hopkins University Press, 1999), 26. See also the similar indexing hypothesis suggested in W. Lance Bennett and David Paletz, eds., *Taken by Storm: The Media, Public Opinion, and U.S. Foreign Policy in the Gulf War* (Chicago: University of Chicago Press, 1994), 25, 82, 186.

16. Sparrow, *Uncertain Guardians*, 133.

17. Ibid.

18. For an excellent discussion of ownership and hegemony, see Calvin F. Exoo, *The Politics of the Mass Media* (Minneapolis–St. Paul: West, 1994).

19. Sparrow, *Uncertain Guardians*, 103, quoting Harold Evans.

20. Hess, "Federalism and News," 2; Tom Teepen, "Apathy Sending Politics South," *Atlanta Journal/Constitution*, 31 January, 1999, B4.

21. Neil Postman, *Amusing Ourselves to Death: Public Discourse in the Age of Show Business* (New York: Penguin, 1985), 80, 29. Richard Reeves provides an insightful definition of "real news" as "the news you and I need to keep our freedom" (quoted in Hess, "Federalism and News"). Cohen is quoted in Sparrow, *Uncertain Guardians*, 7.

If television offers little hope for more vibrant democracy, newer media such as the Internet may. Proponents suggest the possibilities of easily accessible information, interactive dialogue, and even new communities uninhibited by space. Although some skepticism is warranted, at a minimum, the Internet seems to have some utility for organizing.

22. Richard K. Scher, *The Modern Political Campaign: Mudslinging, Bombast, and the Vitality of American Politics* (Armonk, N.Y.: M. E. Sharpe, 1997), 148–49.

23. Jon K. Dalager, "Voters, Issues, and Elections: Are the Candidates' Messages Getting Through?" *Journal of Politics* 58, no. 2. (May 1996): 493, 496.

24. Darrell M. West and Burdett A. Loomis, *The Sound of Money: How Political Interests Get What They Want* (New York: W. W. Norton, 1999), 16, 227–28.

25. Darryl Baskin, *American Pluralist Democracy: A Critique* (New York: Van Nostrand Reinhold, 1971), 176–77.

26. Southerners occupied the White House for fifty of the first sixty-one years of the Republic. Larry J. Griffin, "Why Was the South a Problem to America?" in *The South as an American Problem*, ed. Larry J. Griffin and Don H. Doyle (Athens: University of Georgia Press, 1995), 21.

27. For example, Robert Bellah et al., *Habits of the Heart* (New York: Harper and Row, 1985), call for another movement like the civil rights movement as a means of infusing new life into American democracy. Lichtenstein argues that there has been a "redemptive South" in addition to the better-known conservative and racist South. He suggests that the grassroots civil rights movement is the heir of these progressive Southerners, often religiously influenced, who developed a radical critique not only of modern industrial capitalism but also of racism (Alex Lichtenstein, "Right Church, Wrong Pew: Eugene Genovese and Southern Conservatism," *New Politics* 6, no. 3 [summer, 1997]).

28. C. Vann Woodward, *Tom Watson: Agrarian Rebel* (New York: Oxford University Press, 1938). One of the most prominent and beloved politicians in the state, Watson is memorialized by a statue that stands in front of the state capitol in Atlanta. One cannot help but wonder which Tom Watson, the youthful populist reformer or the elder racist demagogue, is being so honored. Watson is far from alone as an example of progressive Southern politicians. Even during the era of the Solid South, some radical, progressive, or liberal politicians were elected to public office. Representative figures include Hugo Black, Lister Hill, and James Folsom of Alabama; Claude Pepper of Florida; Olin Johnson of South Carolina; the Longs of Louisiana; Albert Gore, Estes Kefauver, and Frank Clement of Tennessee; Brooks Hays of Arkansas; Frank Graham of North Carolina; and Ralph Yarborough of Texas. Michael Goldfield, *The Color of Politics* (New York: New Press, 1997), 297–98.

29. Lawrence Goodwyn, *Democratic Promise: The Populist Moment in America* (New York: Oxford University Press, 1976).

30. Quoted in Alexander P. Lamis, "Southern Politics in the 1990s," in *Southern Politics in the 1990s*, ed. Alexander P. Lamis (Baton Rouge: Louisiana State University Press, 1999), 405–6. Key's words echo remnants of republicanism, a more participatory and deliberative theory of democracy than liberal pluralism, the version of democratic theory that has increasingly held sway in public consciousness in recent decades. See Michael Sandel, *Democracy's Discontent: America in Search of a Public Philosophy* (Cambridge, Mass.: Harvard University Press, 1996).

31. Robert Dreyfuss, "Reform Beyond the Beltway," *American Prospect,* May–June 1998, 51–52, quoting David Donnelly. If the Maine act survives court challenge, it is slated to take effect in the 2000 election cycle at a projected cost of $2.4 million, to be raised through registration fees on lobbyists, fines for violations of the act, candidate qualifying contributions, and citizen tax-return check-offs (ibid., 51–52, 55).

32. The Supreme Court upheld the constitutionality of antifusion laws in *Timmons v. Twin Cities Area New Party,* 520 U.S. 351 (1997). On the wasted-ballot syndrome, see Theodore J. Lowi, "A Ticket to Democracy," *New York Times,* 28 December 1996.

33. Much of the philosophical impetus for deliberative democracy has come from the work of continental theorist Jurgen Habermas and John Rawls in this country (James Bohman, *Public Deliberation* [Cambridge, Mass.: MIT Press, 1996]). Amy Gutmann and Dennis Thompson, *Disagreement and Democracy* (Cambridge, Mass.: Harvard University Press, 1996), have outlined conditions for deliberation. Cass Sunstein, *The Partial Constitution* (Cambridge, Mass.: Harvard University Press, 1993), v, 24; James S. Fishkin, *Democracy and Deliberation* (New Haven, Conn.: Yale University Press, 1991), 1, 2, 87.

34. W. Lance Bennett, *News: The Politics of Illusion,* 3d ed. (White Plains, N.Y.: Longman, 1996).

35. This statement is from Anthony Lewis, *Make No Law: The Sullivan Case and the First Amendment* (New York: Vintage, 1991), 246, who is quoting Liu Binyan, an exiled Chinese journalist. As Lewis notes, James Madison might just as easily have voiced this sentiment.

36. Steven J. Rosenstone and John Mark Hansen, *Mobilization, Participation, and Democracy in America* (New York: Macmillan, 1993), 219; Steven J. Rosenstone, Roy L. Behr, and Edward H. Lazarus, *Third Parties in America: Citizen Response to Major Party Failure,* 2d ed. (Princeton, N.J.: Princeton University Press, 1996).

37. A midterm issues convention was held in 1978 by the Democrats. This innovative practice, however, is an example of the kinds of reform abandoned as elites reasserted themselves in reaction to the popular insurgencies of the 1960s. Samuel P. Huntington, "The Democratic Distemper," *Public Interest* 41 (fall 1975): 36.

38. American Political Science Association, Committee on Political Parties, "Toward a More Responsible Two-Party System," *American Political Science Review* 44 (September 1950); David Broder, *The Party's Over* (New York: Harper and Row, 1972).

39. Lowi, *Personal President,* 195–208.

40. Robert Richie and Steven Hill, *Reflecting All of Us: The Case for Proportional Representation* (Boston: Beacon, 1999).

41. James Q. Wilson, *The Amateur Democrat* (Chicago: University of Chicago Press, 1966); James I. Lengle and Byron E. Shafer, eds., *Presidential Politics: Readings on Nominations and Elections,* 2d ed. (New York: St. Martins's, 1983).

42. These examples, of course, do not definitively establish the efficacy of issue-oriented politics. Many voters in 1994 had never heard of the Contract with America, and in some respects, the ideological Republican Congress of 1995 helped reelect President Clinton in 1996. Conversely, it may not have been the specifics of the contract but the perception that the Republican party "meant business" that

won it votes in 1994, and the Republicans' perceived personal and partisan bickering more than ideological conflict might have helped reelect Clinton. Besides, the Republicans retained the majority in Congress in 1996. Finally, one must consider the possibility that it was the content of the contract, not the fact of clearcut issue stances, that failed to appeal to the American electorate. In my view, the ideologically driven New Right Republicanism has encountered serious limits and even backlash not primarily because it has taken stands per se but because of the stands it has taken.

43. Kenneth M. Dolbeare and Linda J. Medcalf, *American Ideologies Today* (New York: Random House, 1988), provide an insightful analysis of the strengths and limitations of programmatic movements such as civil rights, women's, peace, environmental, and consumer groups. They argue that despite victories on discrete issues, these groups have failed to enunciate a common program that could be a springboard to winning political power. Such a common program would require an in-depth analysis of the workings of American society and political economy to reveal the basis of common problems and shared solutions. On the role of conservative think tanks, see Jean Stefancic and Richard Delgado, *No Mercy: How Conservative Think Tanks and Foundations Changed America's Social Agenda* (Philadelphia: Temple University Press, 1996).

44. L. A. Kauffman, "The Anti-Politics of Identity," *Socialist Review* 20, no. 1 (January–March 1990): 67–80; Carole A. Stabile, "Feminism Without Guarantees: The Misalliances and Missed Alliances of Postmodern Social Theory," *Rethinking Marxism* 7 (1994): 48–61.

45. Robert Huckfeldt and Carol Weitzel Kohfeld, *Race and the Decline of Class in American Politics* (Urbana: University of Illinois Press, 1989), 188.

46. Paul M. Sniderman and Edward Carmines, *Reaching Beyond Race* (Cambridge, Mass.: Harvard University Press, 1997), chs. 3, 4.

47. Ibid., 129, 122, 105, 108, 138.

48. Ibid., 111. Whether programs turn out to be color-blind or color-inclusive is more a matter of practice than of ideology or rhetoric. For discussion of how the controversial issue of affirmative action might be reshaped and defended, see *American Prospect*, September–October 1999. For a more general list of progressive policies, see Ira Katznelson, "Reversing Southern Republicanism," in *The New Majority: Toward a Popular Progressive Politics*, ed. Stanley Greenberg and Theda Skocpol (New Haven, Conn.: Yale University Press, 1997), 261. Goldfield, *Color of Politics*, 362.

49. Goldfield, *Color of Politics*, 283. In my own congressional district, Representative Cynthia McKinney has managed to construct an electoral coalition that adds women, labor, environmentalists, and gays and lesbians to her core African American constituency. She has succeeded in this difficult task not by soft-pedaling controversial issues but by boldly addressing domestic and foreign policy problems of concern to these groups.

50. Sniderman and Carmines, *Reaching Beyond Race*, 119; Sunstein, *Partial Constitution*, 20.

51. David Fott, *John Dewey: America's Philospher of Democracy* (Lanham, Md.: Rowman and Littlefield, 1998), 65.

52. This short sketch necessarily exaggerates how smooth the relationship

between the SAP and the unions has been. For instance, in the late 1970s, when the Landorganisationen pushed for the introduction of wage-earner funds that would have gradually converted the majority of Swedish corporate shares from private to social ownership, the SAP first balked at the controversial proposal, then responded with a watered-down version of this plan. Also, it should be noted that the SAP has in recent years diluted its strong worker orientation. This retrenchment may reflect conflicts among various unions, dissension among party leaders, or a more crucial shift in the balance of class forces in Sweden caused in large part by global economic transformations. Despite these changes, Swedish parties still present that country's voters with a wider range of clear programs and more progressive platforms than are enjoyed by the American electorate. Jonas Pontusson, *The Limits of Social Democracy: Investment Politics in Sweden* (Ithaca, N.Y.: Cornell University Press, 1992).

53. Katznelson, "Reversing Southern Republicanism," 252; Theda Skocpol, *The Missing Middle: Working Families and the Future of American Social Policy* (New York: W. W. Norton, 2000), 53.

54. The free-trade debates are the starkest examples of this subsidiary relationship. President Clinton consistently joined the Republican leadership to push a blank-check, globalist approach to free trade, against the labor movement's insistence that free trade must also be fair trade.

55. Bryant Simon, "Rethinking Why There Are so Few Unions in the South," *Georgia Historical Quarterly* 81, no. 2 (summer 1997): 465–84, argues that the distinctiveness of the South's antiunionism was always a difference more of degree than of kind.

56. Kim Moody, "American Labor: A Movement Again?" *Monthly Review* 49, no. 3 (July–August 1997): 63, retrieved 5 June 1998 from the World Wide Web: *http://cal listo.gsu.edu*; Michael Eisenscher, "Leadership Development and Organization: For What Kind of Union?" *Labor Studies Journal* 24, no. 2 (summer 1999): 3–21; Bennett Harrison, *Lean and Mean* (New York: Basic, 1994); Eileen Appelbaum and Rosemary Batt, *The New American Workplace* (Ithaca, N.Y.: ILR Press, 1994).

57. Immanuel Ness, "The Road to Union Cities," *WorkingUSA*, November–December 1998, 78–86.

58. Richard B. Freeman and Joel Rogers, *What Workers Want* (Ithaca, N.Y.: ILR Press, 1999); Paul C. Weiler, *Governing the Workplace* (Cambridge, Mass.: Harvard University Press, 1990). The classic case for the centrality of participation at work in democracy is Carole Pateman, *Participation and Democratic Theory* (Cambridge: Cambridge University Press, 1970).

59. There is a vast literature evolving on civil society, from both theoretical (e.g., Jean L. Cohen and Andrew Arato, *Civil Society and Political Theory* [Cambridge, Mass.: MIT Press, 1995]) and empirical (e.g., Theda Skocpol and Morris Fiorini, *Civic Engagement in American Democracy* [Washington, D.C.: Brookings, 1999]) perspectives. Robert Putnam attracted much of the early attention to civil society with his "Bowling Alone: America's Declining Social Capital," *Journal of Democracy* (January 1995). In "The Strange Disappearance of Civic America," *American Prospect*, winter 1996, 34–48, Putnam places much of the blame on television for the decay of civil society in this country. Miroff, Seidelman, and Swanstrom, *Democratic Debate*, ch. 5, discuss the effect of the decline of civil

society and "third places" on nonvoting. On worker ownership, see Jeff Gates, *The Ownership Solution* (Reading, Mass.: Addison Wesley, 1998). On neighborhood organizations, see Harry Boyte, *Community Is Possible* (New York: Harper and Row, 1984). Philip Green, *Retrieving Democracy: In Search of Civic Equality* (Totowa, N.J.: Rowman and Allanheld, 1985), offers one of the most thoroughgoing prescriptions for democratic revitalizations anywhere. For a survey of measures to democratize wealth, see Chuck Collins, Chris Harman, and Holly Sklar, *Divided Decade: Economic Disparity at the Century's Turn* (Boston: United for a Fair Economy, 1999), 10–13, retrieved 13 March 2000 from the World Wide Web: *http://www.ufenet.org/press/divided_decade.html.*

60. V. O. Key, Jr., *Southern Politics in State and Nation* (New York: Vintage, 1949); Benjamin Barber, *Jihad vs. McWorld: How Globalism and Tribalism Are Reshaping the World* (New York, Ballantine, 1996), 281–88.

Bibliography

Abramowitz, Alan I., and Kyle L. Saunders. "Party Polarization and Ideological Realignment in the U.S. Electorate, 1976–1994." In *The Parties Respond*, edited by L. Sandy Maisel. 3d ed. Boulder, Colo.: Westview, 1998.

Abramson, Paul R., John H. Aldrich, and David W. Rohde. *Change and Continuity in the 1996 Elections.* Washington, D.C.: Congressional Quarterly, 1998.

Abramson, Paul R., and Charles W. Ostrom, Jr. "Response." *American Political Science Review* 86, no. 2 (June 1992): 481–85.

Adatto, Kiku. "The Incredible Shrinking Sound Bite." In *Voices of Dissent: Critical Readings in American Politics*, edited by William F. Grover and Joseph G. Peschek. 2d ed. New York: HarperCollins, 1996.

Aistrup, Joseph A. *The Southern Strategy Revisited.* Lexington: University Press of Kentucky, 1996.

Aldrich, John H., and Richard G. Niemi. "The Sixth American Party System: Electoral Change, 1952–1992." In *Broken Contract? Changing Relationships Between Americans and Their Government*, edited by Stephen C. Craig. Boulder, Colo.: Westview, 1996.

Alt, James E. "The Impact of the Voting Rights Act on Black and White Voter Registration in the South." In *The Quiet Revolution in the South*, edited by Chandler Davidson and Bernard Grofman. Princeton, N.J.: Princeton University Press, 1994.

American Political Science Association, Committee on Political Parties. "Toward a More Responsible Two-Party System." *American Political Science Review* 44 (September 1950): Supplement, 1–14.

Anderson, William. *The Wild Man from Sugar Creek: The Political Career of Eugene Talmadge.* Baton Rouge: Louisiana State University Press, 1975.

Ansolabehere, Stephen, and Shanto Iyengar. *Going Negative: How Attack Ads Shrink and Polarize the Electorate.* New York: Free Press, 1995.

Appelbaum, Eileen, and Rosemary Batt. *The New American Workplace.* Ithaca, N.Y.: ILR Press, 1994.

Applebome, Peter. *Dixie Rising: How the South Is Shaping American Values, Politics and Culture.* New York: Random House, 1996.

Arsenault, Raymond. "The End of the Long Hot Summer: Air Conditioning

and Southern Culture." *Journal of Southern History* 50 (November 1984): 597–628.

Atleson, James. "Law and Union Power." *Buffalo Law Review* 42 (1994): 463.

Bachrach, Peter, and Morton S. Baratz. *Power and Poverty.* New York: Oxford University Press, 1970.

Bakanic, Von. "I'm Not Prejudiced, but . . . : A Deeper Look at Racial Attitudes." *Sociological Inquiry* 65, no. 1 (February 1995): 67–86.

Baker, C. Edwin. "Giving the Audience What They Want." *Ohio State Law Journal* 58 (1997): 311.

Baldwin, Sidney. *Poverty and Politics: The Rise and Decline of the Farm Security Administration.* Chapel Hill: University of North Carolina Press, 1968.

Bane, Mary Jo. "Welfare as We Might Know It." *American Prospect,* January–February 1997, 47–53.

Barber, Benjamin. *Jihad vs. McWorld: How Globalism and Tribalism Are Reshaping the World.* New York: Ballantine, 1996.

Barone, Michael. "Advantage GOP." Retrieved 1 January 1998 from the World Wide Web: *http://intellectualcapital.com.*

Bartels, Larry M. "Partisanship and Voting Behavior, 1952–1996." *American Journal of Political Science* 44 (January 2000): 35–50.

Baskin, Darryl. *American Pluralist Democracy: A Critique.* New York: Van Nostrand Reinhold, 1971.

Bass, Harold F., Jr. "Background to Debate: A Reader's Guide and Bibliography." In *The End of Realignment? Interpreting American Electoral Eras,* edited by Byron E. Shafer. Madison: University of Wisconsin Press, 1991.

Bass, Jack, and Walter DeVries. *The Transformation of Southern Politics.* New York: New American Library, 1977.

Beatty, Jack. "The Road to a Third Party." *Atlantic Monthly,* August 1995.

Bellah, Robert, et al. *Habits of the Heart.* New York: Harper and Row, 1985.

Bennett, W. Lance. *The Governing Crisis: Media, Money, and Marketing in American Elections.* New York: St. Martin's, 1992.

———. *News: The Politics of Illusion.* 3d ed. White Plains, N.Y.: Longman, 1996.

Bennett, W. Lance, and David Paletz, eds. *Taken by Storm: The Media, Public Opinion, and U.S. Foreign Policy in the Gulf War.* Chicago: University of Chicago Press, 1994.

Berman, William C. *America's Right Turn: From Nixon to Clinton.* 2d ed. Baltimore: Johns Hopkins University Press, 1998.

Bernd, Joseph L. *Grassroots Politics in Georgia.* Atlanta: Emory Research Committee, 1960.

———. "Georgia: Static and Dynamic." In *The Changing Politics of the South,* edited by William C. Havard. Baton Rouge: Louisiana State University Press, 1972.

Bernstein, Jared. "Two Cheers for the Earned Income Tax Credit." *American Prospect,* 19 June–3 July 2000, 64–67.

"Best Places 1997." *Money,* July 1997.

Binder, Sarah. "Going Nowhere: A Gridlocked Congress." *Brookings Review* 18, no. 1 (winter 2000): 16–19.

Binford, Michael. "Georgia: Political Realignment or Partisan Evolution." In *The South's New Politics: Realignment and Dealignment,* edited by Robert Swansbrough and David Brodsky. Columbia: University of South Carolina Press, 1988.

Binford, Michael, Tom Baxter, and David E. Sturrock. "Georgia: Democratic Bastion No Longer." In *Southern Politics in the 1990s,* edited by Alexander P. Lamis. Baton Rouge: Louisiana State University Press, 1999.

Black, Earl, and Merle Black. *Politics and Society in the South.* Cambridge, Mass.: Harvard University Press, 1987.

———. *The Vital South: How Presidents are Elected.* Cambridge, Mass.: Harvard University Press, 1992.

Black, Merle. "Roundtable on the 1996 Election." Presented at the annual meeting of the Southern Political Science Association, Atlanta, 7 November 1996.

Bloom, Jack. *Class, Race, and the Civil Rights Movement.* Bloomington: Indiana University Press, 1987.

Bluestone, Barry, and Bennett Harrison. *The Great U-Turn: Corporate Restructuring and the Polarizing of America.* New York: Basic, 1988.

Bluestone, Barry, and Stephen Rose. "Overworked and Underemployed." *American Prospect,* March–April 1997, 58–69.

Blumenthal, Sidney. *The Permanent Campaign.* New York: Simon and Schuster, 1983.

Boggs, Carl. *The End of Politics: Corporate Power and the Decline of the Public Sphere.* New York: Guilford, 2000.

Bohman, James. *Public Deliberation.* Cambridge, Mass.: MIT Press, 1996.

Borosage, Robert L. "Election 98: The End of the Gingrich Revolution." Campaign for America's Future, 1998. Retrieved 12 November 1998 from the World Wide Web: *http://ourfuture.org/tpoint/98boro.asp.*

———. "Democrats Face the Future." *Nation,* 2 February 1999.

Boyte, Harry C. *Community Is Possible.* New York: Harper and Row, 1984.

Brace, Paul, and Barbara Hinckley. "The Structure of Presidential Approval: Constraints Within and Across Presidencies." *Journal of Politics* 53, no. 4 (November 1991): 993–1017.

Broach, Glen T., and Lee Bandy. "South Carolina: A Decade of Rapid Republican Ascent." In *Southern Politics in the 1990s,* edited by Alexander P. Lamis. Baton Rouge: Louisiana State University Press, 1999.

Broder, David. *The Party's Over.* New York: Harper and Row, 1972.

Brownstein, Ronald. "The Successor Generation: American Politics as a Family Business." *American Prospect,* November–December 1998, 38–44.

Brundage, Fitzhugh. *Under Sentence of Death: Lynching in the South.* Chapel Hill: University of North Carolina Press, 1997.

Bullock, Charles S. III. "Georgia: Election Rules and Partisan Conflict." In *The New Politics of the Old South,* edited by Charles S. Bullock III and Mark J. Rozell. Lanham, Md.: Rowman and Litttlefield, 1998.

Bullock, Charles S. III, and Mark J. Rozell. "Southern Politics at Century's End." In *The New Politics of the Old South*, edited by Charles S. Bullock III and Mark J. Rozell. Lanham, Md.: Rowman and Littlefield, 1998.

Burke, Thomas F. "The Concept of Corruption in Campaign Finance Law." *Constitutional Commentary* 14 (spring 1997): 127.

Burnham, Walter Dean. *Critical Elections and the Mainsprings of American Politics.* New York: W. W. Norton, 1970.

———. *The Current Crisis in American Politics.* New York: Oxford University Press, 1982.

———. "V. O. Key, Jr., and the Study of Political Parties." In *V. O. Key, Jr., and the Study of American Politics*, edited by Milton C. Cummings, Jr. Washington, D.C.: American Political Science Association, 1988.

———. "Critical Realignment: Dead or Alive?" In *The End of Realignment? Interpreting American Electoral Eras*, edited by Byron E. Shafer. Madison: University of Wisconsin Press, 1991.

———. "The Class Gap." In *Voices of Dissent: Readings in American Politics*, 2d ed., edited by William F. Grover and Joseph G. Peschek. New York: HarperCollins, 1996.

———. "The 1996 Elections: Drift or Mandate?" *American Prospect*, July–August 1996, 43–49.

———. "Bill Clinton: Riding the Tiger." In *The Election of 1996: Reports and Interpretations*, edited by Gerald M. Pomper et al. Chatham, N.J.: Chatham House, 1997.

———. "The End of American Party Politics." *Society* 35, no. 2 (January–February 1998): 68–76.

Burns, James McGregor. *Roosevelt: The Lion and the Fox.* Orlando, Fla.: Harcourt, Brace, 1956.

Button, James W. *Blacks and Social Change: The Impact of the Civil Rights Movement in Southern Communities.* Princeton, N.J.: Princeton University Press, 1989.

Caldwell, Christopher. "The Southern Captivity of the GOP." *Atlantic Monthly*, June 1998, 55–72.

Calvert, Clay. "When First Amendment Principles Collide: Negative Political Advertising and the Democratization of Democratic Self-Governance." *Loyola of Los Angeles Law Review* 30 (June 1997): 1539.

Campbell, Angus, Philip E. Converse, Warren E. Miller, and Donald E. Stokes. *The American Voter.* New York: John Wiley and Sons, 1964.

———. *Elections and the Political Order.* New York: John Wiley and Sons, 1966.

Cappella, Joseph N., and Kathleen Hall Jamieson. "News Frames, Political Cynicism, and Media Cynicism." *Annals of American Academy of Political and Social Science* 546 (July 1996): 71–84.

Caraley, Demetrios James. "Dismantling the Federal Safety Net: Fictions Versus Realities." *Political Science Quarterly* 111, no. 2 (summer 1996): 225–58.

Carmines, Edward G., and James A. Stimson. *Issue Evolution: Race and the Transformation of American Politics.* Princeton, N.J.: Princeton University Press, 1989.

Carnoy, Martin, and Derek Shearer. *Economic Democracy.* Armonk, N.Y.: M. E. Sharpe, 1980.

Carter, Dan T. *The Politics of Rage: George Wallace, the Origins of the New Conservatism, and the Transformation of American Politics.* New York: Simon and Schuster, 1995.

Cash, W. J. *The Mind of the South.* New York: Random House, 1941.

Cecelski, David S., and Timothy B. Tyson. *Democracy Betrayed: The Wilmington Race Riot of 1898 and Its Legacy.* Chapel Hill: University of North Carolina Press, 1998.

Center for Responsive Politics. "Who's Paying for This Election?" Retrieved 27 October 1998 from the World Wide Web: *http://www.crp.org/whospay ing/bigpic/intro.htm.*

Christensen, Rob, and Jack D. Fleer. "North Carolina; Between Helms and Hunt No Majority Emerges." In *Southern Politics in the 1990s,* edited by Alexander P. Lamis. Baton Rouge: Louisiana State University Press, 1999.

Cohen, Jean L., and Andrew Arato. *Civil Society and Political Theory.* Cambridge, Mass.: MIT Press, 1995.

Cohn, Jonathan. "Perrier in the Newsroom." *American Prospect,* spring 1995, 15–18.

Collins, Chuck, Chris Hartman, and Holly Sklar. *Divided Decade: Economic Disparity at the Century's Turn.* Boston: United for a Fair Economy, 1999. Retrieved 13 March 2000 from the World Wide Web: *http://ufenet.org/press/divided_decade.html.*

Collins, Chuck, Betsy Leondar-Wright, and Holly Sklar. *Shifting Fortunes: The Perils of the Growing American Wealth Gap.* Boston: United for a Fair Economy, 1999. Retrieved 13 March 2000 from the World Wide Web: *http://www.stw.org/html/shifitn_fortunes_report.html.*

Collins, Ronald K. L., and David M. Skover. *The Death of Discourse.* Boulder, Colo.: Westview, 1996.

Congress and the Nation. Vol. 9. *1993–1996.* Washington, D.C.: Congressional Quarterly Press, 1998.

Cosman, Bernard. *Five States for Goldwater.* University: University of Alabama Press, 1996.

Craver, Charles B. *Can Unions Survive? The Rejuvenation of the American Labor Movement.* New York: New York University Press, 1993.

Crawford, Alan. *Thunder on the Right: The "New Right" and the Politics of Resentment.* New York: Pantheon Books, 1981.

Cronin, Thomas. "The Textbook Presidency." In *The Confused Eagle: Division and Dilemma in American Politics,* edited by Lewis Lipsitz. Boston: Allyn and Bacon, 1973.

———. *The State of the Presidency.* Boston: Little, Brown, 1975.

———. "The Presidency and Its Paradoxes." In *The Presidency Reappraised,*

edited by Thomas E. Cronin and Rexford G. Tugwell. 2d ed. New York: Praeger, 1977.

Cummings, Stephen D. *The Dixification of America: The American Odyssey into the Conservative Economic Trap.* Westport, Conn.: Praeger, 1998.

Dalager, Jon K. "Voters, Issues, and Elections: Are the Candidates' Messages Getting Through?" *Journal of Politics* 58, no. 2 (May 1996): 486–515.

Davidson, Chandler. *Race and Class in Texas Politics.* Princeton, N.J.: Princeton University Press, 1990.

———. "The Recent Evolution of Voting Rights Law Affecting Racial and Language Minorities." In *The Quiet Revolution in the South,* edited by Chandler Davidson and Bernard Grofman. Princeton, N.J.: Princeton University Press, 1994.

DeLuca, Tom. *The Two Faces of Political Apathy.* Philadelphia: Temple University Press, 1995.

DeVries, Walter, and Lance Tarrance, Jr. *The Ticket Splitter.* Grand Rapids, Mich.: William B. Eerdmans, 1972.

Dionne, E. J., Jr. *Why Americans Hate Politics.* New York: Simon and Schuster, 1992.

———. "Why Americans Hate Politics: A Reprise." *Brookings Review* 18, no. 1 (winter 2000): 8–11.

Dolbeare, Kenneth. *Democracy at Risk: The Politics of Economic Renewal.* Chatham, N.J.: Chatham House, 1986.

Dolbeare, Kenneth M., and Linda J. Medcalf. *American Ideologies Today.* New York: Random House, 1988.

Dreyfus, Robert. "Reform Beyond the Beltway." *American Prospect,* May–June 1998, 50–55.

———. "The Turnout Imperative." *American Prospect,* July–August 1998. Retrieved 31 August 2000 from the World Wide Web: *www.prospect.org/ archives/39/39dreyfs.html.*

Duncan, Philip D., and Christine C. Lawrence. *Politics in America 1996.* Washington, D.C.: Congressional Quarterly, 1995.

Edelman, Murray. *The Symbolic Uses of Politics.* Urbana: University of Illinois Press, 1964.

Edelman, Peter. "The Worst Thing Bill Clinton Has Done." *Atlantic Monthly,* March 1997, 43–58.

Edgerton, John. *The Americanization of Dixie: The Southernization of America.* New York: Harper's Magazine Press, 1974.

Edsall, Preston W., and J. Oliver Williams. "North Carolina: Bipartisan Paradox." In *The Changing Politics of the South,* edited by William C. Havard. Baton Rouge: Louisiana State University Press, 1972.

Edsall, Thomas Byrne. *The New Politics of Inequality.* New York: W. W. Norton, 1984.

———. "The Cultural Revolution of 1994." In *Present Discontents: American Politics in the Very Late Twentieth Century,* edited by Byron E. Shafer. Chatham, N.J.: Chatham House, 1997.

Edsall, Thomas Byrne, with Mary D. Edsall. *Chain Reaction: The Impact of Race, Rights, and Taxes on American Politics*. New York: W. W. Norton, 1992.

"Education and Progress in the South." Atlanta: Southern Regional Education Board, 1998. Retrieved 18 June 1998 from the World wide Web: *http://www.sreb.org/temp/1998.html*.

Eisencher, Michael. "Leadership Development and Organization: For What Kind of Union?" *Labor Studies Journal* 24, no. 2 (summer 1999): 3–21.

Elazar, Daniel. *American Federalism*. New York: Thomas Y. Crowell, 1966.

Entman, Robert M. Review of *Out of Order*, by Thomas E. Patterson. *Journal of American History* 8 (1995): 1826–27. Retrieved 14 May 1998 from the World Wide Web: *http://ganymede.galileo.gsu.edu*.

Esping-Andersen, Gosta. *Politics Against Markets: The Social Democratic Road to Power*. Princeton, N.J.: Princeton University Press, 1985.

Exoo, Calvin F. *The Politics of the Mass Media*. Minneapolis–St. Paul: West, 1994.

Fallows, James. "Rush from Judgment." *American Prospect*, March–April 1999, 18–25.

Faulkner, William. *Requiem for a Nun*. New York: Random House, 1951.

Ferguson, Thomas. *Golden Rule: The Investment Theory of Party Competition and the Logic of Money-Driven Political Systems*. Chicago: University of Chicago Press, 1995.

Ferguson, Thomas, and Joel Rogers. "Neoliberals and Democrats." *Nation*, 26 June 1982, 781–86.

Fineman, Howard. "Virtuecrats." *Newsweek*, 13 June 1994, 31–34.

Fiorini, Morris. *Congress: Keystone of the Washington Establishment*. New Haven, Conn.: Yale University Press, 1977.

Fishkin, James S. *Democracy and Deliberation*. New Haven, Conn.: Yale University Press, 1991.

Fleer, Jack D., Roger C. Lowery, and Charles L. Prysby. "Political Change in North Carolina." In *The South's New Politics: Realignment and Dealignment*, edited by Robert Swansbrough and David Brodsky. Columbia: University of South Carolina Press, 1988.

Fott, David. *John Dewey: America's Philosopher of Democracy*. Lanham, Md.: Rowman and Littlefield, 1998.

Foucault, Michel. *Discipline and Punish: The Birth of the Prison*. New York: Vintage, 1977.

Free, Lloyd A., and Hadley Cantril. *The Political Beliefs of Americans*. New York: Simon and Schuster, 1968.

Freeman, Richard B., and Joel Rogers. *What Workers Want*. Ithaca, N.Y.: ILR Press, 1999.

Freidel, Frank. *F.D.R. and the South*. Baton Rouge: Louisiana State University Press, 1965.

Frymer, Paul. *Uneasy Alliances: Race and Party Competition in America*. Princeton, N.J.: Princeton University Press, 1999.

Galphin, Bruce. *The Riddle of Lester Maddox.* Atlanta: Camelot, 1968.

Gamson, Joshua. "Incredible News." *American Prospect,* fall 1994, 28–35.

Gans, Herbert. *The War Against the Poor: The Underclass and Anti-Poverty Policy.* New York: Basic, 1996.

Gates, Jeff. *The Ownership Solution.* Reading, Mass.: Addison Wesley, 1998.

Gaventa, John. *Power and Powerlessness: Quiescence and Rebellion in an Appalachian Valley.* Urbana: University of Illinois Press, 1982.

Gilens, Martin. "'Race Coding' and White Opposition to Welfare." *American Political Science Review* 90, no. 3 (September 1996): 593–604.

Ginsberg, Benjamin, and Martin Shefter. *Politics by Other Means.* 2d ed. New York: W. W. Norton, 1999.

Glaser, James M. *Race, Campaign Politics, and the Realignment in the South.* New Haven, Conn.: Yale University Press, 1996.

Glasser, Theodore. "Objective Reporting Is Irresponsible." In *The Mass Media: Opposing Viewpoints,* edited by Neal Bernards. St. Paul, Minn.: Greenhaven, 1988.

Goldfield, Michael. *The Decline of Organized Labor in the United States.* Chicago: University of Chicago Press, 1987.

———. *The Color of Politics.* New York: New Press, 1997.

Goodwyn, Lawrence. *Democratic Promise: The Populist Moment in America.* New York: Oxford University Press, 1976.

Gordon, David M., Richard Edwards, and Michael Reich. *Segmented Work, Divided Workers.* New York: Cambridge University Press, 1982.

Green, Donald, Bradley Palmquist, and Eric Schickler. "The Coming Democratic Realignment." *PS: Political Science and Politics* 33, no. 2 (June 2000): 199–200.

Green, Philip. *Retrieving Democracy: In Search of Civic Equality.* Totowa, N.J.: Rowman and Allanheld, 1985.

Greider, William. *Who Will Tell the People: The Betrayal of American Democracy.* New York: Simon and Schuster, 1992.

———. "Why the Global Economy Needs Worker Rights." *WorkingUSA,* May–June 1997, 32–44.

Griffin, Larry J., "Why Was the South a Problem to America?" In *The South as an American Problem,* edited by Larry J. Griffin and Don H. Doyle. Athens: University of Georgia Press, 1995.

———. "Southern Distinctiveness, Yet Again: Or, Why America Still Needs the South." *Southern Cultures* (forthcoming).

Gross, Bertram M. *Friendly Fascism: The New Face of Power in America.* New York: M. Evans, 1980.

Gutmann, Amy, and Dennis Thompson. *Disagreement and Democracy.* Cambridge, Mass.: Harvard University Press, 1996.

Hale, Jon F. "The Making of the New Democrats." *Political Science Quarterly* 110 (summer 1995): 207–32.

Handley, Lisa, and Bernard Grofman. "The Impact of the Voting Rights Act on Minority Representation: Black Officeholding in Southern State Legis-

latures and Congressional Delegations." In *The Quiet Revolution in the South*, edited by Chandler Davidson and Bernard Grofman. Princeton, N.J.: Princeton University Press, 1994.

Harrison, Bennett. *Lean and Mean*. New York: Basic, 1994.

Hershey, Marjorie Randon. "The Congressional Elections." In *The Election of 1996: Reports and Interpretations*, edited by Gerald M. Pomper et al. Chatham, N.J.: Chatham House, 1997.

Hess, Stephen. "Federalism and News: Media to Government: Drop Dead." *Brookings Review* 18, no. 1 (winter 2000): 28–31.

Hochschild, Arlie. "The Time Bind." *WorkingUSA*, July–August 1997, 21–29.

Hodgson, Godfrey. *America in Our Time*. New York: Vintage, 1976.

Hoffman, Donna R. "A Theory for All Elections? Realignment Theory and a Changing Electorate." Paper presented at the annual meeting of the American Political Science Association, Atlanta, 2–5 September 1999.

Hout, Michael. "Inequality by Design: Myths, Data, and Politics." Retrieved 27 June 2000 from the World Wide Web: *http://www.russellsage.org/ programs/visiting_scholars/vs9697_2.htm#hout.*

Huckfeldt, Robert, and Carol Weitzel Kohfeld. *Race and the Decline of Class in American Politics*. Urbana: University of Illinois Press, 1989.

Huntington, Samuel P. "The Democratic Distemper." *Public Interest* 41 (fall 1975): 9–38.

Irons, Peter. *Courage of Their Convictions: Sixteen Americans Who Fought Their Way to the Supreme Court*. New York: Penguin, 1990.

Jamieson, Kathleen Hall. *Dirty Politics: Deception, Distraction, and Democracy*. New York: Oxford University Press, 1992.

Judis, John. "Irresponsible Elites." *American Prospect*, May–June 1998, 14–17.

Katz, Michael B. *The Undeserving Poor*. New York: Pantheon, 1989.

Katznelson, Ira. "Was the Great Society a Lost Opportunity?" In *The Rise and Fall of the New Deal Order, 1930–1980*, edited by Simon Fraser and Gary Gerstle. Princeton, N.J.: Princeton University Press, 1989.

———. "Reversing Southern Republicanism." In *The New Majority: Toward a Popular Progressive Politics*, edited by Stanley Greenberg and Theda Skocpol. New Haven, Conn.: Yale University Press, 1997.

———. "The Southern Origins of Our Time." Paper presented at the Center for the History of Business, Technology, and Society, Hagley Museum and Library, Wilmington, Del., 10 December 1998.

Kaufman, L. A.. "The Anti-Politics of Identity." *Socialist Review* 20, no. 1 (January–March 1990): 67–80.

Kayden, Xandra. "Alive and Well and Living in Washington: The American Political Parties." In *Manipulating Public Opinion*, edited by Michael Margolis and Gary A. Mauser. Pacific Grove, Calif.: Brooks/Cole, 1989.

Kazee, Thomas A. "North Carolina: Conservatism, Traditionalism, and the GOP." In *The New Politics of the Old South*, edited by Charles S. Bullock III and Mark J. Rozell. Lanham, Md.: Rowman and Littlefield, 1998.

Kazin, Michael. *The Populist Persuasion*. New York: Basic, 1995.

Keech, William R. *The Impact of Negro Voting: The Role of the Vote in the Quest for Equality.* Chicago: Rand McNally, 1968.

Keech, William R., and Michael P. Sistrom. "North Carolina." In *The Quiet Revolution in the South,* edited by Chandler Davidson and Bernard Grofman. Princeton, N.J.: Princeton University Press, 1994.

Keefe, William J. *Parties, Politics, and Public Policy in America.* 8th ed. Washington, D.C.: Congressional Quarterly, 1998.

Keeter, Scott. "Public Opinion and the Election." In *The Election of 1996: Reports and Interpretations,* edited by Gerald M. Pomper et al. Chatham, N.J.: Chatham House, 1997.

Kennedy, Randall. "Is He a Soul Man? On Black Support for Clinton." *American Prospect,* March–April 1999, 26–30.

Key, V. O., Jr. *Southern Politics in State and Nation.* New York: Vintage, 1949.

———. "A Theory of Critical Elections." *Journal of Politics* 17, no. 1 (February 1955): 3–18.

———. "Secular Realignment and the Party System." *Journal of Politics* 21, no. 2 (May 1959): 198–210.

Kimball, Penn. *Downsizing the News.* Baltimore: Johns Hopkins University Press, 1994.

King, Anthony. "Running Scared." *Atlantic Monthly,* January 1997.

Kousser, J. Morgan. *The Shaping of Southern Politics: Suffrage Restriction and the Establishment of the One-Party South, 1880–1910.* New Haven, Conn.: Yale University Press, 1974.

Kuklinski, James H., Michael D. Cobb, and Martin Gilens. "Racial Attitudes and the 'New South.'" *Journal of Politics* 59, no. 2 (May 1997): 323–49.

Kuttner, Robert. "The Limits of Markets." *American Prospect,* March–April 1997, 28–36.

———. "The New Economy: Where Is It Taking Us?" Lecture at *Providence Journal*/Brown University Public Affairs Conference, Providence, R.I., 12–20 March 1997. Retrieved from the World Wide Web: *http://epn.org.*

Kuzenski, John C., and Michael K. Corbello. "Racial and Economic Explanations for Republican Growth in the South: A Case Study of Attitudinal Voting in Louisiana." *American Review of Politics* 17 (summer 1996): 129–43.

Kytle, Calvin, and James A. Mackay. *Who Runs Georgia?* Athens: University of Georgia Press, 1998.

Ladd, Everett Carll. "Like Waiting for Godot: The Uselessness of 'Realignment' for Understanding Change in Contemporary American Politics." In *The End of Realignment? Interpreting American Electoral Eras,* edited by Byron E. Shafer. Madison: University of Wisconsin Press, 1991.

———. "1996 Vote: The 'No Majority' Realignment Continues." *Political Science Quarterly* 112, no. 1 (1997): 1–23.

Lakoff, George, and Mark Johnson. *Metaphors We Live By.* Chicago: University of Chicago Press, 1980.

Lamis, Alexander P. *The Two-Party South.* 2d ed. New York: Oxford University Press, 1988.

————. "Southern Politics in the 1990s." In *Southern Politics in the 1990s,* edited by Alexander P. Lamis. Baton Rouge: Louisiana State University Press, 1999.

Lasswell. Harold. *Politics: Who Gets What, When, and How.* Cleveland, Ohio: World, 1958.

Lawrence, David G. *The Collapse of the Democratic Presidential Majority.* Boulder, Colo.: Westview, 1996.

Lengle, James I., and Byron E. Shafer, eds. *Presidential Politics: Readings on Nominations and Elections.* 2d ed. New York: St. Martin's, 1983.

Lewis, Anthony. *Make No Law: The Sullivan Case and the First Amendment.* New York: Vintage, 1991.

————. "The Prosecutorial State." *American Prospect,* January–February 1999, 26–32.

Lewis, Justin, Michael Morgan, and Sut Jhally. "Libertine or Liberal? The Real Scandal of What People Know About President Clinton." 10 February 1998. Retrieved 4 April 2000 from the World Wide Web: *http://www.umass.edu/ newsoffice/archive/1998/021098study2.html.*

Lewis, Sinclair. *It Can't Happen Here.* Garden City, N.Y.: Sun Dial, 1935.

Lichtenstein, Alex. "Right Church, Wrong Pew: Eugene Genovese and Southern Conservatism." *New Politics* 6, no. 3 (summer 1977).

Lind, Michael. "Southern Coup." *New Republic,* 19 June 1995, 20–29.

Lipset, Seymour Martin. *American Exceptionalism: A Double-Edged Sword.* New York: W. W. Norton, 1996.

Loesche-Scheller, Brigitta. *Reparations to Poverty: Domestic Policy in America Ten Years After the Great Society.* Bern: Peter Lang, 1995.

Loewen, James. *The Mississippi Chinese: Between Black and White.* 2d ed. Prospect Heights, Ill.: Waveland Press, 1988.

Logan, Charles W., Jr. "Getting Beyond Scarcity: A New Paradigm for Assessing the Constitutionality of Broadcast Regulation." *California Law Review* 85 (December 1997): 1687–1747.

Lowi, Theodore J. *The End of Liberalism: Ideology, Policy, and the Crisis of Public Authority.* New York: W. W. Norton, 1969.

————. *The Personal President: Power Invested, Promise Unfulfilled.* Ithaca, N.Y.: Cornell University Press, 1985.

————. *The End of the Republican Era.* Norman: University of Oklahoma Press, 1995.

Lubell, Samuel. *The Future of American Politics.* 3d ed. New York: Harper and Row, 1962.

Luebke, Paul. *Tar Heel Politics; Myths and Realities.* Chapel Hill: University of North Carolina Press, 1990.

MacKuen, Michael B., Robert S. Erikson, and James A. Stimson. "Question Wording and Macropartisanship." *American Political Science Review* 86, no. 2 (June 1992): 475–81.

Maisel, L. Sandy. "Political Parties on the Eve of the Millennium." In *The Parties Respond,* edited by L. Sandy Maisel. 3d ed. Boulder, Colo.: Westview, 1998.

————. *Parties and Election in America: The Electoral Process*. 3d ed. Lanham, Md.: Rowman and Littlefield, 1999.

Manheim, Jarol. "Packaging the People." In *Debating Democracy*, edited by Bruce Miroff, Raymond Seidelman, and Todd Swanstrom. Boston: Houghton Mifflin, 1997.

Mann, Thomas. "Governance in America 2000: An Overview." *Brookings Review* 18, no. 1 (winter 2000): 4–7.

Mann, Thomas, and Norman Ornstein. "After the Campaign, What? Governance Questions for the 2000 Election." *Brookings Review* 18, no. 1 (winter 2000): 44–48.

Matthews, Donald R., and James W. Prothro. *Negroes and the New Southern Politics*. New York: Harcourt, Brace and World, 1966.

Mayer, William G. *The Divided Democrats*. Boulder, Colo.: Westview, 1996.

————. "Mass Partisanship, 1946–1996." In *Partisan Approaches to Postwar American Politics*, edited by Byron E. Shafer. New York: Chatham House, 1998.

Mayhew, David R. "Why Did V. O. Key Draw Back from His 'Have Nots' Claim?" In *V. O. Key, Jr., and the Study of American Politics*, edited by Milton C. Cummings, Jr. Washington, D.C.: American Political Science Association, 1988.

McConnell, Grant. *Private Power and American Democracy*. New York: Alfred A. Knopf, 1966.

McDonald, Laughlin. "Reapportionment, Racial Gerrymandering, and Georgia's Eleventh District." Lecture at Agnes Scott College, Decatur, Ga., 6 December 1994.

McDonald, Laughlin, Michael Binford, and Ken Johnson. "Georgia." In *The Quiet Revolution in the South*, edited by Chandler Davidson and Bernard Grofman. Princeton, N.J.: Princeton University Press, 1994.

McGinniss, Joe. *The Selling of the President 1968*. New York: Pocket Books, 1968.

McGlennon, John J. "Party Competition in Southern State Legislatures, 1976–1996: The Last Block of the Solid South Crumbles." *American Review of Politics* 17 (1996): 213–24.

McWilliams, Wilson Carey. "The Meaning of the Election." In *The Election of 1996: Reports and Interpretations*, edited by Gerald M. Pomper et al. Chatham, N.J.: Chatham House, 1997.

Mettler, Suzanne. *Dividing Citizens: Gender and Federalism in New Deal Public Policy*. Ithaca, N.Y.: Cornell University Press, 1998.

Miller, Warren E. "Party Identification, Realignment, and Party Voting: Back to the Basics." *American Political Science Review* 85, no. 2 (June 1991): 557–68.

————. "Party Identification and the Electorate of the 1990s." In *The Parties Respond*, edited by L. Sandy Maisel. 3d ed. Boulder, Colo.: Westview, 1998.

Mills, C. Wright. *The Power Elite*. New York: Oxford University Press, 1956.

Minchin, Timothy J. *What Do We Need a Union For?* Chapel Hill: University of North Carolina Press, 1997.

Miroff, Bruce. "Monopolizing the Public Space: The President as a Problem for Democratic Politics." In *Debating Democracy,* edited by Bruce Miroff, Ray Seidelman, and Todd Swanstrom. Boston: Houghton Mifflin, 1997.

Miroff, Bruce, Raymond Seidelman, and Todd Swanstrom. *The Democratic Debate: An Introduction to American Politics.* 2d ed. Boston: Houghton Mifflin, 1998.

Mischel, Lawrence, Jared Bernstein, and John Schmitt. "Dismantling the Myth of the 'New American Economy.'" *WorkingUSA,* September–October, 1998, 8–25.

Moody, Kim. "American Labor: A Movement Again?" *Monthly Review* 49, no. 3 (July–August 1997): 49–66.

Murphy, Reg, and Hal Gulliver. *Southern Strategy.* New York: Charles Scribner, 1971.

Nardulli, Peter F. "The Concept of a Critical Realignment, Electoral Behavior, and Political Change." *American Political Science Review* 89, no. 1 (March 1995): 10–22.

Ness, Immanuel. "The Road to Union Cities." *WorkingUSA,* November–December 1998, 78–86.

Neustadt, Richard. *Presidential Power.* New York: New American Library, 1964.

New York Times. Downsizing of America. New York: Times Books, 1996.

Newman, Katherine S. *Declining Fortunes.* New York: Basic, 1993.

Omi, Michael, and Howard Winant. *Racial Formation in the United States from the 1960s to the 1980s.* New York: Routledge and Keagan Paul, 1986.

Orfield, Gary. *The Reconstruction of Southern Education.* New York: John Wiley and Sons, 1969.

———. "The Growth of Segregation: African Americans, Latinos, and Unequal Education." In *Dismantling Desegregation: The Quiet Reversal of* Brown v. Board of Education, edited by Gary Orfield, Susan Eaton, and the Harvard Project on School Desegregation. New York: New Press, 1996.

Palley, Thomas I. "Goodbye Washington Consensus, Hello Main Street Alternative." Retrieved 5 February 1999 from the World Wide Web: *http://www. fmcenter.org/fmc_superpage.asp?ID+179.*

Panetta, Leon E., and Peter Gall. *Bring Us Together: The Nixon Team and the Civil Rights Retreat.* Philadelphia: Lippincott, 1971.

Parker, Frank R. *Black Votes Count.* Chapel Hill: University of North Carolina Press, 1990.

Pateman, Carole. *Participation and Democratic Theory.* Cambridge: Cambridge University Press, 1970.

Patterson, Kelly D. *Political Parties and the Maintenance of Liberal Democracy.* New York: Columbia University Press, 1996.

Patterson, Thomas. *Out of Order.* New York: Vintage, 1994.

Percy, Leroy. *Lanterns on the Levee: Recollections of a Planter's Son.* New York: Alfred A. Knopf, 1941.

Pettit, Philip. *Republicanism: A Theory of Freedom and Government.* New York: Oxford University Press, 1997.

Phillips, Kevin. *The Emerging Republican Majority.* Garden City, N.J.: Anchor Books, 1969.

———. *The Politics of Rich and Poor: Wealth and the American Electorate in the Reagan Aftermath.* New York: Random House, 1990.

Pigeon, Marc-Andre, and L. Randall Wray. "Did the Clinton Rising Tide Raise All Boats?" Public Policy Brief no. 445, Jerome Levy Institute. Retrieved 11 January 1999 from the World Wide Web: *http://www.levy.org/docs/sumwin98.html.*

Piven, Frances Fox, and Richard A. Cloward. *Why American's Don't Vote.* New York: Pantheon, 1989.

Platt, Suzy ed. *Respectfully Quoted: A Dictionary of Quotations Requested from the Congressional Research Service.* Washington, D.C.: Library of Congress, 1989.

Pomper, Gerald M. "The Presidential Election." In *The Election of 1992: Reports and Interpretations,* edited by Gerald M. Pomper et al. Chatham, N.J.: Chatham House, 1993.

———. "The Presidential Election." In *The Election of 1996: Reports and Interpretations,* edited by Gerald M. Pomper et al. Chatham, N.J.: Chatham House, 1997.

Pontusson, Jonas. *The Limits of Social Democracy: Investment Politics in Sweden.* Ithaca, N.Y.: Cornell University Press, 1992.

Postman, Neil. *Amusing Ourselves to Death: Public Discourse in the Age of Show Business.* New York: Penguin, 1985.

Presidential Commission on the Future of Worker-Management Relations. "Fact Finding Report." Washington, D.C.: U.S. Departments of Commerce and Labor, May 1994.

Prysby, Charles. "North Carolina: Republican Consolidation or Democratic Resurgence?" In *The 1996 Presidential Election in the South: Southern Party Systems in the 1990s,* edited by Laurence W. Moreland and Robert P. Steed. Westport, Conn.: Praeger, 1997.

Public Agenda Foundation. *Prescription for Prosperity: Four Paths to Economic Renewal.* Dayton, Ohio: National Issues Forums Institute, 1992.

Putnam, Robert. "Bowling Alone: The Decline of America's Social Capital." *Journal of Democracy* (January 1995): 65–78.

———. "The Strange Disappearance of Civic America." *American Prospect,* winter 1996, 34–48.

Quadagno, Jill. *The Color of Welfare: How Racism Undermined the War on Poverty.* New York: Oxford University Press, 1994.

Rae, Nicol C. *Southern Democrats.* New York: Oxford University Press, 1994.

———. "Party Factionalism, 1946–1996." In *Partisan Approaches to Postwar American Politics,* edited by Byron E. Shafer. New York: Chatham House, 1998.

Rauch, Jonathan. *Demosclerosis: The Silent Killer of American Government.* New York: Times Books, 1994.

Reed, John Shelton. *The Enduring South*. Chapel Hill: University of North Carolina Press, 1972.

Reeves, Keith. *Voting Hopes or Fears? White Voters, Black Candidates, and Racial Politics in America*. New York: Oxford University Press, 1997.

Reich, Robert B. *The Work of Nations*. New York: Vintage, 1992.

————. "My Dinner with Bill." *American Prospect*, May–June 1998, 6–9.

Reingold, Jennifer. "Executive Pay. *Business Week*, 17 April 2000, 100–12.

Rhodes, Terrel L. *Republicans in the South: Voting for the State House, Voting for the White House*. Westport, Conn.: Praeger, 2000.

Richie, Robert, and Steven Hill. *Reflecting All of Us: The Case for Proportional Representation*. Boston: Beacon, 1999.

Rifkin, Jeremy. *The End of Work?* New York: G. P. Putnam's Sons, 1995.

Ritter, Kurt. "Ronald Reagan's 1960s Southern Rhetoric: Courting Conservatives for the GOP." *Southern Communications Journal* 64 (summer 1999): 333–45.

Rodgers, Harrell R., Jr., and Charles S. Bullock III. *Law and Social Change: Civil Rights Laws and Their Consequences*. New York: McGraw-Hill, 1972.

Rogers, Joel. "The Folks Who Brought You the Weekend." *WorkingUSA*, November–December 1997, 11–20.

Rohde, David W. "The Inevitability and Solidity of the 'Republican Solid South.'" *American Review of Politics* 17 (summer 1996): 23–46.

Rosenstone, Steven J., Roy L. Behr, and Edward H. Lazarus. *Third Parties in America: Citizen Response to Major Party Failure*. 2d ed. Princeton, N.J.: Princeton University Press, 1996.

Rosenstone, Steven J., and John Mark Hansen. *Mobilization, Participation, and Democracy in America*. New York: Macmillan, 1993.

Rushkoff, Douglas. "Media Democracy." In *Debating Democracy*, edited by Bruce Miroff, Raymond Seidelman, and Todd Swanstrom. Boston: Houghton Mifflin, 1997.

Sale, Kirkpatrick. *Power Shift: The Rise of the Southern Rim and Its Challenge to the Eastern Establishment*. New York: Random House, 1975.

Salmore, Barbara G., and Stephen A. Salmore. *Candidates, Parties, and Campaigns: Electoral Politics in America*, 2d ed. Washington, D.C.: Congressional Quarterly Press, 1989.

Sandel, Michael. *Democracy's Discontent: America in Search of a Public Philosophy*. Cambridge, Mass.: Harvard University Press, 1996.

Sawyers, Larry, and William K. Tabb. *Sunbelt/Snowbelt: Urban Development and Regional Restructuring*. New York: Oxford University Press, 1984.

Scammon, Richard M., Alice V. McGillvray, and Rhodes Cook. *America Votes 23, 1998: A Handbook of Contemporary American Election Statistics*. Washington, D.C.: Congressional Quarterly, 1998.

Scammon, Richard M., and Ben J. Wattenberg. *The Real Majority*. New York: Coward, McCann and Geoghegan, 1970.

Schattsneider, E. E. *The Semi-Sovereign People*. New York: Holt, Rinehart and Winston, 1960.

Schell, Jonathan. *The Time of Illusion.* New York: Vintage, 1975.

———. "The Uncertain Leviathan." *Atlantic,* August 1996. Retrieved 4 June 1998 from the World Wide Web: *http://theatlantic.com/96aug/schell/ schell.htm.*

Scher, Richard. *Politics in the New South: Republicanism, Race, and Leadership in the Twentieth Century.* Armonk, N.Y.: M. E. Sharpe, 1992.

———. *Politics in the New South: Republicanism, Race, and Leadership in the Twentieth Century.* 2d ed. Armonk, N.Y.: M. E. Sharpe, 1997.

———. *The Modern Political Campaign: Mudslinging, Bombast, and the Vitality of American Politics.* Armonk, N.Y.: M. E. Sharpe, 1997.

Scher, Richard K., Jon L. Mills, and John J. Hotaling. *Voting Rights and Democracy: The Law and Politics of Districting.* Chicago: Nelson-Hall, 1997.

Schlesinger, Arthur M., Jr. *The Imperial Presidency.* New York: Popular Library, 1974.

Schneider, Paige. "Factionalism in the Southern Republican Party." *American Review of Politics* 19 (summer 1998): 129–48.

Schneider, William. "Realignment: The Eternal Question." *PS: Political Science and Politics* 15, no. 3 (summer 1982): 449–57.

Schor, Juliet B. *The Overworked American.* New York: Basic, 1991.

Schreiber, E. M. "Where the Ducks Are: Southern Strategy vs. Fourth Party." *Public Opinion Quarterly* 35 (1971): 157–67.

Schumhl, Robert. *Statecraft and Stagecraft: American Political Life in the Age of Personality,* 2d ed. Notre Dame, Ind.: University of Notre Dame Press, 1992.

Schwartz, John E. "The Hidden Side of the Clinton Economy." *Atlantic Monthly,* October 1998.

Sears, Donald O., Jim Sidanius, and Lawrence Bobo, eds. *Racialized Politics: The Debate About Racism in America.* Chicago: University of Chicago Press, 2000.

Shafer, Byron E. "We Are All Southern Democrats Now." In *Present Discontents: American Politics in the Very Late Twentieth Century,* edited by Byron E. Shafer. Chatham, N.J.: Chatham House, 1997.

Shaffer, Stephen D., and Monica Johnson. "A New Solid South? The Drama of Partisan Realignment in the Deep South State of Mississippi." *American Review of Politics* 17, no. 2 (summer 1996): 171–91.

Shaffer, Stephen D., et al. "Mississippi: From Pariah to Pacesetter?" In *Southern Politics in the 1990s,* edited by Alexander P. Lamis. Baton Rouge: Louisiana State University Press, 1999.

Shapiro, Bruce. "We, the Jury." *Nation,* 12 December 1998. Retrieved 27 June 2000 from the World Wide Web: *http://www.thenation.com/issue/981130/ 1130SHAP.htm.*

Sherrill, Robert. *Gothic Politics in the Deep South.* New York: Ballantine, 1969.

Shribman, David M. "Era of Pretty Good Feelings: The Middle Way of Bill Clinton and America's Voters." In *The Parties Respond,* edited by L. Sandy Maisel. 3d ed. Boulder, Colo.: Westview, 1998.

Silbey, Joel H. "Beyond Realignment and Realignment Theory: American Political Eras, 1789–1989." In *The End of Realignment? Interpreting American Political Eras,* edited by Byron E. Shafer. Madison: University of Wisconsin Press, 1991.

Silverstein, Mark. *Judicious Choices: The New Politics of Supreme Court Confirmations.* New York: W. W. Norton, 1994.

Simon, Bryant. "Rethinking Why There Are so Few Unions in the South." *Georgia Historical Quarterly* 81, no. 2 (summer 1997): 465–84.

Sindler, Allan P. "Bifactional Rivalry as an Alternative to Two Party Competition in Louisiana." *American Political Science Review* 49, no. 3 (September 1955): 641–62.

Sklar, Holly. *Chaos or Community? Seeking Solutions, Not Scapegoats for Bad Economics.* Boston: South End, 1995.

Skocpol, Theda. *Boomerang: Health Care Reform and the Turn Against Government.* New York: W. W. Norton, 1997.

———. "Democrats at the Crossroads." *Mother Jones,* January–February 1997. Retrieved from the World Wide Web.

———. "Associations Without Members." *American Prospect,* July–August 1999, 66–73.

———. *The Missing Middle: Working Families and the Future of American Social Policy.* New York: W. W. Norton, 2000.

Skocpol, Theda, and Morris Fiorini. *Civic Engagement in American Democracy.* Washington, D.C.: Brookings, 1999.

Skowronek, Stephen. *The Politics Presidents Make: Leadership from John Adams to George Bush.* Cambridge, Mass.: Harvard University Press, 1993.

Smith, Rogers M. "Beyond Tocqueville, Myrdal, and Hartz: The Multiple Traditions in America." *American Political Science Review* 87, no. 3 (September 1993): 549–66.

Sniderman, Paul, and Edward Carmines. *Reaching Beyond Race.* Cambridge, Mass.: Harvard University Press, 1997.

Sparrow, Bartholomew H. *Uncertain Guardians: The News Media as a Political Institution.* Baltimore: Johns Hopkins University Press, 1999.

Stabile, Carole A. "Feminism Without Guarantees: The Misalliances and Missed Alliances of Postmodern Social Theory." *Rethinking Marxism* 7 (1994): 48–61.

Stanley, Harold W. *Voter Mobilization and the Politics of Race.* New York: Praeger, 1987.

———. "Southern Partisan Changes: Dealignment, Realignment or Both?" *Journal of Politics* 50, no. 1 (February 1988): 64–88.

———. "The South and the 1996 Presidential Election: Republican Gains Among Democratic Wins." In *The 1996 Presidential Election in the South: Southern Party Systems in the 1990s,* edited by Laurence W. Moreland and Robert P. Steed. Westport, Conn.: Praeger, 1997.

State of the South 1998. Chapel Hill, N.C.: MDC, 1998.

Stefancic, Jean, and Richard Delgado. *No Mercy: How Conservative Think*

Tanks and Foundations Changed America's Social Agenda. Philadelphia: Temple University Press, 1996.

Stephens, John D. *The Transition from Capitalism to Socialism.* Urbana: University of Illinois Press, 1986.

Stoesz, David. *Small Change: Domestic Policy Under the Clinton Presidency.* White Plains, N.Y.: Longman, 1996.

Stone, Clarence. *Urban Regimes: Governing Atlanta, 1946–1988.* Lawrence: University Press of Kansas, 1989.

Strahan, Randall W. "Partisan Officeholders, 1946–1996." In *Partisan Approaches to Postwar American Politics,* edited by Byron E. Shafer. New York: Chatham House, 1998.

Sturrock, David E. Review of *The Disappearing South,* edited by Robert P. Steed, Lawrence W. Moreland, and Tod A. Baker. *Journal of Politics* 53, no. 1 (February 1991): 238–40.

Sundquist, James L. *Dynamics of the Party System.* 2d ed. Washington, D.C.: Brookings Institution, 1983.

Sunstein, Cass R. *The Partial Constitution.* Cambridge, Mass.: Harvard University Press, 1993.

Teeple, Gary. *Globalization and the Decline of Social Reform.* Atlantic Heights, N.J.: Humanities, 1995.

Teixeira, Ruy A. "Economic Change and the Middle-Class Revolt Against the Democratic Party." In *Broken Contract? Changing Relationships Between Americans and Their Government,* edited by Stephen C. Craig. Boulder, Colo.: Westview, 1996.

Thompson, Dennis F. "Mediated Corruption: The Case of the Keating Five." *American Political Science Review* 87, no. 2 (June 1993): 369–81.

Thompson, Ruth Anne. Review of *Southern Strategies: Southern Women and the Woman Suffrage Question,* by Elna C. Green. H-Net Reviews in the Humanities and Social Sciences. Retrieved 20 April 1999 from the World Wide Web: *http://www.h-net.msu.edu/reviews.*

Tolchin, Susan J. *The Angry American.* 2d ed. Boulder, Colo.: Westview, 1999.

Tolleson-Rinehart, Sue. "Can the Flower of Southern Womanhood Bloom in the Garden of Southern Politics?" *Southern Cultures* 4, no. 1 (April 1998): 78–87.

Uslaner, Eric. *The Decline of Comity in Congress.* Ann Arbor: University of Michigan Press, 1993.

Virtanen, Simo V., and Leonie Huddy. "Old-Fashioned Racism and New Forms of Racial Prejudice." *Journal of Politics* 60, no. 2 (May 1998): 311–32.

Voss, D. Stephen. "Black Incumbents, White Districts: An Appraisal of the 1996 Congressional Elections in Georgia and Florida." Paper presented at the annual meeting of the Southern Political Science Association, Atlanta, 29 October 1998.

Voyles, James Everett. "Don't Cross This Line: A Comparison of the Reagan, Bush, and Clinton Departments of Justice on Majority-Minority Districts." Paper presented at the annual meeting of the Southern Political Science Association, Atlanta, 4 November 1994.

Watson, Stanley J. "Race and Alignment Reconsidered: Issues Evolution in the South Since 1972." *American Review of Politics* 17, no. 2 (summer 1996): 145–70.

Wattenberg, Martin. *Candidate-Centered Politics: Presidential Elections of the 1980s.* Cambridge, Mass.: Harvard University Press, 1991.

———. *The Decline of American Political Parties.* 4th ed. Cambridge, Mass.: Harvard University Press, 1996.

Weiler, Paul C. *Governing the Workplace.* Cambridge, Mass.: Harvard University Press, 1990.

Weiss, Linda. *The Myth of the Powerless State.* Ithaca, N.Y.: Cornell University Press, 1998.

West, Darrell M., and Burdett A. Loomis. *The Sound of Money: How Political Interests Get What They Want.* New York: W. W. Norton, 1999.

Williams, T. Harry. *Huey Long.* New York: Bantam Books, 1969.

Wilson, James Q. *The Amateur Democrat.* Chicago: University of Chicago Press, 1966.

Wilson, William Julius. *When Work Disappears.* New York: Vintage, 1996.

Wirt, Frederick M. *"We Ain't What We Was": Civil Rights in the New South.* Durham, N.C.: Duke University Press, 1998.

Wolman, William, and Anne Colamosca. "The Judas Economy." *Working-USA,* September–October 1997, 51–61.

Woodward, C. Vann. *Tom Watson: Agrarian Rebel.* New York: Oxford University Press, 1938.

———. *Origins of the New South, 1877–1913.* Baton Rouge: Louisiana State University Press, 1951.

———. *The Strange Career of Jim Crow.* 2d ed. New York: Oxford University Press, 1966.

Index